Easy PC security and safety

Other Computer Titles

by

Robert Penfold

BP470 Linux for Windows users
BP484 Easy PC Troubleshooting
BP495 Easy Windows Troubleshooting
BP503 Using Dreamweaver 4
BP504 Using Flash 5
BP507 Easy Internet Troubleshooting
BP518 Easy PC Peripherals Troubleshooting
BP521 Easy Windows XP Troubleshooting
BP523 Easy PC Interfacing
BP527 Using Flash MX
BP530 Using Dreamweaver MX
BP531 Easy PC Upgrading

Easy PC security and safety

Robert Penfold

Bernard Babani (publishing) Ltd
The Grampians
Shepherds Bush Road
London W6 7NF
England
www.babanibooks.com

Please note

Although every care has been taken with the production of this book to ensure that any projects, designs, modifications, and/or programs, etc., contained herewith, operate in a correct and safe manner and also that any components specified are normally available in Great Britain, the Publisher and Author do not accept responsibility in any way for the failure (including fault in design) of any projects, design, modification, or program to work correctly or to cause damage to any equipment that it may be connected to or used in conjunction with, or in respect of any other damage or injury that may be caused, nor do the Publishers accept responsibility in any way for the failure to obtain specified components.

Notice is also given that if any equipment that is still under warranty is modified in any way or used or connected with home-built equipment then that warranty may be void.

First Published - February 2004

British Library Cataloguing in Publication Data

A catalogue record for this book is available from the British Library

ISBN 0 85934 540 8

Cover Design by Gregor Arthur

Printed and bound in Great Britain by Cox and Wyman

Preface

Computer security is a subject that many computer users have ignored in the past, and they were probably taking little risk in doing so. Computer viruses made the news headlines from time to time, but the stories about impending worldwide doom never seemed to come to anything. Some viruses that were about to sweep the world actually turned up on less than a dozen computer systems. The degree of risk for the average computer user was very low, and the press tended to exaggerate the threat posed by the latest super-viruses.

Unfortunately, the computing world has radically changed in recent years and computer security is something that few can now afford to ignore. The speed with which some recent virus and worm attacks have spread around the world demonstrates how widespread use of the Internet has changed things. In the past it was mainly professionals looking after servers or large computer networks that had to worry about computer security, but it is now a subject that all computer users have to take seriously.

Of course, the Internet has been around for many years, but it is now used by many more people and users tend to spend far longer online. Broadband Internet access opens up new possibilities, but it also makes computer systems far more vulnerable than ever before. The increasing use of Email as a quick and easy means of communicating with people all over the world has provided another means for viruses to spread. This threat has actually been the main cause for concern in recent times.

Fortunately, making a PC safe against hackers, viruses, and the like does not have to cost very much and does not require a high level of expertise. This book explains in simple terms the differences between viruses, Trojans, and other harmful files, and how they can be combated. It also covers the use of firewalls to keep your PC free from the attentions of hackers. Other subjects covered include dealing with spam, Email viruses, and pop-up advertisements, keeping children safe online, and using encryption to keep information on your PC secure.

It is not possible to guarantee that any computer system will be totally secure against attacks, and other problems can also result in lost data or damage to the operating system. Consequently, the subjects of backing up your system and disaster recovery are also covered in some detail. A high level of computer expertise is not assumed, but readers do need to be familiar with the basics of using a PC running a modern version of Windows.

Robert Penfold

Trademarks

Contents

5

6

7

1

The basics of security

From all sides

Computer security has been a growth industry in recent years, with ever more ways of protecting PCs being devised in response to increasingly imaginative ways of attacking them. Viruses are the best known form of computer attack, but there are other ways that hackers can mount an assault on your PC. In fact many of the much publicised computer viruses are not, strictly speaking, viruses at all.

In this chapter various aspects of computer security will be explained. Some aspects of security are covered in sufficient depth here, but others are covered in more detail by later chapters. Even for those that take proper security measures there is no guarantee that a virus or some other form of computing disaster will never strike. Therefore, later chapters also deal with the all-important topic of recovering from a computing disaster.

Virus

The non-technical press tend to call any form of software that attacks computers a virus. A virus is a specific type of program though, and represents just one of several types that can attack a computer. Initially, someone attaches the virus to a piece of software, and then finds a way of getting that software into computer systems. These days the Internet is the most likely route for the infection to be spread, but it is important not to overlook the fact that there are other means of propagating viruses. Indeed, computer viruses were being spread around the world long before the Internet came along.

Programs and possibly other files can carry viruses regardless of the source. If someone gives you a floppy disc, CD-ROM, or DVD containing software it is possible that the contents of the disc are infected with a virus. In the early days of personal computing the main route for viruses to spread was by way of discs containing illegally copied programs. Discs containing pirated software are still used to propagate viruses. Avoid any dodgy software if you wish to keep your PC virus-free.

A later development was pirated software placed on bulletin boards so that it could be downloaded by computer users having PCs equipped with a modem. A modem was an expensive piece of equipment in those days, but once someone had downloaded a piece of software they would usually make several copies and distribute them to friends who would in turn make and distribute further copies. Although the old bulletin board system was crude compared with the modern Internet, it was actually remarkably quick and efficient at spreading viruses. The main way in which viruses are now spread is much the same as the bulletin board method, but with the Internet acting as the initial source. Due to the popularity of the Internet it is possible for viruses to rapidly spread around the world via this route.

Anyway, having introduced a virus into a system via one route or another, it will attack that system and try to replicate itself. Some viruses only attack the boot sector of a system disc. This is the part of the disc that the computer uses to boot into the operating system. Other viruses will try to attach themselves to any file of the appropriate type, which usually means a program file of some sort. The attraction of a program file is that the user will probably run the program before too long, which gives the virus a chance to spread the infection and (or) start attacking the computer system.

At one time there were only two possible ways in which a virus could attack a computer. One way was for the virus to attach itself to a program file that the user then ran on his or her computer. The other was for someone to leave an infected floppy disc in the computer when it was switched off. On switching the computer on again the floppy disc was used as the boot disc, activating the virus in the disc's boot sector.

Script virus

These days you have to be suspicious of many more types of file. Many applications programs such as word processors and spreadsheets have the ability to automate tasks using scripts, or macros as they are also known. The application effectively has a built-in programming language and the script or macro is a form of program. This makes it possible for viruses or other harmful programs to be present in many types of data file. Scripts are also used in some web pages, and viruses can be hidden in these JavaScript programs, Java applets, etc. There are other potential sources of infection such as Email attachments.

I would not wish to give the impression that all files, web pages, and Emails are potential sources of script or macro viruses. There are some types of file where there is no obvious way for them to carry a virus or other harmful program. A simple text file for example, should be completely harmless. Even in cases where a harmful program is disguised as a text file with a "txt" extension, the file should be harmless. The system will treat it as a text file and it can not be run provided no one alters the file extension. Similarly, an Email that contains a plain text message can not contain a script virus. Nevertheless, it is probably best to regard all files and Emails with a degree of suspicion. As explained later in this chapter, even though simple text can not carry a true virus, it can carry a virus of sorts.

Benign virus

It tends to be assumed that all viruses try to harm the infected computer system. This is not correct though, and many viruses actually do very little. For example, you might find that nothing more occurs than a daft message appears onscreen when a certain date is reached, or on a particular date each year. Viruses such as this certainly have a degree of nuisance value, but they are not harmful. I would not wish to give the impression that most viruses are harmless. Many computer viruses do indeed try to do serious damage to the infected system. If in doubt you have to assume that a virus is harmful.

A virus that does attack the system will often go for the boot sector of the hard disc drive, and this will usually make it impossible to boot the computer into the operating system. Other viruses attack the FAT (file allocation table) in an attempt to effectively scramble the contents of the disc. Another way of attacking the files on the disc is to take the direct approach and simply alter all or part of their contents. Renaming or simply deleting files are other popular ploys.

Worm

A worm is a program that replicates itself, usually from one disc to another, or from one system to another via a local network or the Internet. Like a virus, a worm is not necessarily harmful. In recent times many of the worldwide virus scares have actually been caused by worms transmitted via Email, and not by what would normally be accepted as a virus. The usual ploy is for the worm to send a copy of itself to every address in the Email address book of the infected system. A worm spread in this way, even if it is not intrinsically harmful, can have serious consequences. There can be a sudden upsurge in the amount of Email traffic, possibly causing parts of the Email system to seriously slow down or even crash. Some worms compromise the security of the infected system, perhaps enabling it to be used by a hacker for sending spam for example.

Trojan horse

A Trojan horse, or just plain Trojan as it is now often called, is a program that is supposed to be one thing but is actually another. In the early days many Trojans were in the form of free software, and in particular, free antivirus programs. The users obtained nasty shocks when the programs were run, with their computer systems being attacked. Like viruses, some Trojans do nothing more than display stupid messages, but others attack the disc files, damage the boot sector of the hard disc, and so on.

Backdoor Trojan

A backdoor Trojan is the same as the standard variety in that it is supplied in the form of a program that is supposed to be one thing but is actually another. In some cases nothing appears to happen when you install the program. In other cases the program might actually install and run as expected. In both cases one or two small programs will have been installed on the computer and set to run when the computer is booted.

One ploy is to have programs that produce log files showing which programs you have run and Internet sites that you have visited. The log will usually include any key presses as well. The idea is for the log file to provide passwords to things such as your Email account, online bank account, and so on. Someone hacking into your computer system will usually look for the log files, and could obviously gain access to important information from these files. Another ploy is to have a program that makes it easier for hackers to break into your computer system. A backdoor Trojan does not attack the infected computer in the same way as some viruses, and it does not try to spread the infection to other discs or computers. Potentially though, a backdoor Trojan is more serious than a virus, particularly if you use the computer for online banking, share dealing, etc.

Spyware

Spyware programs monitor system activity and send information to another computer by way of the Internet. There are really two types of spyware, and one tries to obtain passwords and send them to another computer. This takes things a step further than the backdoor Trojan programs mentioned earlier. A backdoor Trojan makes it easier for a hacker to obtain sensitive information from your PC, but it does not go as far as sending any information that is placed in the log files. Spyware is usually hidden in other software in Trojan fashion.

Adware

The second type of spyware is more correctly called adware. In common with spyware, it gathers information and sends it to another computer via the Internet. Adware is not designed to steal passwords or other security information from your PC. Its purpose is usually to gather information for marketing purposes, and this typically means gathering and sending details of the web sites you have visited. Some free programs are supported by banner advertising, and the adware is used to select advertisements that are likely to be of interest to you.

Programs that are supported by adware have not always made this fact clear during the installation process. Sometimes the use of adware was pointed out in the End User License Agreement, but probably few people bother to read the "fine print". These days the more respectable software companies that use this method of raising advertising revenues make it clear that the adware will be installed together with the main program. There is often the option of buying a "clean" copy of the program. Others try to con you into installing the adware by using the normal tricks.

Provided you know that it is being installed and are happy to have it on your PC, adware is not a major security risk. It is sending information about your surfing habits, but you have given permission for it to do so. If you feel that this is an invasion of privacy, then do not consent to it being installed. The situation is different if you are tricked into installing adware. Then it does clearly become an invasion of your privacy and you should remove any software of this type from your PC. Note that if you consent to adware being installed on your PC and then change your mind, removing it will probably result in the free software it supports being disabled or uninstalled.

Dialers

A dialer is a program that uses a modem and an ordinary dial-up connection to connect your PC to another computer system. Dialers probably have numerous legitimate applications, but they are mainly associated with various types of scam. An early one was a promise of free pornographic material that required a special program to be downloaded. This program was, of course, the dialer, which proceeded to call a high cost number in a country thousands of miles away. In due course the user received an astronomic telephone bill.

A modern variation on this is where users are tricked into downloading a dialer, often with the promise of free software of some description. Users go onto the Internet in the usual way via their dial-up connections, and everything might appear to be perfectly normal. What is actually happening though is that they are not connecting to the Internet via their normal Internet service provider (ISP). Instead, the dialer is connecting them to a different ISP that is probably thousands of miles away and is costing a fortune in telephone charges. Again, the problem is very apparent when the telephone bill arrives.

The increasing use of broadband Internet connections has largely or totally removed the threat of dialer related problems for many. If there is no ordinary telephone modem in your PC, there is no way the dialer can connect your PC to the Internet or another computer system via a dial-up connection. There is a slight risk if your PC is equipped with a telephone modem for sending and receiving faxes. The risk is relatively small though, since you would presumably notice that the modem was being used for no apparent reason.

Hoax virus

A hoax virus might sound innocuous enough and just a bit of a joke, but it has the potential to spread across the world causing damage to computer systems. The hoax is usually received in the form of an Email from someone that has contacted you previously. They say that the Email they sent you previously was infected with a virus, and the Email then goes on to provide information on how to remove the virus. This usually entails searching for one or more files on your PC's hard disc drive and erasing them.

Of course, there was no virus in the initial Email. The person that sent the initial Email could be the hoaxer, or they might have been fooled by the hoax themselves. The hoax Email suggests that you contact everyone that you have emailed recently, telling them that their computer could be infected and giving them the instructions for the "cure". This is the main way in which a hoax virus is propagated. The files that you are instructed to remove could be of no real consequence, or they could be important system files. It is best not to fall for the hoax and find out which.

These hoax viruses demonstrate the point that all the antivirus software in the world will not provide full protection for your PC. They are simple text files that do not do any direct harm to your PC, and can not be kept at bay by software. Ultimately it is up to you to use some common sense and provide the final line of defence. A quick check on the Internet will usually provide details of hoax viruses and prevent you from doing anything silly.

Note that there are other scams that involve hoax Emails. Recently there have been several instances of Emails being sent to customers of online financial companies. These purport to come from the company concerned, and they ask customers to provide their passwords and other account details. A link is provided to the site, and the site usually looks quite convincing. It is not the real thing though, and anyone falling for it has their account details stolen. The success of this scan has been limited, but some accounts have been plundered.

Virus or not?

A true computer virus has the ability to replicate itself, as do some other types of software that attack computers. I suppose the difference with a true virus is that it is not a complete entity in its own right. On its own a virus is just a junk file that does nothing. A virus is attached to another file and it then attaches copies of itself to other files. These then attach copies of themselves to more files, and so on. Apparently a biological virus is not a separate living entity either, and it requires a host cell to reproduce and spread itself. The term "computer virus" is therefore quite apt.

A Trojan is a program that attacks a PC when the program file is run, and it is a complete entity in its own right. Accordingly, it is not really a form of virus. Some Trojans are actually in the form of extra program code added to a Setup file. When the Setup file is run in order to install a piece of software, the extra code places additional files on the hard disc or attacks the computer. This is closer to a being a virus, but it does not result in other files being infected. Hence it is still a form of Trojan rather than a virus, and the same is true of spyware.

The distinction between a virus and some other form of computer nasty might seem to be purely academic, but there is a practical difference. Non-virus attacks are generally easier to detect and eliminate. If you delete a Trojan and any files the program added when you ran it, this will not reverse any damage done to the system, but it will prevent further damage. Similarly, uninstalling or deleting spyware and dialers prevents them from running up big telephone bills or giving away information stored on your PC.

A virus is generally more difficult to deal with because it conceals itself in an existing file on the computer's hard disc. Looking for a particular file or set of files on the computer will work with most Trojans, as well as spyware and dialers. It will not work with a virus because the virus is concealed within an existing file. Potentially, the virus will be within a different file on each computer that is infected. Virus detection programs therefore operate by looking within files for pieces of program code associated with the viruses in their databases. This code is sometimes referred to as the "fingerprint " of the virus.

When an infected file is located there are three normal ways of dealing with it. The obvious one is to simply delete it. Most anti-virus programs are actually a bit reluctant to take this course of action just in case it "kills" the infected file but gives the virus a chance to spread to other files. Many opt for the alternative of quarantining the infected file, which basically means placing it in a special folder on the hard disc drive where no access to the file is permitted, other than via the antivirus program. The third method is to "cure" the infected file. Remember that by deleting or quarantining an infected file you are losing the original file as well as the virus attached to it. Ideally the virus should be removed from the file so that it can go on operating as it did before the infection occurred. Unfortunately, it is often impossible to remove the virus while leaving the original file intact.

Basic measures

The obvious way of protecting a PC from viruses and other harmful programs is to simply keep it away from possible sources of infection. Unfortunately, the quarantine approach is not usually a practical one. If you use a PC to (say) produce letters that are printed out and then sent by post, then the quarantine method should work. Once the computer has been set up ready for use it should not be necessary to put any discs into the floppy or CD-ROM drives, and there is no need for it to connect to the Internet or any other network. It might be necessary to have a CD/RW disc or two for backup purposes, but provided these discs are not used in any other computer there is no significant risk of them introducing a virus into the computer.

Unfortunately, little real world computing is compatible with this standalone approach. I use my PC to produce letters that are sent through the post, but I probably send about 50 times as many Emails. Large numbers of Emails are also received in my Email accounts. My PC is used mainly for generating work that is sent off on CDR discs, but I also receive data discs occasionally, and these have to be read using my computer. I have to use the Internet extensively for research, and I sometimes download software updates. Isolating my computer from the outside world would render it largely useless to me.

Totally removing the threat of attack is not usually possible, but the chances of a successful attack can be greatly reduced by using a few basic precautions.

Email attachments

Some individuals operate a policy of never opening Email attachments. I do not take things that far, but I would certainly not open an Email attachment unless I knew the sender of the Email and was expecting the attachment. Bear in mind that some viruses and worms spread by hijacking a user's Email address book and sending copies of the infected Email to every address in the address book. The fact that an Email comes from someone you know, or purports to, does not guarantee that it is free from infection. Another point to bear in mind is that Email attachments are now the most common way of spreading viruses and computer worms.

Selective downloading

Downloading software updates from the main computer software companies should be safe, as should downloading the popular freebies from their official sources. Downloading just about anything else involves a degree of risk and should be kept to a minimum.

Pirate software

Pirated software has become a major problem for the software companies in recent years. In addition to casual software piracy where friends swap copies of programs there is now an epidemic of commercial copying. Apart from the fact that it is illegal to buy and use pirate software, unlike the real thing, some of it contains viruses, spyware, etc.

Virus protection

Some programs, and particularly those from Microsoft, have built-in virus protection that is designed to block known macro/script viruses. If you have any programs that include this feature, make sure that it is enabled.

P2P

P2P (peer to peer) programs are widely used for file swapping. Even if you use this type of software for swapping legal (non-pirated) files, it still has to be regarded as very risky. In most cases you have no idea who is supplying the files, or whether they are what they are supposed to be. Also, you are providing others with access to your PC, and this access could be exploited by hackers.

Switch off

Some PC users leave their computers running continuously in the belief that it gives better reliability. It did in the days when computers were based on valves, but there is no evidence that it improves reliability with modern computers. It will increase your electricity bills, and it also increases the vulnerability of your PC if it has some form of always-on Internet connection. No one can hack into your computer system if it is switched off.

Prevention

The old adage about "prevention is better than cure" certainly applies to computer viruses. In addition to some basic security precautions, equip your PC with antivirus software and keep it up-to-date. This software will usually detect and deal with viruses before they have a chance to spread the infection or do any damage to your files.

Backup

Always have a least one backup copy of any important data file. This is not just a matter of having a replacement copy if a file should be destroyed by a virus. The hard disc of a computer has a finite lifespan, and hard disc failures are not a rarity. You should backup all important data anyway, just in case there is a major hard disc failure. It is a good idea to backup the entire system from time to time. This makes it easy to restore a working version of the system, applications programs, etc., in the event of any major problem such as a virus attack, corrupted Windows installation, or hard disc failure.

Fault or virus?

When a computer starts giving problems how do you know whether the problem is due to a virus or some other problem? Viruses can be subtle, but in many cases a message will appear on the screen making it clear that your PC has a virus. Many hardware faults are clearly caused by hardware problems and are nothing to do with a virus. Distinguishing between something like a minor hard disc or software problem and one of the more secretive viruses is relatively difficult.

It is unlikely that a virus is to blame if a PC fails to reach the stage where Windows starts to boot. The initial messages that appear on the screen are produced by the BIOS (basic input/output system), which is a program built into the PC's hardware. This does some checks on the PC's memory and other hardware and then starts to load the operating system. The BIOS program is usually stored in FLASH memory and can be upgraded by downloading a newer version and a small utility program that is used to burn the new program into the FLASH memory chip.

A BIOS that can be easily upgraded is clearly desirable, but it does leave the possibility of a virus corrupting the BIOS and rendering the PC unbootable. Some viruses do indeed try to attack PCs in this way. However, any PC made within the last few years should have the BIOS set to the protected mode by default, making it very difficult for a virus to alter the BIOS program. Any problems prior to booting are likely to be due to a hardware problem rather than some form of virus attack.

If a computer fails to boot properly it is possible that a virus is to blame, but unless there is something specific to support the virus theory, it is unlikely to be the cause. Problems with Windows failing to boot properly are not exactly a rarity, especially for users of Windows ME and its predecessors. Windows XP is closer to being crash-proof than Windows ME, but it could not really be accurately described as invulnerable. Also, no matter how stable the operating system might happen to be, problems with the hardware can and do give boot problems from time to time. Memory, processor, and hard disc faults can all produce problems when the computer goes through the boot sequence. Boot problems can also be due to faulty software such as badly written device drivers for video cards, sound cards, and the like.

Chapter 2 covers dealing with viruses, and it provides detailed instructions on how to boot a troublesome PC so that antivirus and other diagnostic software can be used. The basic technique is to boot Windows in what is called Safe Mode. This is a minimal version of Windows that only installs the bare necessities. Some of the hardware, such as the sound generator and the CD-ROM drives will probably not be operational. However, provided antivirus software has been installed on the PC it should be possible to run this software and check for viruses. Note that installing antivirus software on a PC that might have already been infected is not considered a good idea. Installing software gives the infection plenty of opportunities to spread and possible destroy more of your important files. In fact many antivirus programs run some initial checks before they will commence the installation process. The installation will not be commenced if a possible virus is detected.

This emphasises the need to install antivirus software before an infection occurs rather than afterwards. Once an infection has occurred it is likely that damage will have already occurred and some of your files could be lost for ever. Effecting a cure is more difficult once the infection has had a chance to take hold, and by the time you realise there is a problem it is possible that the infection will have spread beyond your PC.

Boot options

If the damage to the operating system is very severe it is possible that the computer will not even boot in safe mode. It should still be possible to boot into a form of MS/DOS from a floppy disc. A boot disc can be made from Windows XP and a Recovery Disc is produced as part of the installation process for Windows ME and 98. With Windows XP it is also possible to boot into some utilities via the installation CD-ROM. Unfortunately, all this is likely to be of limited use if you are trying to deal with a virus.

Some antivirus programs are supplied with a set of floppy discs that can be used to first boot the PC into an MS/DOS style operating system and then provide some virus checks. With other programs the set of emergency discs is made as part of the installation process. Another variation is for the antivirus software to be supplied on a bootable CD-ROM that can be used in a similar way to the set of emergency discs. Note that virus checks made using any form of emergency disc or disc set are likely to be less thorough than those made as part of the normal checking routine. Antivirus software is normally updated over the Internet at least once per month, keeping the installation reasonably up-to-date.

Emergency discs are not usually updated, and it is not possible to update software supplied on an ordinary CD-ROM. In most cases emergency discs will still get you out of trouble, but you might be out of luck if your PC is infected with a recent virus.

Where a virus is detected it might be possible for the antivirus program to completely remove it from the system. In other cases the program will provide a list of instructions explaining how to remove it manually. Unfortunately, the computer might not work normally once the virus has been removed. Removing the virus and repairing any damage it has caused are two totally different things. An antivirus program may do a certain amount of file repair as part of the removal process, but it is unlikely to undo any wholesale damage to files. Some data files might be erased or damaged beyond repair, so it is essential to keep backup copies of important data. It is also possible that the operating system will remain damaged, and that it will have to be reinstalled. The same is true of any applications software installed on the PC.

Even if your antivirus software is fully up-to-date, it is possible that no virus will be detected. In cases where there were clear signs of a virus causing problems, such as an onscreen message stating that a particular virus was present, you clearly have a major problem. The most likely explanation is that the virus is a recent one, and it has not yet made it into the updates for your antivirus software. Using another computer to search the Internet will usually provide information about the virus that is causing problems with your PC, and with luck there will be details for its removal. It is certainly worthwhile visiting the web site for the publisher of your antivirus program to see if they have any information on the mystery virus. Many offer some sort of customer support that includes help with tackling new viruses.

Where there was no obvious sign of a virus and a good antivirus program fails to find any evidence of one, that does not necessarily mean that no virus is present. If possible, try scanning using another antivirus program, and check the Internet to determine whether other people are having similar problems with a new virus. Being realistic about things, there is little point in spending large amounts of time looking for a virus that is almost certainly not there.

In cases where a fair amount of effort has failed to find any real evidence of a virus it is reasonable to assume that there is another cause of the problem. It is then a matter of going through the usual processes to repair the operating system, locate the hardware fault, or whatever. This goes beyond the scope of this publication, but these books from the same publisher and author as this book provide information on fixing Windows and hardware problems:

BP484	Easy PC troubleshooting
BP495	Easy Windows troubleshooting
BP521	Easy Windows XP troubleshooting

Where a virus has caused massive damage to the operating system or there is no certain way of removing it, drastic measures can be required. Some PC users have been known to throw away the infected hard disc drive and fit a new one. This is a good excuse for upgrading to a bigger and faster drive, but it is not really necessary. Reformatting the existing drive will remove all data from it, together with the operating system, applications software, and any other contents including the virus.

Everything can then be reinstalled from scratch, which will probably be very time consuming. The quicker method is to use a program such as Drive Image or Norton Ghost to take regular backup images of the hard disc drive. The hard disc drive can then be restored to the exact state it had at the time the backup was made. There is a potential flaw in this method in that many viruses have a built-in delay, and this can be quite a long delay of several months or even more. With a virus of this type it is possible that the backup image will contain the virus. This will not matter provided it is possible to neutralise the virus before the restored backup becomes damaged by the activities of the virus. It is a good idea to keep old backup copies. If the main backup is infected you then have the option of using an older backup, which is likely to be quicker than installing everything “from scratch”.

Clean discs?

It is as well to bear in mind that detecting a virus on the hard disc of your PC and removing the infection does not always mean that your computer equipment is totally clear of the infection. It used to be quite common for people to remove a virus only to find it return soon afterwards. The problem was usually that the virus had been introduced to the computer via an infected floppy disc. The virus would usually spread to other floppy discs used with the computer. Using any of the infected discs with the “cured” PC could reintroduce the virus to the computer.

Modern computing practices mean that floppy discs are now less likely to give this problem with reinfection. It is still a good idea to check any discs used with the PC in the last few weeks to see if any are carrying the virus. CDR and CD/RW discs should also be checked, especially if any files have been copied to them from the hard disc drive. The infection can not be spread to an ordinary pressed CR-ROM, but it might be worthwhile checking these as well just in case one of them is the source of the infection.

Other discs such as Zip types are potential carriers of infection, and I suppose that these days you also need to check any drives that are actually in the form of memory devices connected to a USB port, or something of this nature. Anything used to store a file is a potential source of infection, and an infection can be spread to any type of rewritable device.

IE settings

In order to make a PC really secure when using the Internet it is necessary to have some hardware and (or) software to protect the system. However, you can improve security by using the computer in the correct manner when online and by having the best settings in Internet Explorer. The best way of avoiding trouble is to keep away from dubious web sites that offer pirated music, programs, or whatever. If you restrict your surfing to respectable sites and avoid downloading anything that might be a bit dubious you will greatly increase your chances of staying out of trouble. Avoid P2P and similar forms of file swapping, which are a common source of viruses, Trojans, etc.

Be very careful if you find a file on your PC and you do not know what it is or how it found its way onto the hard disc. Opening some form of document file (PDF, DOC, and so on) or running some form of program file (EXE or COM) could activate some form of attack. Simply deleting a mystery file is not a good idea because it might be a file you need but have forgotten about. It is better to first copy the file to a floppy disc, CD/RW, or whatever, and then delete the original. The normal Delete function of Windows puts erased files in the Recycle Bin rather than deleting them straight away. This could leave a Trojan or similar file still on the hard disc. In order to genuinely delete a file it is first selected using Windows Explorer, and then the Delete key is pressed while holding down the Shift key. The file will appear to have been deleted in the normal way, but it will be conspicuously absent from the Recycle Bin.

Up-to-date

Many viruses and worms are designed to exploit a security flaw in an applications program or the operating system itself. Sometimes these flaws have already been covered by software updates, but not everyone has bothered to update their PCs and the infection is able to spread. In fairness to amateur PC users, there have been worms that have exploited old security "holes" in the operating systems of servers. The professionals maintaining the affected servers had not bothered to routinely update their systems. Some worms and viruses exploit previously unknown security flaws, but patches to fix the problem are soon made available when this sort of thing occurs.

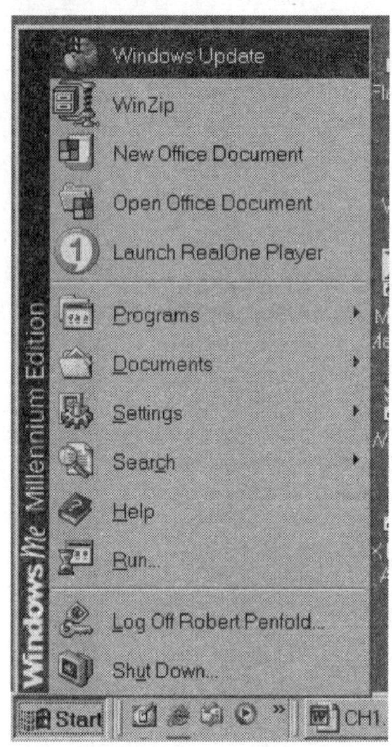

Fig.1.1 The Windows update option

Some applications programs now have an automatic update facility, as does the Windows operating system. A system such as this could be regarded as a potential security risk itself, but manual updates are usually available from the software publisher's web site if you do not trust the automatic approach. In the case of Windows it is possible to launch the automatic update facility via the Windows Update option in the start menu (Figure 1.1). The computer used in this example is running Windows ME, but the process is exactly the same for Windows XP users. Of course, the PC must have an active Internet connection in order to use any form of online update system.

The Windows update system produces the Welcome screen of Figure 1.2, and the first step is to operate the Scan for Updates link near the middle of the page. The scanning process is usually quite quick and produces a list of available updates in the left-hand section of the screen

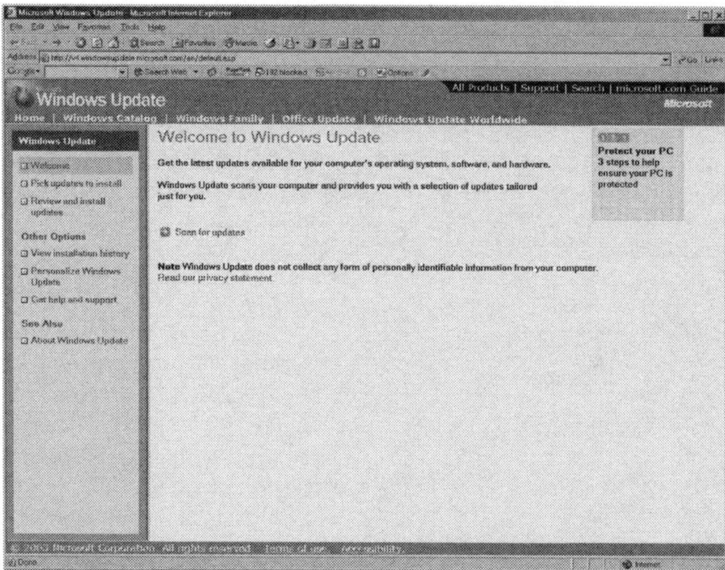

Fig.1.2 The Welcome screen of the Windows Update facility

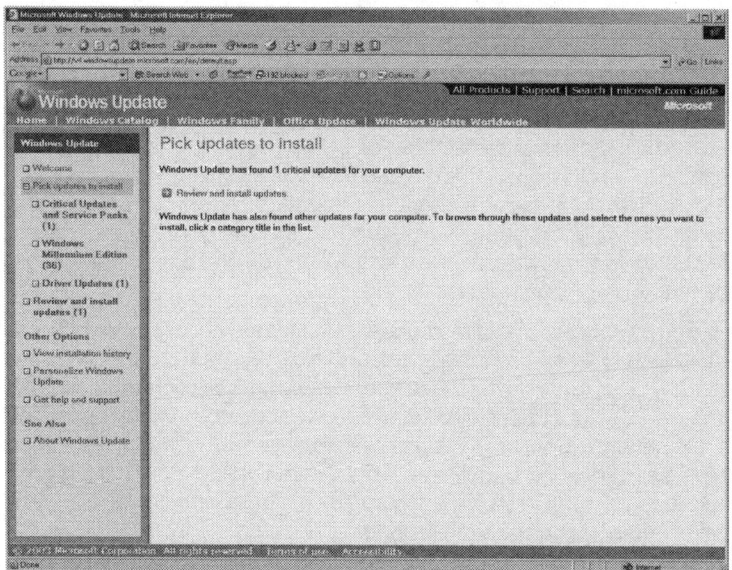

Fig.1.3 The availalable updates are list down the left of the window

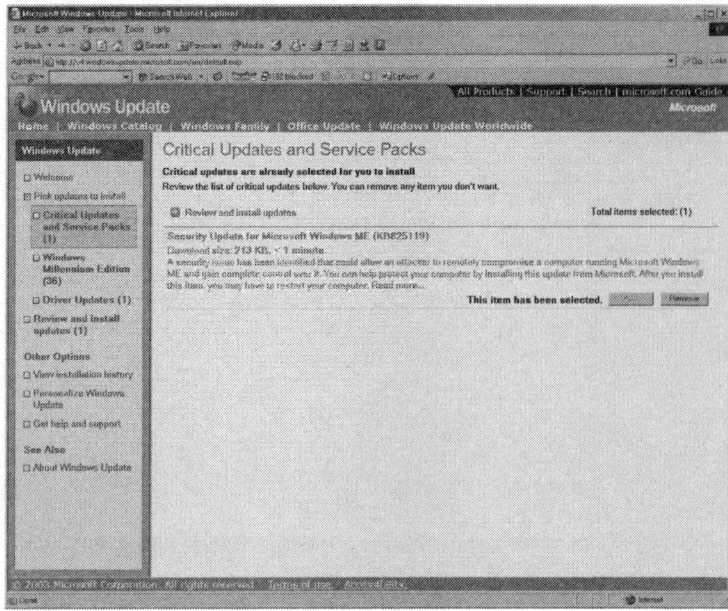

Fig.1.4 Selecting a category provides more details

(Figure 1.3). Left-clicking an entry brings up a list of available updates in that category. The list, together with details of each update, is displayed in the main section of the window, as in Figure 1.4. In this example only one update is listed, but this is a security type that needs to be installed. It is as well to look through the other categories to see if there is anything worth installing, but you will probably find that many of the updates are not of relevance to the Windows installation you are using. There might be foreign language updates for example.

Having selected the required updates via the Add and Remove buttons, activate the Review and Install Updates link in the left-hand section of the window. Then operate the Install button in the main section of the window (Figure 1.5). The updates will then be installed and a small window will show how the process is progressing (Figure 1.6). Once the updates have been installed you will be asked if you would like to reboot the computer. It is not essential to do so, but the updates will not take effect until the computer has been rebooted.

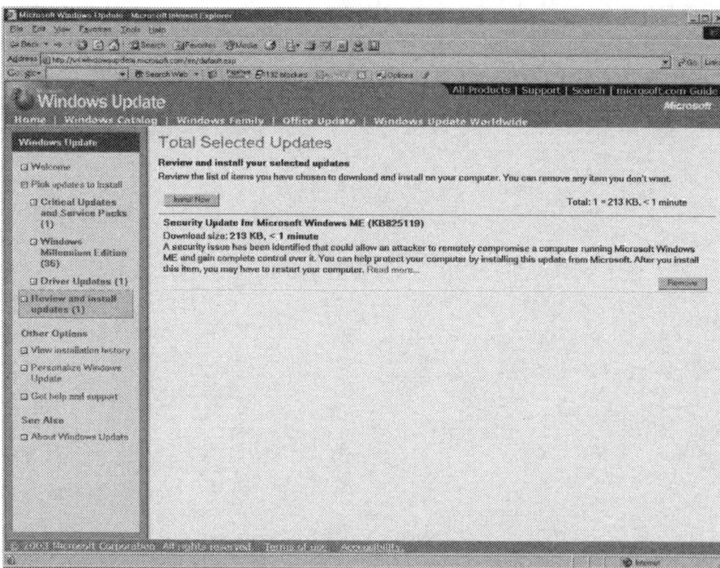

Fig.1.5 Operate the Install button to go ahead with the updates

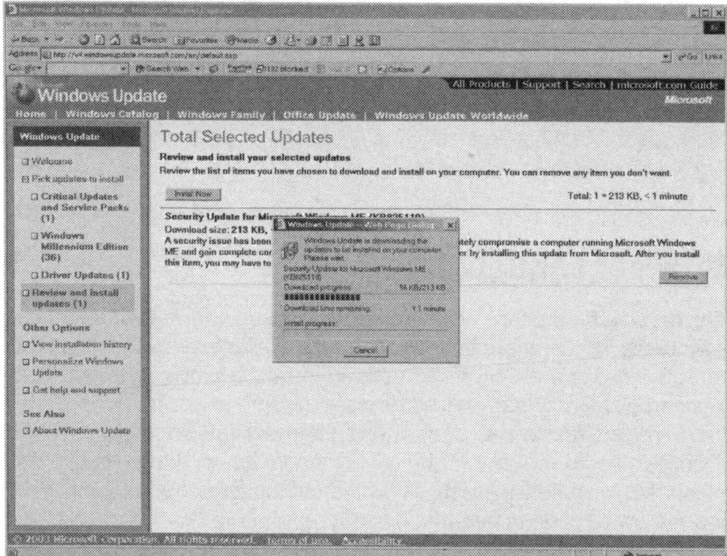

Fig.1.6 The small window shows how things are progressing

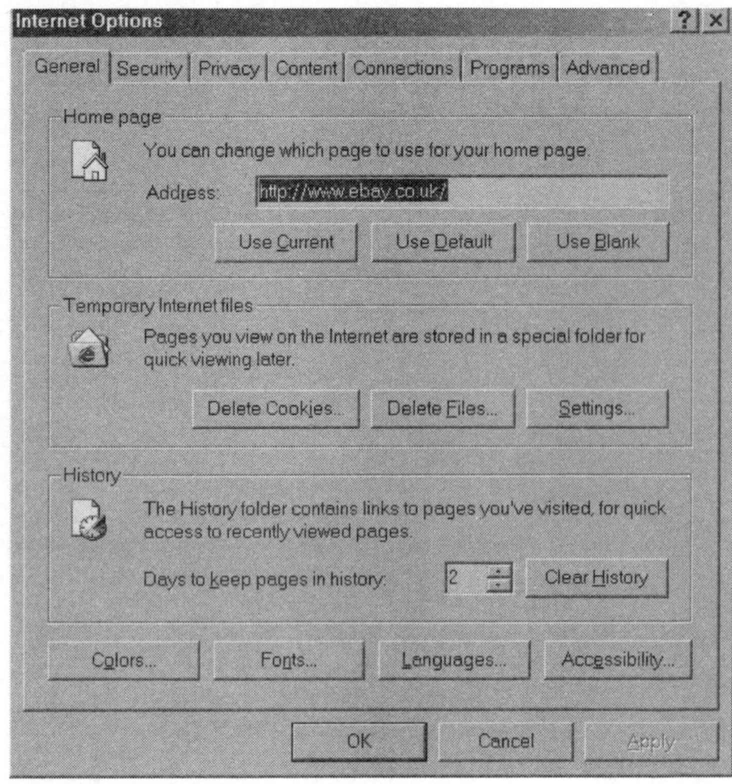

Fig.1.7 The Internet Options window

Browser configuration

The Internet Explorer browser program has some built-in safeguards to help protect your computer from an attack via the Internet. It is possible to vary the degree of protection provided by the browser, which might seem to be an odd way of doing things. Surely it would be safer to have the browser automatically set for the highest possible degree of security? Clearly it would, but the total security approach to things would also mean that many useful features would fail to work. For example, with the maximum level of security it is not possible to download any files, which is a major limitation. You probably use web sites that require users to log on, but most of these sites have a facility that automatically

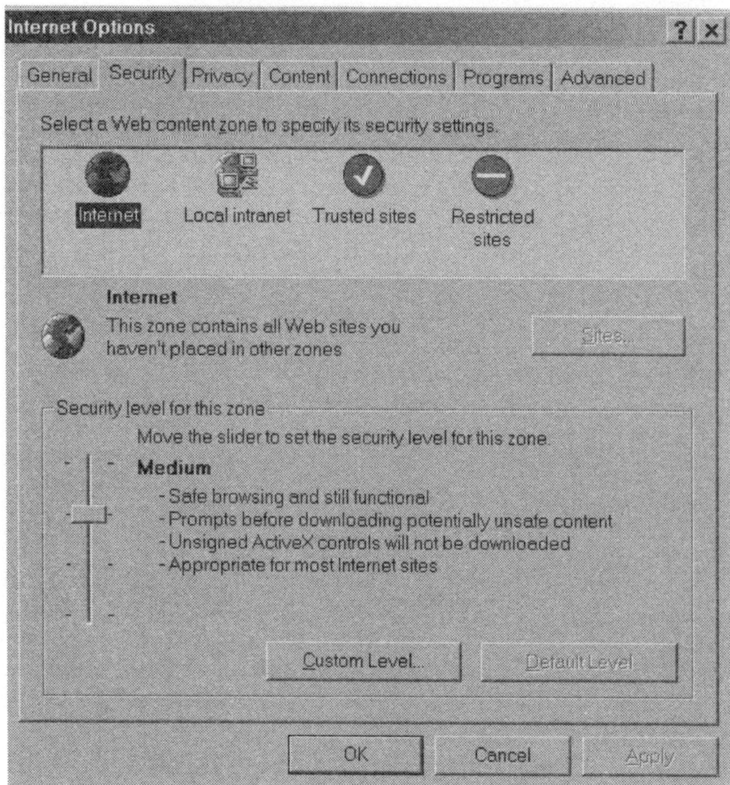

Fig.1.8 The Security options

logs users onto the system. Facilities of this type will not work if a browser is set for maximum security.

The easy way of altering the security setting of Internet Explorer is to run the program and then select Internet Options from the Tools menu. This produces a window like the one of Figure 1.7, and by default the General tab will be selected. The General section is used for altering the homepage and other basic tasks, but it is the Security page that is of interest in the current context. Selecting the Security tab produces a window like the one in Figure 1.8. The degree of security is selected by way of the slider control, which has four settings. These settings are Low, Medium-Low, Medium, and High. The text next to the slider control gives brief details of each setting, but in practice it is really a matter of

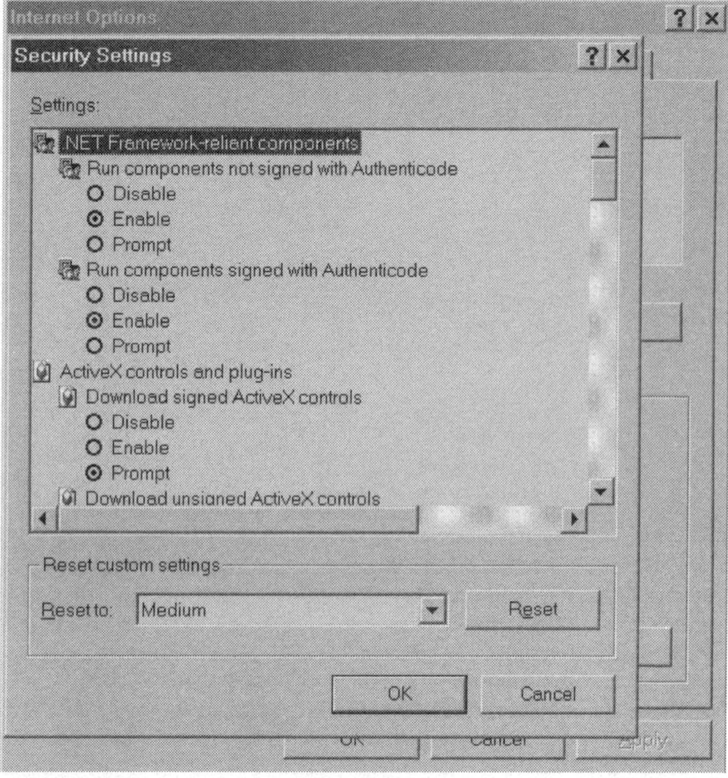

Fig.1.9 More precise control is available if you need it

using the "suck it and see" method. Use the highest level of security that does not result in any features you use being disabled.

Cookies

More precise control over the security settings can be obtained by operating the Custom Level button. A new window (Figure 1.9) is then launched, and this has radio buttons that are used to individually control each aspect of security. In order to use the custom settings properly it is necessary to understand the terminology involved. One of these terms is "cookies", and with older versions of Windows these are controlled via the Custom Level feature. In Windows ME and XP they are controlled

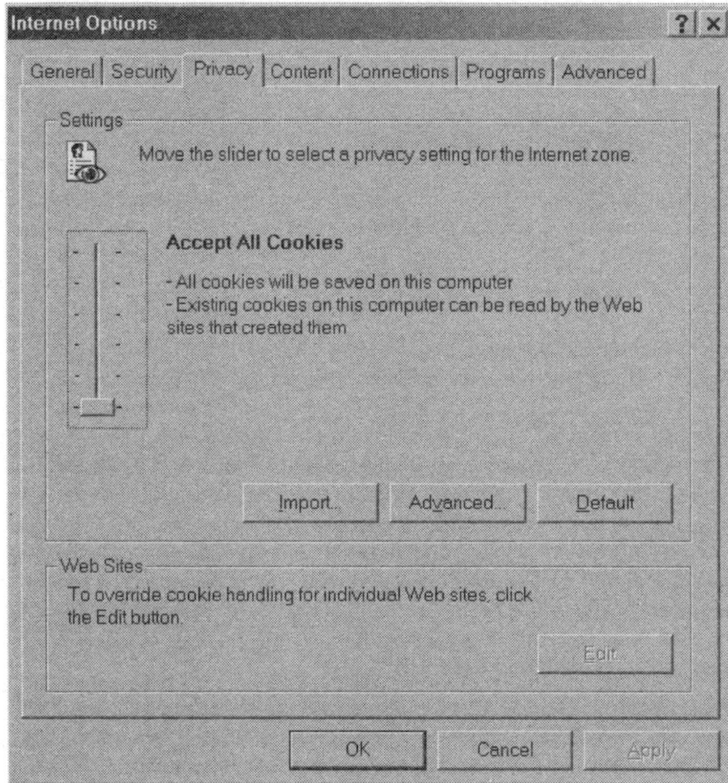

Fig.1.10 The Internet Options Privacy page

separately by way of the Privacy page, and operating this tab switches the window to look like Figure 1.10.

A cookie is just a text file that is deposited on the hard disc drive of your PC when certain web sites are visited. In most cases the use of cookies is optional, but without them you will find that certain features of the site do not work properly. With a few sites you can only use its facilities if your PC is set to accept cookies. Since a cookie is just a small text file it should be completely innocuous. There is a special folder on the hard disc drive for cookies (usually C:\Windows\Cookies), and if you take a look at its contents there will usually be a large number of files there. On my PC I found over 1800 cookies in this directory!

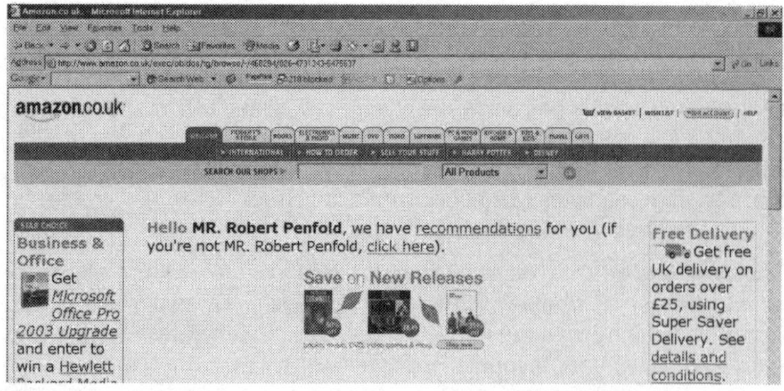

Fig.1.11 Some web sites use cookies for automatic identification

The main use of cookies is to enable a site to automatically identify you on each visit. When I visit www.amazon.co.uk for example, I am greeted with the message “Hello MR. Robert Penfold” (Figure 1.11). The site identifies me by looking for a cookie left on the hard disc during a previous visit to the site. The site will not know who I am if that cookie is deleted or I use a different PC to access the site. Indeed, if I use a PC belonging to someone else and that person has used the Amazon site, it is the greeting for that person that I will receive.

This is a slight drawback of cookies. Anyone gaining access to your PC can take advantage of the cookies it contains. In practice cookies do not give automatic access to anything important. The site of your Email provider might recognise you via a cookie, but you still have to use a password in order to gain access to your Email account. Consequently, someone gaining access to your computer and the cookies it contains should not permit them to access any important accounts. However, never leave passwords anywhere on your PC. Storing passwords on a PC is a bit like locking a door but going off and leaving the key in the lock.

In some cases cookies will provide automatic entry to subscription or other password protected sites. Bear in mind that anyone gaining access to your PC will also gain access to these sites if you opt for the convenience of automatic entry. Furthermore, they will gain access to the sites via your account and in your name. Fortunately, it is unlikely that they will be able to do any real harm since things such as online bank accounts require users to login properly at each visit. Do not opt for automatic entry to any site that contains personal information.

One slight problem with cookies is that they tend to build up on your hard disc drive, especially if you use the Internet for research and visit many sites per day. I think that the importance of this tends to be exaggerated somewhat, since the files are small and will each consume whatever the minimum amount per file happens to be for your PC. Eventually some 25 to 50 megabytes could be used, but with most hard discs having a capacity of 20,000 megabytes this is rather less important than in the days of 500 megabyte discs.

The "belt and braces" approach to removing unwanted cookies is to simply remove all cookies from your PC. This will clearly remove the useful ones along with the rubbish, but the useful ones will be restored on signing in to your favourite web sites again. In order to remove all cookies it is just a matter of launching Internet Explorer, selecting Internet Options from the Tools menu, and then operating the Delete Cookies button in the middle section of the window. Operate the Yes button when asked if you are sure that you wish to delete the cookies.

Many PCs are supplied complete with a suite of utility programs, or you might have bought and installed one. Many of these suites include a utility that helps to identify cookies so that you can remove any that are for sites that are no longer of any interest. There are also shareware utilities that provide this function, and these can be downloaded and tried for free. You only pay for the program if you intend to go on using it. Many cookie related programs can be found at www.shareware.com and similar sites.

In addition to programs that enable unwanted cookies to be deleted there are programs that delete a cookie once the current session has been ended. Some cookies are automatically deleted anyway, and these are known as "session-only" or "per-session" cookies. These programs effectively turn any desired cookie into a session-only type. If you visit a site where cookies are mandatory, a program that has this facility provides an easy way of removing the cookies once you have exited the site.

Cookie options

The cookie control in the Internet Options window has six settings from Accept All Cookies to Block All Cookies. The text to the right of the control briefly explains the effect of each setting. As cookies are relatively harmless, there is probably no significant danger in using Accept All Cookies setting. Cookies do provide a means for your browsing habits to be monitored, so you may prefer to use a higher setting on privacy

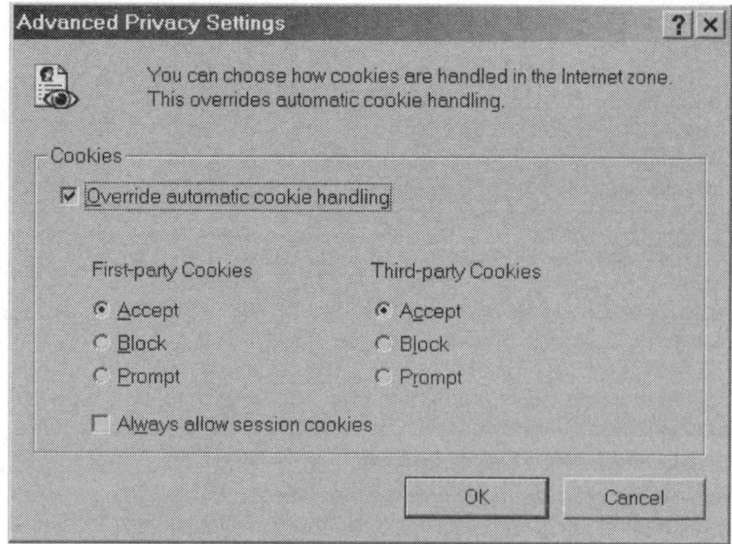

Fig.1.12 The Advanced Privacy Settings window

rather than security grounds. Bear in mind though, that with the higher settings you will almost certainly find that some of the facilities at your favourite sites fail to work, and all or part of a few sites might be inaccessible.

It is possible to override automatic handling of cookies by operating the Advanced button in the Privacy section of the Internet Options window. This produces a window like the one shown in Figure 1.12, and the checkbox near the top must be ticked in order to make the other options active. First and third party cookies can be blocked, allowed to pass, or you can be prompted each time a site tries to use a cookie. There is a lot to be said for the prompting method, which ensures that only cookies you agree to use find their way onto the hard disc. In practice it might mean a lot of hassle though. Per-session cookies will always be allowed if the checkbox near the bottom of the window is ticked. There is probably nothing to be gained by blocking this type of cookie so it makes sense to tick this checkbox.

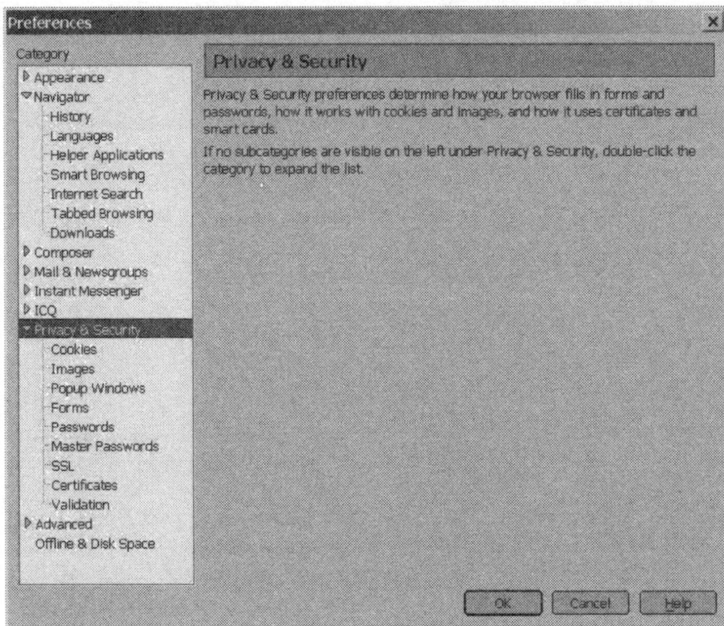

Fig.1.13 Entries can be expanded to show the constituent parts

Netscape

Internet Explorer is by far the most popular browser, but there are others in use, and they have different means of controlling privacy and security settings. Netscape Navigator is the main rival to Internet Explorer, and it has some useful settings that govern privacy and security. These can be accessed by first selecting Preferences from the Edit menu, which launches the Preferences window. Then double-click the Privacy & Security entry in the list down the left-hand side of the window. This will expand the entry to show its constituent parts (Figure 1.13). You can then double-click one of these parts to bring up the appropriate options in the right-hand section of the Preferences window (Figure 1.14). You can control the way in which cookies and pop-ups are handled, whether or not passwords should be remembered, and so on.

Further facilities for handling cookies are available from the Cookie Manager which is accessed via the Tools menu. In addition to the ability to accept cookies, there is a manager facility for stored cookies (Figure

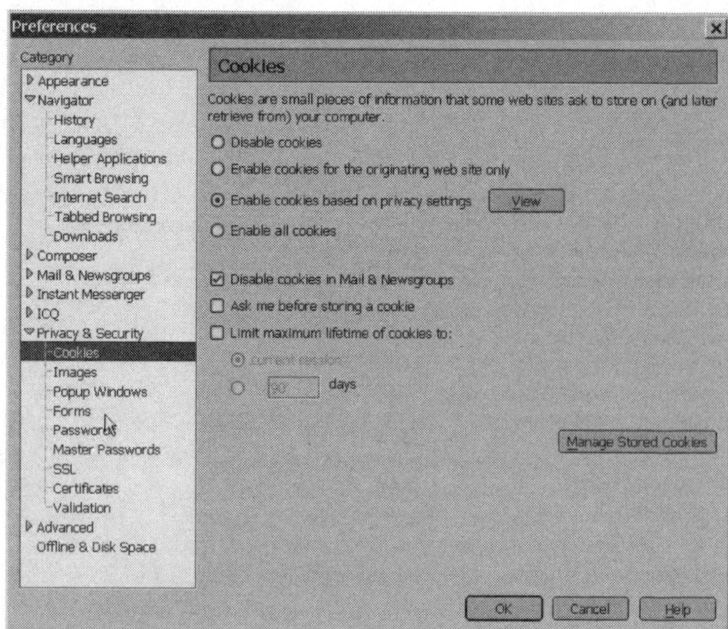

Fig.1.14 Double-clicking an entry brings up the corresponding options

1.15). This shows a list of cookies, together with the site that stored each one. This makes it easy to find and remove unwanted cookies, and there is also a button that enables all the stored cookies to be removed.

Firewalls

A considerable amount of protection can be provided by using the most secure browser settings, but only at the expense of some facilities becoming difficult or impossible to use. There is an alternative in the form of a firewall, which can be either a piece of hardware or a program. A firewall's basic function is much the same whether it is implemented in software or hardware.

Although some people seem to think that a firewall and antivirus programs are the same, there are major differences. There is often some overlap between real world antivirus and firewall programs, but their primary aims are different. An antivirus program is designed to scan files on discs and the contents of the computer's memory in search of viruses and other potentially harmful files. Having found any suspect files, the program will usually deal with them. A firewall is used to block access to your PC, and in most cases it is access to your PC via the Internet that is blocked. Bear in mind though, that a software firewall will usually block access via a local area network (LAN) as well.

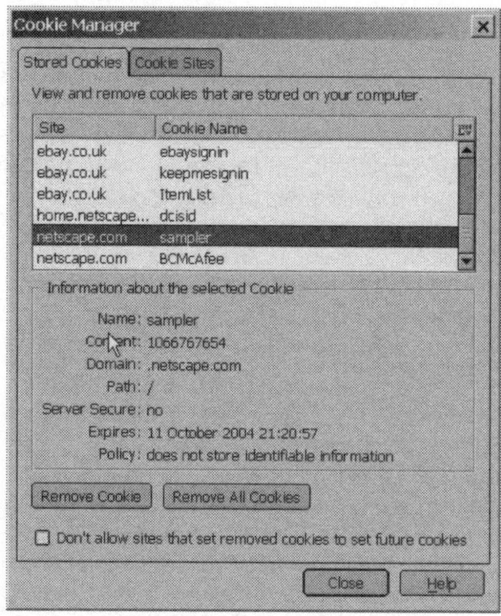

Fig.1.15 There is a facility for managing cookies stored on the PC

Of course, a firewall is of no practical value if it blocks communication from one PC to another and access via the Internet. What it is actually doing is preventing unauthorised access to the protected PC. When you access an Internet site your PC sends messages to the server hosting that site, and these messages request the pages you wish to view. Having requested information, the PC expects information to be sent from the appropriate server, and it accepts that information when it is received. A firewall does not interfere with this type of Internet activity provided it is set up correctly.

It is a different matter when another system tries to access your PC when you have not instigated the initial contact. The firewall will treat this attempted entry as an attack and will block it. Of course, the attempt at accessing your PC might not be an attack, and a firewall can result in legitimate access being blocked. Something like P2P file swapping is likely to fail or operate in a limited fashion. The sharing of files and resources on a local area network could also be blocked. A practical firewall enables the user to permit certain types of access so that the computer can work normally while most unauthorised access is still blocked. However, doing so does reduce the degree of protection provided by the firewall.

Broadband

Using a firewall is considered to be much more important when using some form of broadband Internet access. One reason for this is simply that with a high-speed connection it will be less obvious if someone is accessing your PC. With a slow dial-up connection the additional flow of data would slow things down and be more readily apparent. Another, and perhaps more important reason, is that with most types of broadband connection you are provided with a fixed Internet address. Having found your PC it is possible for a hacker to go back to it again whenever it is switched on. With a dial-up connection your Internet service provider (ISP) normally provides a new Internet address each time you logon to their system.

Another point to bear in mind is that with a broadband connection the PC is usually connected to the Internet all the time that it is operating, and not just when you decide to go online and do some surfing. With many PCs this means that there is a connection to the Internet virtually all day every day. Even if you are provided with a new Internet address each time the PC is switched on, it will probably be operating with that address for many hours before it is switched off again. This still leaves it relatively vulnerable to attack.

With some types of modem the Internet connection does not close down when the PC is switched off. The modem remains connected to the Internet all the time unless it is switched off, which most users do not bother to do. With this setup the system retains the same address for what could easily be weeks or even months. This effectively gives the system a permanent address.

Hardware or software?

For users of ordinary dialup connections there is probably no inexpensive hardware option available, and a software firewall has to be used. For broadband users the hardware option is usually available at reasonable cost, and it is one that is worth serious consideration. If you use an external broadband modem that connects onto one of your PC's USB ports, or an internal modem, there may be no way of implementing a hardware firewall without also switching to a different type of modem. It is still worth looking to see if anything suitable is available. New computer gadgets are being introduced all the time, and Internet security is something of a growth industry.

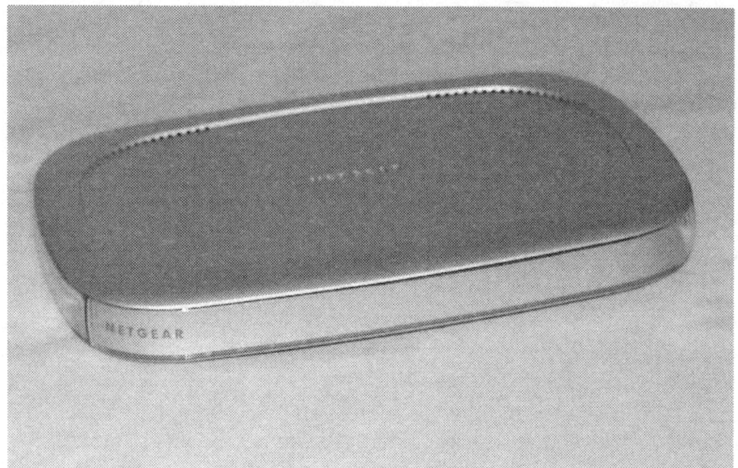

Fig.1.16 This modem has a built-in router and hardware firewall

A hardware firewall is a relatively easy option for those using a modem that connects to the PC via a standard Ethernet. In fact some modems of this type have a built-in firewall. The Netgear DG814 modem shown in Figure 1.16 includes a versatile DSL modem, but it also includes a four- way router, or switcher as this piece of equipment is also known. In other words, up to four PCs can be connected to the unit via ordinary Ethernet ports (Figure 1.17), and each one will appear to have its own

Fig.1.17 There are network inputs for four PCs

Internet connection. In fact the PCs are sharing a single connection, and the router ensures that the received data is sent to the correct PC. It also ensures that any data sent from one PC is kept separate from any data from the other PCs.

The router uses a process known as network address translation (NAT), and it provides the firewall action as a by-product of the sharing process. The only device in the system that can be recognised externally is the router. Anything on the other side of the router is "invisible" to the outside world. The router uses the real Internet address provided by your ISP, but the PCs in the system use a sort of fake address based on the real one. The router makes the necessary adjustments to incoming and outgoing data so that everything runs smoothly.

I tested the firewall capability of the TG814 by going to a website that runs tests that are supposed to shock you by showing how vulnerable your PC is to Internet attacks. In fact the site was unable to access any of the PCs in the system, and was unable to detect a computer at the appropriate Internet address. This lack of success was due to the fact that the system at the test site was "talking" to the router and not the PCs on the other side of the router. There is no point in trying to hack into a PC that is not there.

It is unlikely that this or any other type of firewall can ever be one hundred percent effective against hackers, but it certainly makes it very difficult to hack into one of the PCs in the system. This is probably all you need to do in order to avoid attacks from hackers. If your PC system proves to be difficult to penetrate it is likely that any hackers will go elsewhere in search of easier pickings.

Note that it is not necessary to have a network of several PCs in order to use this type of firewall. The firewall action is still obtained with a single PC connected to the TG814 or a similar unit because the translation process is still used. Also, the modem and the router do not have to be in the form of a single unit. However, unless you are reasonably expert with networking it is definitely a good idea to opt for the modem and router/firewall in a single unit. Setting up the system is very straightforward using equipment of this type.

Software firewall

Broadband is becoming more popular, but most private individuals still use an ordinary dialup connection or a form of broadband where a hardware firewall is not a very practical proposition. Software firewalls are consequently the more popular type with home Internet users. There are a number of well known firewall programs available, and a program of this type is sometimes included in suites of utility programs. Fortunately, these personal firewall programs, unlike the highly sophisticated business firewalls, are reasonably inexpensive. In fact one or two free firewall programs are available. Software firewalls all operate in essentially the same manner and use the same techniques.

One of these techniques is to monitor Internet activity and alert the user if a non-authorised program tries to access the Internet. Initially there might be alerts when running programs that involve legitimate Internet access, but once you have set up the firewall to recognise legitimate Internet traffic this should no longer be a problem. This form of monitoring is guarding against software such as Trojans and spyware that tries to send information obtained from your PC to another system on the Internet.

Note that a hardware firewall will not guard against this type of thing, because it will consider any Internet access that originates from your PC to be legitimate. A software firewall that provides this type of monitoring will detect and block Internet activity from any program that you have not granted Internet access. Although a hardware firewall is very good at guarding against external attacks, it will not prevent an internal attack if you should download a Trojan or similar program. For the ultimate in security a hardware firewall therefore has to be backed up by appropriate software protection. In some cases this additional protection is built into the firewall's hardware, but in most instances a program running on the PC is required.

Another technique used by software firewalls is essentially the same as the one used by routers. The vast majority of incoming messages are in response to a request sent from the PC. The firewall inspects received packets of data and blocks them unless they are the result of a request for data sent by the PC. This method gives excellent security, but some facilities might be lost because they require the initial contact to come from the remote system. Like hardware firewalls, the software variety normally has a facility that permits exceptions to be specified so that these facilities can be reinstated. Of course, this could slightly compromise security, but some types of Internet activity are blocked unless these exceptions are made.

Ports

When dealing with firewalls you are almost certain to encounter the term "ports". In a computer context this normally means a socket on the PC where a peripheral of some kind is connected. In an Internet context a port is not in the form of any hardware, and it is more of a software concept. Programs communicate over the Internet via these notional ports that are numbered from 0 to 65535. It enables several programs to utilise the Internet without the data for one program getting directed to another program.

Firewalls usually have the ability to block activity on certain ports. The idea is to block ports that are likely to be used by programs such as backdoor Trojans but are not normally used for legitimate Internet traffic. A Trojan could be set to "listen" on (say) port 80, and send the data it has collected once it receives a message from a hacker. By blocking any activity on port 80, the firewall ensures that the Trojan can not send any data, and that it will not be contacted in the first place.

Note that most software firewall programs will block this type of activity anyway, because the firewall will detect that an unauthorised program is trying to use the Internet. It will alert the user and only permit the data to be sent if the user authorises it. Presumably the user would "smell a rat" and deny permission for the Trojan to access the Internet. Most hardware firewalls would prevent the message from the hacker from reaching the Trojan, and would also prevent the attack from succeeding. Even so, it is useful to block ports that are likely to be used for hacking the system. Doing so makes it that much harder for someone to "crack" your system, which is what Internet security is all about.

False alarms

Many of the early firewall programs had a major problem in that they were a bit overzealous. While you were trying the surf the Internet there were constant interruptions from the firewall informing you of attacks on the system. In reality these attacks were wholly or largely nonexistent. What the programs were actually detecting was normal Internet activity, and many of the false alarms could be prevented by setting up the program to ignore certain programs accessing the Internet. Some of these programs were virtually unusable though.

Modern firewall programs mostly operate in a rather less "in your face" fashion, and produce fewer interruptions. Even so, it is usually necessary to go through a setting up process in order to keep down the number of false alarms, and further tweaking may be needed in order to get things working really well. Of course, if you would like to be informed about every possible attack on the system, most firewalls will duly oblige

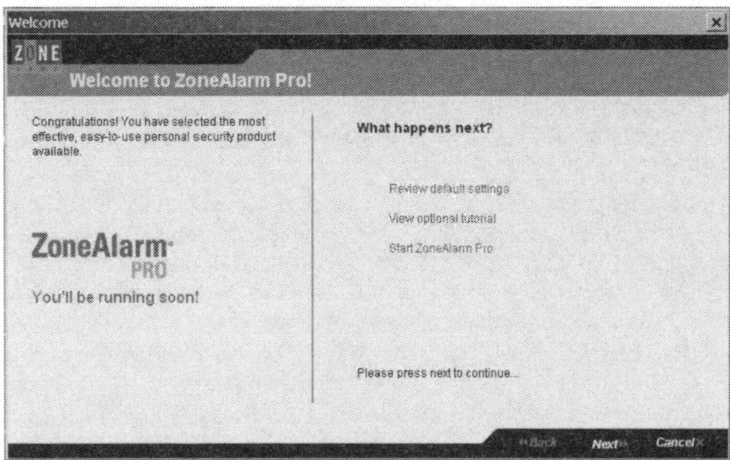

Fig.1.18 The initial screen of Zone Alarm Pro

provided the appropriate settings are used. This certainly gives the ultimate in security, but it could make surfing the Internet a very slow and tedious process.

Zone Alarm

There are plenty of software firewalls to choose from, and most of them are capable of providing your PC with a high degree of security. Black Ice Defender is a popular program that has the advantage of requiring little setting up before it is ready for use. Zone Alarm is another popular firewall, and it exists in free, trial, and full commercial versions. It is quite easy to set up and use, and the free version represents a good starting point for private users wishing to try a good quality firewall at minimum cost. All versions of this program are reasonably easy to set up. Zone alarm Pro will be used for this example, and this program has a few more facilities than the basic (free) version.

Figure 1.18 shows the initial window produced once the installation process has been completed. This simply explains that there are a few processes to complete before the program is ready for use. The options available at the next screen (Figure 1.19) are for two of Zone Alarm Pro's optional extras. One of these is a routine that blocks pop-up advertisements and it also blocks third-party "spy" cookies. Pop-ups

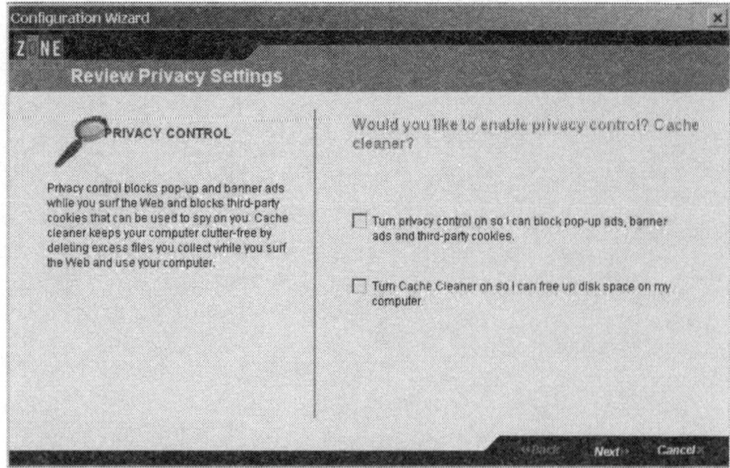

Fig.1.19 Two optional extras are available

are now so widespread on the Internet that they have become a major nuisance. Apart from being irksome, they can effectively slow down your Internet connection by increasing the amount of data that has to be downloaded. This can be a serious drag on your surfing if you do not

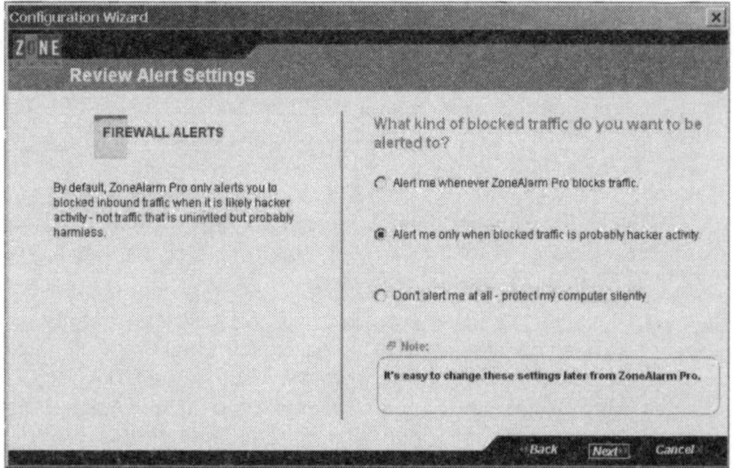

Fig.1.20 Here you select the level of alerts that will be produced

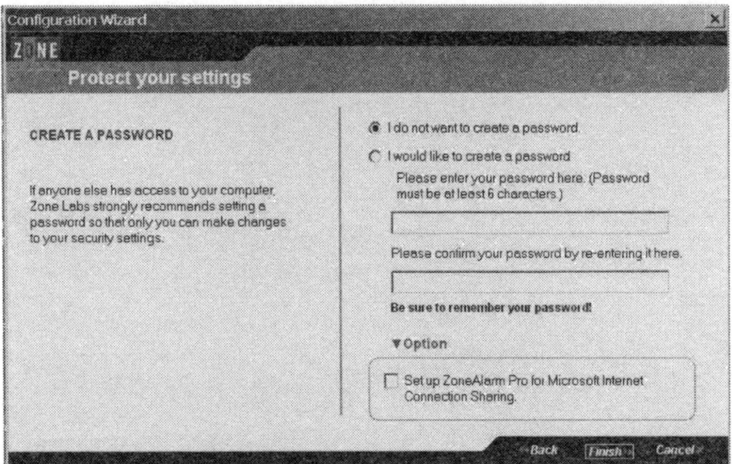

Fig.1.21 If required, the program can be password protected

have some form of broadband connection. A pop-up blocker is therefore a very useful feature.

Cache cleaning is the other option. Copies of many Internet files are kept on a PC so that they do not have to be downloaded again when the relevant pages are revisited. Anyone undertaking a lot of surfing is likely to end up with many megabytes of cached Internet files on their PC's hard disc. These files should eventually be removed by Windows, but the cache cleaner provides a neater solution by preventing a massive build-up from occurring in the first place.

Things then move on to a window (Figure 1.20) where you choose the types of Internet access that will produce alerts. You can opt to have an onscreen message appear when any access is blocked, or for no alerts to be issued. Note that the program will still continue to block Internet access as and when it sees fit, even if the alerts are completely switched off. The middle option results in an alert being produced when the program considers that attempted access is probably the result of an attack by a hacker. This is the default option and is probably the best choice.

The next window (Figure 1.21) enables the program to be password protected. This is only necessary if someone else has access to your PC. This is followed by the screen of Figure 1.22. Here Zone Alarm lists programs that it thinks will need Internet access. The list will include the

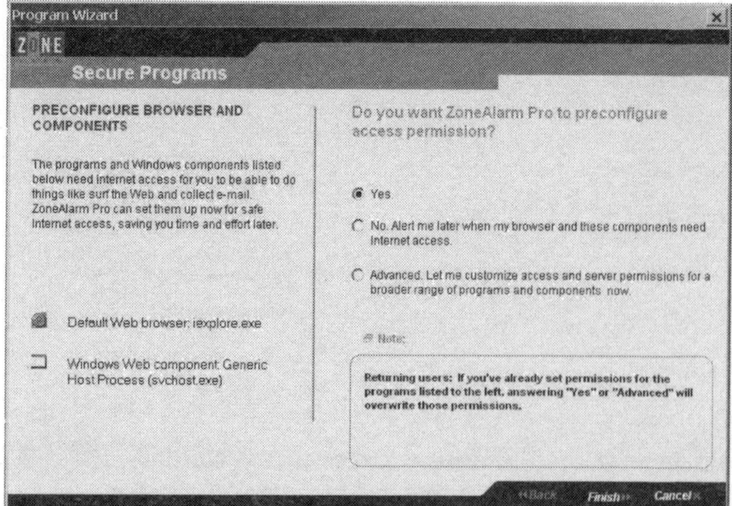

Fig.1.22 You can choose which programs are granted Internet access now or later

default browser and any other programs that are required for normal Internet access. By default, these programs will be given Internet access, but other programs will produce a warning message if they attempt to

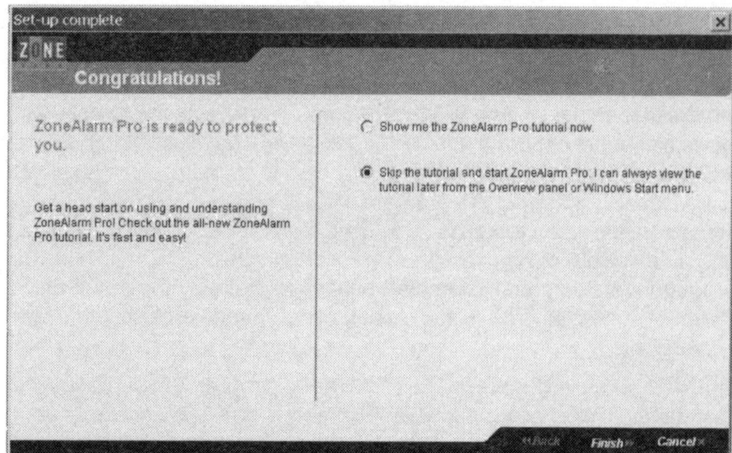

Fig.1.23 You can start the program or view a tutorial

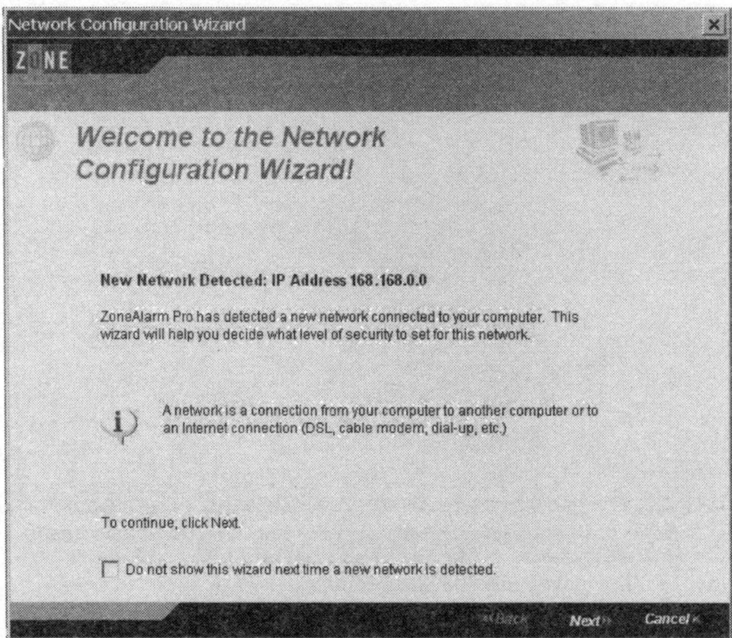

Fig.1.24 The program has detected a network, and it has to be configured so that Zone Alarm will permit file sharing

use the Internet. Access will then be allowed only if you give permission. You might prefer to choose which programs will be granted access during the setting up process rather than dealing with it later as programs try to access the Internet. As most programs do not require Internet access, it is probably easier to grant access as and when necessary.

The next window (Figure 1.23) gives the option of starting the program or viewing a quick tutorial. It is definitely a good idea to look at the tutorial, but it can be viewed at any time by running Zone Alarm Pro and operating the Tutorial button.

Network

The PC used for this demonstration has its Internet connection provided by a broadband modem that has a built-in router, with two other PCs connected to the router. This network was detected by Zone Alarm Pro

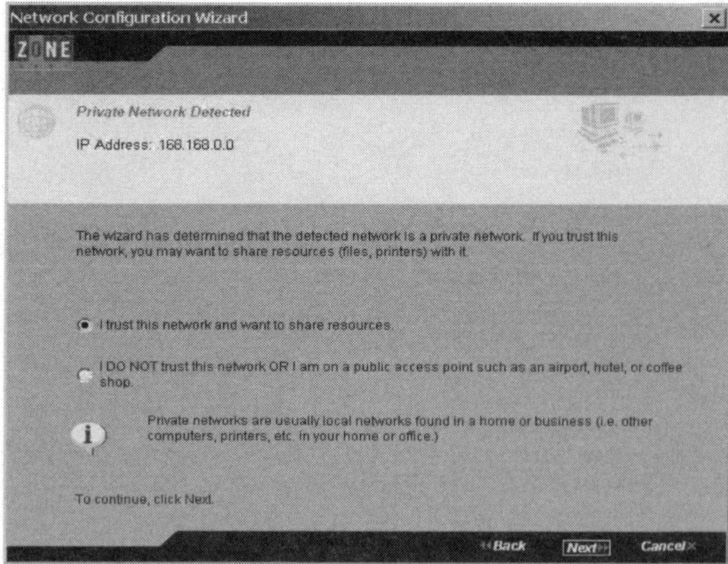

Fig.1.25 The network can be enabled or blocked

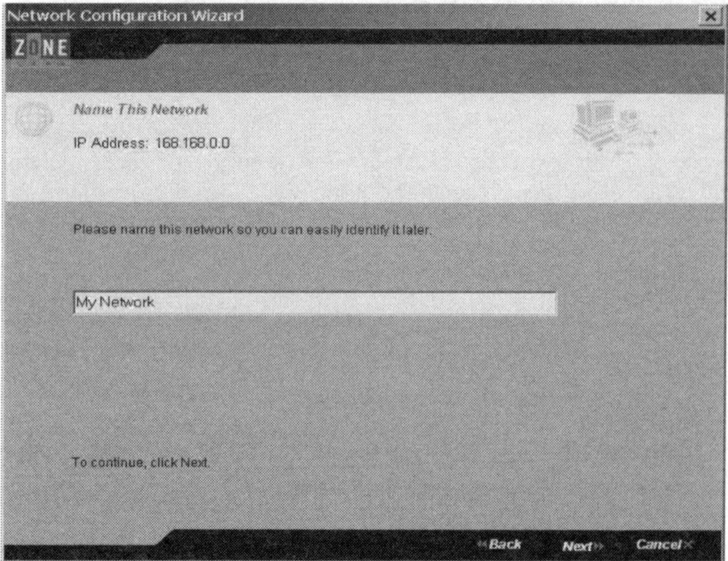

Fig.1.26 Here you can give the network a name or accept the default

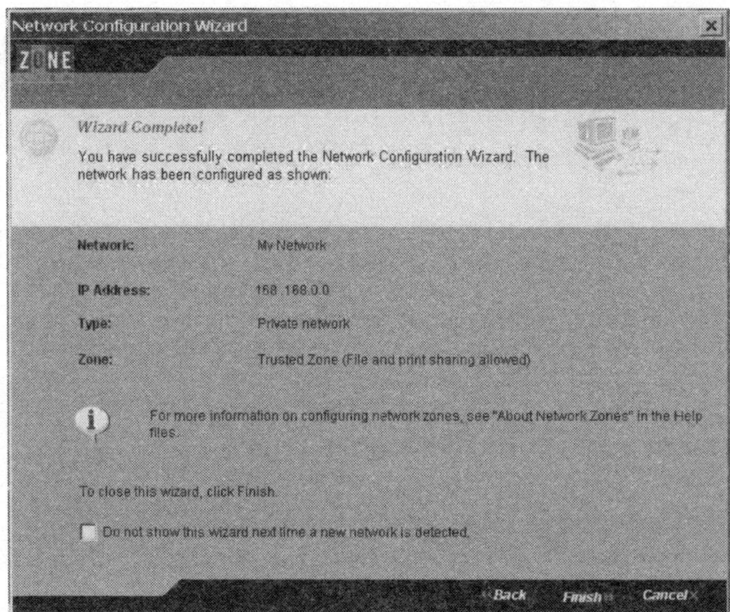

Fig.1.27 Use this window to review the selected settings

(Figure 1.24), and the Network Configuration Wizard was launched. Remember that a firewall will block any network access, including the LAN (local area network) variety, unless instructed otherwise. At the next screen (Figure 1.25) you have the option of enabling this network or blocking it. Obviously it must be enabled in order to permit the system to go on working properly.

The window of Figure 1.26 enables the network to be given a name of your choice, or you can simply settle for the default name. The next window (Figure 1.27) simply shows the settings you have chosen and provides an opportunity to go back and change them. Finally, the program is run (Figure 1.28). In normal use the program runs in the background and it is only necessary to go to this screen if you need to make changes to the setup or view the statistics produced by the program.

Operating the Firewall tab switches the window to look like Figure 1.29, and the degree of security in each zone can then be adjusted via the slider controls. Unless there is good reason to change the setting for the Internet Zone, it should be left at High. The other tabs permit easy control

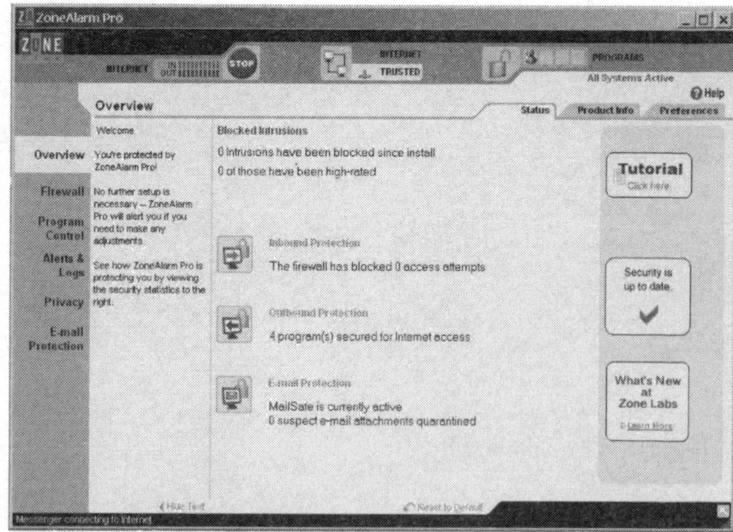

Fig.1.28 Finally, the program is operational

of other aspects of the program, such as alerts (Figure 1.30). Therefore, if you find any of the initial settings unsatisfactory it is easy to change them.

In use it is likely that the program will initially query potential problems that are really just a normal part of PC's operation. In the example of Figure 1.31 an alert has been triggered by an image editing program trying to access the Internet. Although there is no obvious reason for such a program requiring the Internet, many programs these days use the Internet to regularly look for program updates. Operate the Yes button to permit Internet access or the No button to block it. Tick the checkbox if you would like this answer to be used automatically each time the program tries to access the Internet.

Sometimes the alert will genuinely find something that is amiss. In Figure 1.32 the alert shows that a file called msbb.exe has tried to access the Internet. Some delving on the Internet revealed that this is part of the Ncase adware program, which was supposedly uninstalled from the PC a few weeks earlier. Clearly it had not been successfully uninstalled, and some further work was needed in order to banish it from the system.

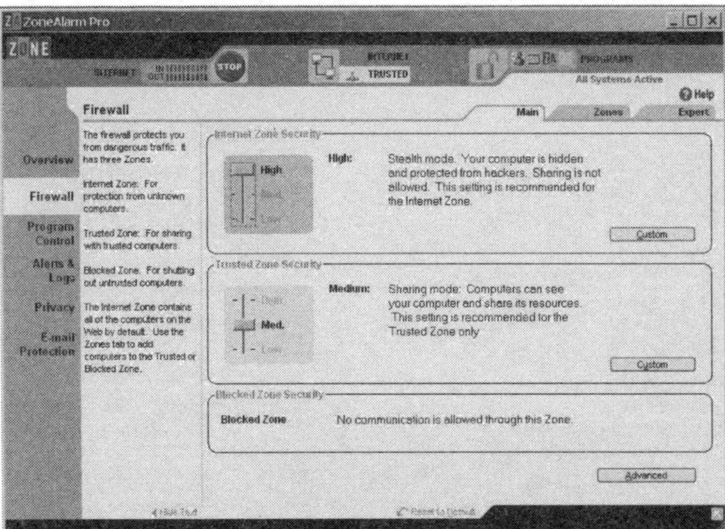

Fig.1.29 Here the Firewall tab has been operated

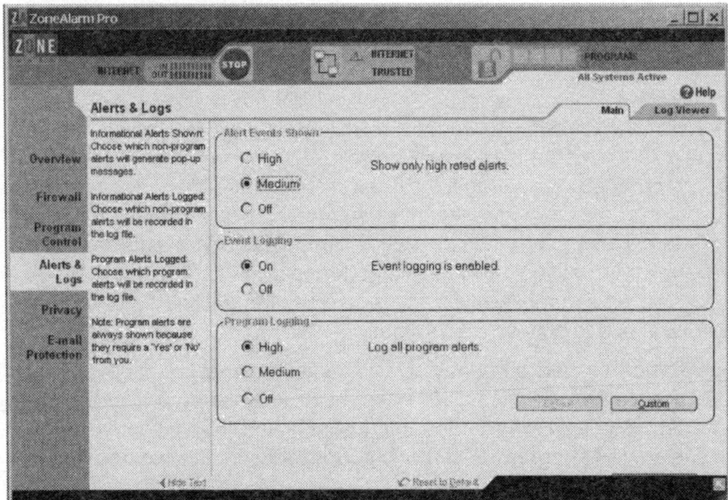

Fig.1.30 You are not stuck with the options selected during installation. The settings available via this tab enable the alert settings to be changed

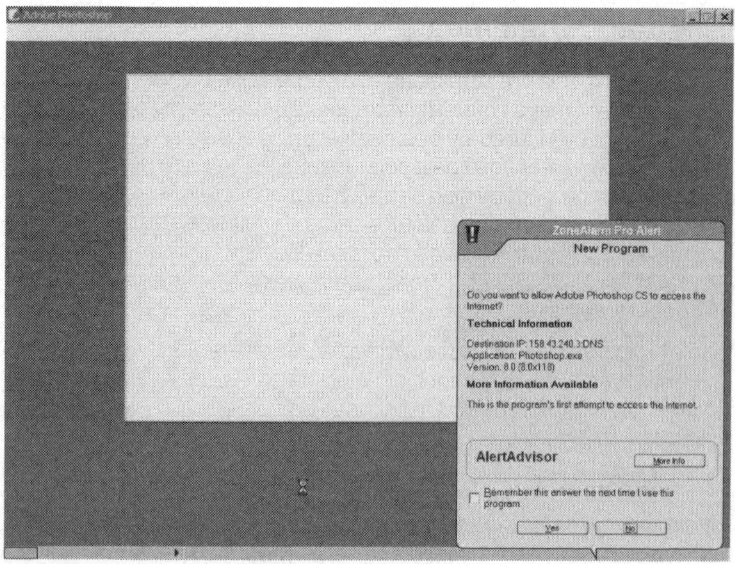

Fig.1.31 An alert produced by a program trying to access the Internet

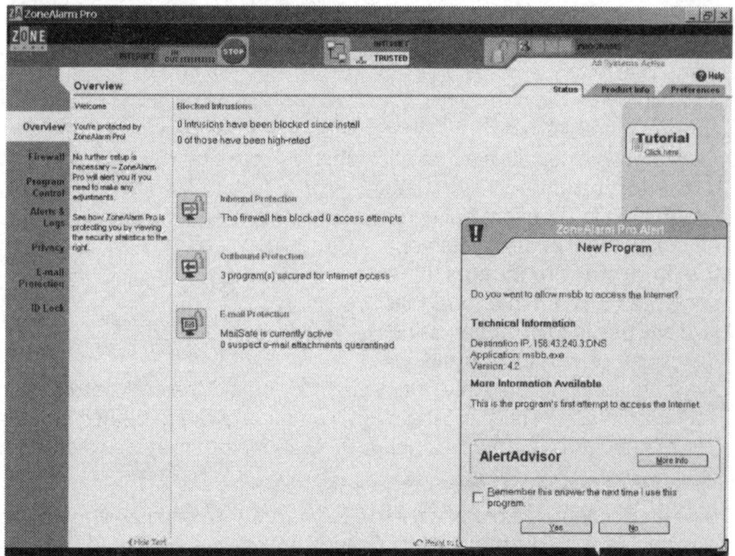

Fig.1.32 This alert was produced by an adware component

Digital Certificates

Digital certificates are something that you are likely to encounter on the Internet from time to time. The purpose of the certificate is to guarantee the identity of an individual or organisation, and they could be regarded as the digital version of a passport. Having the identity of the person or organisation properly verified should in turn guarantee that you can safely download their program, use their site, or whatever. Typically a digital certificate is encountered when downloading a player program to permit a media file to be played. Digital certificates are also used much used for secure web sites.

In order to be of any value the certificate must be issued by a recognised certificate authority (CA) such as VeriSign. Certificates have an expiry date and must be renewed from time to time. Occasionally a warning message might be produced as you enter a site, due to the certificate having been allowed to lapse. There is probably nothing to worry about if the site is one that is tried and tested. The certificate has probably been allowed to lapse due to an oversight. If the site is not one that you have used regularly in the past it is probably a good idea to give it a miss until the certificate is renewed.

Secure site?

Many web sites claim that they are secure and that any information that you supply to them is hacker-proof, but how do you know if a site is actually a secure type? For that matter, what exactly is a secure site? Sites that take sensitive information such as credit card details normally use encryption so that your information is safe from hackers. A hacker might actually intercept the information, but as it is encrypted it is not in a form that is of any use to them. Even using the most powerful computers available today it would take many years to "crack" the code and extract your credit card details, or whatever. No one is going to bother, and the information would probably be well out of date by the time it was recovered by a hacker.

Fig.1.33 The lock icon of Internet Explorer

By default, Internet Explorer will tell you when you are entering and leaving a secure site. This can get a bit irritating, so most users switch off these messages. Even where they are still operational, it can be difficult to keep track of things if the messages keep popping up. Fortunately it is very easy to determine whether or not a secure site is being accessed using Internet Explorer. A tiny padlock icon appears near the bottom right-hand corner of the window when visiting a secure site (Figure 1.33). If this icon is absent, the site is not secure, even if it contains claims to the contrary. Netscape browsers use a similar system, but the padlock icon (Figure 1.34) is normally the same colour as the background, and it turns yellow once into a secure site.

Fig.1.34 Netscape's version of the lock icon

The encryption and decryption process is very complex, but can be handled very rapidly by modern computers. Information sent from your PC to a secure site is mathematically manipulated using a very large number as the basis of the changes. This number is not secure, and a hacker could gain access to it. The "trick" of this system is that the encryption code is not enough to decrypt the data that you send. An additional code number is required, and this is known only at the secure site. These codes are known as the private and senders keys.

Although simple in principle, it took many years for someone to actually come up with a practical system of this type. The degree of security provided by the current systems is so high that there is no realistic chance of anyone intercepting and decrypting your credit card details, etc. It would be easier to steal the information by more conventional means. Do not send sensitive information to a site that is not secure. Note that older browsers can not handle the current level of encryption (128-bit), but this should not be a major problem unless you are using a real "golden oldie" version of Netscape, Internet Explorer, or whatever. For the ultimate in security it is advisable to always use the most up-to-date version of a browser that your PC can run. Check for updates that will improve various aspects of your browser's security including encryption.

Points to remember

The term "virus" tends to be used to describe a wide range of harmful files, but strictly speaking it refers to a specific type of threat. A virus attaches itself to other files and tries to spread across the system. It may or may nor cause severe damage to the system, and in practice most viruses do try to damage data and (or) the operating system.

A Trojan is a program that purports to be one thing but is actually something else. Some Trojans attack the system, much like viruses, but can not replicate and spread like a virus. A backdoor Trojan helps hackers to penetrate your computer system, either with a view to causing damage or to steal information.

A worm looks for security "holes" in other systems in an attempt to attack that system and spread from it. Some of the worst computer attacks in recent times have been from worms that are spread by Emails, and replicate by sending copies of themselves to every address in the address book of the attacked system.

Prevention is better than cure. A good antivirus program can cost little or nothing and will immediately spot most viruses. New viruses are appearing all the time, so remember to keep the antivirus program up-to-date.

Antivirus programs are of limited use against hackers. In order to keep hackers at bay it is essential to use either a software or hardware firewall. Ideally, both should be used if you have some form of broadband connection, especially if it is of the "always on" variety.

Visiting dodgy sites and using "pirated" software are good ways of introducing viruses and other harmful files to your PC. Using peer-to-peer programs to swap files is another good way of doing it.

Use common sense and never take anything on the Internet at face value. If something looks too good to be true then it probably is.

Secure sites are now so secure that there is no realistic chance of a hacker stealing information you send to this type of site. Do not send credit card details or other sensitive information to sites that are not secure. A lock icon appears in the status bar of your browser when you access a secure site.

2

Antivirus software

Be prepared

Many computer users take the view that they do not need antivirus software until and unless a virus attacks their PC. This is a rather short-sighted attitude and one that is asking for trouble. As explained in the previous chapter, by the time that you know a virus has infected your PC it is likely that a substantial amount of damage will have already been done to the system files and (or) your own data files. Using antivirus software to help sort out the mess after a virus has struck is "shutting the stable door after the horse has bolted". The virus may indeed be removed by the antivirus software, but there may be no way of correcting all the damage that has been done.

Another point to bear in mind is that your PC could be rendered unbootable by the virus. Many viruses attack the operating system and will try to make the system unbootable. If the system is not bootable, you can not install antivirus software. As pointed out in the previous chapter, most antivirus programs do some basic checks as part of the installation process. The program will not be installed if any hint of a virus is detected. The reason for this is that the installation process involves copying numerous files onto the hard disc and making changes to some of the Windows system files. This can provide an opportunity for the virus to spread and do further damage.

Many antivirus programs can be used once a virus has attacked a PC, and even if the PC can not be booted into Windows. One approach is to either have a set of boot floppy discs supplied as part of the package, or for these rescue discs to be produced during installation. If the PC becomes unbootable at some later date and a virus is thought to be the cause, the PC is booted from the first disc in the set. A series of checks are then performed, with the other discs being used as and when required.

A more modern alternative to this method is for the installation disc to be a boot type. The basic facilities provided are generally much the same as when using a set of boot discs, but there is no need to keep changing discs. Also, the high capacity of a CD-ROM means that more facilities are easily included in the program suite, if required. The drawback of both methods is that the discs will be something less than fully up-to-date, and may not be able to handle some of the more recent viruses.

Other options

There are other ways of handling things that do not involve any form of antivirus rescue disc. Where there is a recent backup of the system and all your data it makes sense to simply wipe the hard disc clean by reformatting it and then restoring the backup. This will completely destroy any infected files and should provide you with an infection-free system. However, in this situation it would be a good idea to run some antivirus scans on the restored system just in case the backup copy is infected. Remember that viruses are often designed to lay dormant for some time. The virus could have infected the PC many weeks prior to it showing any obvious signs of the infection.

Another approach is to again wipe the hard disc of all its contents but to then reinstall everything “from scratch”. It is important to realise that with this method any data on the hard disc drive will be lost. Depending on the importance of the data on the disc, and whether backup copies are available, it might be necessary to rescue the data on the disc first, or to attempt a rescue anyway. It might not be possible to rescue anything in cases where the damage to the contents of the disc is severe. Unless you have a backup of the system there is no alternative to reinstalling everything “from scratch”. Any data that has not been backed up will be lost, which is why you should always have at least one backup copy of any important data.

For those prepared to mess around with the hardware, another method is to add a hard disc to the PC. This disc is set as drive C (the boot disc) and it has Windows installed in the normal way, complete with some antivirus software. The original disc is used as drive D in the new setup, but it is not installed until everything has been fully installed on the new drive C. With this setup it is possible to boot into the fresh copy of Windows on drive C, run the antivirus software, and then use it to scan the infected drive D.

Provided the infected disc can be repaired, the hardware setup can be restored to its original configuration. If not, the new drive can be retained as the boot drive and the applications programs are installed onto it. Any undamaged data files can be copied from the old disc to the new one, and the old disc can then be reformatted. Either way the expense of the new hard disc is incurred, but you have an additional disc that can be more than a little useful for backup purposes.

A method that can not be wholeheartedly recommended is to remove the infected hard disc from the PC and set it to operate as drive D in another PC. The antivirus software on the other PC can then be used to scan the infected disc and, hopefully, produce a cure. There is nothing fundamentally wrong with this way of handling things, and it has a good chance of success. It is difficult to recommend it though, because there is a definite risk of the infection being spread to the second PC rather than being removed from the first one. I suppose that there is little to lose if the second PC is an old one that is not used in any serious applications, and it does not contain any important data. Other methods are preferable unless this is the case.

Topics such as data recovery, making backups, and reinstalling Windows "from scratch" are covered in subsequent chapters. This chapter covers the use of antivirus software and similar programs that are designed to keep your PC clean of any form of infection. Correct use of the appropriate software does not guarantee that the operation of your PC will never be seriously disrupted by a virus or similar infection, but it does greatly reduce the chances of serious problem developing.

Background

Software firewalls were considered in the previous chapter, and Zone Alarm Pro was used as an example of how these programs are set up and used. In order to perform its task properly a software firewall has to run as a background task, monitoring the Internet activity of the PC. With Zone Alarm Pro you have the option of bringing up the program window, but this is mainly done to alter the default settings or view the statistics generated by the program.

An antivirus program does not have to run as a background task, but it does have to do so in order to be as effective as possible. You could simply use the program to periodically scan the drives of your PC, and antivirus programs invariably have this mode of operation. In fact most can be set up to provide automatic scans at a certain time on a given day of each week. This way of handling things has a big limitation though. It is possible for a virus to be on the system for nearly a week before the discs are scanned and there is any possibility of it being detected. In that time the virus could become well entrenched and would probably start to attack the files on the hard disc drive. More frequent scans could be scheduled, but the computer would then spend much of its time looking for viruses. This would probably be inconvenient, and would significantly reduce the operating life of the hard disc drive.

Most antivirus programs have two or three different modes of operation. In addition to the scanning mode, most can operate in real-time, and many have some form of rescue mode that tries to cure problems if a virus should find its way onto the hard disc. It is the real-time mode that is probably the most important. Like a firewall, the program runs in the background and monitors Internet activity. In fact most programs do rather more than that, and also monitor the interchangeable disc drives such as the floppy and CD-ROM drives.

The general idea is to have the program spot a virus as soon as it enters the system, and to then alert the user to its presence before it has time to spread. This greatly reduces the chances of the PC coming to grief, but there is a slight downside with both software firewalls and real-time antivirus programs. They both operate continuously in the background and utilise some of the computer's resources. In particular, they take up a certain amount of the PC's processing time and its memory. This tends to make the computer run applications programs a little slower.

In the past this problem was certainly more of an issue than it is now. The best PCs of ten years ago were far less powerful than an even an inexpensive PC of today. There was often a very marked loss of performance when a firewall or antivirus program was installed on a PC. These days it is unlikely that a noticeable reduction in performance will occur, but there will be some reduction in speed. Another problem with many of the early antivirus programs was that

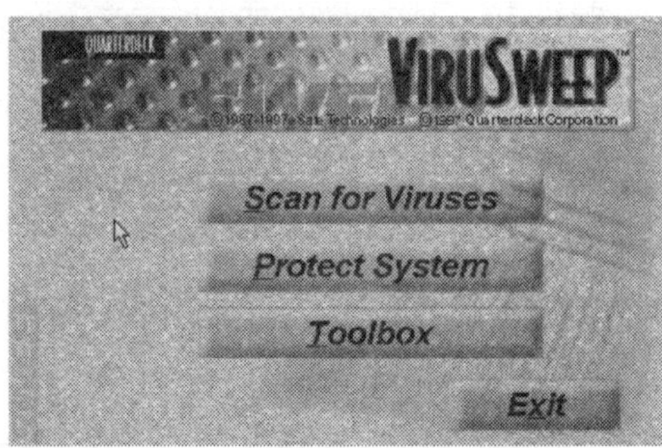

Fig.2.1 The ViruSweep startup screen

they tended to take over the PC. Most were more than a little intrusive in operation, and some produced over-protective warnings whenever you tried to do practically anything. Fortunately, most modern antivirus programs are much more discreet and remain unseen in the background most of the time.

Real world programs

There are a number of "big name" antivirus programs, and any of these should provide your PC with excellent protection against viruses and other harmful files. These programs provide broadly the same functions but are different in points of detail. We will consider a few representative examples here. It is worth emphasising the point that it is not a good idea to have more than one of these programs installed on your PC at any one time. Antivirus programs are less intrusive than they used to

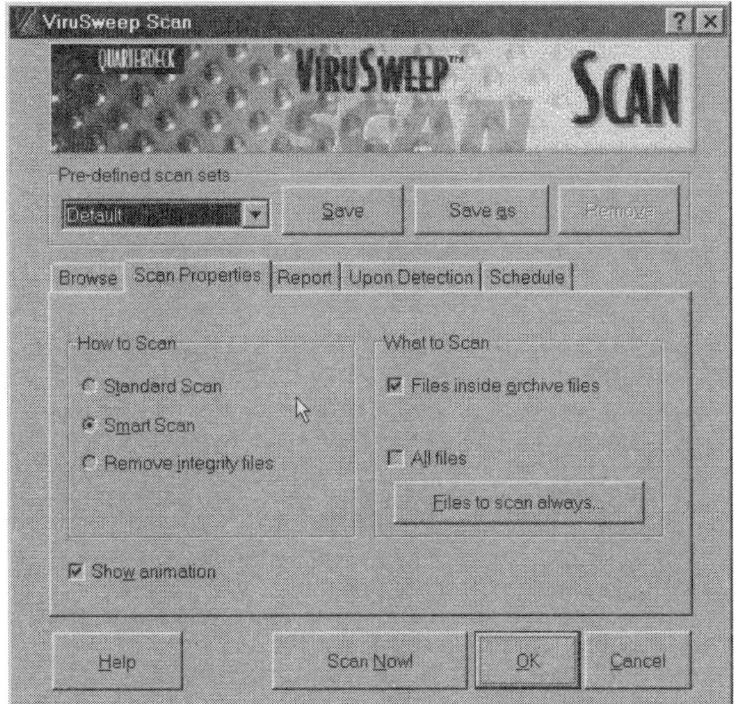

Fig.2.2 The first ViruSweep screen after scanning for viruses

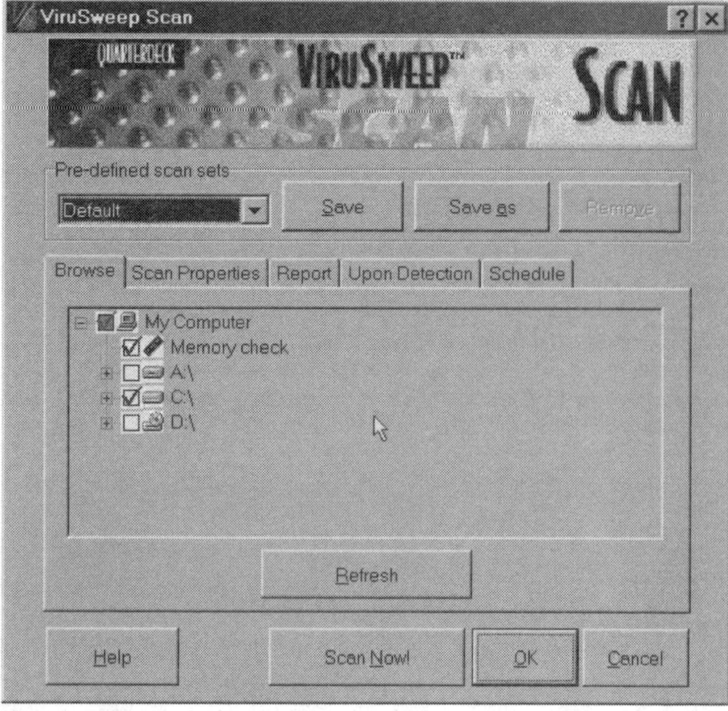

Fig.2.3 This screen enables the type of scan to be selected

be, but they still operate continuously in the background monitoring the PC's activity.

Having two of the programs operating simultaneously can easily produce conflicts that can easily result in the PC crashing. With many of the older antivirus programs you never actually managed to get that far. Having two of them installed on a PC usually resulted in it failing to boot into Windows. It might seem reasonable to have two or three antivirus programs installed, since this gives a better chance of a virus being detected. In practice it does not work very well when applied to real-time monitoring. It can be useful to have the ability to scan using two or three antivirus programs in succession, but having more than one operating at a time is definitely something to be avoided.

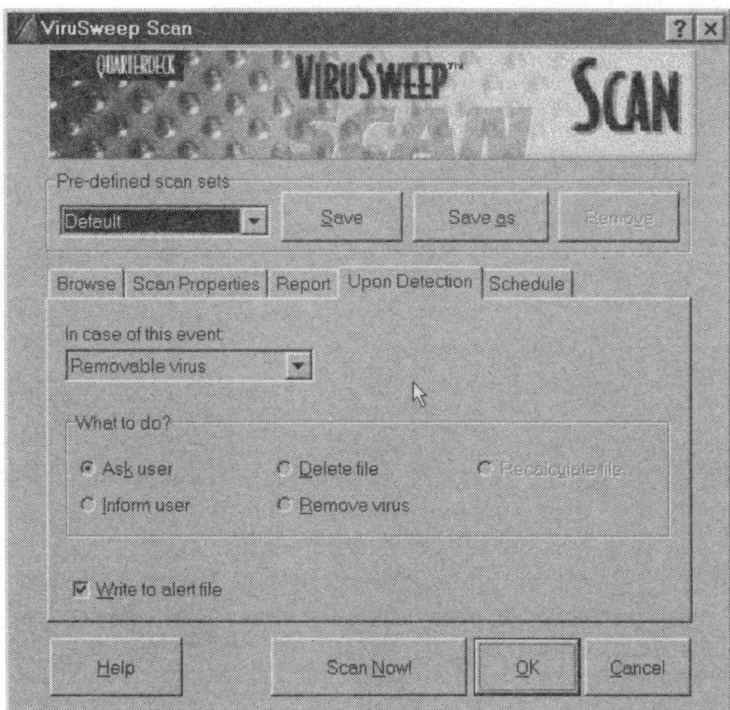

Fig.2.4 This screen gives control over the action taken when a virus is detected

Figure 2.1 shows the start up screen for the Quarterdeck ViruSweep program, and operating the "Scan For Viruses" button takes the user into further screens that permit various options to be selected. The first screen (Figure 2.2) permits the user to select the parts of the system that will be checked. Viruses can exist in memory as well as in disc files, so checking the memory is normally an option. Further screens enable the type of scan to be selected (Figure 2.3), and the action to be taken if a virus is detected (Figure 2.4). Most antivirus software has the option of removing a virus rather than simply indicating that it has been detected. Note though, that in some cases it might not be possible to automatically "kill" a virus. The program will then usually give details of how to manually remove the virus.

Things are likely to be very difficult if you do not use antivirus software and your PC becomes infected. On the face of it, you can simply load

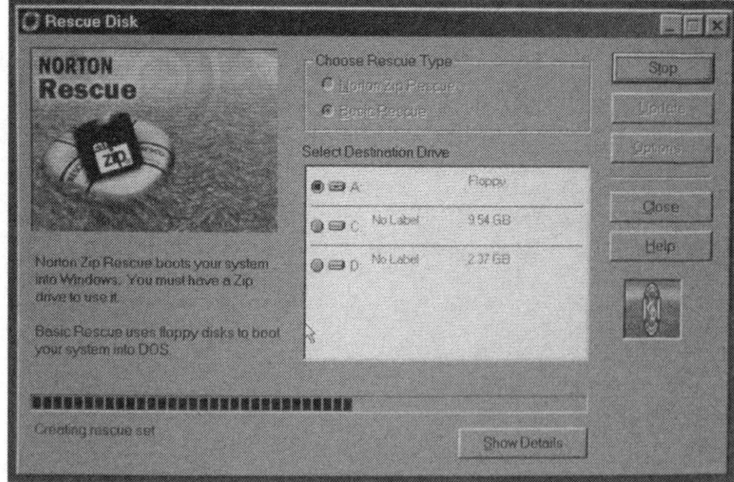

Fig.2.5 Many antivirus programs can make recovery discs. Norton Antivirus makes a set of five recovery discs

an antivirus program onto the hard disc and then use it to remove the virus. As explained previously, it is definitely not advisable to try this method, and most software of this type will not load onto the hard disc if it detects that a virus is present. There would be a very real danger of the antivirus program itself spreading the infection and becoming damaged itself.

Boot disc

The method offered by many (but not all) antivirus suites is to boot from a special floppy disc that contains antivirus software. With this method there is no need to load any software onto the hard disc, and consequently there is no risk of the antivirus software causing the virus to be spread further over the system. With the Norton Antivirus program a boot disc plus four support discs are made during the installation process (Figure 2.5). If boot problems occur at a later date, the PC can be booted using the Norton boot disc, and with the aid of the other discs a comprehensive range of virus scans can be undertaken (Figure 2.6). In some cases the virus can be removed automatically, and it might also be possible to have any damage to the system files repaired automatically as well.

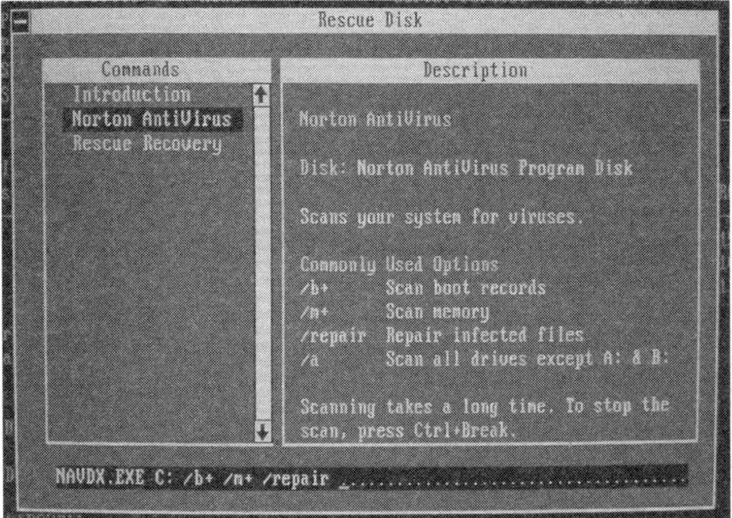

Fig.2.6 Virus scanning using the Norton Antivirus recovery discs

Free check-up

Antivirus software does not rate as one of the more expensive types, and a good antivirus program can be quite inexpensive. It does not have to cost anything at all and there are various free options available if you would prefer not to buy one of the mainstream commercial products. The best source for this type of software is undoubtedly the cover-mounted discs provided "free" with computer magazines. There seems to be a steady stream of antivirus software provided on these discs. Some of these programs are actually only time-limited trials that are of no use for long-term use.

There is a catch with many of the others in that the program is free, but a subscription has to be paid in order to keep the virus database up to date. Note that even with full commercial products the updates are usually only available free of charge for one year. After that time you either have to buy the new version of the program or subscribe to updates. Of course, you can simply continue to use out of date antivirus software, and it will still detect many viruses. However, if a new virus infects your PC it is unlikely that an out-of-date antivirus will be able to detect it.

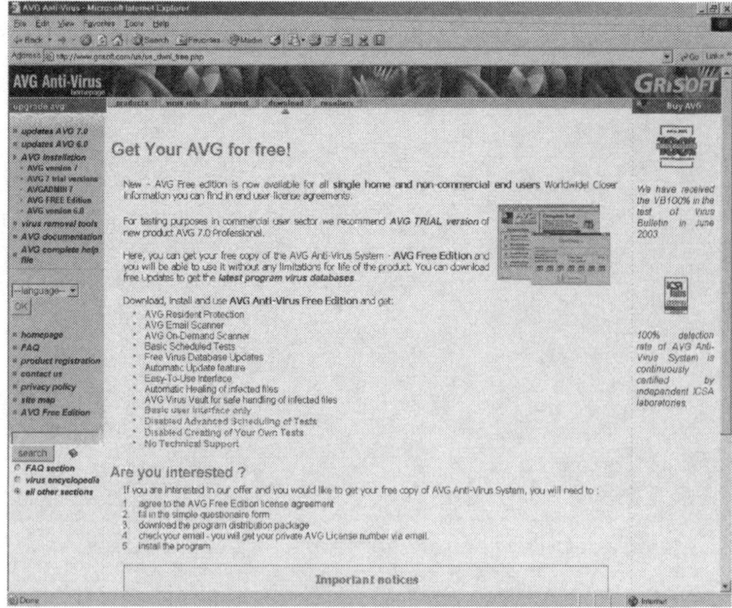

Fig.2.7 AVG 6.0 is available from the Grisoft web site

There are one or two totally free antivirus programs available on the Internet, where you do not even have to pay for monthly online updates to the database. AVG 6.0 from Grisoft is one that is certainly worth trying. The Grisoft site is at:

www.grisoft.com

On the home page there should be a link in the list down the left-hand side called something like "AVG Free Edition". Activating this link will bring up a page like the one in Figure 2.7. This gives some information about the free version of the AVG antivirus program and provides a link that enables it to be downloaded. You do have to go through a registration process, but it is worth the effort. Monthly updates to AVG are available free of charge. This program has a reputation for being very efficient, and it certainly detected a couple of backdoor Trojan programs on my system that a certain well-known commercial program had failed to detect. It is one of the best freebies on the Internet.

It does have one major limitation, which is that it does not have a rescue mode of the type provided by Norton Antivirus and some other programs.

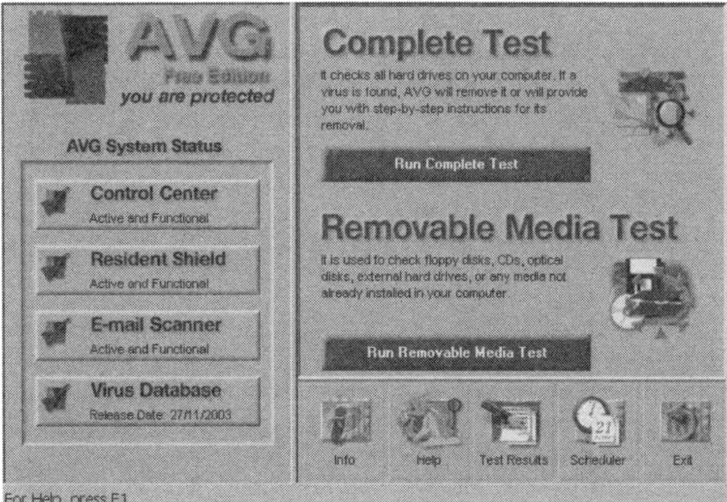

Fig.2.8 The main screen of AVG 6.0

There is a facility to backup important system files so that they can be restored if the originals become damaged by a virus. There is no facility to boot from a floppy disc or CD-ROM drive and run virus checks. The program works effectively in the background detecting the vast majority of viruses, Trojans, etc., so there is little likelihood of a rescue mode being required. However, if you should get unlucky it might be necessary to resort to another antivirus program in order to clear an infection.

AVG does have a useful range of facilities and in other respects it is a very capable program. In common with most antivirus programs you can set it to scan the system on a regular basis, and it also has an automatic update facility. Manual scanning is also available, and this is another standard feature for this type of software. If you suspect that there might be a virus infection somewhere in the PC you can get the program to do a complete scan of the entire system. Another standard option is to scan one or more of the interchangeable disc drives such as a floppy or CD-ROM drive. This is useful in cases where you suspect that a disc someone has given you might contain a virus.

AVG normally runs automatically at start-up and then runs in the background until the PC is shut down, but it can be started in the normal way from the Start menu. It then appears in a window like the one

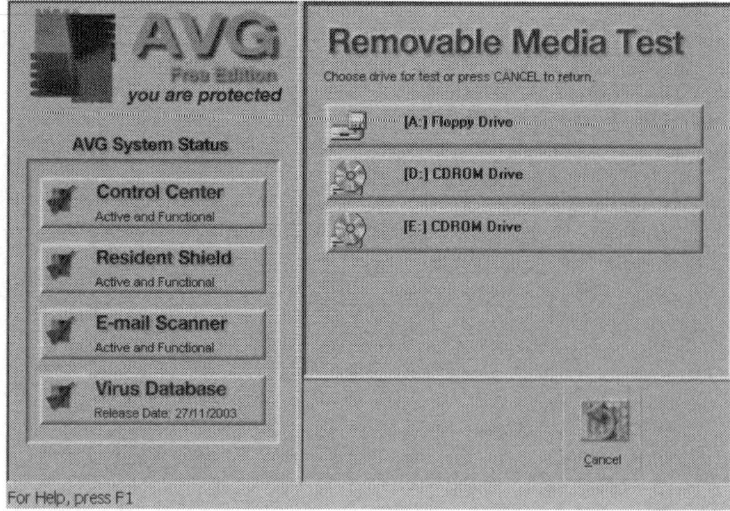

Fig.2.9 Removable media can be scanned for viruses

shown in Figure 2.8. One of the large buttons gives access to the full system scan and the lower one permits the removable media to be checked. Operating the lower button changes the window to look something like Figure 2.9, which has a button for each removable disc fitted to the computer. Operating one of the buttons runs a check on the appropriate drive, and a window showing the results (Figure 2.10) is produced when the process has been completed.

The test results will show what action was taken if one or more viruses were detected. The action taken depends on how the program is set up and precisely what it finds. It will leave the infected file unchanged, delete it, or quarantine the file by moving it to the secure folder that is called the "Virus Vault" in AVG terminology. Alternatively, it will do nothing and ask the user to select the required option.

When running in the background the program is represented by a small button on the toolbar at the bottom of the Windows desktop. Double-clicking the button brings up the control window of Figure 2.11, and this is typical of the way antivirus programs operate. Using this it is possible to alter a number of settings, including the types of scan that are provided. Unless there is good reason to do otherwise it is probably best to leave

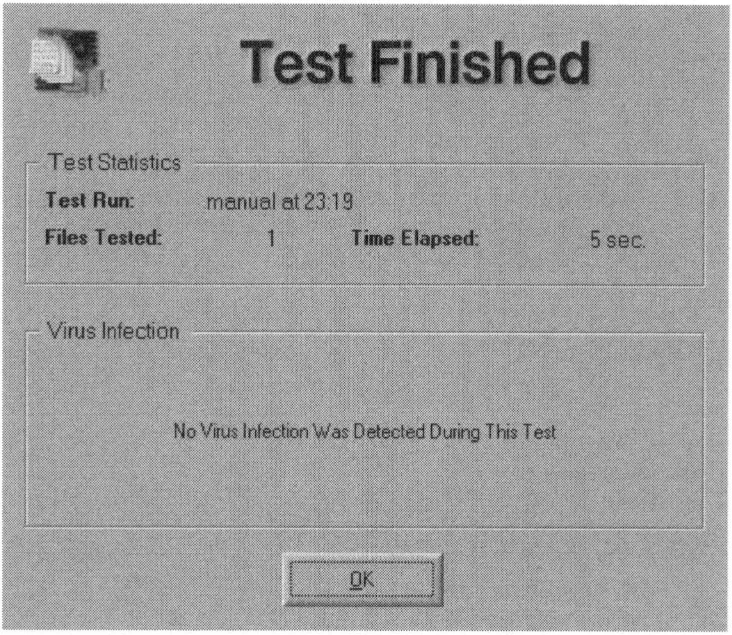

Test Finished

Test Statistics

Test Run: manual at 23:19

Files Tested: 1 **Time Elapsed:** 5 sec.

Virus Infection

No Virus Infection Was Detected During This Test

OK

Fig.2.10 The test results after checking a floppy disc

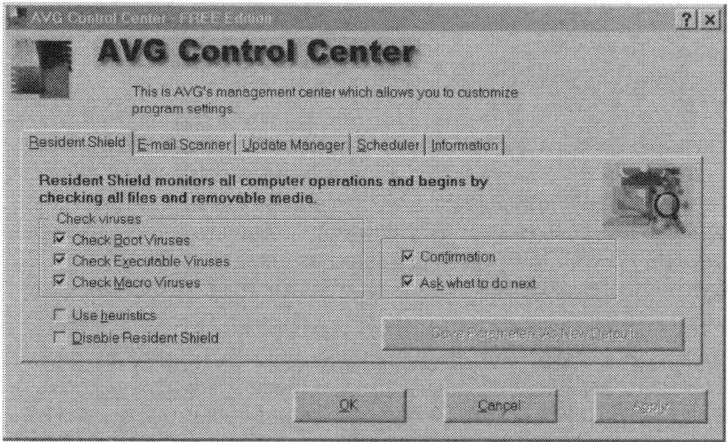

Fig.2.11 Many of AVG's settings can be changed via the Control Center

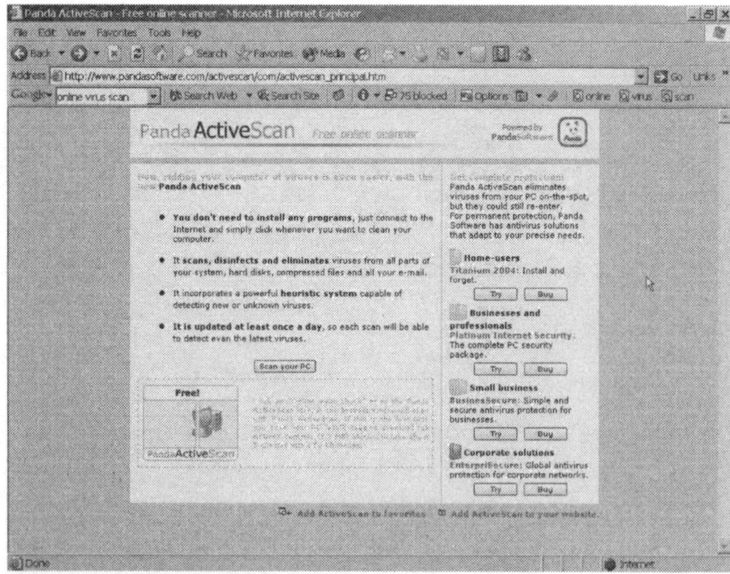

Fig.2.12 Panda Software offer a free online virus scan via their ActiveScan system

the default settings. It is definitely not a good idea to reduce the types of scan that are provided since this could obviously leave security holes in the system.

Online scan

There are various companies that offer online virus scanning facilities, and most of these are free. Although online scanning might seem an attractive option in cases where a PC has a virus infection but you have no antivirus software, there is a drawback to their use in this situation. Obviously the PC must be largely operational before it can go online and be used with this type of scanning. Assuming it can get that far, the main problem is that online scanning is not exactly online scanning.

The name suggests that a program running at the server scans your PC for viruses, but in most cases very little of the software runs at the other end of the Internet link. The usual arrangement is for an antivirus program to be downloaded to your PC, temporarily installed, run, and then erased. The problem with this method is that it is not really much different to

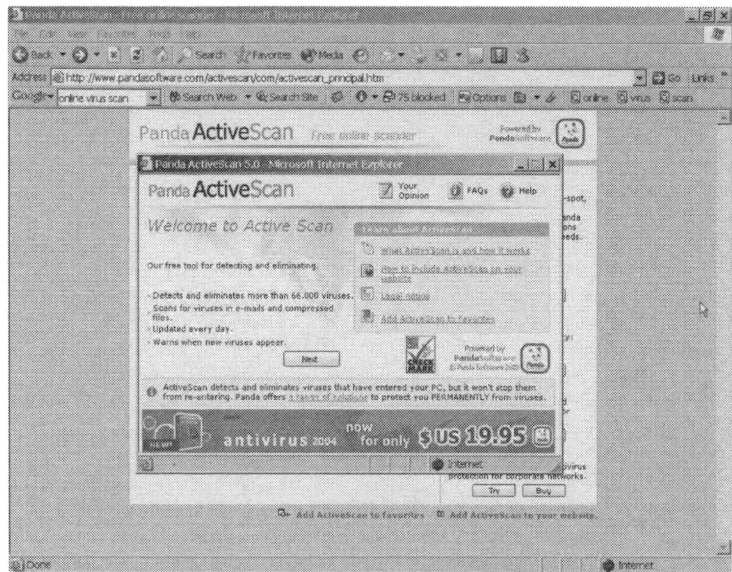

Fig.2.13 The first window provides a brief explanation of ActiveScan

installing an antivirus program and running it in the usual way. The file copying provides opportunities for any virus to propagate, and going online provides spyware and backdoor Trojans with an opportunity to "do their thing".

If you suspect that there could be a problem with a virus but have no definite proof, then it might be worth the risk if you do not have a better alternative. Online testing is also worthwhile if you do not intend to use normal antivirus software, but it is certainly not a genuine alternative to normal antivirus software. A program such as AVG 6.0 will monitor your PC and provide real-time protection. Any virus entering the system is likely to be detected immediately. With occasional online scanning there could be a significant gap between the infection occurring and the virus being detected. Even a few days or hours could be long enough for the virus to spread and damage your files.

I suppose online testing might be worthwhile if you are at the stage where you are desperate enough to try anything, but as far as possible it is best to avoid getting into that situation. Installing a free antivirus program on your PC is far better than getting into difficulties and then trying to recover the situation.

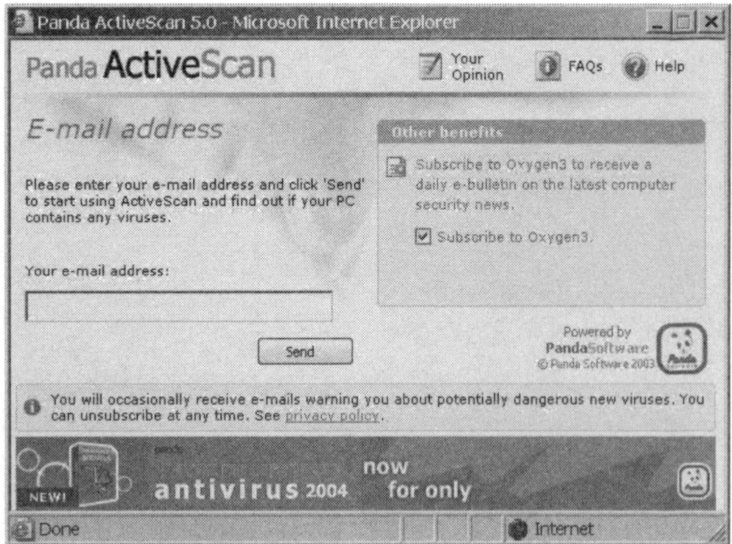

Fig.2.14 An Email address must be provided in order to proceed

An important point if you do try online virus scanning is to make sure that you use the services of a reputable company. In the early days of computer viruses it was quite common for infections to be spread via antivirus software that was actually a Trojan. This method has rather gone out of fashion, but the possibility of someone coming up with an online version can not be ruled out. Only using the services of a "big name" company should ensure that the scanning detects and removes any viruses rather than adding a few!

Panda Software is well known for its security oriented software suites, and they offer online scanning in the form of the ActiveScan facility (Figure 2.12). Operating the Scan Your PC link brings up the initial window of Figure 2.13, which briefly explains what ActiveScan does. Operating the Next button moves things on to the window of Figure 2.14 where you have to enter your Email address. If you do not wish to use your normal Email address for this type of thing it is just a matter of setting up an account with Hotmail, Yahoo!, or one of the other online Email providers. This account can then be used when obtaining free online services, which almost invariably require a valid Email address.

At the next window (Figure 2.15) you have to state your country and (possibly) area within that country. Things then move on to the stage

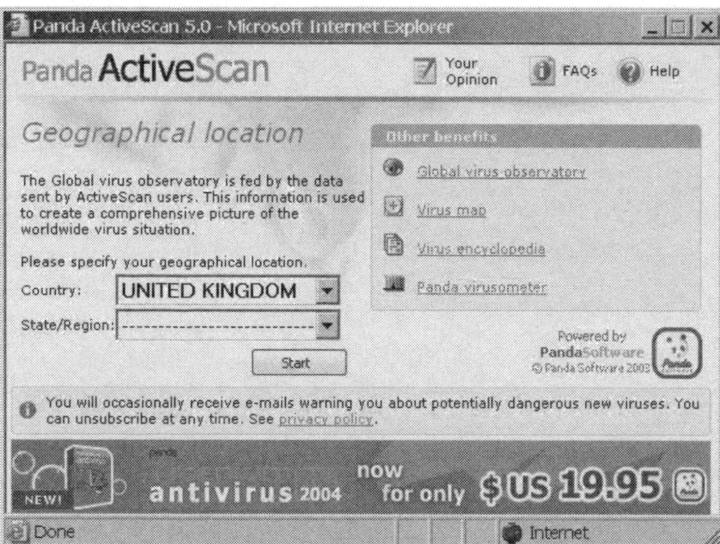

Fig.2.15 The simple registration process also requires your location

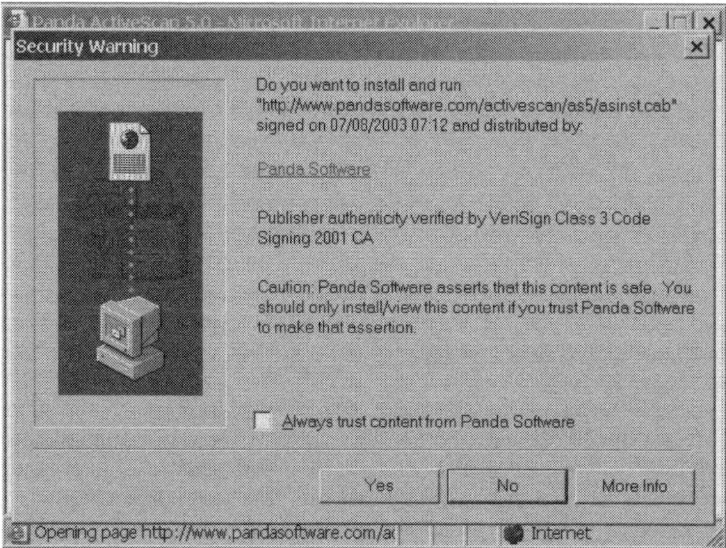

Fig.2.16 A download is required in order to carry out the scan

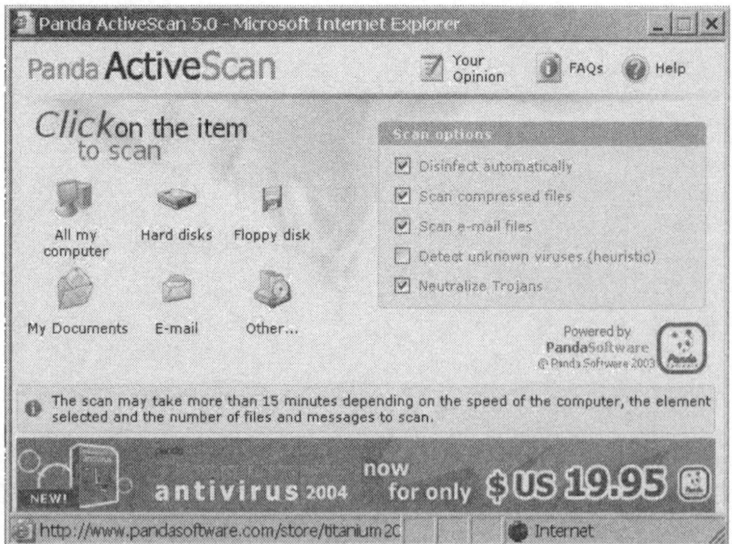

Fig.2.17 The required type of scan is selected using this wndow

where the software is downloaded, and the security warning of Figure 2.16 might appear. Operate the Yes button to go ahead with the download. The window of Figure 2.17 appears once the program has been downloaded and temporarily installed. The buttons near the top left-hand corner of the screen enable various parts of the system to be tested, and for this example the All My Computer option was used. The checkboxes in the right-hand section of the window give some control over the type of scan that is undertaken. You can opt to have Trojans neutralised for example.

A window like the one in Figure 2.18 is produced once the scan is under way. This has a bargraph display to show how far the scan has progressed. A table of results is included, and this shows things like the number of files tested, and any actions taken by the program. Note that it is not necessary to remain online while the scanning takes place, but that the PC must be online before the final results can be produced. As with any antivirus scanning, it can take some time if there is a large and largely full hard disc drive to check. Eventually the scan will be completed though (Figure 2.19) and a full set of results will then be shown.

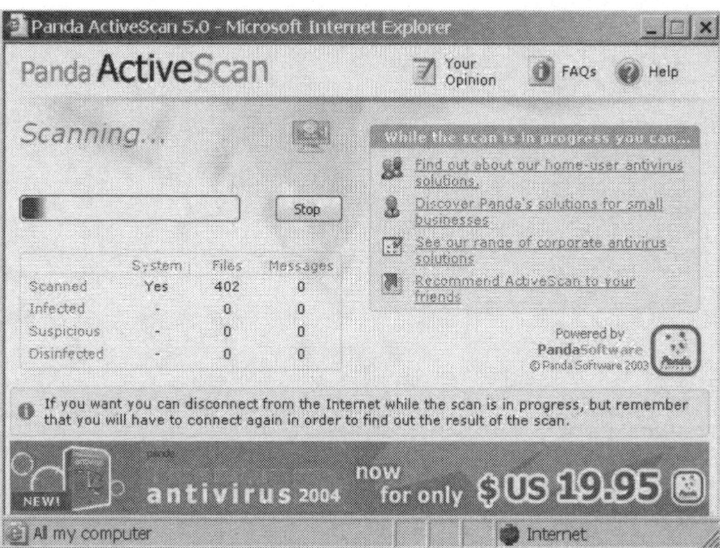

Fig.2.18 Finally, the scan is under way

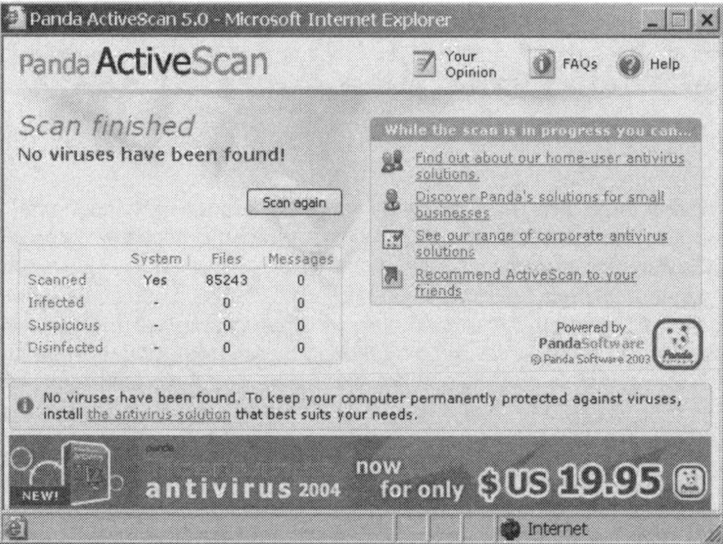

Fig.2.19 The list of results produced by the scan

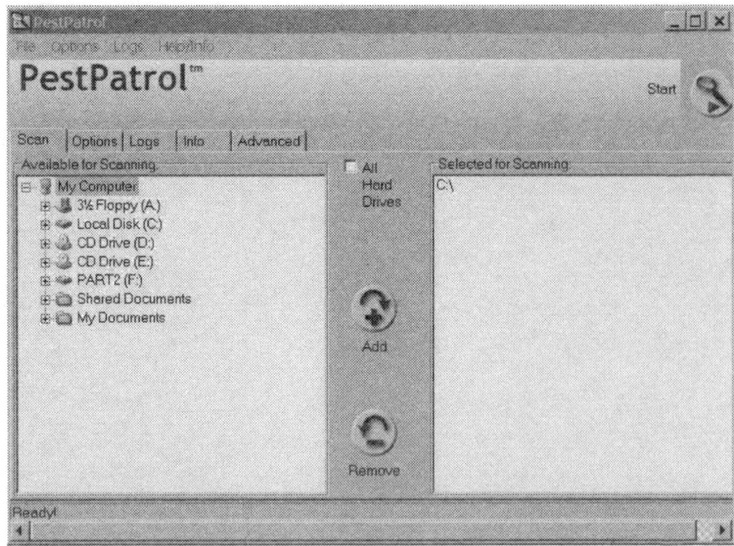

Fig.2.20 The first task is to select the drives to be scanned

The program is much like an ordinary antivirus program in operation, and this is essentially what it is. However, when you exit the program it will effectively be uninstalled, and it can not be run in the usual fashion.

Non-virus

Antivirus programs, as their name suggests, are primarily concerned with the detection and removal of viruses. Most will actually detect a wider range of threats, including most Trojans, spyware, and backdoor Trojans. How well these types of threat are detected varies somewhat from one program to another. Antivirus programs are not usually designed to detect what could be termed nuisance programs, such as adware programs and their related files. However, there are programs that are designed to deal with this type of thing, and they will mostly detect some of the more serious threats such as spyware.

Pest Patrol is one of the best known programs of this type, and it is the one that will be used as the basis of this example. The initial screen of Pest Patrol is shown in Figure 2.20, and the first task is to select the drives that will be scanned. This is just a matter of selecting the required

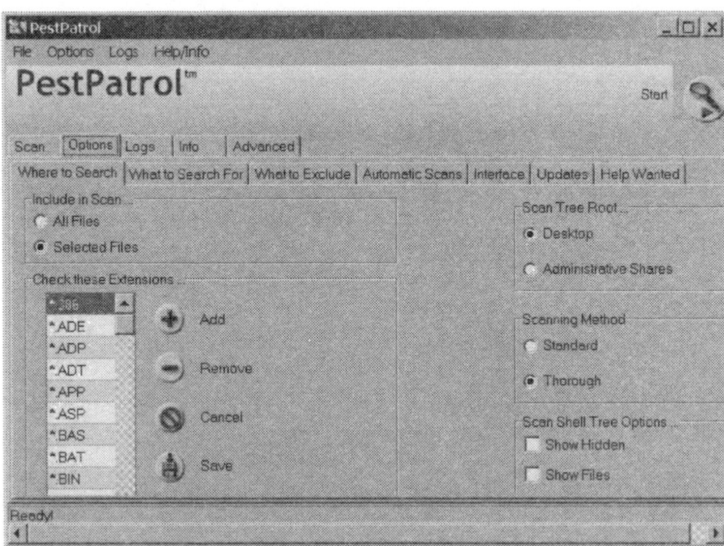

Fig.2.21 You can control how thoroughly Pest Patrol scans and the types of file it seeks

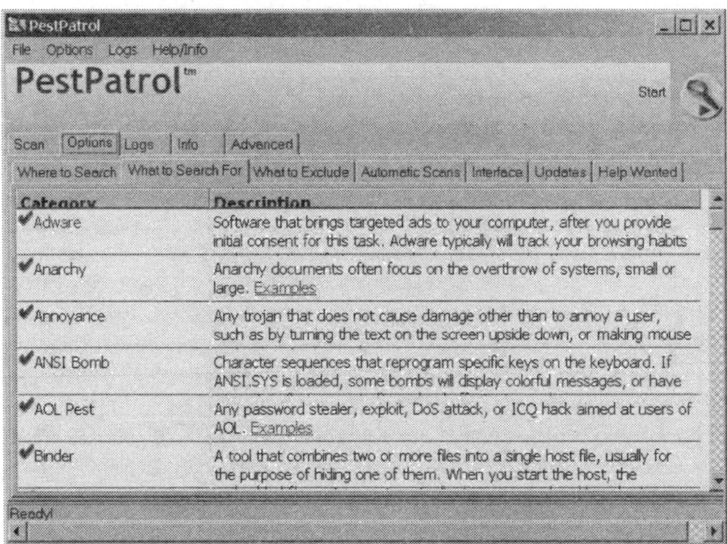

Fig.2.22 You can control the types of "pest" that the program seeks

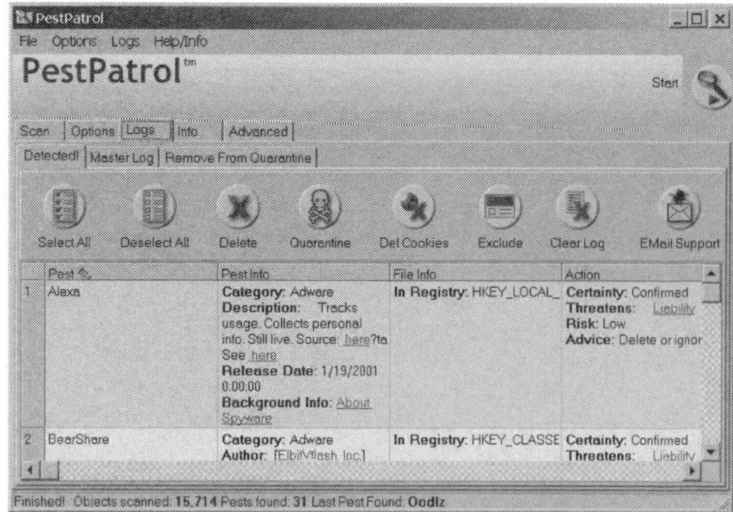

Fig.2.23 A list of "pests" is produced once the scan has been completed

drives in the panel on the left using the standard Windows methods. The Add button is then left-clicked in order to add the drives to the list in the right panel. A drive can be removed from the list by selecting its entry and operating the Remove button. Simply tick the checkbox if you wish to check all the hard drives.

Operating the Options tab produces a further row of tabs, and these give access to a range of options that control the way Pest Patrol scans the disc. There are standard and thorough options for example (Figure 2.21), and you can also set the program to only look for certain types of "pest" (Figure 2.22). It is by no means essential to do any "fine tuning" though, and the program should work well enough if it scans the discs using the default settings. To go ahead with a scan it is just a matter of operating the Start button in the top right-hand corner of the window.

You are presented with a scrollable list of results once Pest Patrol has finished the scan (Figure 2.23). It is essential to look down the list, item by item, even in cases where there are a large number of entries. What you and Pest Patrol consider to be "pests" could be rather different. Remember that removing adware files could result in any programs supported by that adware becoming inoperative. You are unlikely to get away with installing supported software, disabling the associated adware, and then continuing to use the supported software. Blocking adware

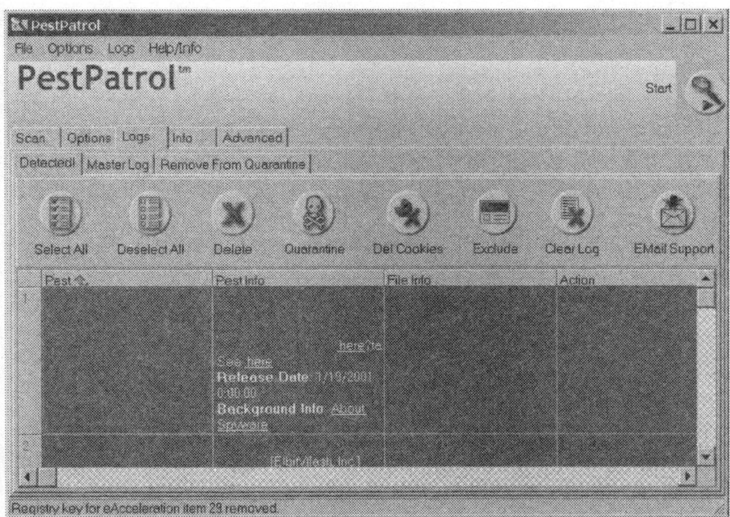

Fig.2.24 Pest Patrol confirms that the offending files have been deleted

with a firewall does sometimes leave the supported application fully operational, but this is a morally dubious practice.

Having decided the fate of the various entries, it is just a matter of selecting each batch and then operating the appropriate button. In this example none of the detected files were required, so they were all deleted. The list changes to show what has been done to each file (Figure 2.24). Note that the program may be unable to delete some files and folders. It will then show the location of the relevant files or folders and recommend manual deletion.

Email scams

The advice about Emails used to be along the lines that there is no risk from a simple text Email, and that the real threat from Emails comes from attachments that are not what they are supposed to be. These days it is necessary for this type of advice to be heavily qualified, since many Email problems now stem from the text contained in an Email. To be brutally frank, in many cases the problems also stem from the naivety of the recipients. It is essential for anyone receiving Emails to act as the main defence against the various scams and hoaxes that are becoming increasingly common.

The subject of hoax viruses was covered in chapter 1. This type of hoax is not exclusive to Emails, but this method of transmission is used for practically all hoax viruses. If someone sends you an Email saying that they have accidentally sent a virus to you in an Email or attachment, do some checking to ensure that there really is a virus. When someone sent a hoax virus to my sister suggesting that a couple of files needed to be erased in order to eradicate it, about 30 seconds of checking on the Internet was sufficient to establish that it was indeed a hoax. Remember that it is unwise to trust this type of thing simply because the Email carries a sender's address that you know. The sender's address could be about as genuine as the virus, and there is also the possibility that the sender has been fooled and is unwittingly spreading the hoax.

Email scams have been on the increase in recent years. The first one to come to fame was the Nigerian scam where you pay money to help a Nigerian business man to get his money out of the country. In return for your help you supposedly get large sums of money, but there is no prize for guessing how much you actually get back. There is no prize either with another common scam where you are told that you have won a competition but you need to pay a fee in order to get the prize. Usually there is no prize, but occasionally there is a worthless prize. This scam is just the Email equivalent of one that will be familiar to recipients of ordinary junk mail.

A more recent and potentially costly scam (known as phishing or carding) is where an Email is received from a financial organisation of some kind. Yahoo's PayPal system for transferring funds was the first to be targeted, but several online banks were targeted later. The Email asks you to sign in at the site and confirm your password and other details. There is a link on the Email that leads to what looks very much like the real site, and the address is very similar to the real thing. However, the link actually leads to a fake site where you give away your account details if you sign in and provide the requested information.

So far this scam has not been particularly successful. Most recipients of the Emails realised that there was something amiss and either ignored or reported it. Others ignored the link and went to the relevant page in the usual way, thus avoiding the fake site. To avoid anything of this type it is just a matter of not supplying passwords or any other sensitive information in answer to Emails or telephone calls. As many online organisations go to great lengths to point out, they will never ask you for your password.

This general type of scam is not really all that new. Some Internet service providers (ISPs) and AOL in particular, used to have problems with new users getting communications of one type or another asking them to confirm their passwords. The crooks were trying to get the passwords so that they could obtain Internet access at the expense of the legitimate user. This practice died out due to changes in the way that Internet access is provided, but it does demonstrate the point that you should never divulge passwords for any Internet service, not just the financial variety.

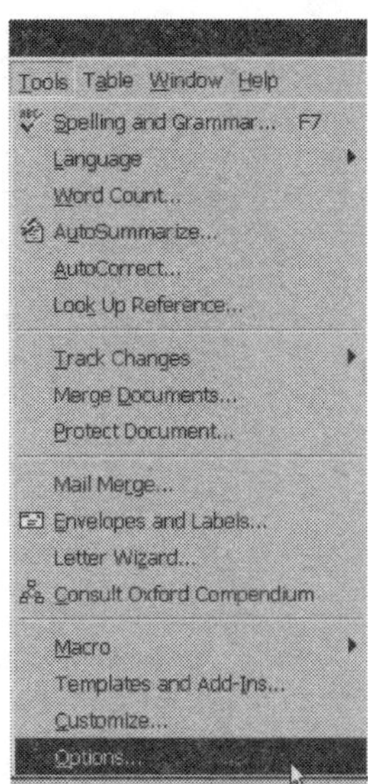

Fig.2.25 The Tools menu

Attachments

Although they are not the only threat, attachments remain the most likely route for a serious Email attack. In recent years a number of Email viruses have rapidly spread around the world. These Email viruses utilise the automation features that are built into Microsoft Office and other programs. These facilities are intended to provide a means of doing clever things that make life easier for users, but they can also hand over control of the PC to a virus.

If you do not need these facilities, disabling them is a simple but effective means of removing this threat to your PC. Microsoft has a useful download for Outlook 98 and 2000 that provides protection against viruses such as ILOVEYOU and Melissa. It disables the ability to download attachments that could contain a virus. The download and further information are available from this web page:

http://office.microsoft.com/downloads/2000/Out2ksec.aspx

Another tactic is to turn off the automatic running of scripts in Word, Access, and Excel. First select Options from the Tools menu (Figure 2.25), and then operate the General tab in the window that appears (Figure 2.26). Make sure that the checkbox for Macro virus protection is ticked.

It makes sense to have the security settings of Internet Explorer as high as possible, or failing that as high as possible without preventing the programs from providing the functions you require. Adjusting these settings was covered in the previous chapter so it will not be covered again here. This is a simple aspect of Internet security that many users

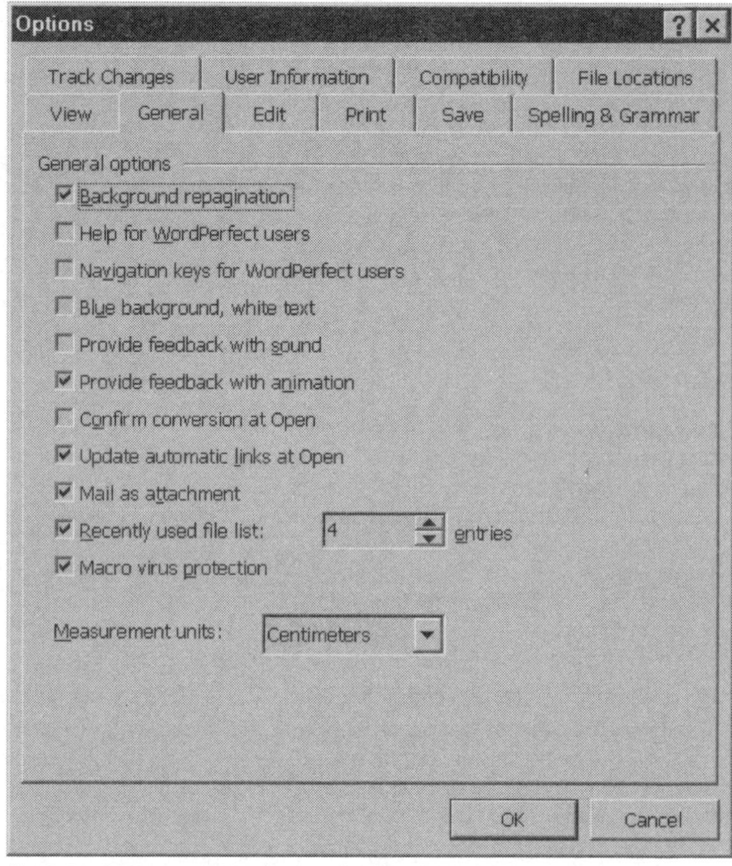

Fig.2.26 Make sure that the box for Macro Virus Protection is ticked

seem to overlook, so make sure that you use the most secure settings that do not block or seriously hinder the facilities you wish to use.

Email antivirus

There are protection programs designed specifically to deal with Email viruses and other infections carried by scripts. Obviously this type of program has to run in real-time, and it produces a warning if it detects something suspicious happening. Figure 2.27 shows a warning message

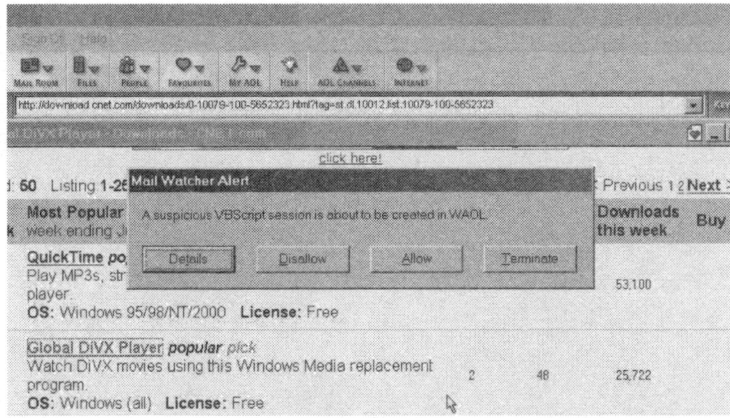

Fig.2.27 A warning message is produced by suspicious events, but many of these are just part of the PC's normal operation

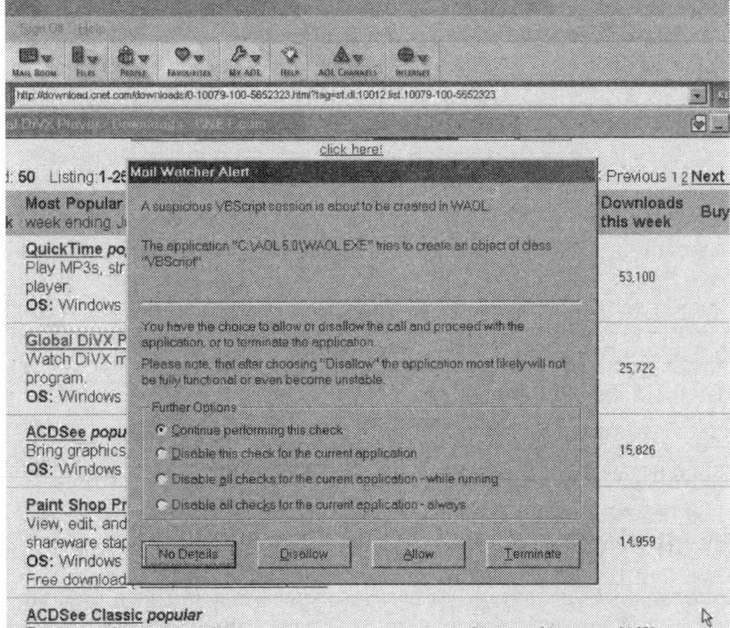

Fig.2.28 More details of the current operation can be obtained

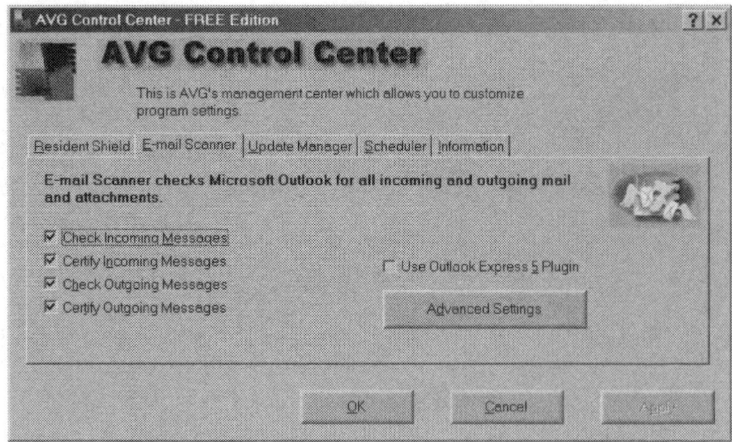

Fig.2.29 Antivirus programs often include Email scanning facilities

produced by Mail Watcher from Computer Associates, which detects attempts to access the Email system. Since many of the events detected by the program are perfectly legitimate it does not block them, but instead provides a simple control panel. The Terminate button is pressed if it is felt that the detected action is possibly a virus. Operating the Allow button enables things to proceed normally. Left-clicking the Details button opens a new window (Figure 2.28) that gives more details of the current operation and the options for dealing with it.

Most antivirus suites now include a program that can check Emails or have this facility built into the main program. AVG 6.0 has a built-in Email scanning facility, and it is possible to select the required checks from the Email section of its Control Center (Figure 2.29). This type of thing is fine if you are using Outlook or Outlook Express as the Email client, but these days many people use Internet based Email services such as those provided by Hotmail or the Yahoo!. These do not usually make use of Outlook, Outlook Express, or any similar program, but instead have their facilities built into the system. An antivirus program such as AVG does not usually provide any protection with a fully Internet base Email service.

This is not to say that no protection is available for users of these services. Some Email service providers have facilities for checking attachments prior to downloading them. Figure 2.30 shows an Email that is being viewed using the Yahoo.com Email service. This has a ZIP file attachment

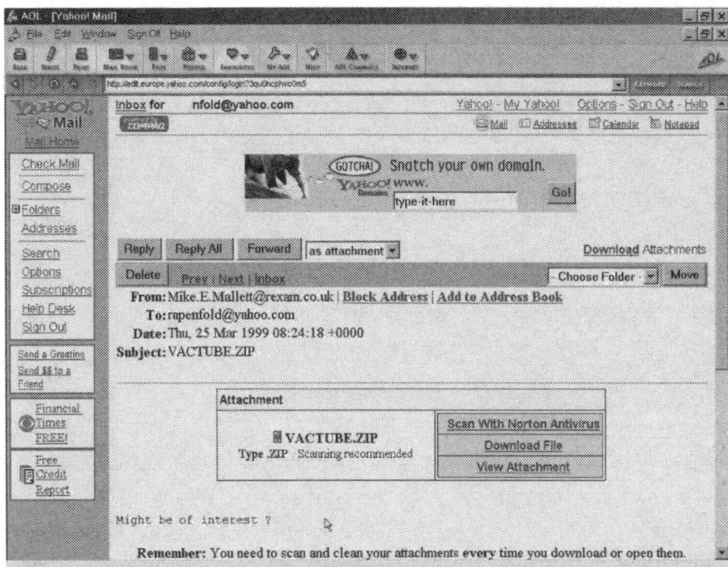

Fig.2.30 This Email has a ZIP file attachment

and one option for dealing with the attachment is to simply download it regardless of the risk. Another option is to scan it using the system's built-in Norton antivirus program. The scanning process is very rapid because the file is being checked while it is still on the server. The Email, complete with its attachment, can be erased if a problem is discovered. In this way the file never reaches your PC and can not infect it. Usually everything will be all right and a reassuring message will appear (Figure 2.31).

A third option is available, and this enables the attachment to be viewed so that you can check that it is genuine and not an impostor. Obviously this is not of much use with all types of file, but it is useful with something like a Word DOC file that could contain a macro virus. The system will accurately interpret the document so that it appears much the same as it would when viewed using Word itself (Figure 2.32). This method does not guarantee that the attachment is virus-free, but you can at least check that it is a proper document from someone you know.

If you need to work on the document in Word it must be downloaded, but this is not necessary if you only need to read its contents. Having viewed and read the contents the Email and attachment can be deleted.

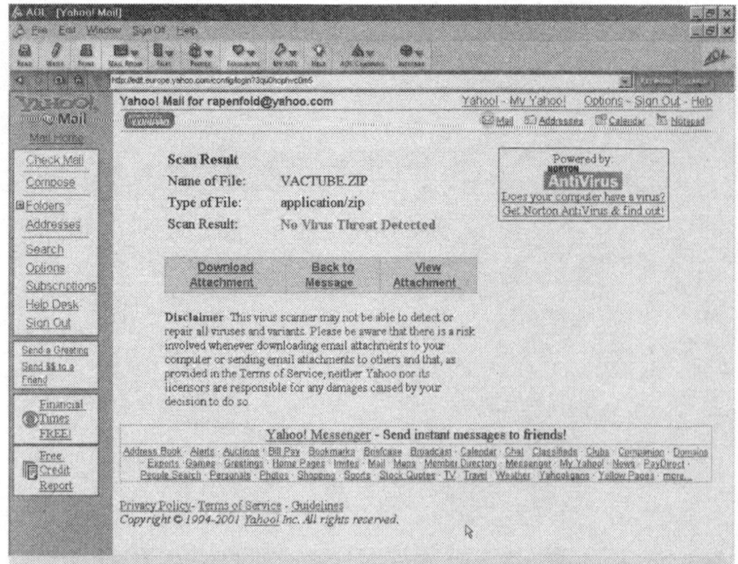

Fig.2.31 On this occasion the scan has not found an infection

Another possibility is to cut and paste the text from the Email viewer to Word. Select the required text and press the Control and C keys to copy the text to the clipboard. Open Word and then press the Control and V keys to copy the text into Word from the clipboard. With this method any clever tricks in the original document will be lost, but so will any macro virus.

If you need to exchange formatted text documents via Email attachments it is worth considering the rich text format. Documents in this format can have the usual types of Windows formatting including alignment, different fonts, text colours, etc. It does not support any type of macro language, so files that use this format can not contain a macro virus. Plain text files are also safe, but have no formatting capability. Of course, these files are only safe when they are what they purport to be. Any data file needs to be checked for authenticity before you download it.

Many people now take the "belt and braces" approach of simply refusing to open any Email attachments. I suppose that this is a practical approach for anyone that has no real need to exchange anything other than plain text by Email, but it is not practical if you need to receive images, formatted

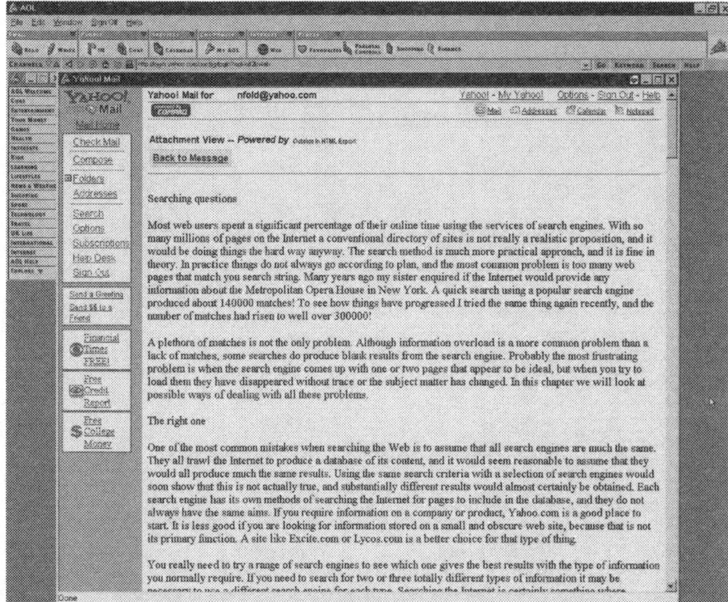

Fig.2.32 A Word file being displayed by the built-in viewer program

documents, etc., via this route. It still makes sense not to open attachments if you do not know the sender and (or) are not expecting an Email with an attachment. Where necessary, check that the Email and attachment genuinely come from the supposed sender, and only open the attachment once you have verified their authenticity. Unfortunately, these days anything received via Email has to be treated with a degree of suspicion.

Internet resource

When dealing with a computer virus remember that the Internet carries a vast amount of information about dealing with many viruses and other forms of infection. Some of the information is general in nature, but there is also a large amount of information about specific viruses. This can be very useful where you know that a PC is infected with a certain virus but you are having difficulties in dealing with it. Using the name of the virus in a search engine, perhaps with the words "computer" and

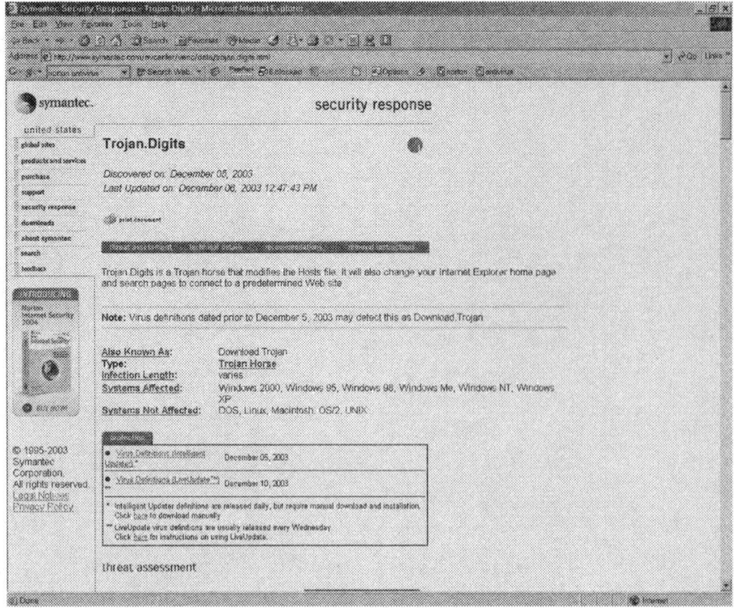

Fig.2.33 The Symantec site contains a great deal of information about numerous viruses, including the newest ones

"virus", should produce some helpful information. There might even be a utility program that helps to remove the virus and repair damaged files.

As always though, proceed with caution and as far as possible stick with the sites of well-known companies. The Symantec site (www.symantec.com) contains a great deal of information about numerous viruses (Figure 2.33). Details of newly discovered viruses are given prominence on this site, and the sites of the other companies involved in producing antivirus software.

Manual removal

When some form of infection occurs on a PC there is a natural tendency to look for a program that will remove it for you. Being realistic about it, a program such as a virus or Trojan is not going to be removable via the normal route, because it will not install itself into Windows as a normal program. It will do its best to stay hidden, and you will probably need

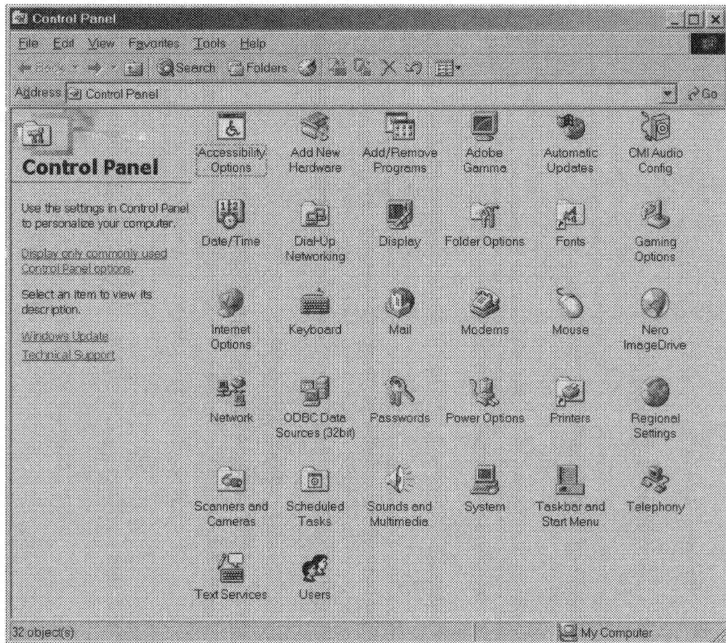

Fig.2.34 The Windows Control Panel

some help in order to locate and remove the relevant file or files. With some of the more minor problems it is not necessary to resort to some form of antivirus or "pest control" program.

For example, many adware programs are installed without it being made clear to the user that they are being added to the system, but most of them are installed in the normal way. Consequently, they can be uninstalled in the usual way. This means going to Settings in the Start menu and selecting Control Panel in the submenu that appears. The exact appearance of the Control Panel depends on how the computer is set up, but it will probably look something like Figure 2.34. Double-click the Add/Remove Programs icon or text entry, as appropriate.

This launches a new window like the one of Figure 2.35, which includes a scrollable list of all the programs installed on the computer. Look down this to see if the program that is giving problems is installed, or if there is anything that should not be there. To uninstall a program it is necessary to first left-click its entry in the list to select it. Then operate

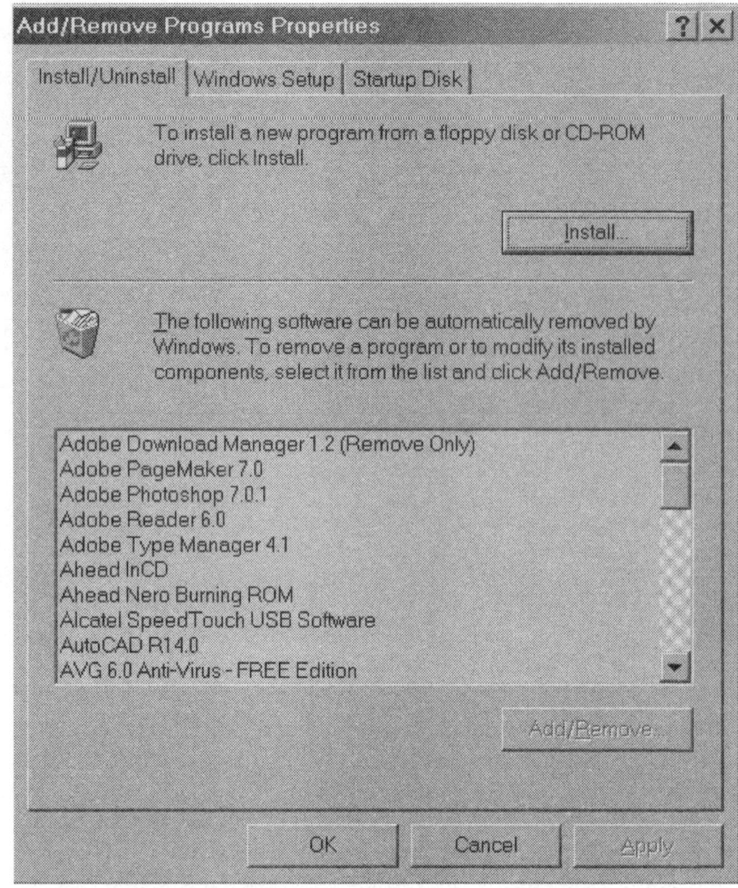

Fig.2.35 A full list of all the installed programs is provided

the Add/Remove button and go through the additional steps needed to remove the program. These tend to be slightly different from one program to another, but it is usually just a matter of confirming that you wish to remove the program.

In the case of adware it is likely that there will be a warning to the effect that the software it supports will not operate properly if the program is removed. Unfortunately, in most cases the supported program will not be named, but you will probably be able to deduce this for yourself. It is

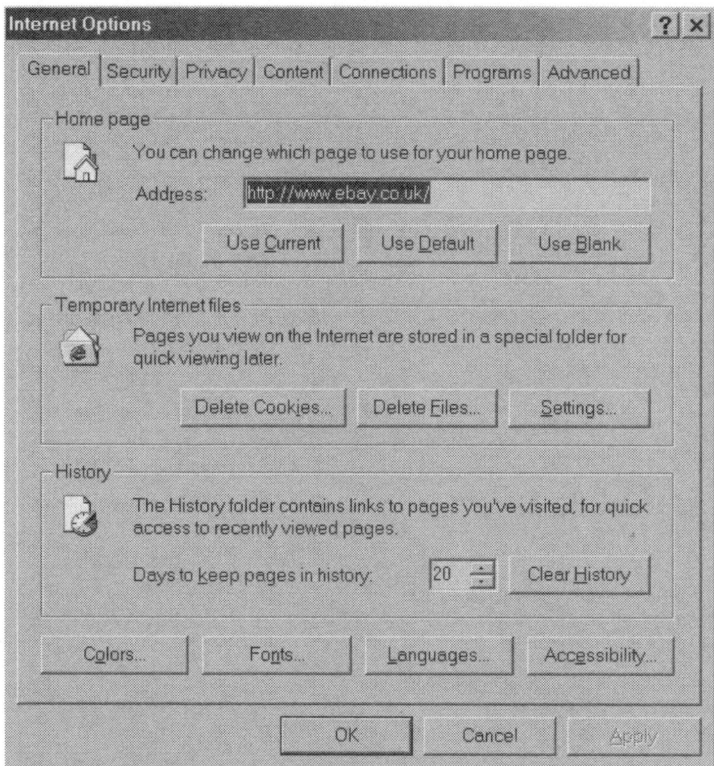

Fig.2.36 The Internet Options window enables the homepage to be changed

up to you whether to remove the program anyway or put up with it. You might get a warning message saying that shared files are no longer needed by other applications and asking whether you wish to remove them. In theory it should be all right to operate the Yes button, but the No button is the safer option. Leaving shared files in place should still result in the program being properly uninstalled and rendered inoperative.

Some web sites play clever tricks that alter the home page of your browser. Each time the browser is launched you typically find either a pornography site or some form of directory or search engine. In most cases it is possible to set the homepage back to its original setting using the normal facilities of the browser. In the case of Internet Explorer select Internet Options from the Tools menu when running the program from the Windows Control Panel. Either way a window like the one shown in Figure 2.36 will appear. Simply change the text in the Address textbox to the required web address.

Sometimes you can find that the homepage address keeps reverting to the one you have just removed. There can also be problems with a new toolbar appearing, often offering something like a search facility for pornography sites. A toolbar can be switched off by going to the View menu and selecting Toolbars (Figure 2.37). Find the offending toolbar in the list and remove the tick next to its name. This should suppress it, but it does not remove the toolbar from the system.

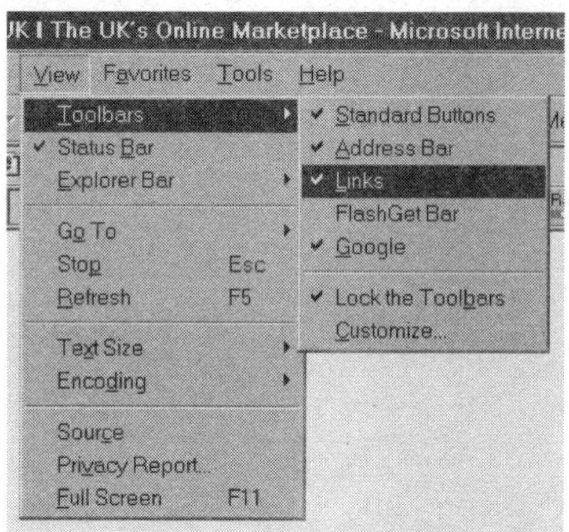

Fig.2.37 Toolbars are easily turned on and off

In theory a toolbar should have an entry in the Add/Remove Programs window, but one added to the system without your consent is unlikely to make itself as easy to remove as this. With a computer running under Windows ME or XP it is worth using the System Restore facility to take the system back a day or two. It is assumed here that the offending toolbar or homepage change entered the system within the last day or two. Taking the system settings back a couple of days should undo the changes and leave the system as it was previously. There is no guarantee that this will work or that no re-infection will occur, but in most cases it seems to do the trick. Note that any changes you have made to the system within the last couple of days will also be undone and will have to be reinstated. Using the System Restore facility is covered in more detail in a later chapter.

Points to remember

It is important to have antivirus software installed on a PC before it succumbs to an infection. Installing antivirus software on an infected PC is inadvisable because it entails file copying and changes to system files. Both of these can help a virus to spread across the hard disc drive. With a good antivirus program installed it is unlikely that a virus will manage to take hold in the first place.

Some antivirus suites include a set of bootable floppy discs or a bootable CD-ROM so that antivirus checks can be made on a PC that does not have antivirus software installed. Using this type of software, checks can be made on a PC even if it can not be booted into Windows. One drawback of this method is that the antivirus software will not be fully up-to-date.

Antivirus software usually scans for more than viruses, and other harmful files such as Trojans and spyware will usually be found. Things such as adware will not be detected though, as they are often installed legitimately. Programs such as Pest Patrol will scan for adware and the like, and will remove them if required.

Provided you are using up-to-date software there should be no risk of your PC being infected if you open and read an Email. Attachments are a different matter, and are now a common means of trying to spread viruses.

Do not take Emails at face value, even if they supposedly come from an address that you normally deal with. With the aid of some common sense you have to act as the first line of defence against malicious and scam Emails.

Where possible, check your Email attachments for viruses before downloading them to your PC. Never open Email attachments if the sender is unknown to you, or you are not expecting a file from that particular person. You can always Email the supposed sender of the file to check its authenticity.

Programs for scanning Emails are available and this facility is included in many antivirus suites. These programs work with Outlook and Outlook Express but do not normally work with fully Internet based Email services. However, these services sometimes have built-in virus scanning facilities.

3

Data rescue

Learning the hard way

Ideally every PC would be equipped with good antivirus software and would be largely immune from attack. In the real world there are still plenty of PCs that are not properly protected. Probably only a small percentage of those PCs will actually come to grief, but that is little comfort if your PC is one of the unfortunate few. It is of even less comfort if you are left with a PC that refuses to boot into Windows, leaving you with data on the hard disc drive that is not backed up and no obvious way of accessing it.

One potential way around the problem is to try reinstalling Windows on top of the existing installation. With luck, this will effectively repair the damaged installation. This works because Windows detects the existing installation and tries to merge the new installation with the old one. Unfortunately, this merging will not always be successful. There must be enough of the old installation left intact for the Setup program to be able to identify it and use its settings. If there are not enough of the old Windows files on the disc the new installation will be started "from scratch". This should work and your data should be intact, but all the applications software has to be reinstalled and (where appropriate) customised again.

What often happens is that the new installation uses some of the configuration files from the existing Windows set-up, complete with errors. Consequently, the new installation has exactly the same failings as the old one. Anyway, reinstallation over the existing Windows files is worth trying provided the hard disc drive is actually in a fully working state. This method is not possible if the virus has messed up the formatting of the drive, making it impossible to read or write files. The only option with the disc in that state is to reformat the disc and install everything "from scratch". Reinstalling Windows XP is covered in chapter 5, and reinstalling Windows ME is the subject of Chapter 6. Chapter 4 covers backing up the system and restoring it after disaster has struck.

Note that it is sometimes possible to recover data from a hard disc that is not readable. However, this is not an easy task. It is possible to obtain software that can help with the task, but programs of this general type are mainly aimed at those having a fair amount of requisite technical knowledge. The better option for those lacking the necessary know-how is to use one of the specialist data recovery services, but these can be quite expensive. Obviously the cost involved could be well worthwhile if the hard disc contains the only copy of data that took months of work.

It is perhaps worth making the point that it is not only a virus that can result in a hard disc drive becoming unusable. If you use PCs for some years you are almost certain to experience a hard disc failure due to a faulty drive or the drive's hardware simply wearing out. A complete failure of the disc usually means that all the data it contains is lost. A data recovery service might be able to recover some or all of its contents, but there is definitely no guarantee that anything will be recoverable. The cost of recovering data from a faulty disc is too high for many users anyway.

As a minimum, any important data files should be backed up onto floppy discs, CDRs, or any suitable media, so that they can be restored onto a new hard disc if the old unit fails. Ideally, the entire contents of the hard disc drive should be backed up using a program that enables it to be properly restored onto a new hard disc. This is very much quicker and easier than having to reinstall and configure the operating system, and then reinstall all the applications programs and data. Also, any customisation of the operating system or other software will be automatically restored. If you have heavily customised software, after reinstallation it can take a great deal of time to get it set up to your satisfaction.

Hardware fault

Having a backup copy of the hard disc's contents is not only insurance against a loss of valuable data if there is a hardware failure or a virus strikes. It can greatly simplify things if there is a major problem with the operating system. Problems with Windows "going walkabout" have probably been somewhat exaggerated over the years. On the other hand, they are not exactly a rarity. Provided the PC was fully operational when the backup copy was made, resorting to the backup will quickly provide a fully functioning PC again. It does not matter whether the problem was due to a virus, ordinary Windows mishap, or a disc fault. Things will be quickly put back in full working order. Of course, in the case of a hardware fault there is the minor matter of replacing the faulty disc first, but with that done it is easy to get the PC back in full use again.

Full backup software enables the system to be quickly restored to a previous and fully working configuration, but bear in mind that any data generated since the last backup session can not be restored. Any data files produced since the backup was taken will therefore be lost. A full backup is normally only undertaken every month or so, making it important to keep backup copies of data files as they are produced. A lot of data is otherwise left at risk, especially as the time for the next backup approaches. Provided data files are regularly saved to some form of backup disc there should be no difficulty in reinstating any missing data once a full backup has been restored.

Backup or Restore?

The Windows XP Backup utility installs the system from scratch and therefore loses any recently produced data. The System Restore facility operates in a different way, and it undoes changes to system and program files so that the system is effectively wound back to an earlier time. In this way the data files are left intact. Of course, System Restore is only usable if the file system is largely undamaged. Backup software is still usable even if the contents of the hard disc has been completely erased.

When a major problem with the operating system occurs and some form of restoration option is available, it is almost certainly best to resort to this method sooner rather than later. There is little point in spending large amounts of time trying to repair a damaged installation if it can be replaced with a backup copy quite quickly and easily. It is certainly worthwhile spending a small amount of time first to check for any minor problems that are easily sorted out. The backup method is "using a sledgehammer to crack a nut" if the problem is something minor that is easily corrected. If a search for any obvious problems proves to be in vain, it is time to resort to the backup software. The backup program's manual should give detailed instructions on maintaining an up-to-date backup and restoring the hard disc's contents.

The problem with the full backup method is that it takes a fair amount of time to maintain an up-to-date copy of the hard disc. Also, it is only feasible if your PC is equipped with some form of mass storage device that can be used for backup purposes, such as a CDR writer or a Zip drive. It could otherwise require well in excess of a thousand floppy discs to do a full backup of the hard drive! Even using some form of mass storage it can take a long while to backup the gigabytes of programs and data stored on many modern hard disc drives. The quickest and easiest way of providing a backup is to opt for a second hard disc drive. Due to the current low cost of hard discs, this could well be the cheapest method as well. However, bear in mind that a second hard disc drive is as vulnerable to attack from viruses unless it is disconnected after the backup has been made.

Split discs

Many PC users now split their large hard drives into two logical drives, which usually become drives C: and D: as far as the operating system is concerned. Drive C: is then used in the normal way and drive D: is reserved for backup purposes. This method is useless in the event that the hard drive develops a serious fault, because the main and backup drives are the two halves of one physical drive. If one becomes faulty it is unlikely that the other will be usable either. It is also of limited use if a virus strikes. If one drive is attacked it is unlikely that the other will escape. There is obviously no way of disconnecting one logical drive and leaving the other in operation.

The point of the split disc system is that the backup copy on drive D: is usable if there is a software problem rather than a fault in the hardware or a virus attack. Since most users have far more problems with the software than with hard disc faults or viruses, this method should get the user out of trouble more often than not. It is of little use as an antivirus measure though.

Some users take a compromise approach and make a backup copy of the hard disc when it contains a newly installed operating system having all the hardware properly integrated into the operating system and fully operational. Ideally the disc should also have the applications programs installed, and any customisation completed. Any important data is backed up separately as it is generated. If the operating system becomes seriously damaged it is then easy to resort to the backup which should be reasonably compact, but gives you a basic system that is fully customised and ready to use. Any essential data can also be restored, but there is no need to restore any data files that are no longer needed on the hard disc.

Clean copy

An advantage of this method is that it returns the PC to a "clean" copy of the operating system. Over a period of time most modern operating systems seem to become slightly "gummed up" with numerous files that no longer serve any purpose, and things can generally slow down. By returning to a fresh copy of the operating system you will probably free up some hard disc space and things might run slightly faster. By not bothering to restore any unimportant data files you free up further hard disc space.

If you lack a proper backup copy of the hard disc and only have copies of the data files, all is not lost. In this situation you might prefer to put a fair amount of effort into fixing the damaged Windows installation rather than simply reinstalling everything. Even if you only use a few applications programs, reinstalling Windows and the applications software is likely to be pretty tedious and time consuming. If there are numerous programs to reinstall, the process is likely to be very tedious and time consuming.

Looking on the bright side, if everything does have to be restored from scratch you will have a "clean" copy of the operating system that should provide optimum performance. In fact many users habitually take the reinstallation route and consider any extra time and effort involved being well worthwhile.

The value of this approach depends on the amount of software you install and remove. It is probably doing things the hard way if you rarely or never make changes to the PC once it is set up to your satisfaction. It might be the only practical approach if you try every program you can lay your hands on.

I would not go as far as to advocate reinstalling everything at the first sign of trouble, but I would definitely advise against the opposite approach of always repairing the original set up regardless of the amount of damage and the time involved. Apart from the fact this could be a very time consuming approach, an installation that has been patched up on numerous occasions, and perhaps had a number of programs added, upgraded, and removed over a period of time, is unlikely to provide peak performance. In fact, I have encountered several installations of this type that took an eternity to go through the boot-up sequence, in one case taking almost 10 minutes to complete the process! Once booted, PCs of this type seem to give the hard disc drive a "hammering" at every opportunity. This is the most common symptom of a system that is operating well below par.

Apart from making the computer slow and irksome in use, this type of thing increases the wear on the hard disc drive and presumably shortens its operating life. It should be possible to discover the sources of the problem and improve results. There are Windows "cleaner" programs that can help to streamline a Windows installation and remove clutter from the hard disc. However, reinstalling everything "from scratch" is the solution favoured by most when this situation arises. This should always ensure optimum performance and might be quicker anyway.

If a virus strikes a system that is operating well below par, it might be a good time to "make a virtue of a necessity" and install everything "from scratch". Some actually advocate this approach after any virus attack, and there is a potential advantage. By obliterating the contents of the drive you are assured that the new and totally fresh installation will be free from viruses. Unfortunately, the virus could be reintroduced as soon as you start installing the old data files. There is less chance of reinfection with the "clean sweep" approach, but ultimately you are reliant on the original infection being fully killed off.

Preliminaries

If you do decide to go ahead with reinstallation "from scratch", it is essential to backup any important data files first. If you are using heavily customised applications programs it is also a good idea to make copies of the configuration files so that the customisation files are easily reinstated. In fact, any files that are unique to your particular installation should be backed-up, including things like speech profiles of voice recognition programs. Some of your applications programs may have facilities for saving and reinstating customisation files, and if so you should already have backups. In other cases simply overwriting the default files with your customised versions will probably have the desired effect. However, there is no guarantee that this will work. There can be problems due to anomalies between the backup file and the entries in the Registry.

It is worth emphasising that backing-up important files should not be left until the hard disc is hit by a rampant virus. With a very serious attack it could be impossible to recover any files from the disc. Recovering files is unlikely to be "plain sailing" even if the disc is readable. With the computer not booting into the operating system properly you are unlikely to have proper access to all the drives and applications programs. Provided Safe Mode is functioning properly you can boot into a version of Windows, but one where drives other than the hard and floppy discs will not be fully functioning. In most cases the CD-ROM drive or drives can be used for read operations, but writing to the CD writers is unlikely to be possible. This severely limits your backup options. There are ways of making a backup of a hard disc drive in an emergency, but this might involve buying some additional hardware. It is better to avoid getting into situations where drastic measures are needed in order to recover the situation. The methods described here will usually get you out of trouble, but they should not be regarded as recommended ways of handling things. They are what you have to do in a "last resort" situation.

Floppy discs

Floppy discs are suitable for backup purposes where only a limited amount of data is involved. The upper limit depends on how many floppy discs you are prepared to use, a factor that is probably a reflection of how desperate you are! Backing up 30 megabytes of data onto about 20 or so floppy discs will be quite time consuming, but is still well within the bounds of reason. Backing up several hundred megabytes onto dozens of floppy discs is not a very practical proposition, and the discs could well cost more than some more convenient backup systems! In terms of megabytes per pound, floppy discs are not very competitive these days. Also, they are being phased out, although most PCs still seem to have a drive of this type.

Where floppy discs are suitable, there is a potential problem in that some of the files you wish to copy may be too big to fit on a single floppy disc. The capacity of a high-density 3.5-inch floppy disc is 1.44 megabytes when the standard PC disc format is used. Things like DTP and graphics files can be substantially larger than this. The normal copying facilities of Windows XP can not spread a large file across one or more discs. If you try to copy a file that is too large to fit onto the disc an error message to that effect will be produced. Fortunately, there are several Windows programs that can handle this problem. The later versions of the popular Winzip program for example, will compress and copy large files to several floppy discs if necessary. You can even copy a collection of files and save them as one large archive file spread across several discs.

Large scale

If floppy discs are not up to the task it is clearly necessary to resort to some form of mass storage device. It is highly unlikely that any installed device of this type will work in Safe Mode. It might be possible to get non-standard PC drives (Zip, etc.) to operate in MS-DOS. Where this is possible, the manufacturer's literature should give instructions for making an MS-DOS boot disc. However, booting from an MS-DOS floppy disc will not enable the hard disc drive to be read if it uses the NTFS filing system. The hard disc drive should be readable provided it uses the FAT or FAT32 filing system.

Second disc

If you have large amounts of data to backup and no mass storage device, your choices are limited. One option is to simply keep trying to repair the Windows installation until you are successful. Any Windows installation should be repairable, and persistence should eventually pay off. With a badly damaged system it will be necessary to reinstall Windows first to at least get something close to a complete and working system.

You may get lucky and fix the problem fairly quickly, or a great deal of time could be involved in locating and removing the problem. The biggest drawback of this method is that you will still have no backup of the hard disc's contents, limiting your options if there are further problems with the Windows installation. Also, the contents of the disc will probably be lost forever if the drive becomes faulty while you are struggling to get Windows working.

Many users save data onto a hard disc thinking that their work is safe and secure, but this is definitely not the case. Having data on a hard disc is sometimes likened to hanging paper documents by a thin thread over an open fire. Modern hard drives are relatively reliable, but if used for long enough a hard disc drive will go wrong, and you will probably end up throwing away the drive together with all your hard work.

A better option is to add some form of mass storage device. An external (parallel port) Zip drive is not particularly expensive, and in an emergency it should work quite happily with the computer booted into MS-DOS. A few Zip discs can store several hundred megabytes of data, which should be sufficient to backup any important data files, configuration files, etc. However, as pointed out previously, the hard disc will not be accessible from MS-DOS if it uses the NTFS file system. Note that any form of USB or SCSI storage device is unlikely to work with Windows in Safe mode or with MS/DOS. This is simply because the interface will not be recognised in Safe Mode or in MS-DOS, rendering the drive "invisible" to the operating system.

My preferred option is to add another hard disc drive. These days this probably represents the cheapest means of adding large amounts of extra storage capacity to a PC, and a hard disc also has the advantage of being very fast. Read and write speeds are measured in megabytes per second, unlike some other storage systems where it is specified as so many megabytes per minute. A further advantage of the hard disc approach is that the disc should work properly with Windows booted in Safe Mode or into MS-DOS. It should even work using Windows XP booted into the command prompt version of Safe Mode or into the Recovery Console. A hard disc drive is one of the standard PC drives, and as such it does not require any special drivers for basic operation. This makes life easier at the best of times, but greatly eases things when the Windows installation is damaged.

Adding a drive

Fitting a second hard disc drive obviously requires the lid or side panel of the PC to be removed, followed by some delving around inside the computer. It is not one of the more difficult upgrades, but unless you are reasonably practical it would be advisable to have the upgrade done professionally. Most shops that sell hard disc drives also offer an upgrade service, but it will almost certainly cost substantially more to have the drive fitted for you. However, this extra cost is preferable to damaging the PC and having to pay a hefty repair bill. Assuming you feel confident enough to go ahead with the upgrade yourself, the first task is to open the PC to determine the current configuration.

With older PCs the top and two sides of the case are in one piece, and are released by removing four or six screws at the rear of the unit. Be careful, because there will probably be other screws here that hold other things in place, such as the power supply unit. With the right screws removed, the outer casing should pull away upwards and rearwards, but it will probably take a certain amount of force to pull it free. More modern cases have removable side panels, and with most types these are again held in place by four or six screws at the rear of the unit. Both panels must be removed in order to give full access to the drive bays. If your PC has one of the more unusual case styles it will be necessary to carefully examine the exterior in order to "crack" it.

A modern PC has the hard disc interface on the motherboard rather than provided by an expansion card. In fact, there are two hard disc interfaces on the motherboard, or possibly four on a modern PC. These are known as IDE interfaces, and this simply stands for integrated drive electronics. In other words, most of the electronics for the hard disc drive controller is built into the drive itself. At one time the IDE interfaces were strictly for hard disc drives, but in a modern PC they can be used for other types of drive. These multipurpose interfaces are more

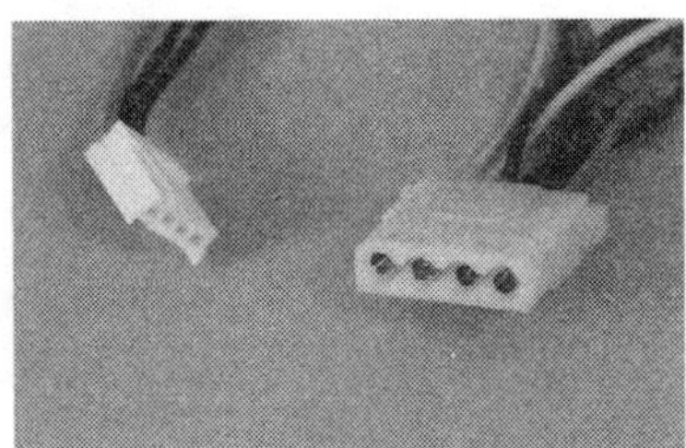

Fig.3.1 3.5-inch (left) and 5.25-inch (right) power connectors

accurately called EIDE interfaces, which stands for enhanced integrated drive electronics. In practice they are still often referred to as just plain IDE interfaces, and by other names such as "ATA". Many types of drive can be used with an EIDE interface, including CD-ROM, Zip, and LS120 drives.

In a typical PC the hard disc drive is connected to IDE port 1 and the CD-ROM drive is wired to IDE port 2. However, each IDE interface supports up to two devices, so the hard disc and CD-ROM drive could be connected to IDE port 1 via a single cable. A more common configuration with modern PCs is to have the hard disc on one IDE interface, with a CD-ROM or DVD drive and a CD writer on the other interface. Provided your PC has no more than three internal drives, excluding any floppy drives, it should certainly be able to support another hard drive.

If you look at the cabling inside the PC you should find some wide cables, know as "ribbon" cables, that connect the drives to the motherboard. With some modern PCs these leads are normal the normal round variety. Either way they should be easy to find as they are the only cables that connect between the hard drives and the main board. With luck, at least one of these cables will have an unused connector that can be used with the new drive. Note that any spare connector on the drive that connects to the floppy disc drive is of no use with a hard disc drive. The floppy variety uses a completely different interface having a smaller connector. A suitable power supply lead and connector is also needed. The connectors come in two sizes, which are a larger one for 5.25-inch drives and a smaller one for the 3.5-inch variety (Figure 3.1). However, all the hard disc drives I have encountered use the larger connector regardless of whether they fit 3.5-inch or 5.25 in bays.

If you are out of luck, one or other of the required leads and connectors will not be present. If the hard disc and CD-ROM drive share an IDE interface, the other IDE interface will be available for the additional drive, but it will not be fitted with a cable. Another possibility is that the existing drives are connected to separate IDE interfaces using single cables rather than types having two connectors for drives. In either case a standard twin IDE data lead is needed in addition to the drive (Figure 3.2).

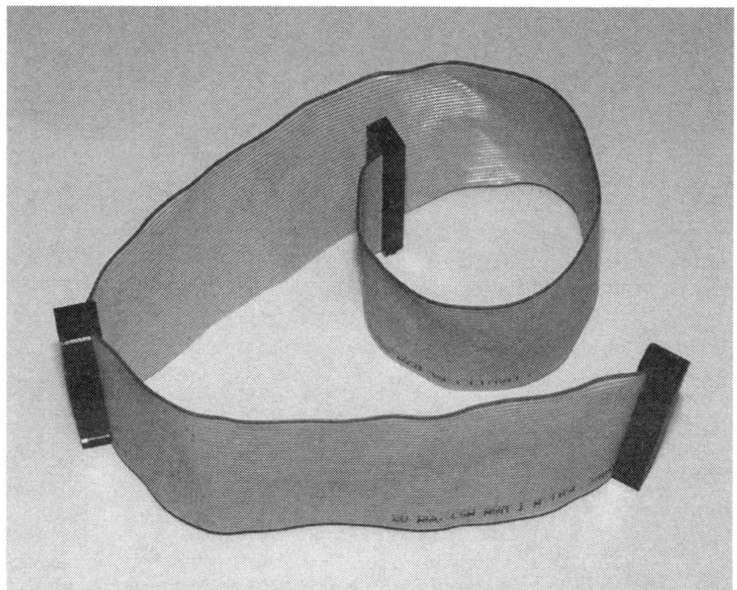

Fig.3.2 A standard twin IDE data lead

Hard drives are available in so called "bare" and "retail" or "boxed" versions. A bare drive may consist of nothing more than the drive itself. However, it will usually include an instruction manual and a set of fixing screws, but no data cable. Incidentally, if you find yourself with a hard drive but no matching manual, the web sites of most hard disc manufacturers include downloadable versions of the manuals for most of their hard disc units. Unless you are dealing with a very old or unusual drive, the information you require should be available on the manufacturer's web site.

The retail versions of hard drives normally include a cable in addition to a set of fixing screws and a more comprehensive manual. There may be other items such as a mounting cradle to permit a 3.5-inch drive to be used in a 5.25-inch drive bay. With modern drives there may well be two data cables included with the drive. One of these is a standard IDE cable that can be used with any IDE drive and any IDE interface. The other cable enables the drive to be used with a modern IDE interface that supports the UDMA66 and UDMA100 standards. UDMA66 and UDMA100 have the potential of faster data transfers than older standards such as the UDMA33 variety, but they can only be used if they are supported by the motherboard, the drive itself, and the correct cable is used. The instruction manual for your PC should state whether or not it supports anything beyond UDMA33.

If in doubt, the safe option is to use a standard IDE cable. This may provide something less than the ultimate in performance, but the disc should still work very well. It should certainly work well enough for making a backup of the main drive. Some advise against using a UDMA33 device together with a UDMA66 or UDMA100 device and cable. It is generally considered safer to use a UDMA33 cable when using a UDMA66 or UDMA100 device on the same interface as a UDMA33 drive. In my experience a UDMA66/100 cable works just as well in this situation, but either way the fast drive will be reduced to UDMA33 operation.

Of course, it is perfectly all right to have UDMA33 devices on one IDE interface and UDMA66 or UDMA100 devices on the other. Rationalising things, this is probably the best solution. The new drive will presumably support UDMA66/100 operation, so you need to pair it with another UDMA66/100 drive in order to obtain optimum results. This normally means pairing it with the existing hard drive, because most CD-ROM drives only support UDMA33 operation. In theory there is some advantage in having devices on different IDE interfaces where it will be necessary to copy large amounts of data from one to the other. In practice this advantage might be outweighed if having the second drive on the other IDE interface downgrades it to UDMA33 operation. Anyway, in this situation I would pair the two hard drives on the first IDE interface.

If the PC only supports UDMA33 operation, the new drive will also operate in this mode whichever IDE interface it is connected to. Where there is a spare channel available on the second IDE interface, this is the best place to install the new drive. This places it on a different interface to the main hard drive, which might help to speed up data transfers between the two.

Static

If you buy virtually any computer add-on to fit inside a PC it will be supplied in packaging plastered with dire warnings about the dangers of static electricity. Some of these are a bit "over the top", and suggest that going anywhere near the device without the protection of expensive anti-static equipment will result in it being instantly zapped. In reality the risks of static induced damage occurring are probably quite small. On the other hand, computer add-ons have yet to fall in price so far that they are in the "two a penny" category, and the risk of damage occurring is a real one.

The likelihood of damage can be reduced to insignificant proportions by observing a few simple rules. Rule number one is to leave the device in its packaging until it is time to install it. The plastic bags, foam lined boxes, etc., used for computer bits and pieces are not just for physical protection. They are designed to keep static electricity at bay. In some cases the packaging is designed to insulate the contents from high voltages. In others it is designed to conduct electricity so that no significant charge can build up between any two points in the device being protected. Any charges of this type will be almost instantly short-circuited by the conductive packaging.

Rule number two is to make sure that you are not charged with a high static voltage that could damage the device when you remove it from the packing. When working on computers do not wear clothes that are known to be good generators of static electricity. Manmade fibres are the most prolific static generators, but most modern clothes are usually made from natural fibres or a mixture of manmade and natural fibres, so this is not the major problem that it was at one time.

To make quite sure that both yourself and the device being installed are charge free, hold the device in its packing in one hand, and touch something that is earthed with the other hand. Any charge in you or the device should then leak away to earth. The metal case of the computer is a convenient earth point. With the cover or side panels removed there should be plenty of bare metal to touch. Touching the paintwork will not provide reliable earthing since most paints are excellent electrical insulators. Note that the computer must be plugged into the mains supply, but it does not have to be switched on.

Rule number three is to keep the work area free of any large static charges. Any obvious sources of static charges should be removed from the vicinity of the computer. Television sets and computer monitors are good static generators, which means that the computer must be moved away from the monitor before you start work on it. This will normally be necessary anyway, because with the computer's base unit in its normal location it will probably be difficult to get proper access to the interior of the unit. It needs to be placed on a table where there is good access to the interior and plenty of light so that you can see what you are doing. The table should preferably be one that it not precious, but if necessary the top can be protected with something like a generous quantity of old newspapers. It is a good idea to have the PC plugged into the mains supply but switched off at the mains socket. The earthed metal chassis of the computer will then tend to earth any static charges in its vicinity, preventing any dangerous charges from building up.

If you follow these simple rules it is very unlikely that the add-on device will be damaged by static charges. When dealing with hard disc drives it is as well to bear in mind that they are relatively delicate physically. Modern drives, although more intricate, are not as vulnerable as the early types. Even so, dropping a hard disc drive onto the floor is definitely not a good idea!

Jumpers

An IDE device has configuration jumpers that are used to set whether the unit will be used as the master or slave device on its IDE channel. Even if there is only one device on an IDE channel, that device must still be set as the master or slave unit. By convention, a single drive on an IDE channel is set as the master device. Therefore, if you are adding the new disc to an IDE channel that already has one device installed, the new drive must be set to operate as the slave device. If the new drive will be the sole device on its IDE channel, it must be set for master operation.

The rear of most CD-ROM drives and some IDE hard disc drives look something like Figure 3.3. The connector on the left is the power input and the one on the right is for the data cable. In between these are three pairs of terminals that can be bridged electrically by a tiny metal and plastic gadget called a jumper. A jumper can be seen in place in Figure 3.4. The "cable select" option is not used in a PC context, so only two pairs of contacts are relevant here. You simply place the jumper on the master or slave contacts, depending on which option you require. The configuration jumper should be supplied with the drive incidentally, and is normally set at the master option by default on a hard disc drive.

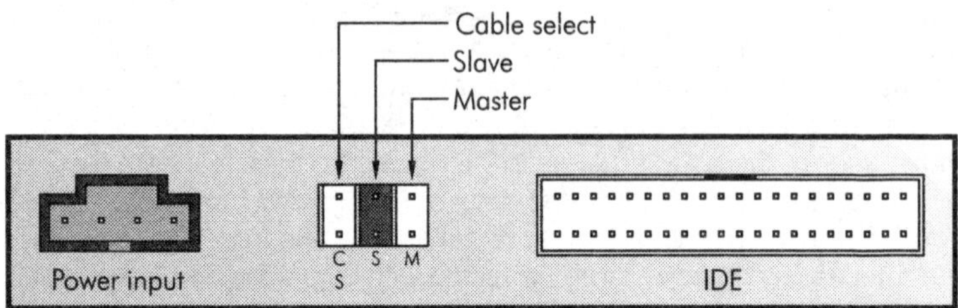

Fig.3.3 Typical layout for the rear of an IDE drive

Fig.3.4 A jumper fitted to a drive

With hard disc drives matters are not always as simple as the arrangement shown in Figure 3.3. There is often an additional set of terminals, and these are used where the drive will be used as the only device on an IDE channel. Using this setting will allow a lone drive to be correctly identified and used by the PC. If the drive has these additional terminals (or they are fitted in place of the cable select pins), you must use them for a sole IDE drive. It is very unlikely that the drive will be picked up properly by the BIOS if the normal master setting is used. Getting it wrong is not likely to produce any damage, but the drive will be unusable until the mistake has been corrected. The manual supplied with the drive should give details of the configuration settings available.

If the new drive is used as the slave device on the primary IDE channel, the other hard drive will presumably be the master device on this channel. The existing drive will need its configuration setting altered if it is set to operate as the sole IDE device on its channel. The manual supplied with the PC should give details of the configuration settings. Alternatively, it should be possible to identify the drive from its markings, and it will almost certainly be possible to find its instruction manual on the Internet.

If there is no device on the secondary IDE channel, or only a single CD-ROM, and the motherboard only supports UDMA33 operation, it would probably be best to add the new drive on this channel. If a CD-ROM is present on this channel, adding the new drive as the secondary slave device is unlikely to require any configuration changes to the CD-ROM drive. If no device is already present, simply add the new drive as the master device or sole device, as appropriate. As pointed out previously, in theory data exchanges between the two hard discs will be quicker if they are on different IDE channels. Where possible, it is therefore better to arrange things this way when using UDMA33 IDE ports.

It is definitely a good idea to check the configuration setting of the new drive, and where necessary alter it, prior to fitting the drive in the case. Once the drive is fitted inside the case it can be difficult to get at the jumper and terminals, and it can be very difficult indeed to see what you are doing when adjusting the jumper. Note that you do not have to look at the jumpers on the existing drives to determine their master/slave settings. The BIOS usually shows which drive is present on each IDE channel during the startup routine.

Getting physical

It is not essential to install the new hard drive in the computer as a fixture. You may prefer to simply connect the new drive to the data and power cables, do the backup, reinstallation and restoration, and then disconnect the drive again. It can then be stored safely away somewhere in case it is needed at some later date. With the drive in storage rather than in use it should not wear out, and should be ready for use if it is needed a few years "down the line". I used this method successfully with a couple of PCs for many years, although not strictly out of choice. Before removing the new drive you could use it to clone the fully restored main drive. If there are major problems with the hard disc at a later date, use the cloned drive in place of the original. This gets the PC almost instantly back in full working order.

If your PC has one of the minimalist cases you may find that there are no spare bays for another hard disc drive. Note that it is possible to use a 3.5-inch drive in a 5.25-inch drive bay using an adapter. This is just a metal cradle into which the drive is bolted, and the whole assembly then fits into the drive bay just like a 5.25-inch drive. This adapter should be available from any large computer store. As pointed out previously, it is sometimes (but not always) included with boxed retail versions of hard disc drives.

When temporarily connecting a drive it is essential to make sure that no exposed connections on the unit come into electrical contact with the metal case, expansion cards, etc. Some drives are fully enclosed, but most have the underside of the circuit board exposed (Figure 3.5). Often the easiest way of keeping the drive safe is to place it on top of the computer with some newspaper to insulate the drive from the case. With a PC that has some form of tower case it is usually easier to work on the unit if it is placed on its side. The drive can then be placed on the side of the drive cage, again with newspaper being used to provide insulation.

Probably most users will wish to use the additional disc as a permanent feature. This is essential if you wish to use it to make frequent backups or you will be making backup copies of data files as they are generated. If you are using a drive bay that has no front opening, the new drive

Fig.3.5 Connections on the underside of a drive

must be slid in from the rear. Any expansion cards that get in the way must be removed temporarily. Remove the screws that fix the cards to the rear of the chassis and it should then be possible to pull the cards free. The sockets on the drive are at the rear, so the other end is pushed into the rear of the drive bay. The manufacturer's name, etc., are marked on the top plate of the drive, so this side should be facing upward. In most cases the drive can be fully pushed into the bay, but it is sometimes necessary to ease it back slightly to get the mounting holes in the drive and the bay to match up properly.

In days gone by it was necessary to use plastic guide rails to mount the drives in the case, but most PCs made within the last eight years or more have drive bays that take the drives without the need for these rails. There are some exceptions, and these use an updated version of the guide rail system. With the old system there were two guide rails, and one was bolted on each side of the drive. The drive was then slid into place and the rails were bolted to the chassis. The new system has one guide rail per drive, and it usually just clips into place. One side of the drive is bolted to the chassis in the normal way, while the other simply clips into place. The point of this is that there is often limited access to one side of the drive bay. Using the clip-on rail on the appropriate side of the drive avoids the difficulty of fitting the mounting bolts on the awkward side. Your PC should have been supplied with one or two spare rails if it uses this type of drive mounting system

Four mounting bolts are normally supplied with the drive, and with the standard method of mounting these are used to secure the drive to the bay. If no fixing screws were supplied with the drive, the PC may have been supplied with some odds and ends of hardware. If so, there will probably be some suitable screws in amongst these. Failing that, you will have to buy some metric M3 screws about 6 millimetres long. Note

Fig.3.6 Polarised IDE connectors on a motherboard

that the mounting screws must be quite short, and should not protrude more than a few millimetres into the drive. Longer mounting bolts could easily damage something inside the drive.

With a so-called "external" drive bay, it might be easier to insert the drive from the front. Where the interior of the computer is very crowded this can avoid having to remove expansion cards to get the drive in place. An external bay is really intended for use with a floppy drive, CD-ROM drive, or some other type where access is needed to the drive for changing discs. However, an external bay is perfectly suitable for a wholly internal drive such as a hard disc unit.

The plastic cover at the very front of the bay can be carefully prised out using a flat bladed screwdriver, and it might then be possible to slide the drive in through the front of the case. There will probably be a metal plate behind the plastic cover though. It may be possible to remove this by first removing two or three fixing screws, but in most cases the plate has to be repeatedly twisted backwards and forwards until the thin pieces of metal holding it in place fatigue and break. With the drive in place, the plastic cover plate can be clipped back into position.

Cabling

The ribbon cable used to provide the data connection has three identical connectors. There is no specific connector for the motherboard and each drive, but because the cable is quite short it will probably have to connect everything together in a particular way in order to reach everything. It should not take too long to fathom out the best way of using the cable. Things are much easier when the new hard drive is the sole device on an IDE channel. The cable should then connect the motherboard to the drive without difficulty.

The connectors must be fitted to the motherboard and drives the correct way round. In theory the connectors are polarised and can only be fitted the right way round. There is a protrusion on the lead's connectors and a matching groove in the connectors on the motherboard and drives. Figure 3.6 shows the polarising keys in the two IDE connectors on a motherboard.

Unfortunately, some connectors, and mainly those on motherboards, are sometimes a bit too minimalist and are not properly polarised. In addition, some IDE connectors lack the polarising key. A search through the appropriate instruction manuals should show which is pin 1 on each connector. This information is often marked on the motherboard and the drives themselves. To make things easier, the ribbon cable has one red lead while the other 39 are grey. The convention is for the red lead to carry the pin 1 connection. Provided this lead is adjacent to pin 1 on the connector for the motherboard and both drives, everything will be connected together properly. With round data cables there should be clear markings to show pin 1 of each connector.

A spare power cable is needed for the new drive, and if there is a spare drive bay there should really be a spare power lead as well. However, it might be fitted with the smaller connector for 3.5-inch floppy drives, whereas it is the larger power connector that is required for hard disc drives, whether they are of the 3.5-inch or 5.25-inch variety. A large computer store should be able to provide a 3.5 to 5.25-inch power connector adapter. If there is no spare power cable, a splitter adapter is available. This provides two power connectors from a single power lead. Disconnect the power lead from the existing hard disc drive and connect it to the splitter. The two remaining connectors of the splitter are then connected to the hard disc drives. The power connectors are fully polarised and can only be connected the right way around. They are also quite stiff, and often need a certain amount of force in order to get them properly connected or disconnected again.

BIOS Setup

Having physically installed the hard disc it will be necessary to go into the BIOS Setup program and set the appropriate parameters for the new disc. The BIOS is something that most PC users never need to get involved with, but for anyone undertaking PC upgrading it is likely that some involvement will be needed from time to time. It is certainly something that can not be avoided if you add a second hard disc drive. In days gone by it was necessary to have a utility program to make changes to the BIOS settings, but this program is built into a modern PC BIOS.

A modern BIOS Setup program enables dozens of parameters to be controlled, many of which are highly technical. This tends to make the BIOS intimidating for newcomers and even to those who have some experience of dealing with PC technicalities. However, most of the BIOS

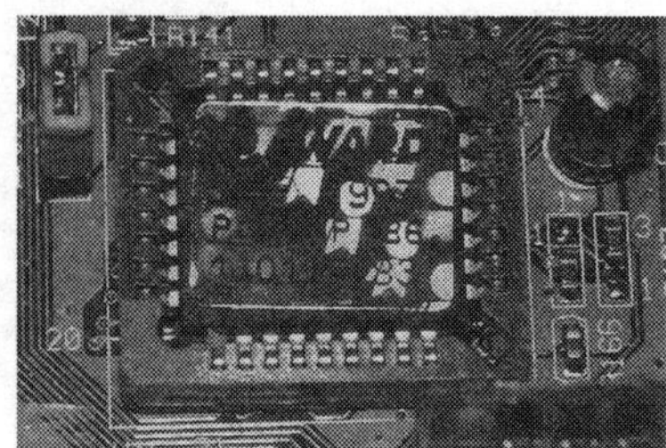

Fig.3.7 A modern BIOS chip

settings are not the type of thing the user will need to bother with, and very few are relevant to the hard disc drives.

BIOS basics

Before looking at the BIOS Setup program it would perhaps be as well to consider the function of the BIOS. BIOS is a acronym and it stands for basic input/output system. Its primary function is to help the operating system handle the input and output devices, such as the drives, and ports, and also the memory circuits. It is a program that is stored in a ROM on the motherboard. These days the chip is usually quite small and sports a holographic label to prove that it is the genuine article (Figure 3.7). Because the BIOS program is in a ROM chip on the motherboard it can be run immediately at start-up without the need for any form of booting process. It is the BIOS that provides the test procedures when a PC is switched on, and the BIOS also starts the boot process.

The BIOS can provide software routines that help the operating system to utilise the hardware effectively, and it can also store information about the hardware for use by the operating system, and possibly other software. It is this second role that makes it necessary to have the Setup program. The BIOS can actually detect much of the system hardware and store the relevant technical information in memory. Also, a modern BIOS is customised to suit the particular hardware it is dealing with, and the defaults should be sensible ones for the hardware on the motherboard. However, some parameters have to be set manually, such as the time and date, and the user may wish to override some of the default settings.

The Setup program enables the user to control the settings that the BIOS stores away in its CMOS memory. A backup battery powers this memory when the PC is switched off, so its contents are available each time the PC is turned on. Once the correct parameters have been set it should not be necessary to change them unless the hardware is altered, such as a new hard disc drive being added or the existing hard disc being upgraded. In practice, the BIOS settings can sometimes be scrambled by a software or hardware glitch, although this is a very rare problem with modern PCs.

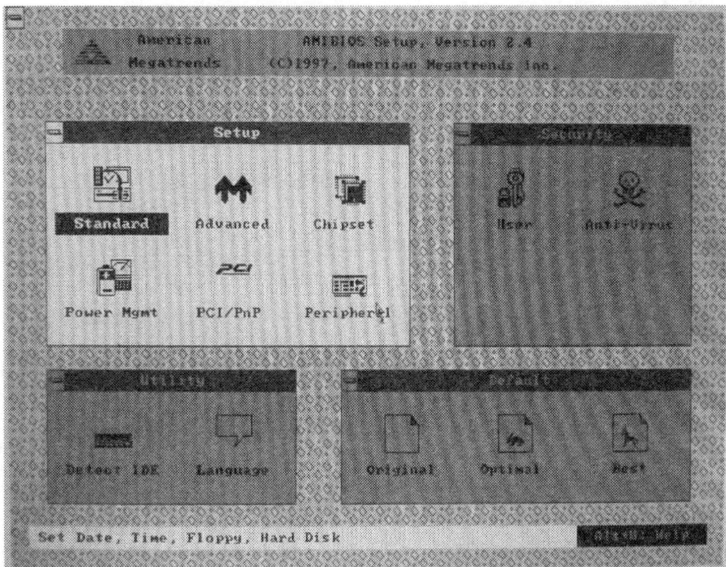

Fig.3.8 The initial screen of an AMI BIOS Setup program

Entry

In the past, there have been several common means of getting into the BIOS Setup program, but with modern motherboards there is only one method in common use. This is to press the Delete key at the appropriate point during the initial testing phase just after switch-on. The BIOS will display a message, usually in the bottom left-hand corner of the screen, telling you to press the “Del” key to enter the Setup program. The instruction manual should provide details if the motherboard you are using has a different method of entering the Setup program. The most common alternative is to press the “Escape” key rather than the “Del” key, but numerous alternatives have been used over the years, and no doubt some of these are still in use.

Every PC should be supplied with a manual that has a section dealing with the BIOS. Actually a lot of PCs are supplied with a very simple “Getting Started” style manual, but this is usually augmented by the manufacturers’ manuals for the main components. It is then the motherboard manual that will deal with the BIOS. It is worth looking through the BIOS section of the manual before you actually go into the BIOS program. This will give you an idea of how things work, but do not

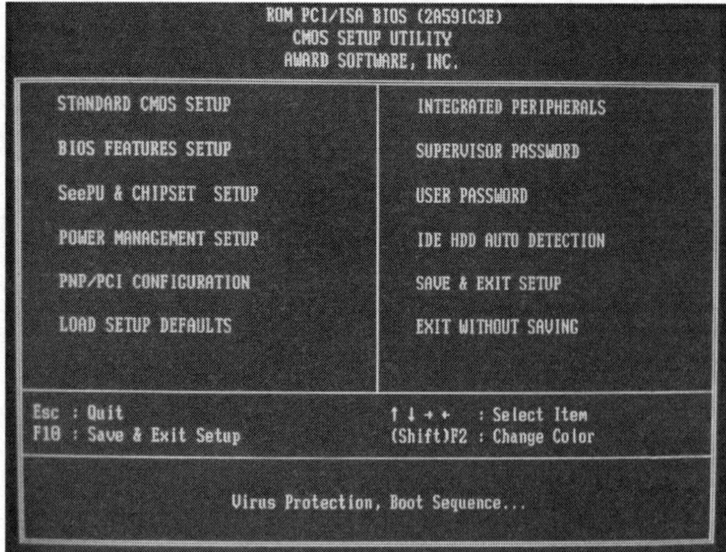

Fig.3.9 The initial screen of an Award BIOS Setup program

bother too much about the more obscure settings. In the current context it is only some of the Standard CMOS settings that are of interest. Do not expect the manual to give detailed explanations of the various settings. Most motherboard instruction manuals assume the user is familiar with all the BIOS features, and there will be few detailed explanations. In fact, there will probably just be a list of the available options and no real explanations at all. This does not really matter, and you really only need to know how to get into the BIOS, make a few changes, save the changes, and exit the program.

There are several BIOS manufacturers and their BIOS Setup programs each work in a slightly different fashion. The Award BIOS and AMI BIOS are two common examples, and although they control the same basic functions, they are organised in somewhat different ways. A modern AMI BIOS has a Setup program that will detect any reasonably standard mouse connected to the PC, and offers a simple form of WIMP environment (Figure 3.8). It can still be controlled via the keyboard if preferred, or if the BIOS does not operate with the mouse you are using. The Award BIOS is probably the most common (Figure 3.9), and as far as I am aware it only uses keyboard control.

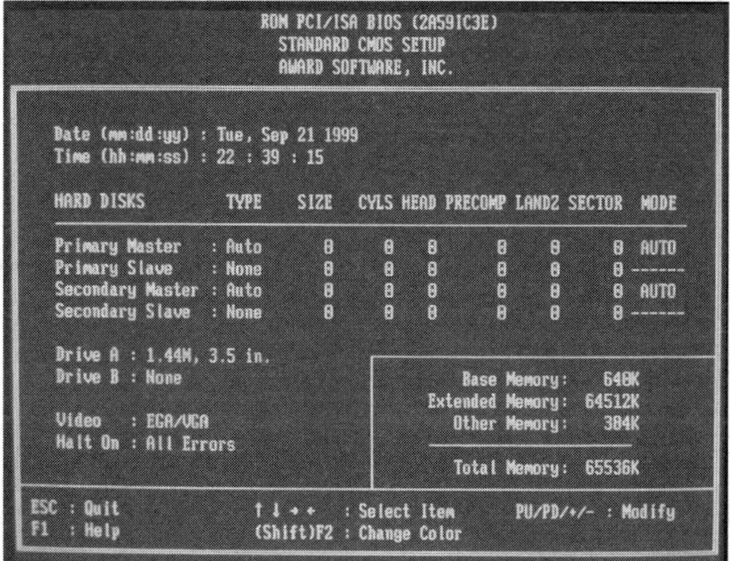

Fig.3.10 A typical Standard CMOS Setup screen

Apart from variations in the BIOS due to different manufacturers, the BIOS will vary slightly from one motherboard to another. This is simply due to the fact that features available on one motherboard may be absent or different on another motherboard. Also, the world of PCs in general is developing at an amazing rate, and this is reflected in frequent BIOS updates. Fortunately, the Standard CMOS section has not changed much over the years, so it should not differ significantly from the one described here unless you are dealing with a computer than falls into the "antique" category.

Standard CMOS

There are so many parameters that can be controlled via the BIOS Setup program that they are normally divided into half a dozen or more groups. The most important of these is the "Standard CMOS Setup" (Figure 3.10), which is basically the same as the BIOS Setup in the original AT style PCs. The first parameters in the list are the time and date. These can usually be set via an operating system utility these days, but you can still

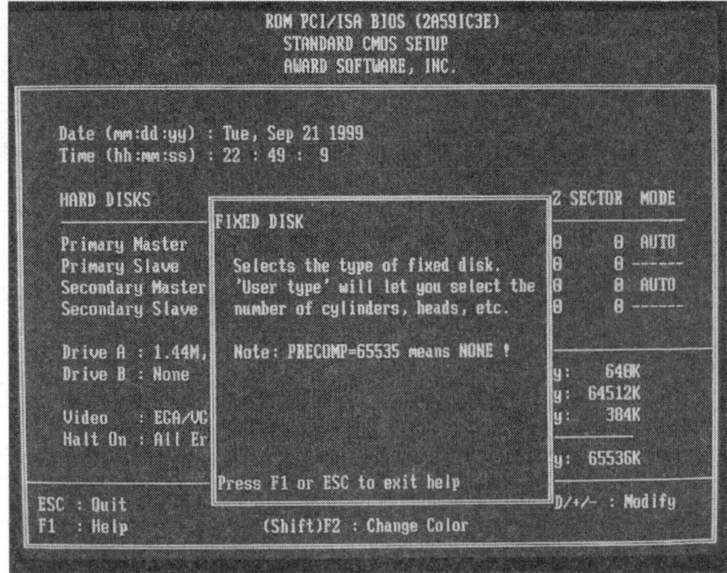

Fig.3.11 Most Setup programs provide context sensitive help

alter them via the Setup program if you prefer. There are on-screen instructions that tell you how to alter and select options. One slight oddity to watch out for is that you often have to use the Page Up key to decrement values, and the Page Down key to increment them.

With virtually any modern BIOS a help screen can be brought up by pressing F1, and this will usually be context sensitive (Figure 3.11). In other words, if the cursor is in the section that deals with the hard drives, the help screen produced by pressing F1 will tell you about the hard disc parameters. It would be unreasonable to expect long explanations from a simple on-line help system, and a couple of brief and to the point sentences are all that will normally be provided.

Drive settings

The next section is the one we need, and it is used to set the operating parameters for the devices on the IDE ports. The hard disc is normally the master device on the primary IDE channel (IDE1), and the CD-ROM is usually the master device on the secondary IDE channel (IDE2). However, to avoid the need for a second data cable the CD-ROM drive is sometimes the slave device on the primary IDE interface. You might have fitted the new drive as any of the four available devices apart from the primary device on IDE1, which will be the original hard disc drive. If in doubt, this table should help you decide which device it is:

IDE No./device	If the new drive is...
IDE1 secondary	on the same cable as the original hard drive
IDE2 primary	the sole device on the opposite channel to the original hard disc
IDE2 secondary	on the same cable as the CD-ROM drive (or other device such as a CD writer)

Having decided how the new drive fits into the overall scheme of things you can set the appropriate parameters. The drive should really be supplied with a manual that provides the correct BIOS settings, but it is usually possible to get by without it. One of the parameters is the hard disc's type number. In the early days there were about 40 standard types of hard disc drive, and it was just a matter of selecting the appropriate type number for the drive in use. The BIOS would then supply the correct parameters for that drive. This system was unable to cope with the ever increasing range of drives available, and something more flexible therefore had to be devised. The original 40-plus preset drive settings are normally still available from a modern BIOS, but there is an additional option that enables the drive parameters to be specified by the user. This is the method used with all modern PCs and their high capacity hard disc drives, so choose the Custom setting and ignore the drive numbers.

The drive table parameters basically just tell the operating system the size of drive, and the way that the disc is organised. Although we refer to a hard disc as a singular disc, most of these units use both sides of two or more discs. Each side of the disc is divided into cylinders (tracks), and each cylinder is subdivided into several sectors. There are usually other parameters that enable the operating system to use the disc quickly and efficiently. You do not really need to understand these parameters, and just have to make sure that the correct figures are placed into the drive table. As pointed out previously, the manual for the hard drive should provide the correct figures for the BIOS. If you do not have the manual, it can probably be downloaded from the disc manufacturer's web site.

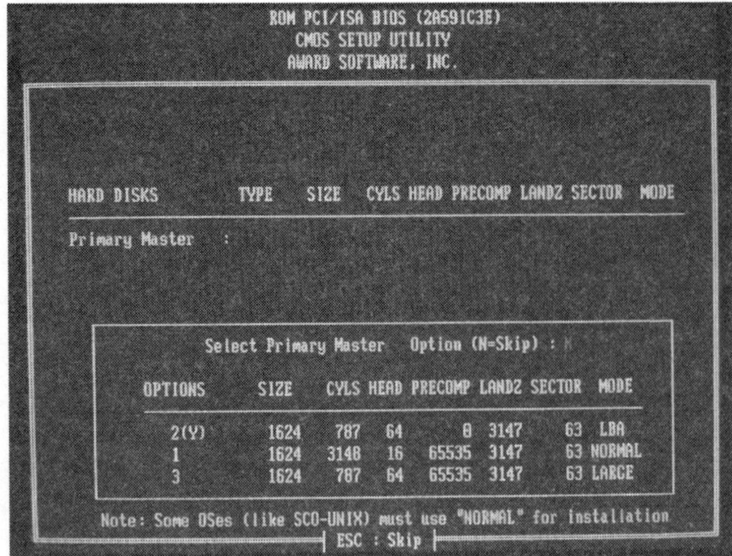

Fig.3.12 An IDE auto-detection screen

If you do not have the manual or prefer to take an easier option, a modern BIOS makes life easy for you by offering an "Auto" option. If this is selected, the BIOS examines the hardware during the start-up routine and enters the correct figures automatically. This usually works very well, but with some drives it can take a while, which extends the boot-up time. If the PC has been set up with this option enabled, the drive table will be blank.

There is an alternative method of automatic detection that avoids the boot-up delay, and any reasonably modern BIOS should have this facility. If you go back to the initial menu you will find a section called something like "IDE HDD Auto Detection" (Figure 3.12), and this offers a similar auto-detection facility. When this option is selected the Setup program examines the hardware on each IDE channel, and offers suggested settings for each of the four possible IDE devices. If you accept the suggested settings for the hard disc drive (or drives) they will be entered into the CMOS RAM. There may actually be several alternatives offered per IDE device, but the default suggestion is almost invariably the correct one. If you do not know the correct settings for a drive, this facility should find them for you.

It is perhaps worth mentioning that with an IDE drive the figures in the drive table do not usually have to match the drive's physical characteristics. Indeed, they rarely if ever do so. The electronics in the drive enable it to mimic any valid physical arrangement that does not exceed the capacity of the drive. In practice it is advisable to use the figures recommended by the drive manufacturer, as these are tried and tested, and should guarantee perfect results. Other figures can sometimes give odd problems such as unreliable booting, although they are within the acceptable limits.

The last parameter for each IDE drive is usually something like Auto, Normal, LBA (large block addressing), and Large. Normal is for drives under 528MB, while LBA and Large are alternative modes for drives having a capacity of more than 528MB. Modern drives have capacities of well in excess of 528MB, and mostly require the LBA mode. The manual for the hard drive should give the correct setting, but everything should work fine with "Auto" selected.

If you are using an up-to-date PC or one that is using automatic detection of the drives, it is possible that you will be able to ignore the BIOS. The BIOS will simply detect the new drive and configure itself accordingly. The PC will then boot normally and the new drive will be recognised by the operating system. The situation is different if the PC boots normally but the operating system does not recognise the new drive, or error messages are produced prior to booting. It is then essential to go into the BIOS and sort things out.

It is increasingly common for modern motherboards to have four rather than two IDE interfaces. With a motherboard of this type it will usually be possible for the added hard disc drive to have its own IDE interface even if the PC already is already fitted with something like one hard disc drive, a CD-ROM drive and a CD writer. Finding a spare IDE channel for the new drive should be that much easier, but in other respects things are essentially the same as when dealing with a twin IDE port motherboard. Motherboards that have more than two IDE ports usually have some form of RAID controller, and these provide clever facilities such as the ability to automatically backup data written to one drive on another drive. It is clearly worthwhile investigating any facilities of this type, which could clearly be more than a little useful in the current context.

Drive letters

Some users get confused because they think a hard drive that will have more than one partition should have separate entries in the BIOS for each partition. This is not the case, and as far as the BIOS is concerned each physical hard disc is a single drive, and it has just one entry in the CMOS RAM table. The partitioning of hard discs is handled by the operating system, and so is the assignment of drive letters. The BIOS is only concerned with the physical characteristics of the drives, and not how data will be arranged and stored on the discs. There is usually no point in using more than one partition if you are adding a drive for backup purposes. The only, and fairly obvious exception, is where the drive you are backing up has been partitioned to operate as two or more logical drives. It is then advisable to have the partitioning of the backup drive match that of the main drive as closely as possible.

The other Standard CMOS settings are concerned with the floppy discs and the default display type, and should simply be left as they are. The same is true of the settings in the other pages of the BIOS Setup program. Do not be tempted to start playing around with these unless you know exactly what you are doing. Entering silly settings is unlikely to damage anything, but could well prevent the PC from operating properly until normality is restored. The BIOS will probably have options that enable the previous settings to be reinstated, or default settings to be used. These can be useful if you should accidentally scramble a few parameters.

Note though, that no settings are actually altered unless and until you select the Save Parameters and Exit option, and then answer Yes when asked to confirm this action. This is clearly the route you should take if everything has gone according to plan. Take the Exit Without Saving option if things have not gone well. Simply switching off the PC or pressing the reset button should have the same effect.

Strategies

With the early PC hard disc drives it was necessary to do low level formatting of the drive before it could be partitioned and the high level formatting could be undertaken. Modern hard drives are supplied with the low level formatting already done. If there is a low level formatting option in the BIOS Setup program, never use it on an IDE hard disc drive. Do not use any similar facility in any utility suites that you might have.

No low level formatting is required, but with operating systems such as Windows 9x, and Windows XP the hard disc drive must be partitioned and high-level formatted before it can be used. We will consider Windows XP first.

The best way to proceed with the data recovery depends on the condition of the Windows XP installation. You options are very limited if it is not even possible to boot in Safe Mode. Probably the only way of tackling the problem is to have the new drive set as the master on the primary IDE channel and the original hard disc on any available IDE channel. Windows XP is then installed from scratch onto the new drive. It should then be possible to boot into the new installation and copy the files you need from the original hard disc. Any high capacity backup devices fitted to the computer should work properly with the new installation in place. It is then possible to copy the files to the new hard disc or the backup devices.

Where it is possible to boot into Windows in Safe Mode an alternative strategy is available. The existing hard disc drive can be left as the boot drive and the second hard disc is then placed on any available IDE channel. With the computer booted in Safe Mode the required files on the main hard drive can then be copied to the second drive. Windows XP can be installed from scratch onto the main drive, which will result in all the files on the main drive being erased. The rescued files on the second drive can then be copied back to the main drive. This is the best method to use if you do not wish to use the new drive as the main one. For example, if you obtain a cheap backup drive that has a much lower capacity than the main one, you will probably not wish to use the new drive as the main one. The second hard drive can be removed once the file recovery has been completed, but it is probably better to leave it in place as a backup drive for important files.

Partitioning

The new drive can be partitioned from within Windows XP and then formatted using the FAT32 or NTFS file system. If you wish to use the FAT32 file system for some reason, Microsoft recommend partitioning and formatting drives larger than 32 gigabytes using Windows 9x rather than Windows XP. This is simply because Windows XP is not fully equipped to deal with the partitioning and formatting of large discs using this format. Partitioning and formatting using Windows 9x and XP will be described here, starting with Windows 9x.

In order to partition and format the disc using Windows 9x it is not necessary to install Windows 9x onto the drive. All that is needed is a Startup disc, and one of these is normally produced as part of the Windows 9x installation process. If you do not have a Startup disc, one can be made using a system that runs Windows 9x. Start by going into

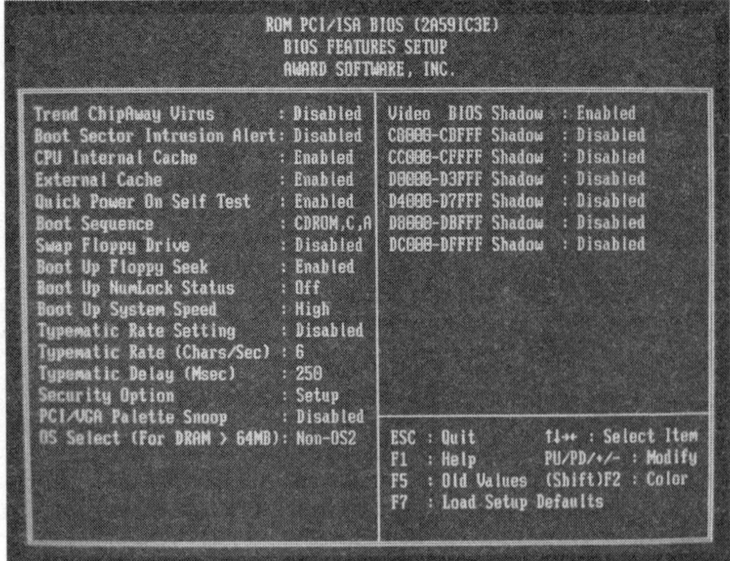

Fig.3.13 An example BIOS Features Setup screen. Amongst other things, this is used to set the required boot option

the Windows Control Panel, and one route to this is to operate the Start button, and then select Settings and Control Panel. Once in the control panel double-click on the Add/Remove Programs icon, select Startup Disk, and finally operate the Create Disk button. Then follow the onscreen prompts. A blank 1.44 megabyte floppy disc is required. Note that you will be asked to insert the Windows 95/98/ME CD-ROM into the CD-ROM drive, because some of the files required are not normally stored on the hard disc. The method of making the disc is exactly the same for all three operating systems (95, 98, and ME) incidentally.

Having obtained the Startup disc, it should be used to boot the computer into the Windows 9x version of MS-DOS. It is probable that the BIOS will already be set to boot from the floppy disc drive, but if necessary you must use the BIOS Setup program to set the floppy drive as a boot device. There will be a page in the BIOS called something like BIOS Features Setup (Figure 3.13), and this should enable various boot sequences to be chosen. Choose one that has the floppy disc (drive A:) as the first boot device, and hard drive C: as the second. Any subsequent boot options are irrelevant, since the PC will always boot from one or other of the first two options.

With the computer booted-up and running MS-DOS or the Windows 95/98/ME equivalent of MS-DOS, the new hard drive will not be accessible. Until it has been partitioned it will be largely "invisible" to the operating system. Note that a drive using the NTFS format will also be largely "invisible" to the system, so make sure that you process the right disc drive. Once the new drive is partitioned the operating system will be more willing to admit to its existence, but it will still be of no use until high-level formatting has been performed using the MS-DOS FORMAT program. However, you must first prepare the disc using the FDISK partitioning program. The Windows Startup disc contains copies of both FDISK and FORMAT, which are automatically placed on the disc for you when the Startup disc is created.

FDISK

FDISK is used to create one or more DOS partitions, and with discs of 2.1 gigabytes or less you may wish to have the whole of the disc as a single partition. Assuming the original hard disc has one partition, the new hard disc drive then becomes drive D:. By creating further partitions it can also operate as drive E:, drive F:, etc. The primary partition is normally the boot disc, and this is where the operating system would be installed. Obviously this does not apply to a second hard drive, and the primary partition is simply the first partition on the disc.

The MS/DOS and Windows 95 file systems set the 2.1-gigabyte partition limit. There is also an 8.4-gigabyte limit on the physical size of the drive. With Windows 98 or ME and any reasonably modern BIOS these limits do not apply, but you must use the FAT32 file system. To do this simply answer yes when FDISK is first run, and you are asked if you require support for large hard disc drives. Even if you do not wish to have a large disc organised as one large partition, it is still best to opt for large hard disc support. FAT32 utilises the available disc space more efficiently and reduces wastage. Note that if you only require a single partition you must still use the FDISK program to set up this single partition, and that the FORMAT program will not work on the hard drive until FDISK has created a DOS partition.

Some hard discs are supplied complete with partitioning software that will also format the disc and add the system files, which will be copied from the boot disc. Where a utility program of this type is available it might be better to use it instead of the FDISK and FORMAT programs. These MS-DOS programs are fairly straightforward in use, but using the software supplied with the drive will almost certainly be even easier.

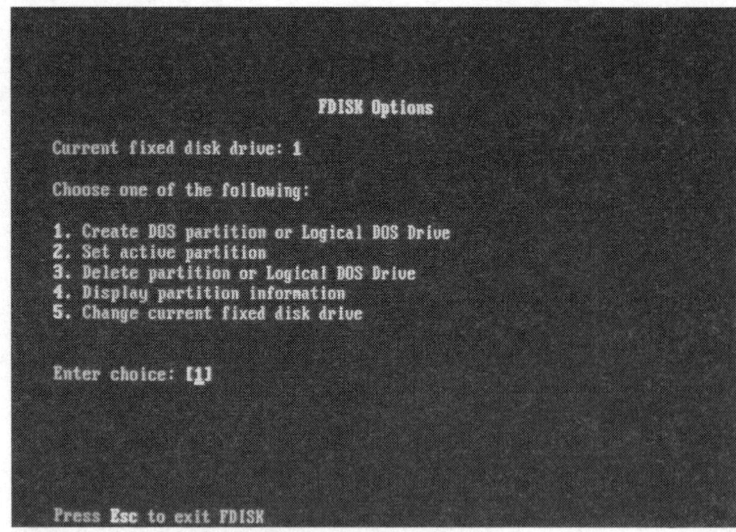

Fig.3.14 The main menu of the FDISK program

The only problem is that the software might be intended for use with drive C:, and might give problems if you try to use it with drive D:. The instructions supplied with the software should make it clear whether the software is suitable for use with a second hard disc drive. If the program insists on placing the system files on drive D:, this is not really a major problem. The system files will waste a small amount of disc space, but should not give any problems when the system is booted provided the boot options are set correctly in the BIOS. If in doubt, simply use FDISK and FORMAT.

Using FDISK

Once you are in FDISK there is a menu offering these five choices (see also Figure 3.14):

1. Create DOS partition or logical DOS drive
2. Set the active partition
3. Delete partition or logical DOS drive
4. Display partition information
5 Change current fixed drive

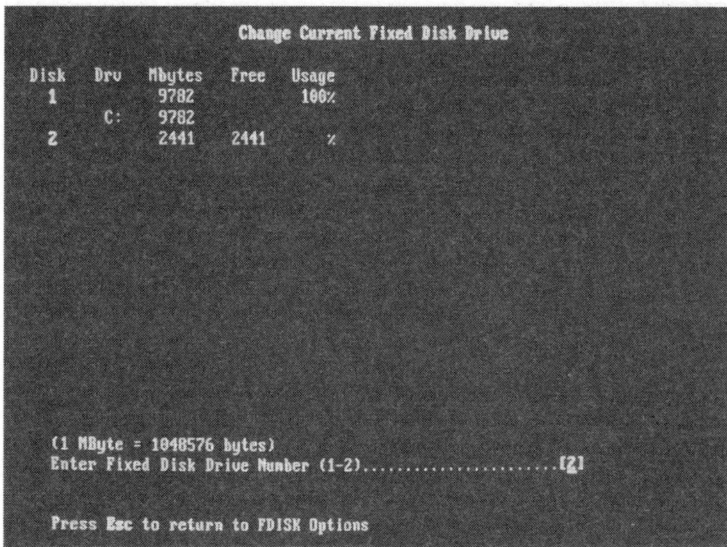

Fig.3.15 The partition information screen

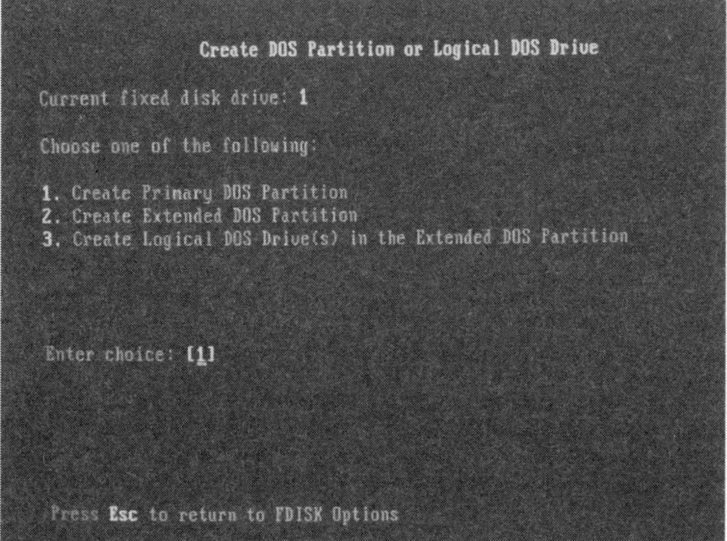

Fig.3.16 Creating a partition on a new hard disc

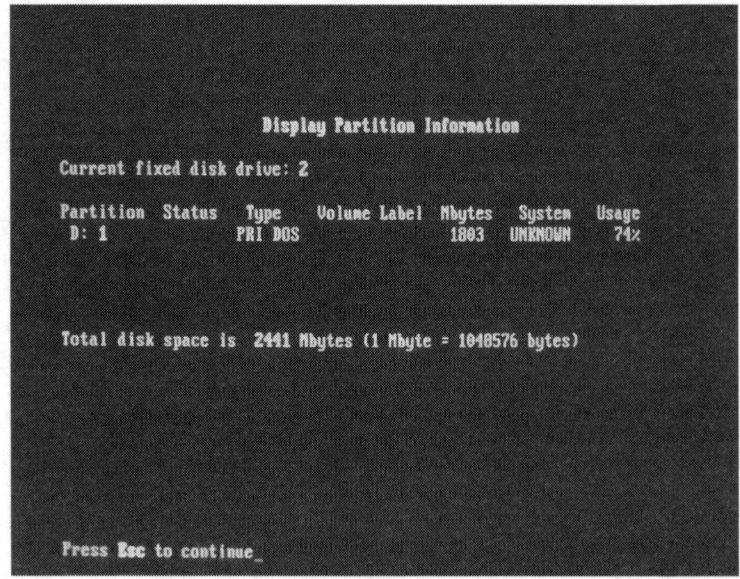

Fig.3.17 Checking that the new partition has been created

Normally the first thing we need to do is create a DOS partition using option one, which is the default. However, in this case we are dealing with an additional hard drive, and we must first make sure that it is the one FDISK is dealing with. It is very important that you do not accidentally use FDISK with the wrong drive, since to do so would almost certainly remove all the data from the disc you are trying to backup! Select option 5, which should bring up a screen like that in Figure 3.15. The original hard disc unit is drive 1 and the new hard disc is drive 2. In this example drive 1 (C:) is the original drive of about 10 gigabytes in capacity, and drive 2 is the additional rescue drive having a capacity of about 2.4 gigabytes. Drive 2 will eventually be drive D:, but at this stage it has not yet been assigned a drive letter. If the current disc is drive 1, enter 2 for this parameter and press the Enter key to go back to the main screen.

Once drive 2 has been set as the current drive it can be partitioned, and option 1 can be selected. This takes you into a further menu offering these three options (Figure 3.16):

1. Create primary DOS partition
2. Create extended DOS partition
3. Create logical DOS drive(s) in the extended DOS partition

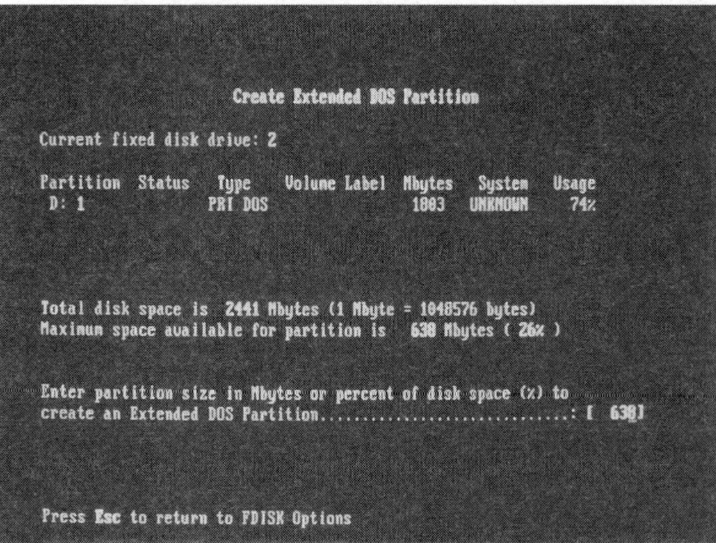

Fig.3.18 Provided there is some spare capacity, one or more additional partitions can be added

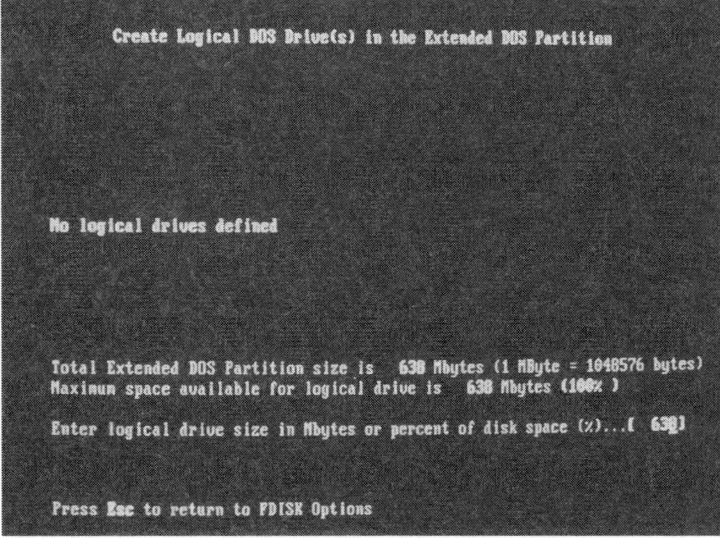

Fig.3.19 An extended partition must be given a drive letter

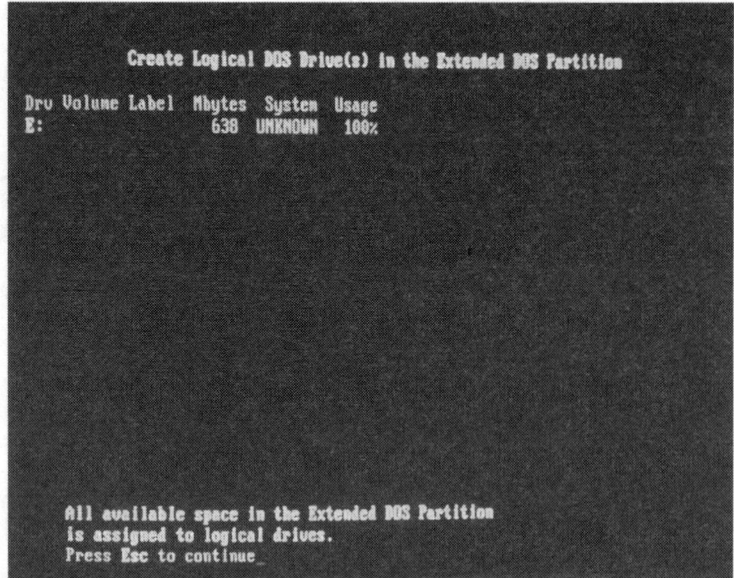

Fig.3.20 If all goes well, a screen showing the drive letter of the new partition will appear

It is a primary DOS partition that is required, so select option one, which should again be the default. After the disc has been given a quick test you will be asked if you wish to use the maximum space for the partition. If you answer yes, the whole disc, or as much of it as FDISK can handle, will be used for the partition. If you answer no, you will then have to specify the size of the primary partition in megabytes. After a further quick check of the disc the new partition will be created. Having created the partition, press the Escape key to return to the original menu. It is a good idea to select option four to check that the partition has been created successfully (Figure 3.17).

If a further partition is required select option one, and then option two, which is "Create extended DOS partition" (Figure 3.18). Enter the size of the partition you require and press the Return key to create the partition. Then press the Escape key, which will bring up a message saying "No logical drives defined" (Figure 3.19). In other words, you have created a partition, but as yet it does not have a drive letter. Assuming you require all the space in the partition to be one logical drive, simply press the Return key. This will make the partition drive E:, and a screen giving

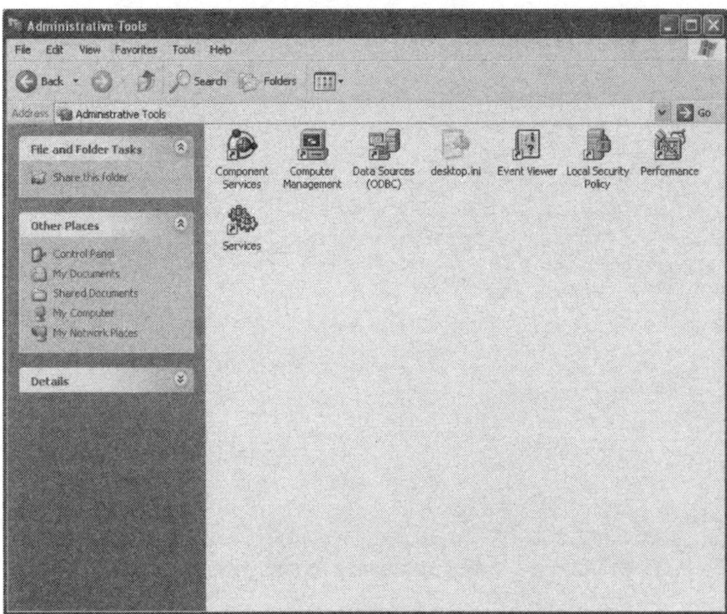

Fig.3.21 The Administrative Tools window

this information will appear (Figure 3.20). Press the Escape key to return to the main menu, and use option four to check that the partition has been created successfully.

It has been assumed here that the original hard disc has a single FAT32 partition. If it has more than one partition these will be drives C;, D;, etc., and the drive letter or letters for the additional drive will be moved up accordingly. For example, if the original disc is used as drives C: and D:, partitions of the new drive would become drives E:, F:, etc. These MS-DOS drive letters are not really of much importance once Windows XP is in use, since it will assign its own drive letters.

Formatting

Having created the partitions you require, the "FORMAT" command can then be run. First you will have to press the Escape key twice to exit FDISK, and then the computer must be rebooted so that the new partition information takes effect. Make sure you format the correct disc, because

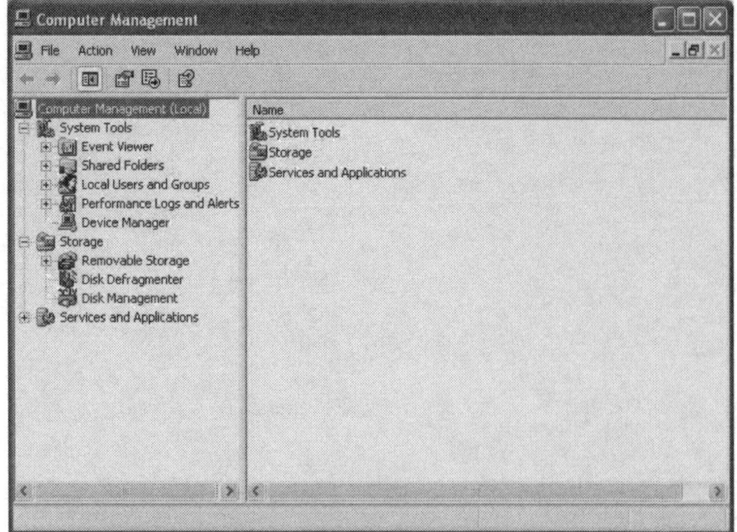

Fig.3.22 The Computer Management window gives access to several utilities

formatting a disc that is already in use will destroy any data it contains. To format drive D: use this command:

format D:

This will bring up a warning to the effect that all data in drive D: will be lost if you proceed with the format. As yet there is no data to lose, so answer yes to proceed with the formatting. It might take several minutes to complete the task, since there are a large number of tracks to be processed and checked. If the hard disc has more than one partition and is operating as drive D:, drive E:, etc., each partition must formatted using a separate "FORMAT" command. To format drive F: for example, this command would be used:

format F:

The new hard disc drive should then be fully operational, and it should appear in My Computer, etc., if you boot the computer in Safe Mode. The files you wish to rescue can then be copied to the new drive using Windows Explorer with Copy and Paste facilities. Windows XP is then installed from scratch onto the original hard disc and the rescued files can then be copied back to this drive.

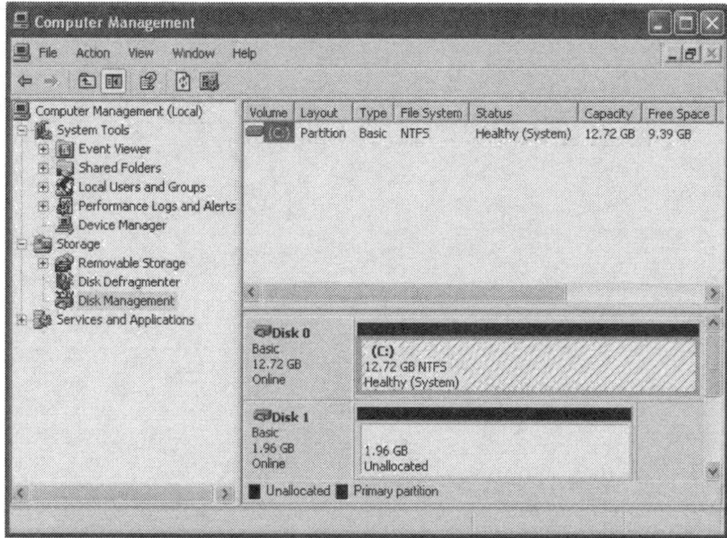

Fig.3.23 The window with the Disk Management utility selected

Computer Management

Partitioning and formatting from within Windows XP is achieved with the aid of the Computer Management utility. This can be run by going to the Windows Control Panel and double clicking the Administrative Tools icon. This produces a window like the one of Figure 3.21, and double clicking the Computer Management icon produces the new window of Figure 3.22. Several utilities are available from the Computer Management window, but the one

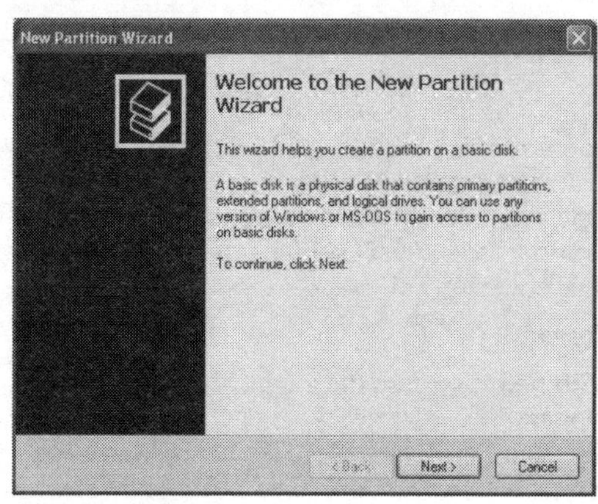

Fig.3.24 The opening screen of the Partition Wizard

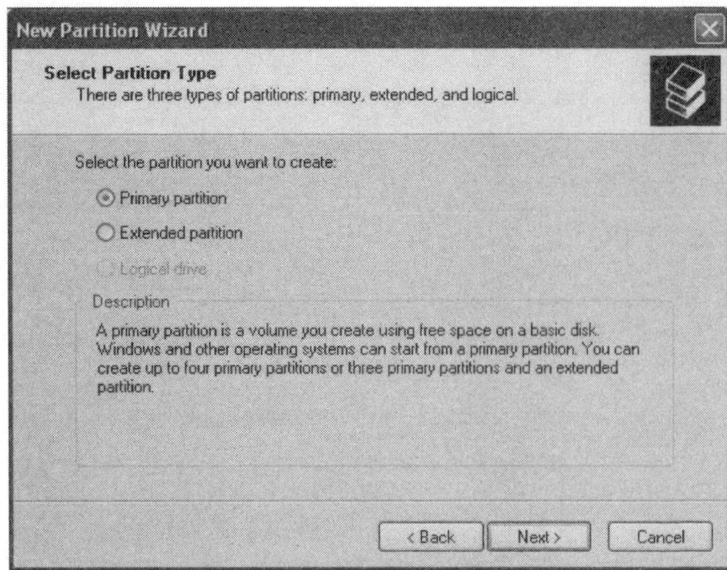

Fig.3.25 Use this window to select the partition type

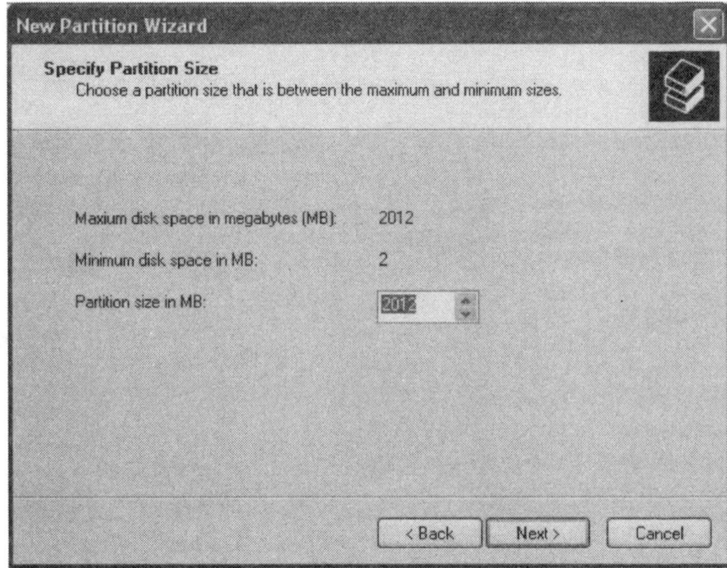

Fig.3.26 This window is used to set the partition size (in megabytes)

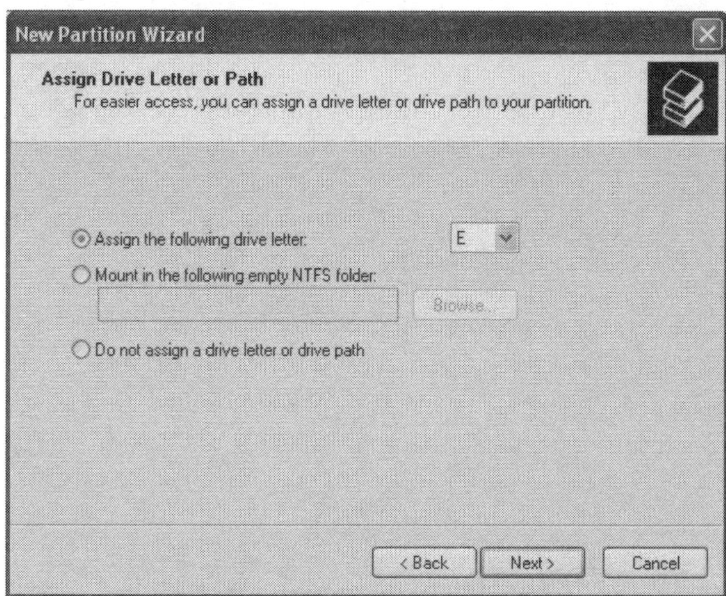

Fig.3.27 Here a drive letter is assigned to the new partition

required in this case is Disk Management. Left-clicking this entry in the left-hand panel changes the window to look something like Figure 3.23.

Details of the boot drive are given at the top of the right-hand panel. The bottom section gives details of both drives, and the new backup drive is Disk 1. This is described as "Unallocated", which means that it is not partitioned or formatted at this stage. The black line to the right of the Disk 1 label and icon also indicates that it is not partitioned. To partition the disc, right-click on the black line and then select the New Partition option from the popup menu. This launches the New Partition Wizard (Figure 3.24). Windows XP can use two types of disc, which are the basic and dynamic varieties. The New Partition Wizard only handles basic discs, and these use conventional partitions that are essentially the same as those used by MS-DOS and earlier versions of Windows. For simple backup purposes a basic disc is perfectly adequate.

Operate the Next button to move on with the partitioning, and a window like the one in Figure 3.25 should appear. Either an extended or a primary partition can be selected using the radio buttons, and in this case it is a

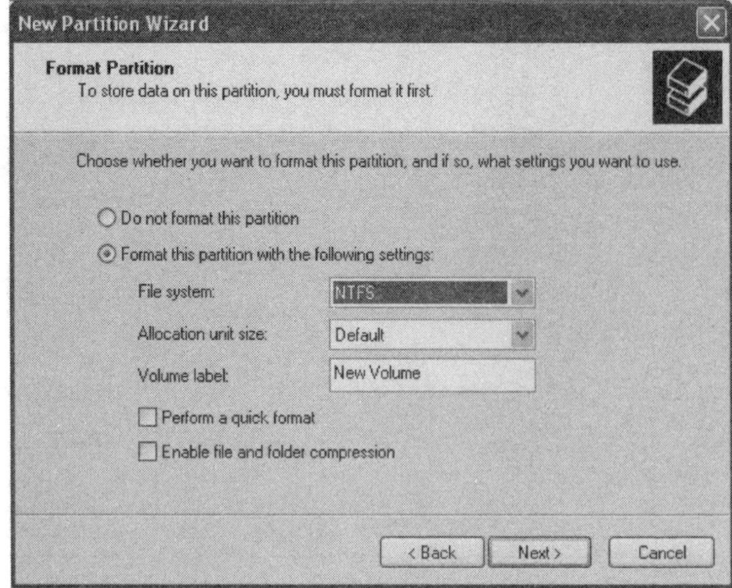

Fig.3.28 The partition can be formatted as a NTFS, FAT, or FAT32 type

primary partition that is needed. The size of the partition is selected at the next window (Figure 3.26), and the maximum and minimum usable sizes are indicated. All the available disc space will be used by default, but a different size can be used by typing a value (in megabytes) into the textbox. Operating the Next button brings up the window of Figure 3.27 where a drive letter is assigned to the new partition. Unless there is a good reason to do otherwise, simply accept the default drive letter.

At the next window (Figure 3.28) you have the choice of formatting the new partition or leaving it unformatted. Since the partition will not be usable until it is formatted, accept the formatting option. One of the menus offers a choice of FAT, FAT32, or NTFS formatting. Settle for the default option of NTFS formatting unless you need compatibility with another Windows operating system. Also settle for the default allocation unit size, which will be one that is appropriate for the partition size. A different name for the drive, such as "Backup", can be entered into the textbox if desired. Tick the appropriate checkbox if the capacity of the disc is barely adequate to backup your files, and you wish to enable file and folder compression.

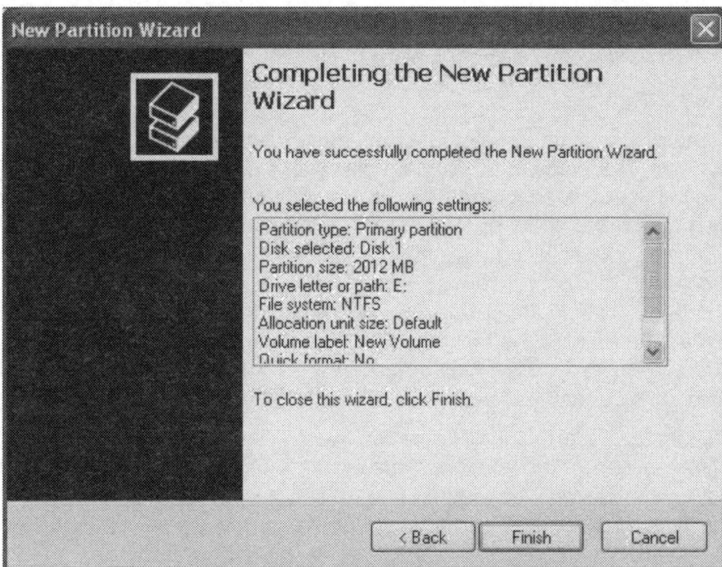

Fig.3.29 This window lists all the parameters that have been selected

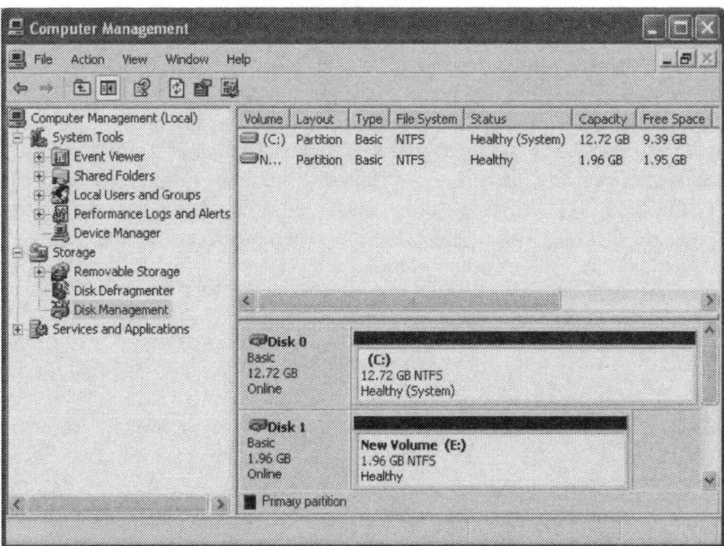

Fig.3.30 The Disk Management window shows the new partition

Left-click the Next button when you are satisfied with the settings. The next window (Figure 3.29) lists all the parameters that have been selected, and provides an opportunity to change your mind or correct mistakes. If necessary, use the Back button to return to earlier windows and change some of the settings. Operate the Finish button if all the settings are correct. The partition will then be created, and it will appear as a blue line in the Disk Management window. It will then be formatted, and this may take half an hour or more for a large partition. The area below the blue line indicates how far the formatting process has progressed. Eventually the formatting will be completed, and the Disk Management window will show the new disc as containing a primary partition using the appropriate file system (Figure 3.30). Once the formatting has been completed, files on the main drive can be copied to the new partition using the Cut and Paste facilities of Windows Explorer.

If space has been left for a further partition on the disc, right-click on the black section of the line that represents the vacant disc space. Then select the New Partition option from the popup menu, and go through the whole partitioning and formatting process again. A maximum of four primary partitions can be used on each physical disc.

Windows 98/ME

The hard disc must be formatted and partitioned using a recovery disc if you are using Windows 98 or ME. This process was fully described previously. The new disc can be used as drive D with PCs that are bootable in Safe Mode, and the appropriate files and folders are then copied from drive C to drive D. If the PC can not be booted into Windows, the best option is to have the new drive as C and the original set as drive D. Then reinstall Windows onto drive C and copy the data files from drive D to drive C. The original drive can then be reformatted to clear its contents so that it can be used as a backup drive.

Points to remember

Do not wait for a virus to strike before backing up data. It should be possible to rescue your data if the operating system becomes seriously damaged, but it might be expensive to have it rescued from a faulty hard drive.

Data rescue services are available, but there is no guarantee that data will be retrievable from a damaged hard drive or one that has been trashed by a virus.

Not all backup devices will work with Windows in Safe Mode or in MS-DOS. Lack of operation in either of these modes does not render a backup device useless, but life is easier when using a more accommodating drive. An NTFS partition is "invisible" to the system if the computer is booted into MS-DOS.

If you find yourself with a Windows installation that seems to be impossible to repair, and no usable device to backup masses of important data, there are three options. Carry on trying to repair Windows for as long as it takes, abandon your data and reinstall Windows from scratch, or add a suitable backup device so that the data can be rescued prior to reinstalling Windows.

Another hard drive is the most practical option when disaster has struck and an emergency backup of data is required. These days a hard disc drive is a relatively cheap backup option that will work in both Safe Mode and MS/DOS since it is a standard MS-DOS and Windows drive. Hard discs are also relatively fast in operation.

A modern PC can have at least four IDE drives (hard discs, CD-ROM drives, etc.) and will usually be able to accept an additional hard drive. If necessary, you can temporarily disconnect a CD-ROM drive to make way for the backup drive.

If the PC will not even boot into Safe Mode, probably the best rescue method is to add a new hard drive as disc C: and have the original hard disc as drive D:. In other words, set the new drive as the primary master and the original drive as the primary slave. Install Windows XP onto the new drive and then copy your data from the old drive.

A hard disc drive has to be partitioned and then high-level formatted before it is ready for use. This can be done using a Windows 9x Startup disc and the FDISK and FORMAT commands if a FAT32 disc is required. Even with Windows XP, this is the best method for discs having a capacity of 32 gigabytes or more. FDISK must be used even if the disc will be organised as one large partition. No low-level formatting is required with a modern hard disc drive, since this formatting is done at the factory.

The Windows XP Disk Management utility can be used to create partitions and format them using the FAT, FAT32, and NTFS file systems. However, this utility is only available if the computer can be booted into Windows XP, either normally or in Safe Mode.

Proper backup software can be used to backup your data, but Windows Explorer enables data to be easily copied from one drive to another. Complete directory structures can be copied using the Copy and Paste facilities and the usual dragging techniques.

4

Backup and Restore

Shutting the stable door

At one time the threat of attack from viruses was greatly exaggerated, and the risk for most users was strictly limited. In the pre-Internet era I was looking after three or four PCs for many years, and prior to that I used various computers such as the Amiga. The total number of attacks on those computers was precisely zero. The situation is certainly different for anyone currently using a computer on the Internet. Rather than an outside chance, the odds of running into trouble over a period of years are probably less than evens.

Many users get into difficulties first, and then buy antivirus software and take other measures to secure and backup their computers. This is really a case of "shutting the stable door after the horse has bolted". An antivirus program should really be considered an essential piece of software for any PC system that is used on the Internet. Bear in mind though, that even with a good program of this type installed, even if it is kept up-to-date, there is no guarantee that it will keep your PC free from viruses. There is inevitably a lag between a new virus appearing and the antidote being made available. You would have to be very unlucky to be one of the first to get a new virus on your PC, but it could happen.

In order to guard against undetected attacks it is necessary to have at least one backup copy of any important data. If the worst comes to the worst and the contents of the hard disc drive have to be erased and everything then reinstalled from scratch, you should have everything necessary to complete the task. It will be a long job that could take a day or two, but you should eventually get everything running much as it did before the attack, complete with all your data.

The job can be greatly speeded up if a full backup of the hard disc is taken. Simply copying all the files on the hard disc to CDRs or another form of mass storage will not enable the system to be restored to its original condition. The files can be copied back to the hard disc, but they will not be in the same places on the restored disc. As a result of this the PC will not be able to boot from the disc. In order to precisely restore a disc to its previous state it is necessary to produce what is termed an image of the disc. It requires special software to produce the image file and restore the disc from this file. Power Quest's Drive Image and Norton's Ghost are two popular programs of this type. There is a rather less sophisticated backup and restore feature included as part of the Windows operating system.

Partitions

With the current low cost of hard disc drives it is quite common for a large drive to be divided into several partitions. In effect, a large disc becomes two or more smaller discs. One partition is often used to store a backup of the main (boot) partition. Another ploy is to have a second physical drive, which is a clone of the main drive. Either way, any new data placed on the main drive is copied to the backup partition/drive. If the Windows installation is seriously damaged it is just a matter of restoring it from the relevant partition of the backup drive. The PC should then much as it did problem occurred, complete with your data.

Having a second physical drive gives even greater security because it guards against a catastrophic failure of the main drive. If the main drive should fail it is just a matter of installing a new one and installing the backup image onto it. As an emergency measure it is possible to set the backup drive to operate as the boot disc, and you can then go on using the PC while a new disc is obtained.

Although backup drives successfully guard a PC against many types of disaster, they do not necessarily help if a virus strikes. The virus might only attack the boot drive, but it is quite likely that it will damage the contents of all the drives and partitions it can find. Having restored the contents of the hard disc you might find that the PC works no better than it did previously. In order to guard against a virus attack it is necessary to have the image file on CDRs or some other form of storage that is kept separate from the PC. Even the most sophisticated of computer viruses is unable to attack files that are on CDRs stored in drawer or cupboard.

Due care must be taken in order to avoid reinfection. Ideally the hard disc should be reformatted to remove its entire contents, which will ensure that the virus infection is removed along with everything else. The computer should then be switched off to clear the contents of its memory. It is then switched back on and by one means or another, everything is restored to the hard disc. In practice there will often be data on the hard disc that has not been backed up to floppy discs, CDRs, or some other form of external storage. You may quite reasonably decide to rescue this data before wiping the disc by reformatting it. Before doing so you need to be sure that the virus has been fully eliminated, or the infection might be introduced to the restored system by way of the rescued files.

System Restore

Windows ME has a useful facility called System Restore, and essentially the same feature is present in Windows XP. It has to be emphasised that this is not a conventional backup program, and it can not be used to make a set of backup discs for use in the event of a hard disc failure. This is simply because it uses the main hard disc to store the backup files, and if the hard disc fails, the backup files are inaccessible. System Restore is designed specifically to deal with problems in the operating system, and on the face of it you should be able to restore a hacked system if your PC has been attacked by a virus.

Unfortunately, the System Restore facility has its limitations, and it is possible that it will have been targeted by the virus. It might be worthwhile trying it as a quick fix before reinstalling everything from scratch. After all, you will have lost nothing other than a small amount of wasted time if it fails to work. If it should work, a great deal of time reinstalling everything will have been saved. The chances of success are probably not good though.

The purpose of the System Restore facility is to take the system back to a previous configuration. In the current context the idea is to take the PC back to a state somewhere prior to the virus starting its attack. Since a virus does its best to stay concealed, it would be unrealistic to expect System Restore to remove the virus. The virus must be removed prior to using System Restore. Ideally you should periodically add new restore points so that if something should subsequently go wrong with the operating system, it can be taken back to a recent restore point. However, Windows adds restoration points periodically, so it is not essential to routinely add your own.

The main reason for adding your own restoration points is that there is increased likelihood of problems occurring. The most common example

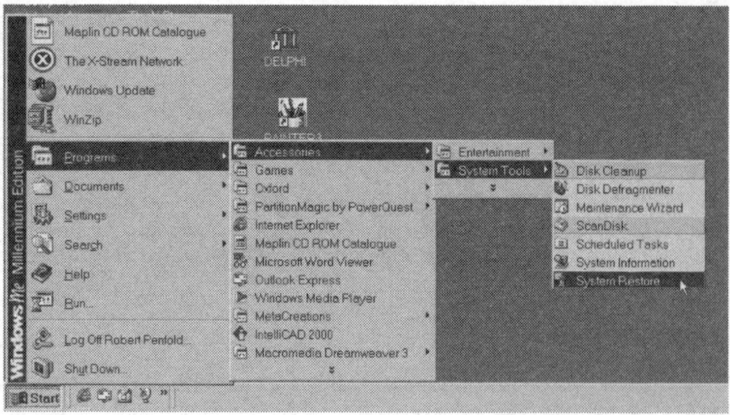

Fig.4.1 The System Restore program is deep in the menu structure

of this is adding a restore point prior to installing new software. If anything should go horribly wrong during the installation process, going back to the restoration point should remove the rogue program and fix the problem with the operating system. You can then contact the software publisher to find a cure to the problem, and in the mean time your PC should still be functioning properly. In the present context you could add a restoration point prior to doing anything that could introduce a virus into the system, such as downloading a file over a P2P system.

When going back to a restoration point the program should remove any recently added programs, but it should leave recently produced data files intact. Of course, with any valuable data that has not been backed up already, it would be prudent to make backup copies before using System Restore, just in case things do not go according to plan. The program itself does provide a way around this sort of problem in that it does permit a restoration to be undone. If a valuable data file should vanish "into thin air" it should be possible to return the PC to its original configuration, backup the restored data, and then go back to the restoration point again. Any programs lost during the restoration have to be reinstalled from scratch.

In use

The System Restore program is buried deep in the menu structure (Figure 4.1), but it can be started by going to the Start menu and then selecting Programs, Accessories, System Tools, and System Restore. The program

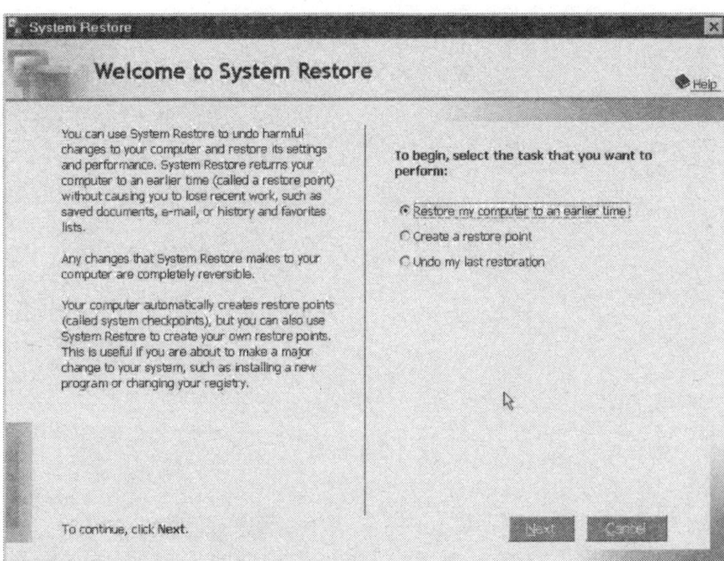

Fig.4.2 The Welcome screen of the System Restore program

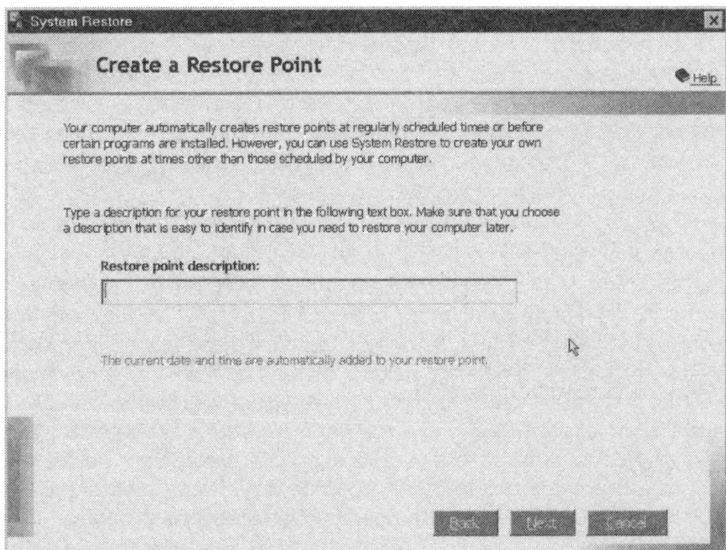

Fig.4.3 The system creates restore points but you can add your own

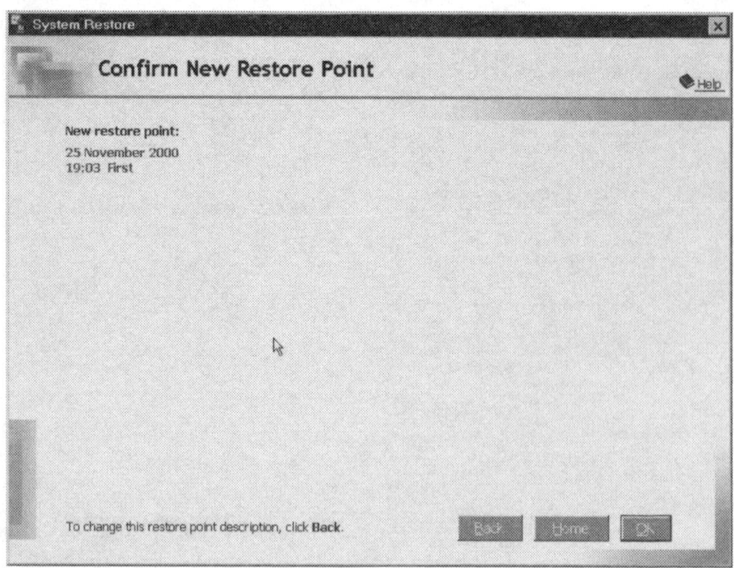

Fig.4.4 You can check things before creating a restoration point

is controlled via a wizard, so when it is run you get the screen of Figure 4.2 and not a conventional Windows style interface. The radio buttons give three options, which are to go back to a restoration point, create a new one, or undo the last restoration. When the program is run for the first time there is no restoration to undo, so this option will not be present.

As pointed out previously the system will automatically create restoration points from time to time, but you will probably wish to create your own before doing anything risky or that will make large changes to the system. Start by selecting the "Create a restore point" option and then operate the Next button. The next screen (Figure 4.3) asks the user to provide a name for the restore point, and it is helpful if the name is something that will be meaningful. There is no need to bother about including a date, as the program automatically records the date and time for you. There will be a delay of at least several seconds when the Next button is pressed, and then a screen like the one shown in Figure 4.4 will appear. This gives you a chance to check that everything is correct before the restoration point is created. If everything is all right, operate the OK button to create the restoration point and terminate the program.

To go back to a restoration point, run the program as before, and select the Return my computer to an earlier time option. Operate the Next

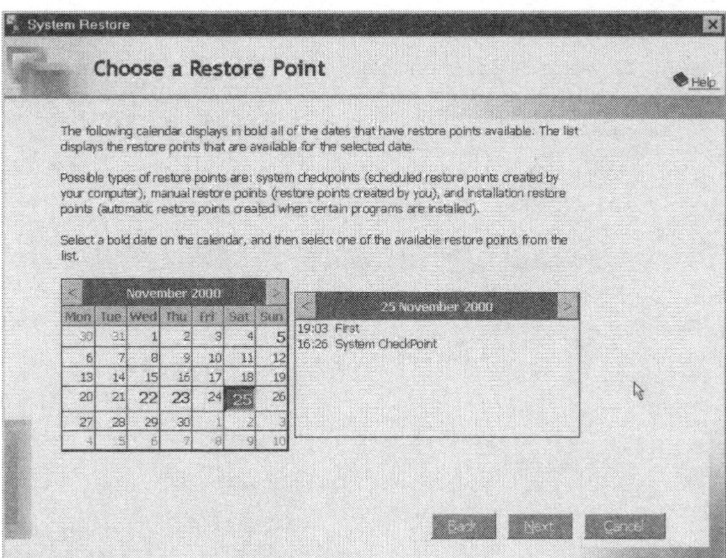

Fig.4.5 Choosing a restoration point

button, and after a short delay a screen like the one of Figure 4.5 will appear. If there are a number of restore points available you can use the arrow heads in the calendar to find the one you require. The dates on the calendar in larger text are the ones that have restore points. Left-clicking on one of these will show the available points in the screen area just to the right of the calendar. Left-click on the required restore point and then operate the Next button. This brings up a screen and warning message, like Figure 4.6. Left-click the OK button to remove the warning message, and close any programs that are running. If you are satisfied that the correct restore point has been selected, operate the Next button and the program will begin the restoration process. A screen showing how things are progressing will appear (Figure 4.7).

Heed the warning on this screen, and do not do anything that will alter, open or delete any files while the program is running. Just sit back and do not touch the computer until the program has finished its task. Once the restoration has been completed the computer will reboot, and a message will appear on the screen (Figure 4.8). This confirms the point to which the computer has been returned, and indicates the options if the PC fails to operate properly using this restore point. Left-click the

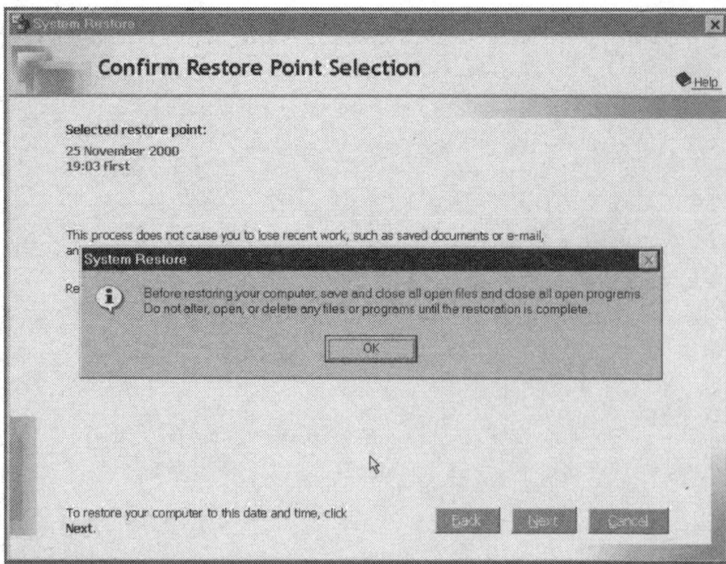

Fig.4.6 A warning message gives you a chance to change your mind

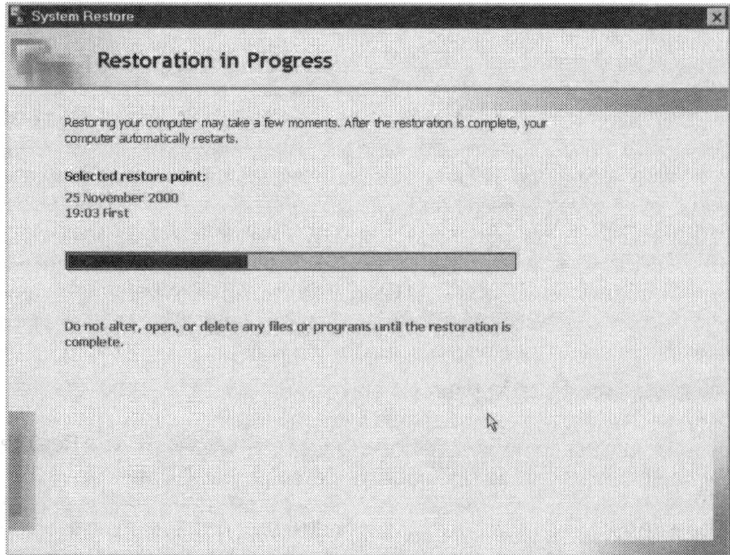

Fig.4.7 You can see how the restoration process is proceeding

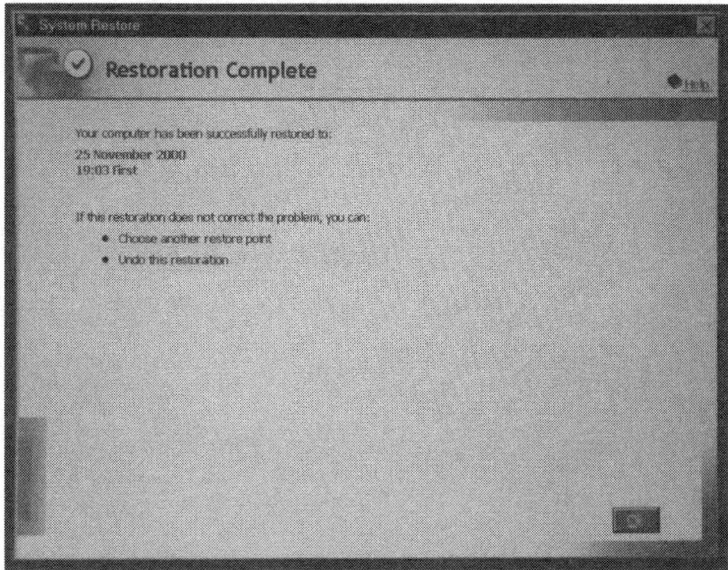

Fig.4.8 This message appears once the process has been completed and the computer has rebooted

OK button to finish the boot process, and the computer should then have shifted back in time to the appropriate restoration point.

There is never any guarantee that the System Restore facility will work, and an error message stating that it can not restore the selected point will sometimes be obtained. You can try a different restoration point, but it is quite likely that none will be available if one of them fails. In my experience it works properly in the majority of cases, but a seriously damaged system is likely to be within the minority of failures. As already pointed out, there is not a lot to lose by trying it in cases where the only alternative is to wipe the hard disc and reinstall everything.

Windows Backup

It is definitely better to have a proper backup in case the System Restore utility can not fix the problem. For anything beyond backing up data files it is best to resort to some sort of backup program. With these it is possible to save selected directories or directory structures, or the entire contents of the hard disc drive. I think I am correct in stating that every

Fig.4.9 The initial window of the Backup and Restore Wizard

version of Windows is supplied complete with a backup program that has the imaginative name of Backup. Although basic compared to some programs of this type it does the job well enough for most users. Its lack of popularity possibly stems from the fact that the equivalent facility in Windows 3.1 was something less than user friendly, causing many users to look elsewhere for a backup utility.

Perhaps the problem is simply that the Backup program is a part of Windows that has often been easy to overlook. Anyway, the Windows XP version is more user friendly and powerful than previous versions, and it is definitely there if you seek it out. With the Professional version of Windows XP it is installed by default, but with the Home Edition it will probably have to be installed from the Valueadd\Msft\Ntbackup folder on the installation CD-ROM.

Backup Wizard

Once installed, the Backup program is run by selecting All Programs from the Start menu, followed by Accessories, System Tools, and then

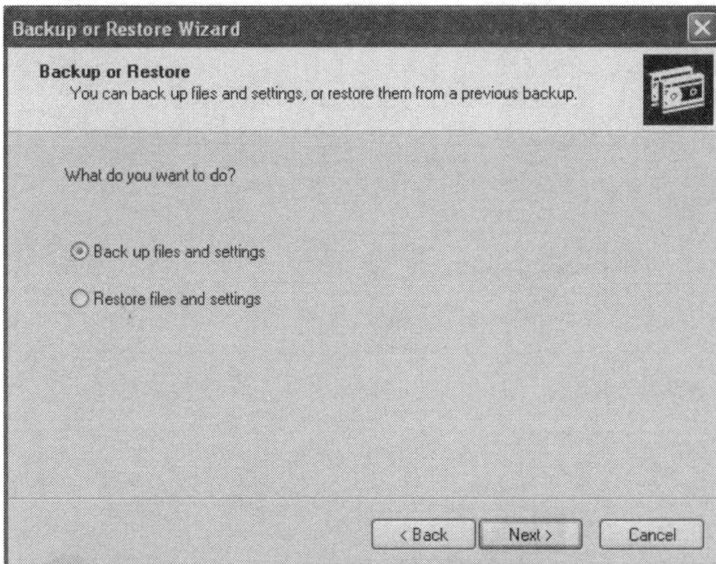

Fig.4.10 This window provides backup and restore options

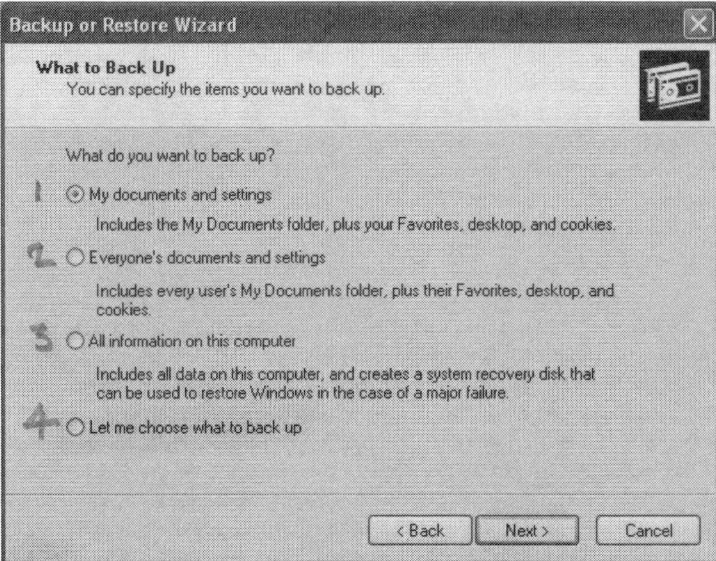

Fig.4.11 Use this window to choose what you wish to backup

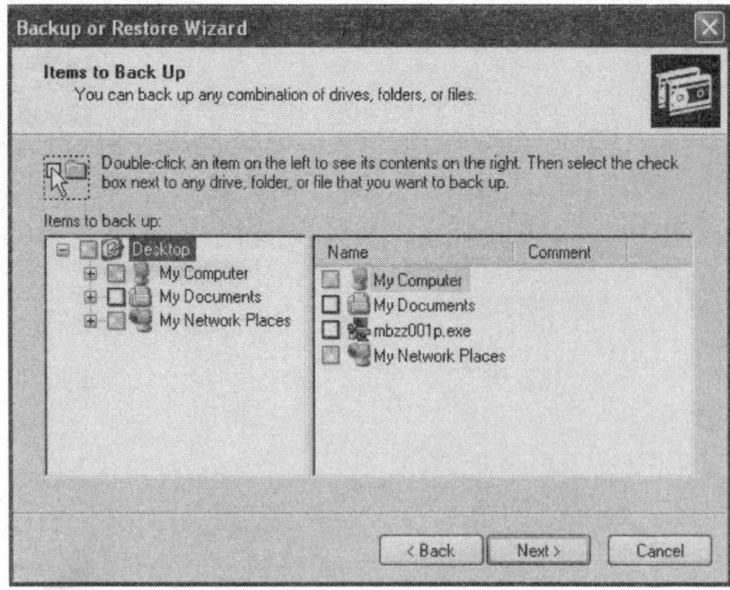

Fig.4.12 Select the files or folders you would like to backup

Backup. By default the Backup Wizard (Figure 4.9) runs when this program is launched, and initially it is probably best to use the wizard. Operate the Next button to move on to the first stage of using the Backup Wizard (Figure 4.10). Here you have the choice of backing up or restoring data, but it is obviously necessary to produce a backup disc before anything can be restored. Therefore, initially the Backup radio button has to be selected.

The next window (Figure 4.11) is used to select the data to be backed up. The top option produces a backup of the My Documents folder plus some system settings and cookies. The second option is similar, but it provides a backup of the documents and settings for all users. Using the fourth option produces a file browser (Figure 4.12) so that the user can select the files and folders that will be backed up. The third option is the one that is of most use if the system becomes seriously damaged or the hard disc becomes unusable. It permits the whole system to be backed up, and it also produces a recovery disc that enables it to be easily restored again. In fact the restoration process is almost totally automated. It is the third option that will be considered here.

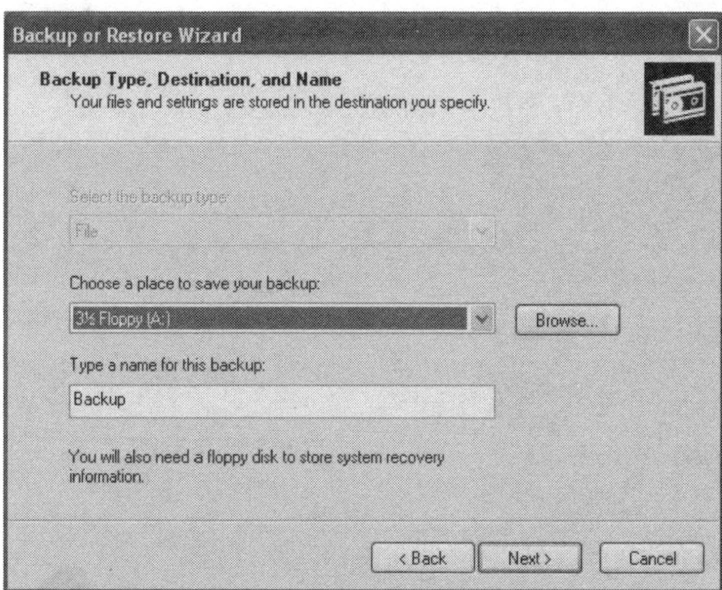

Fig.4.13 Use this window to select the backup drive

The next window (Figure 4.13) enables the backup drive to be selected, and a variety of drive types is supported. These include Zip discs, local hard drives, and some tape backup systems. Unfortunately, CD writers are not supported. Sometimes there are ways of working around this limitation, but it is probably best to opt for a third-party backup program if you wish to use CD-R or CD-RW discs to hold the backup files. Use the menu or the Browse option to select the correct drive. If you select a device that is not supported by the Backup program, an error message will be produced when Windows tries to create the file. This will simply state the backup file could not be produced.

In the current context the best option is to have a second drive as the backup device. However, in order to keep it safe from viruses the backup drive should have the power and data leads disconnected once the backup has been completed. Of course, the power should be switched off before the drive is disconnected. The drive is reconnected again if you need to restore the backup copy at some later time.

By default, the backup file is called "Backup" but the name in the textbox can be changed to any valid filename. Operating the Next button moves things on to a window like the one in Figure 4.14. This shows the options

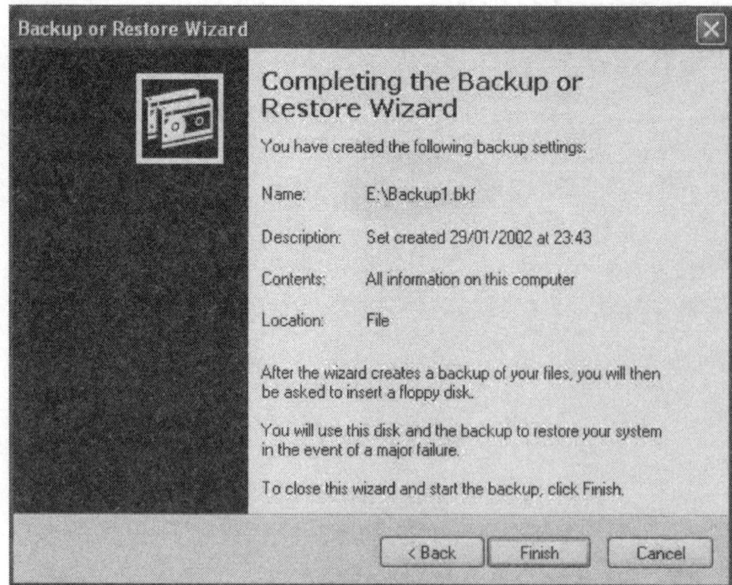

Fig.4.14 The selected options are shown before the backup is started

that have been selected, and provides an opportunity to change your mind or correct mistakes. Use the Back button if it is necessary to return to earlier windows to make changes, or operate the Finish button to go ahead and make the backup file.

A window like the one shown in Figure 4.15 will appear, and this shows the progress made by the Backup program. It provides an estimate for the time remaining until the task is completed, and this will vary massively depending on the amount of data to be saved and the speed of the backup device. With many gigabytes of data to backup it is definitely a good idea to use a fast backup device such as a second hard disc drive. With a slow backup device the process can take many hours. Where appropriate, you will be prompted when a disc change is necessary. With multiple disc backups, always label all the discs clearly. You will then be able supply the right disc each time when restoring the backup copy. Do not worry if the size of the backup file is substantially less than the total amount of data on the hard disc. The backup file is probably compressed, or perhaps no backup copies are made of standard files that are available from the Windows XP installation disc. Anyway, it is quite normal for the backup file to be significantly smaller than the source.

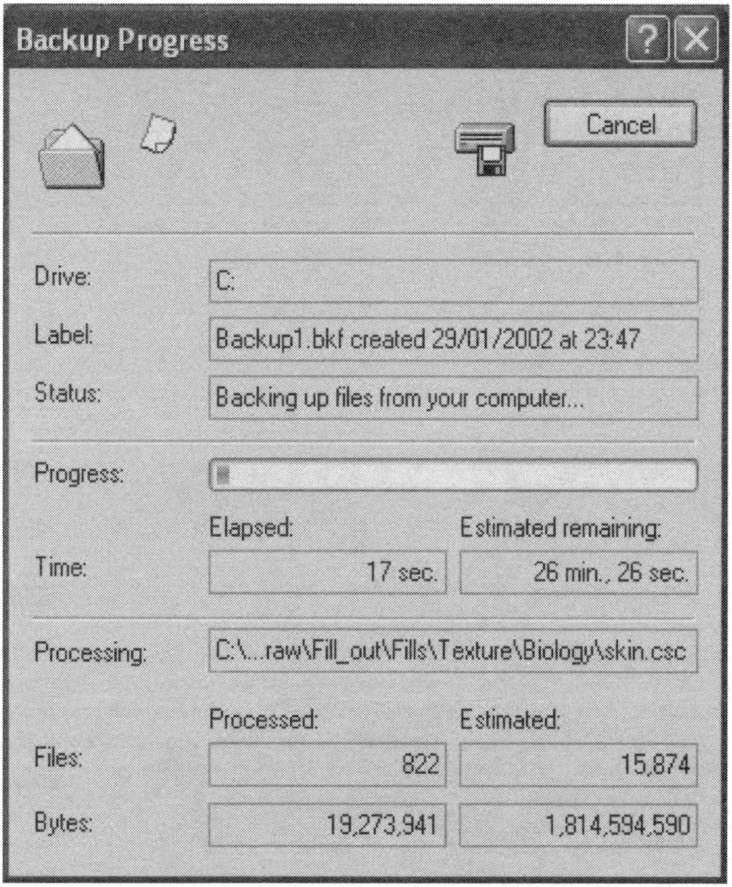

Fig.4.15 This window shows how the backup is progessing

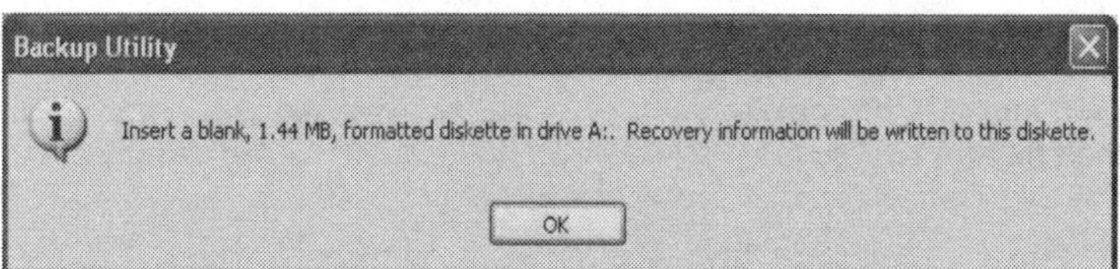

Fig.4.16 The floppy disc is inserted into drive A: when this message appears

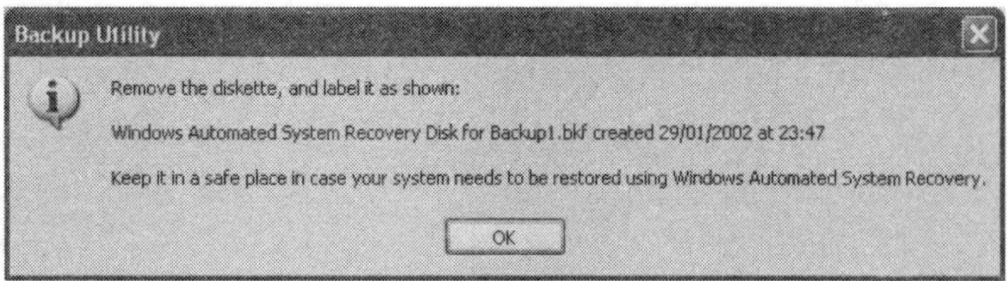

Fig.4.17 This message indicates that the backup has been completed

The message shown in Figure 4.16 will appear towards the end of the backup process. The floppy disc is needed to make an automatic recovery disc. This disc is needed in order to restore the system from the backup disc, and the backup is of relatively little value without the

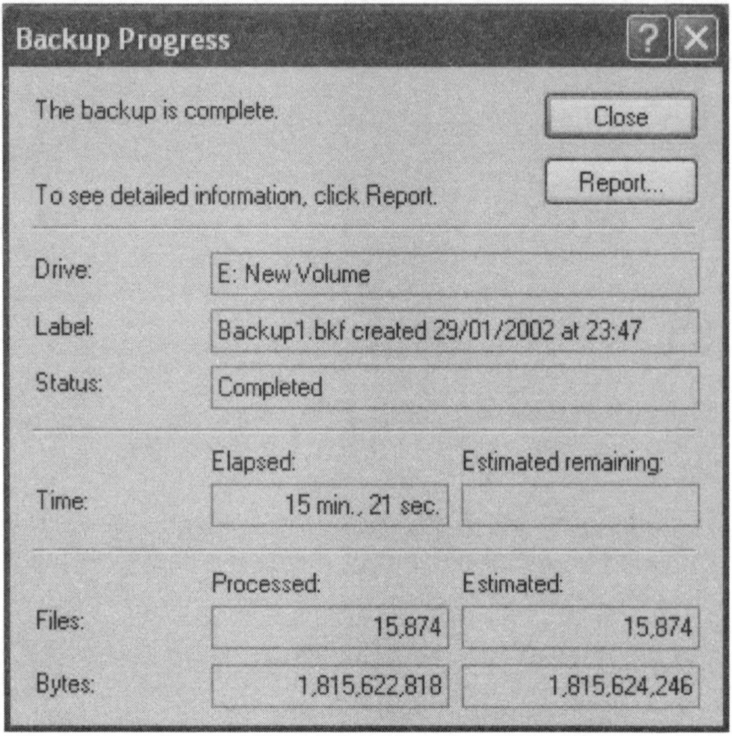

Backup Progress

The backup is complete. | Close

To see detailed information, click Report. | Report...

Drive:	E: New Volume	
Label:	Backup1.bkf created 29/01/2002 at 23:47	
Status:	Completed	
	Elapsed:	Estimated remaining:
Time:	15 min., 21 sec.	
	Processed:	Estimated:
Files:	15,874	15,874
Bytes:	1,815,622,818	1,815,624,246

Fig.4.18 The Backup Progress window provides some statistics

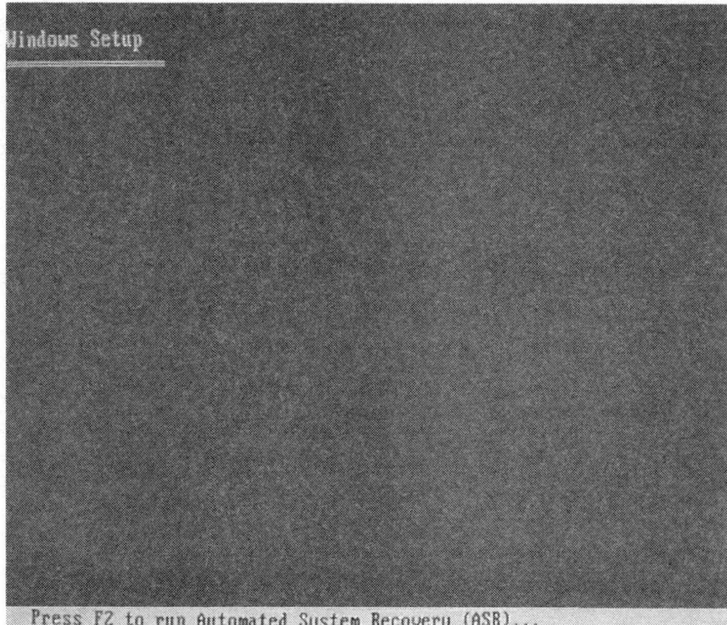

Fig.4.19 Press the F2 key as soon as this message appears at the bottom of the screen

recovery disc. Insert a 1.44-megabyte floppy disc into drive A: and operate the OK button. The message of Figure 4.17 appears once the recovery disc has been completed. Label the disc as indicated in the message and store it safely. The automatic recovery process is not possible without this disc. Finally, you are returned to the Backup Progress window (Figure 4.18), which should indicate that the backup has been completed successfully.

Restoring

There is little point in having a means of restoring the backup that requires the computer to boot normally into Windows XP, since this will often be impossible when the restoration feature is needed. The Windows XP method of restoring a full system backup is more straightforward than the Windows 9x equivalent. In fact the Windows XP method makes the process about as simple as it is ever likely to be. It is termed the

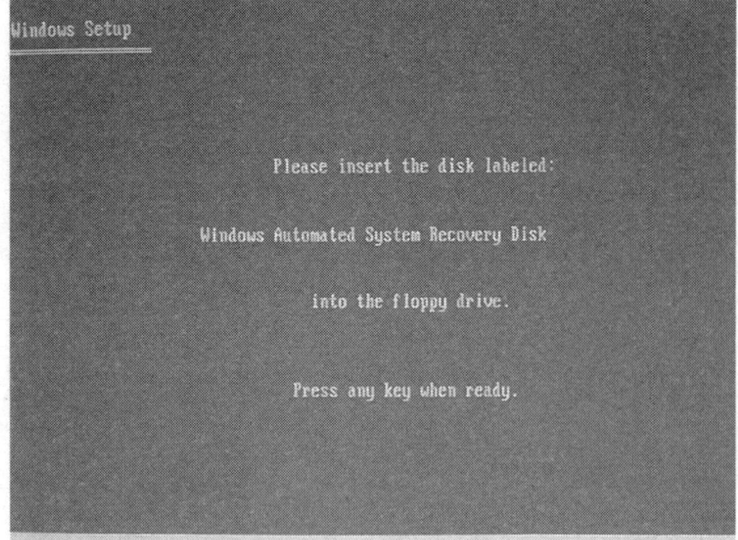

Fig.4.20 Insert the backup disc in drive A: when this prompt appears

Automated System Recovery, and it certainly lives up the automated part of its name.

The first task is to boot from the Windows XP installation CD-ROM, and the BIOS must be set to boot from the CD-ROM drive before it tries to boot from the hard disc drive. If the boot sequence is the other way around, the computer will probably start to boot from the hard drive and the CD-ROM drive will be ignored. With the installation disc in a CD-ROM drive and the correct BIOS settings, a message saying "Press any key to boot from CD-ROM" will appear for a few seconds at the beginning of the boot process. Press any key while this message is displayed or the computer will revert to booting from the hard disc drive.

Messages appear along the bottom of the screen when the computer starts booting from the CD-ROM. Look for the one that says "Press F2 to run Automated System Recovery (ASR)", as in Figure 4.19. This message only appears briefly, so press F2 as soon as it appears. After some disc activity the message of Figure 4.20 will appear, and the floppy disc produced when the backup was made must be placed in drive A:. Then press any key to continue. The restoration process requires little intervention from the user, but it is as well to keep an eye on things in

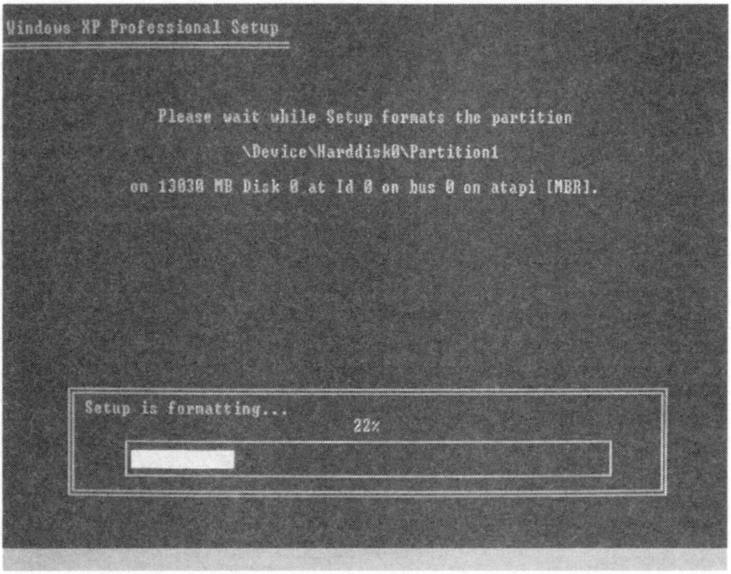

Windows XP Professional Setup

Please wait while Setup formats the partition

\Device\Harddisk0\Partition1

on 13030 MB Disk 0 at Id 0 on bus 0 on atapi [MBR].

Setup is formatting...

22%

Fig.4.21 Formatting erases all the data stored in the disc partition

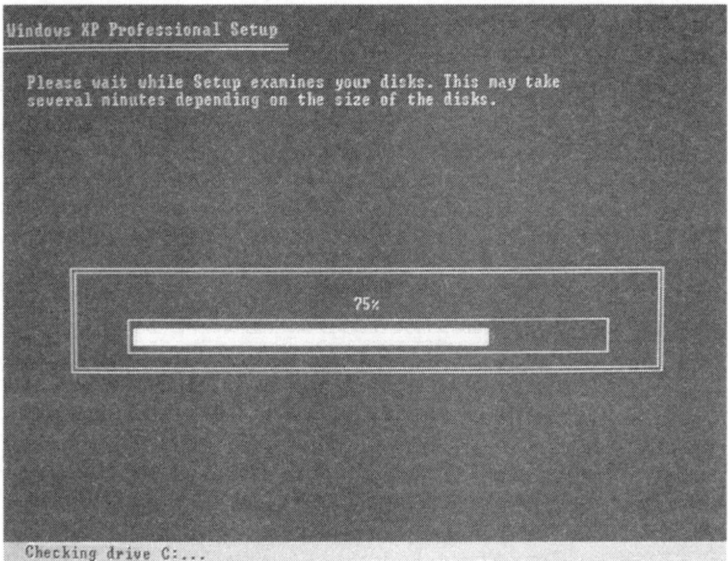

Fig.4.22 The Setup program briefly examines the disc drives

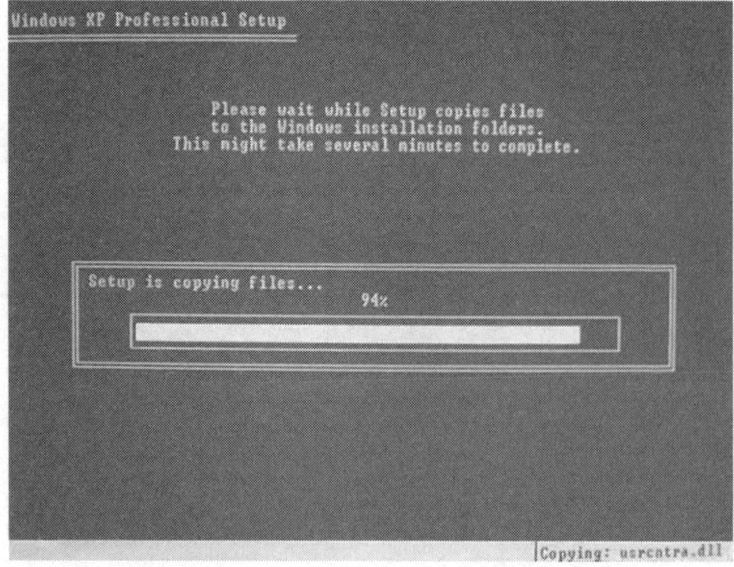

Fig.4.23 It takes a few minutes for the installation files to be copied

case something goes wrong. First the partition used by the system is formatted, which effectively wipes all data from the partition. If there is any data on the disc that has not been backed up, it is lost forever at this stage. The formatting will take several minutes, and an onscreen "fuel gauge" shows how far the formatting has progressed (Figure 4.21).

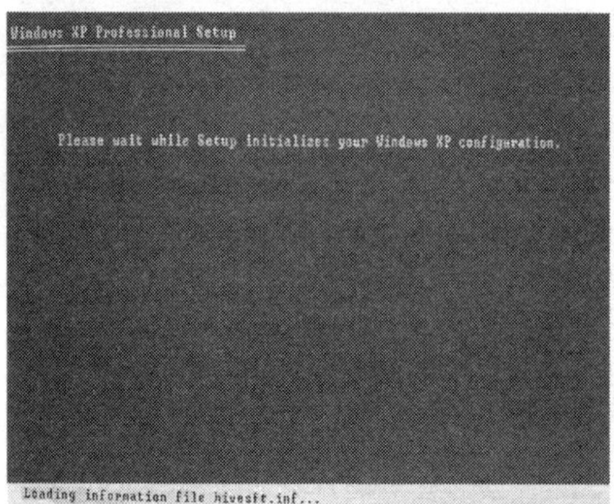

Fig.4.24 More files are loaded

A similar gauge is used at the next screen (Figure 4.22), where the program examines the disc drives. This is usually much quicker than formatting the restoration partition, and this screen may only appear for a second or two. A further gauge appears on the next screen (Figure 4.23), and here the program copies some files to the hard disc. Next the program loads some more files (Figure 4.24). The computer is then rebooted, and it will reboot after several seconds even if you do not press Return to restart the computer (Figure 4.25). Note that the Automated System Recovery disc in drive A: must be removed at this stage. The computer might try to boot from

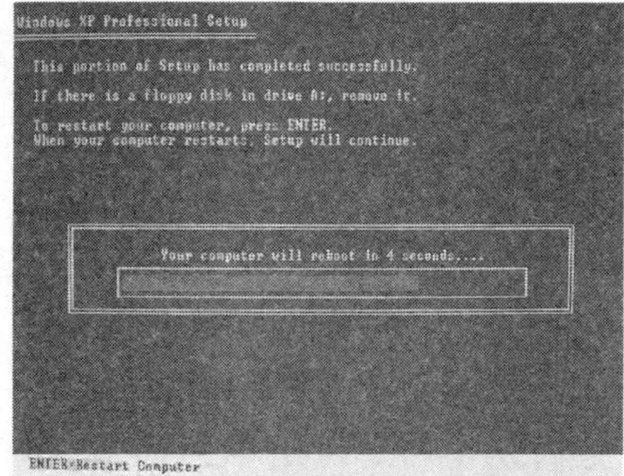

Fig.4.25 The computer will reboot automatically if the Return key is not operated

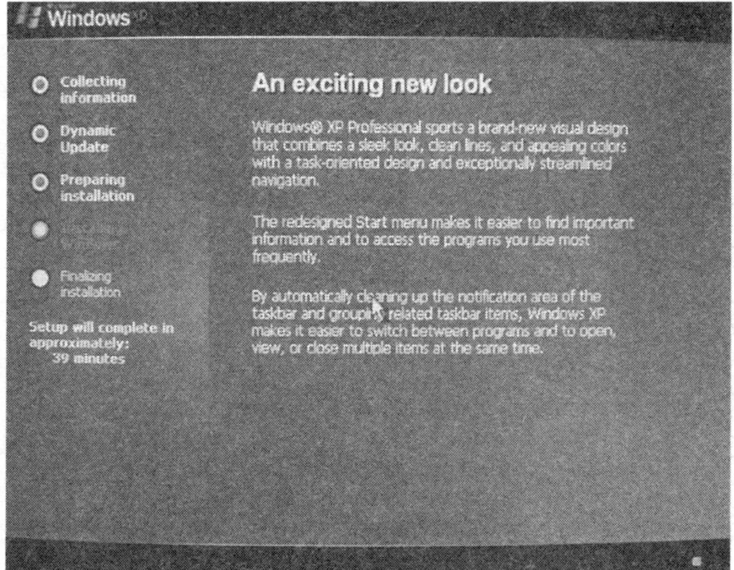

Fig.4.26 Installation starts in earnest once the computer has rebooted

Fig.4.27 The Automatic System Recover Wizard runs once Windows XP has been reinstalled

this disc if it is left in the drive, and this would probably prevent the computer from rebooting properly. If the reboot should stall because the disc is left in drive A:, removing it and pressing any key should get things underway again.

Windows is installed on the appropriate partition when the computer has rebooted, and a screen like the one in Figure 4.26 shows how the installation is progressing. Once Windows has been installed, the Automated System Recovery Wizard runs (Figure 4.27). This does not require any input from the user though, and you can just sit back and watch while your files are restored to the hard disc (Figure 4.28). Once this has been completed, the usual login screen (Figure 4.29) appears. You login using your normal password, and the computer then goes into Windows XP (Figure 4.30). This should look the same and have the same settings that were in force when the backup was made. Any programs, data, etc., on the partition that was backed up should be included in the restored installation.

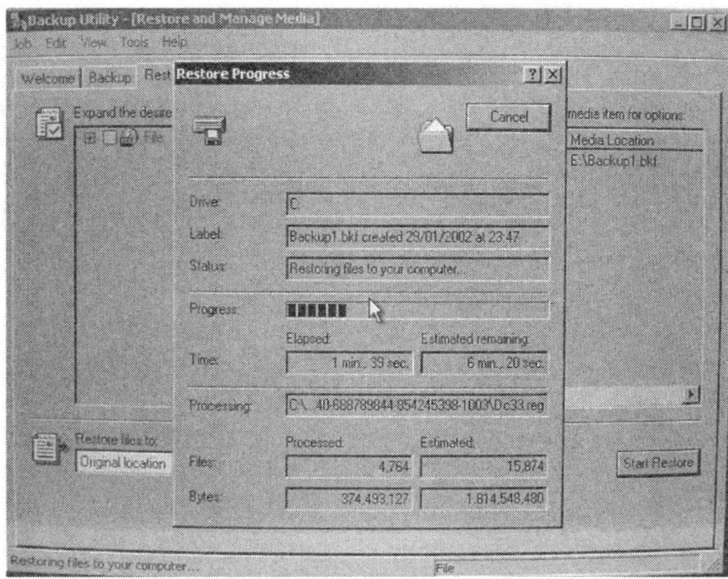

Fig.4.28 The Restore program copies files to the hard disc

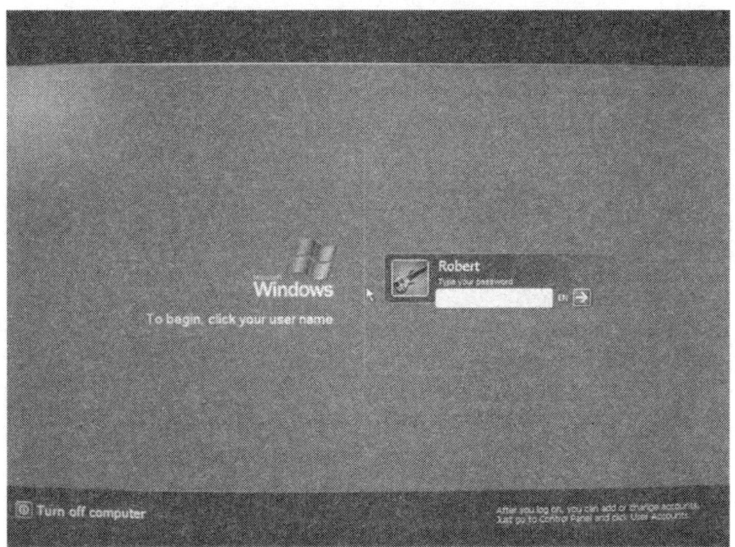

Fig.4.29 Login normally once the files have been restored

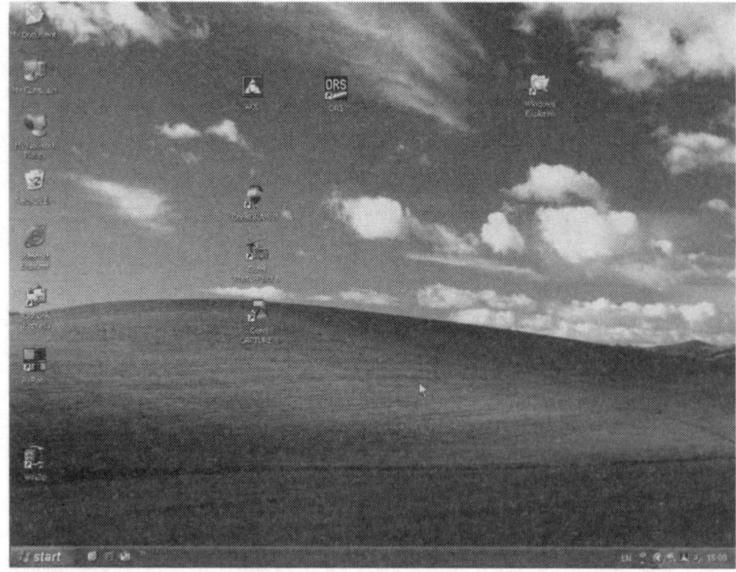

Fig.4.30 Windows XP should now look and work as before

In practice there might be one or two minor differences to the system. In particular, any passwords or other data hidden on the disc in "invisible" files will not have been placed on the backup disc. Files of this type are very secure, but they are "invisible" to the Backup program. It is therefore unable to save them in the backup file. This should not be of any major consequence, because the relevant applications can be run, and the passwords (or whatever) can be stored on the hard disc again. Of course, any data files produced after the backup was made will not be automatically restored to the hard disc. They must be restored manually, and it is essential to make sure that any recent data files are backed up before you start the restoration process.

Advanced mode

Use of the Backup Wizard is not mandatory, and the Backup program can be controlled directly by the user. Start running the program in the usual way, but left-click on the "Advanced mode" link. This produces a window like the one in Figure 4.31, and two of the buttons give access to more advanced versions of the Backup and Restore wizards. The

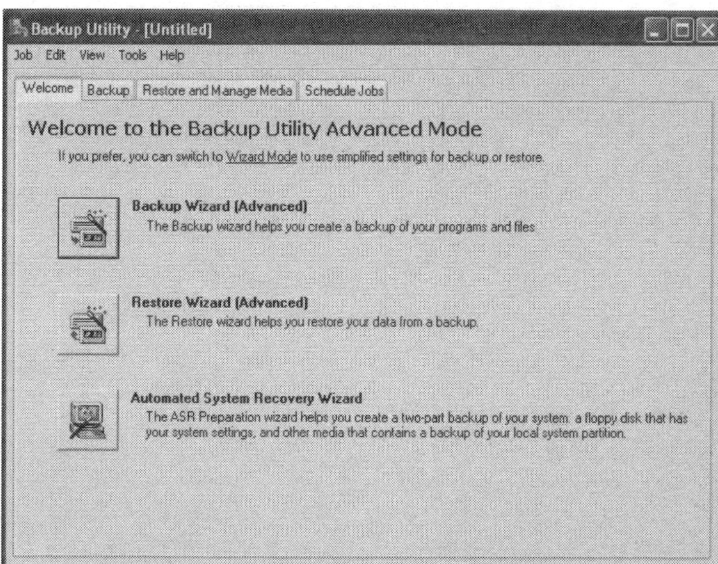

Fig.4.31 Three options are offered when Advanced Mode is selected

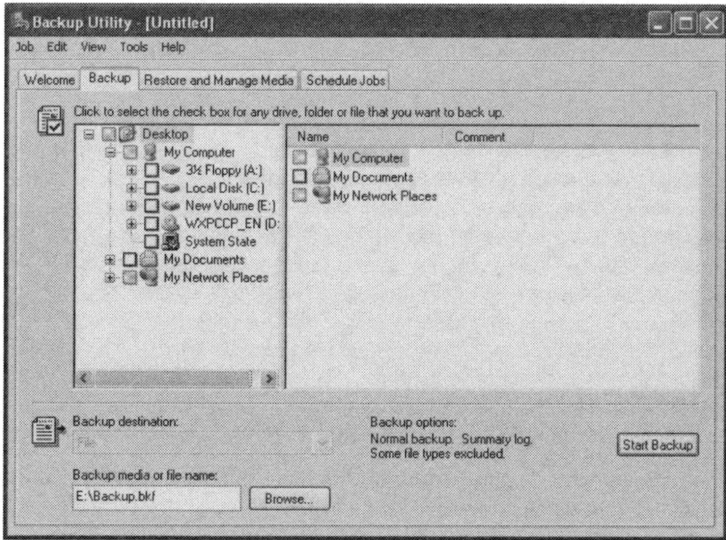

Fig.4.32 The Backup program enables the source files to be selected easily

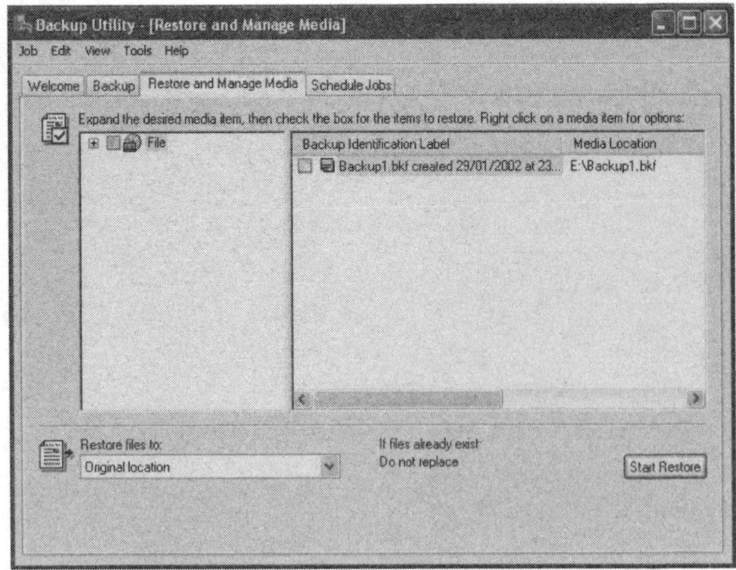

Fig.4.33 The Restore program enables the backup file and destination to be selected

third button provides another route to the Automated System Recovery Wizard. The tabs near the top of the window provide manual operation of the Backup and Restore programs, and to scheduled backups.

Figure 4.32 shows the window for the Backup program. The files and folders to be backed up are selected in the upper section of the window, while the backup drive and filename are entered in the textbox near the bottom left-hand corner of the window. The usual Browse facility is available here. Once everything has been set up correctly, the Start Backup button is operated. The Restore program's window is shown in Figure 4.33. The upper section of the window is used to locate and select the backup file, and the lower section is used to select the destination of the restored backup. This will usually be the original location, but it can be restored to an alternative location. Once everything has been set correctly, the Start Restore button is operated.

The Backup and Restore programs are not difficult to use, and are certainly more user friendly than the equivalent functions in some previous versions of Windows. However, except where some very simple backup and restore operation is required, it is probably best to use the wizards.

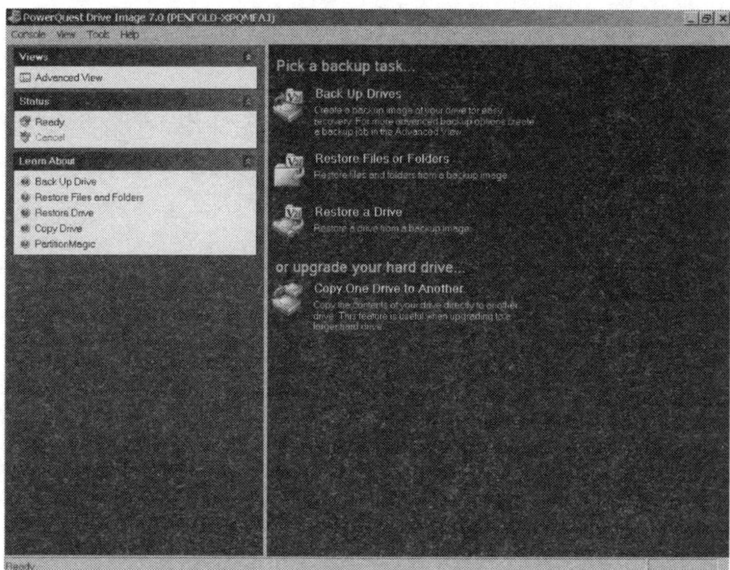

Fig.4.34 The initial screen of Drive Image

These should ensure that you do not overlook anything, and that backup files can always be successfully restored. The Automated System Restore facility is an invaluable facility, and one that it is well worth using. In the past it has been slow, difficult, and expensive to implement this type of backup system. With this facility and an inexpensive hard disc added to the PC, the entire system can be backed up quite rapidly and restored again with ease.

Alternatives

Ideally a backup should be made onto CDR or CDRW discs, but this needs a third party backup program. CDRW discs have the advantage that they can be reused, but they are more expensive than CDR discs. Another point to bear in mind is that an ordinary CDR can be read using any form of CD-ROM drive without the need for any special drivers. The same is not true for CDRW discs. Most other forms of high capacity disc also need special driver software in order to get the disc drive functioning properly.

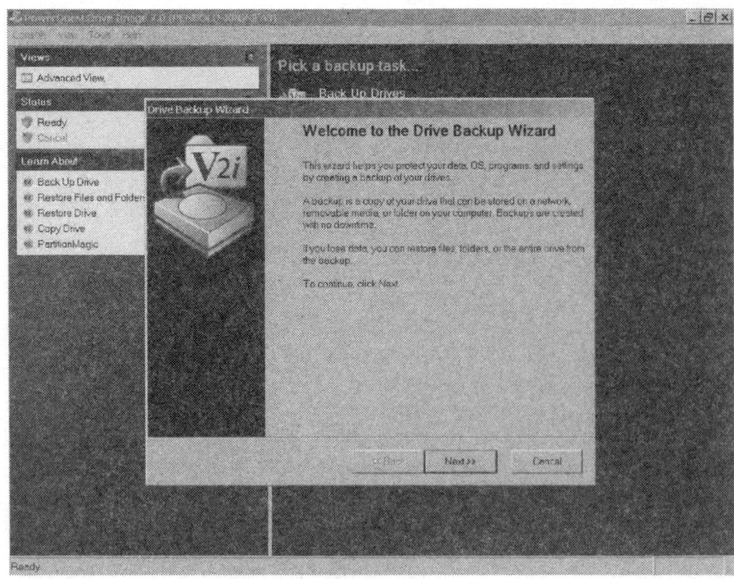

Fig.4.35 The Backup Wizard makes it easier to produce the backup file

This is no problem when you have a fully working computer that is running Windows, but it might be problematic if you have a computer that will not boot into Windows. You need to do some careful checking before using any form of backup that relies on anything other than a standard form of disc for storage. There is no point in carefully producing sets of backup discs if the image they contain can never be restored to the PC. If in doubt, stick to standard disc types, which really means a hard drive or CDRs.

Power Quest's Drive Image 7 is used in this example of producing a backup to CDRs and restoring it. There are other backup programs that no doubt work very well, and I am using Drive Image 7 here simply because it is the one installed on my PC. When this program is run under Windows XP it is possible to produce a backup from within Windows. With other backup programs and other versions of Windows it is often necessary to exit Windows and reboot into a MS/DOS or a similar operating system. This ensures that Windows does not restrict access to any files on the disc, but is obviously not very convenient. However, with most modern backup programs the reboot into a basic operating system is taken care of by the program, and the process may well be completely automatic.

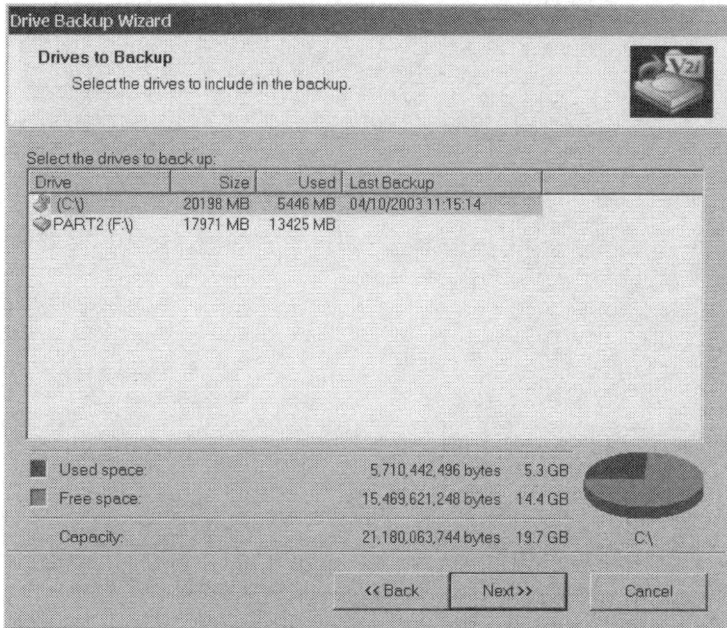

Fig.4.36 The first step is to select the drive to be backed up

Launching Drive Image 7 produces the initial screen of Figure 4.34, and the Backup Drives option is selected in order to start the backup process. Making the backup is made easier by the use of a wizard (Figure 4.35). Operating the Next button moves things on to the window of Figure 4.36 where the drive to be backed up is selected. Actually, in a multi-drive system it is possible to select more than one drive if desired. In this example only the boot drive (drive C) will be backed up, because the other hard drive is itself a backup drive.

The destination for the backup is selected at the next window (Figure 4.37). The Local File option is used when the backup will be onto another hard disc drive. Obviously the Network option is used where the PC is on a local area network (LAN) and the backup will be placed elsewhere on the network. In this case the backup will be made to a CDRW drive, so it is the third option that is selected. The required drive can be selected using the usual file browser if the Browse button is operated.

The required type of compression is selected at the next window (Figure 4.38). Data compression enables more data to be placed on each disc

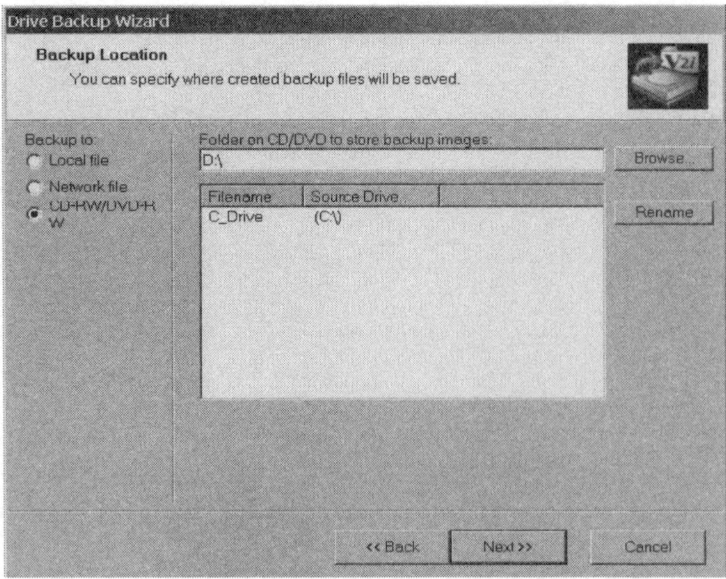

Fig.4.37 This window is used to select the destination for the file

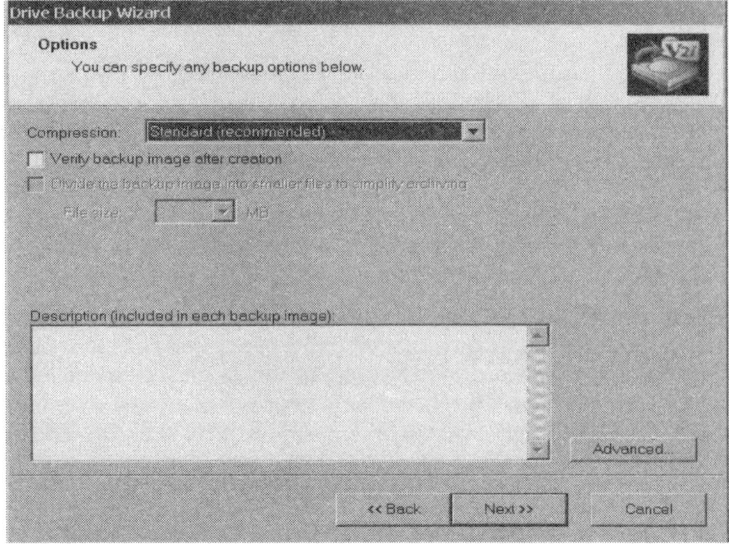

Fig.4.38 Next the type of data compression is selected

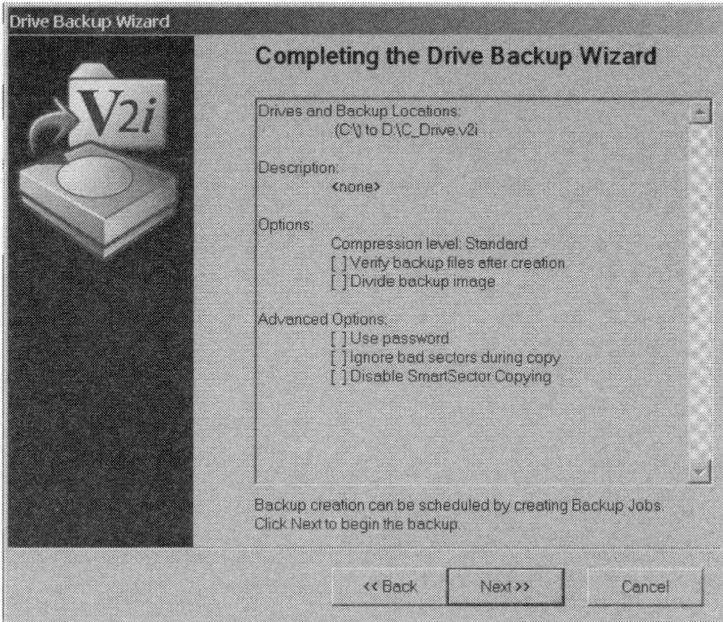

Fig.4.39 This window shows a summary of the selected options

in the backup set. When making a backup to CDR or CDRW discs the compression has the beneficial effect of reducing the number of discs required. With a relatively slow backup device it can also reduce the time take to create and restore a backup. Some types of data compress more readily than others. Some files on the disc may already be in compressed form and will not be amenable to further compression. On the other hand, things like program and simple text files will often compress by a factor of three or more. In practice compression roughly halves the number of discs required. Opt for the Standard method of compression. If required, a description can be added in the textbox in the bottom section of the window (e.g. "Full backup of drive C").

The next window (Figure 4.39) simply provides a summary of the options that have been selected. If necessary, use the Back button in order to return to an earlier window so that a correction can be made. Then use the Next button to return to this window. When the right options have been selected, operate the Next button to start making the backup.

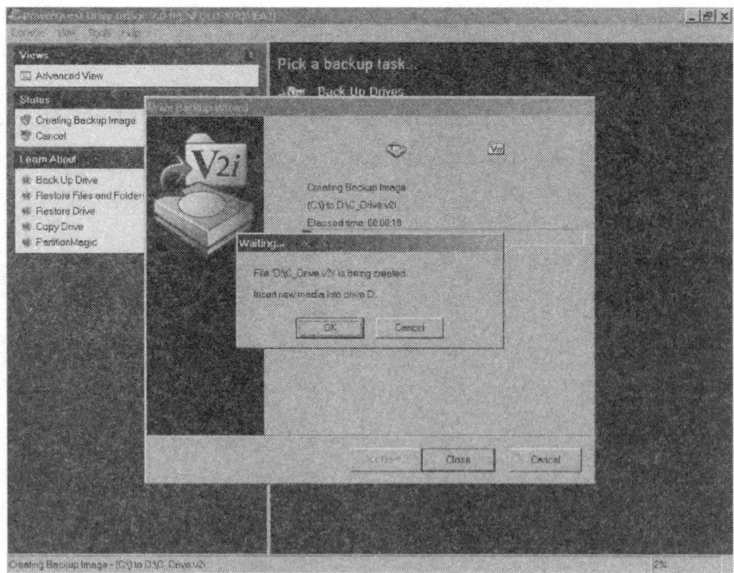

Fig.4.40 Insert the first disc and get the backup under way

Eventually a message like the one in Figure 4.40 will appear, and the first disc is then placed in the CDR drive and the backup process starts.

A full backup is likely to require about six to twelve discs, and could obviously require substantially more than this if a large and almost full disc is being backed up. The program will prompt you each time a change of disc is required. Carefully number each disc because they must be used in the correct order when the backup is used to restore the contents of the hard disc drive. Eventually the program will indicate that the backup has been completed, and you are then returned to the main screen of Drive Image 7.

Restoring

There are facilities in the main Drive Image program for restoring data, but this route is not usable in the current context. Instead, the computer is booted using either a set of boot discs made using the program or via the Drive Image installation CD. These days practically any PC can be booted from a suitable CD-ROM, and it is probably best to use this method where the option is available. Note that this option is not available with earlier versions of Drive Image and with some other backup programs. With some PCs it might be necessary to alter the BIOS settings in order to boot from a CD-ROM. The computer's operating manual should explain how to do this. Using a set of bootable floppy discs is one way around the problem if you do not feel confident about dealing with the BIOS Setup program.

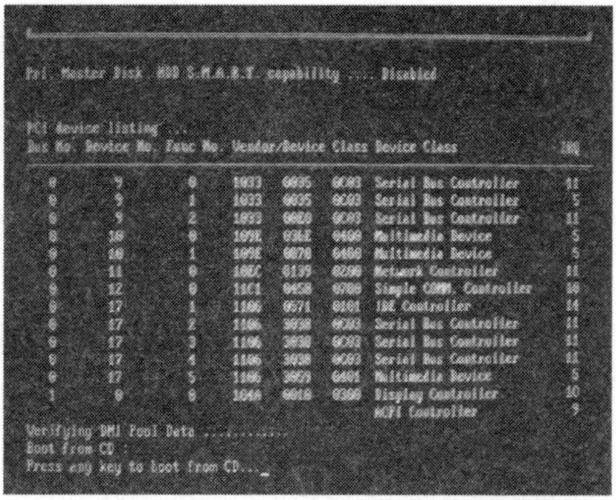

Fig.4.41 Press F2 if this message appears

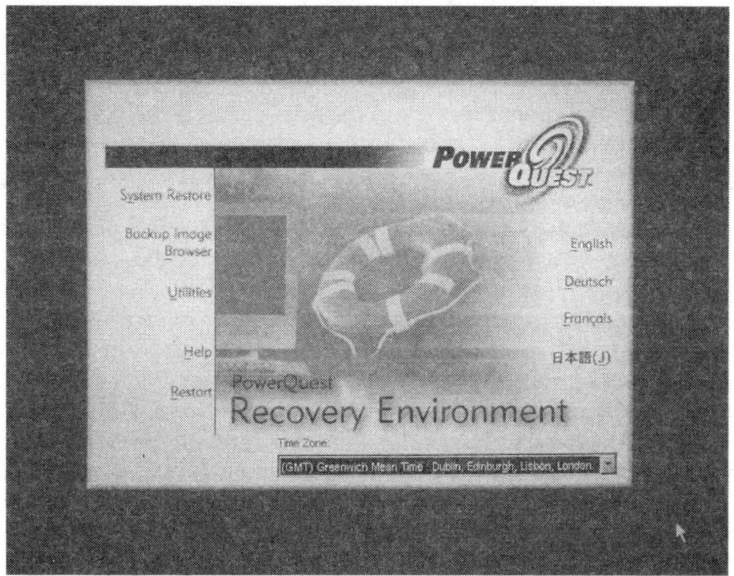

Fig.4.42 The options available from the Recovery program

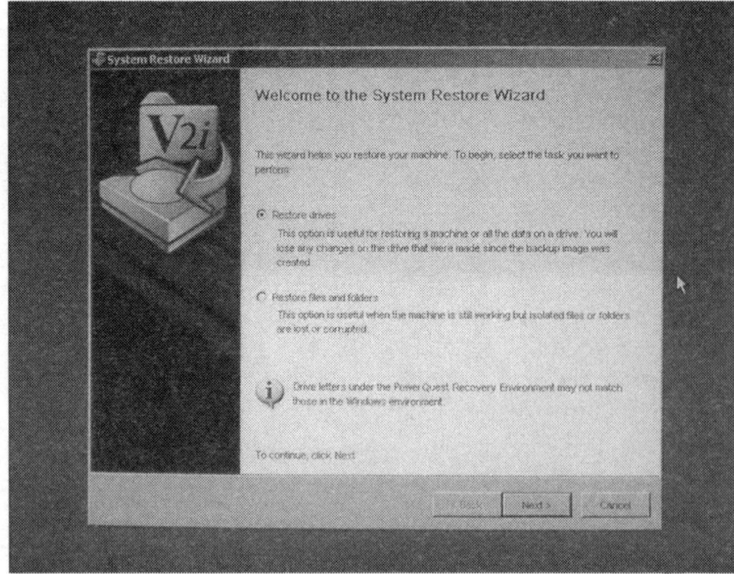

Fig.4.43 A full or partial restoration can be selected

The computer will usually start booting from the CD-ROM or bootable floppy disc without any preamble. Depending on the BIOS used in your PC, it might instead try to boot into the damaged operating system on the hard disc unless you press a key at the right time. If a message like the one in Figure 4.41 appears at the bottom of the screen, immediately press F2 or whatever key the message indicates. The PC should then boot into the operating system contained on the bootable CD-ROM or floppy disc.

This will usually be MS-DOS or something similar, but the Restore program usually includes a simple Windows style user interface. Some messages will probably appear on the screen giving a brief explanation of what the program is doing. When using the floppy disc method there will usually be a boot disc and one or more program discs. Change discs when prompted. The boot process can be quite long, because the Restore program will probably scan the PC's hardware so that it can operate with the mouse, etc., you are using. Where appropriate, networking might be activated so that the hard disc can be restored from an image file stored on another PC on the network.

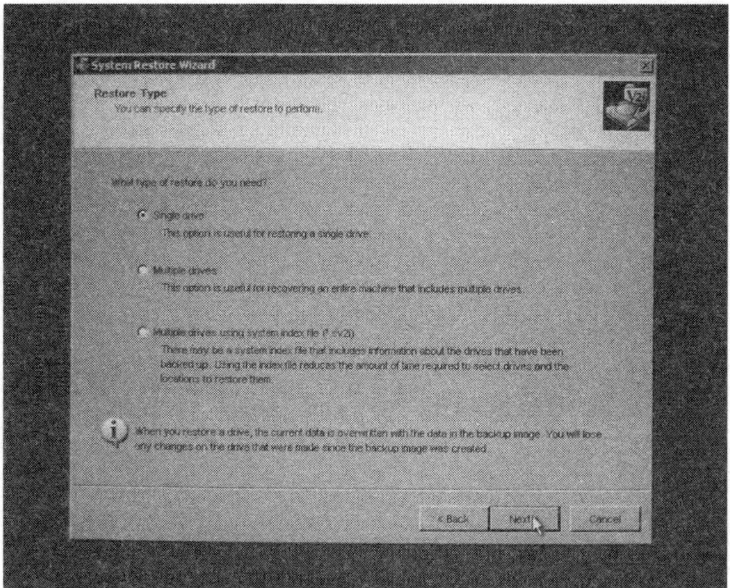

Fig.4.44 One or multiple drives can be restored

Eventually the boot and loading processes should come to an end and a screen like the one of Figure 4.42 will then be obtained. A number of options are available, but it is the System Restore facility that is needed in this case. Selecting this option moves things on to the screen of Figure 4.43 where the radio buttons provide two options. One is used to restore only certain files or folders, and the other is used to restore a complete drive. It is obviously the latter that is required here. The next screen (Figure 4.44) provides the option of restoring one drive or multiple drives. In this example it is only drive C that is being restored, so the single drive option is selected.

At the next screen the backup file is selected, and a file browser is available via the Browse button. Having pointed the program to the drive containing the first disc in the backup set, a message like the one in Figure 4.45 will appear. It is normal for programs that use multi-disc sets to require the first and last discs in the set before proceeding. After the program has read from the last disc you will be prompted to replace the first disc in the drive. You should then have something like Figure 4.46, with the screen showing the location of the backup file and some basic information for it.

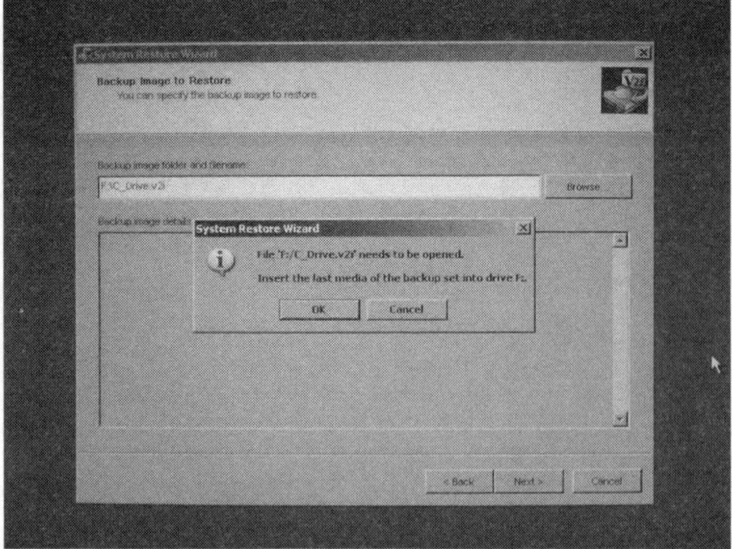

Fig.4.45 Initially the first and last discs in the set are required. This is quite normal for programs that use multi-disc sets

Figure 4.47 shows the next screen, and here you must select the drive to be restored. You must be careful to choose the right disc if there is more than one hard drive or partition. Restoring the image to the wrong drive or partition will erase all the data it contains. It is then just a matter of following the onscreen prompts, and changing discs when necessary. The discs in the backup set must be numbered so that you can provide them in the correct order. The program will detect the error if you should get the discs muddled-up, and it will not proceed until the right disc has been placed in the drive.

Once the restoration has been completed, remove the boot CD-ROM or floppy disc from the drive and reset the computer. It should then boot into the newly restored operating system. The PC should then operate exactly as it did at the time the backup was made. There can be minor problems such as stored passwords being lost, and automatic login facilities failing to work in consequence. This is due to the password being concealed on the disc in a hidden file that the backup program misses. You have to login manually and then reinstate the automatic facility. Of course, and data or programs added since the backup was made must be reinstated in order to bring the installation fully up to date.

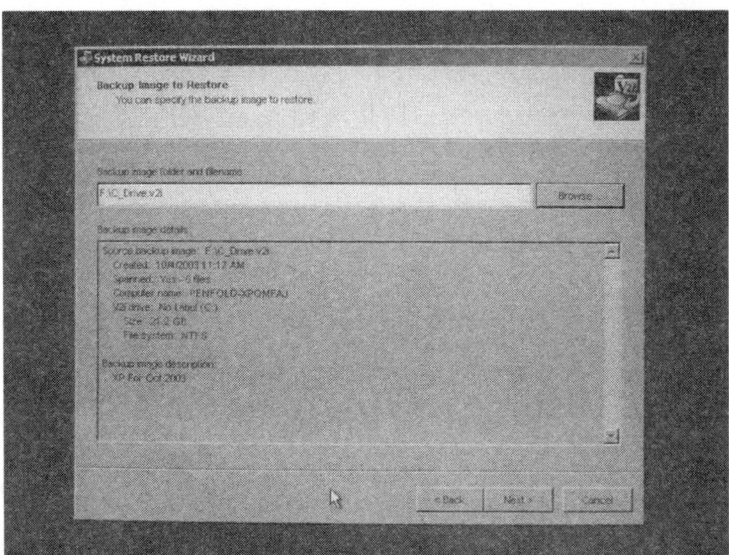

Fig.4.46 This screen shows the backup's location, etc.

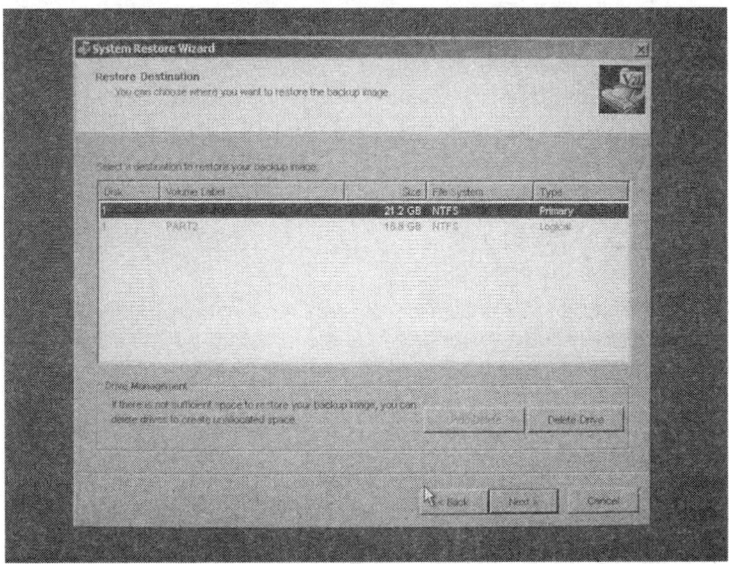

Fig.4.47 Be careful when selecting which drive to restore

Points to remember

Backing up data and (or) system information to another drive is the only way to guard against a serious attack from a virus, a hard disc failure, or other major catastrophe. Backing up system information to the main hard drive is only sufficient to guard against problems with the operating system.

Floppy discs are inadequate to cope with the large amounts of data produced by many modern applications. A CD writer, Zip drive, additional hard disc, or some other form of mass storage device is required. Note that some backup programs (including the Windows XP Backup program) are not compatible with CD writers.

It is only necessary to save important data and configuration files, but it is much quicker to get things back to normal if you make a full backup of the hard drive.

Plenty of third party backup software is available, but the Windows XP Backup utility is adequate for most purposes. Combined with an additional hard disc drive, this provides a fast and cost-effective method of providing a full system backup.

The Windows Backup program can be used to backup selected files, or a full backup of the hard disc can be provided. Regularly backing up the full contents of a hard disc is relatively time consuming, but restoring a full backup is the quickest way to get the computer into full working order again if a major problem occurs.

The Windows XP Backup program can be used without wizards, but for most purposes the wizards provide the easiest and most reliable means of handling backup and restore operations.

It is necessary to buy a backup program such as Drive Image in order to make a backup copy on CDR discs. This method has the advantage of placing the backup copy beyond the reach of viruses. Another advantage is that the cost is quite low provided your PC already has a CD writer (as most do). It is relatively slow though.

5

Reinstalling XP

Clean sweep

Ideally you should never get into the situation where it is necessary to reinstall Windows from scratch and then install all your applications programs together with any templates, data, etc., that you use. It should not be necessary provided you have the complete system backed up onto CD-ROMs or some other media that is stored beyond the reach of viruses. If you ignore the warnings about making adequate backups and a bad virus strikes, it is quite likely that you will be left with a non-bootable system, or even a hard disc drive that can not be read at all.

The situation is dire if you have important data on an inaccessible disc and no backup copies. Even if you do not backup the entire system, always take regular backup copies of important data and store it on CDRW discs, Zip discs, or some other media that can be removed from the PC. All is not necessarily lost if the only copy of important data is on an unreadable hard disc drive. There are specialist companies that can try to recover the data, but their services are likely to be quite expensive and there is no guarantee of success.

The reinstallation process is rather different depending on whether the PC runs under Windows XP or ME. We will start by considering the reinstallation of Windows XP. Where the hard disc is working but the Windows installation is damaged badly damaged, there is the option of reinstalling Windows on top of the original installation. The Windows Setup program effectively tries to repair the existing installation, and it might to a large extent return the PC to its previous condition. Obviously it can not reinstate applications programs, data, and other material lost due to the infection, but it should at least be able to get the basic Windows installation working again. Where the disc is unreadable there is no option to reinstalling everything from scratch. Note that any information on the disc will be lost forever once Windows has been reinstalled from scratch.

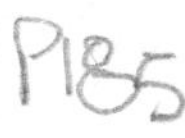

Where possible I would certainly recommend trying to fix Windows by reinstalling it on top of the broken version. If this fails to cure the problem,

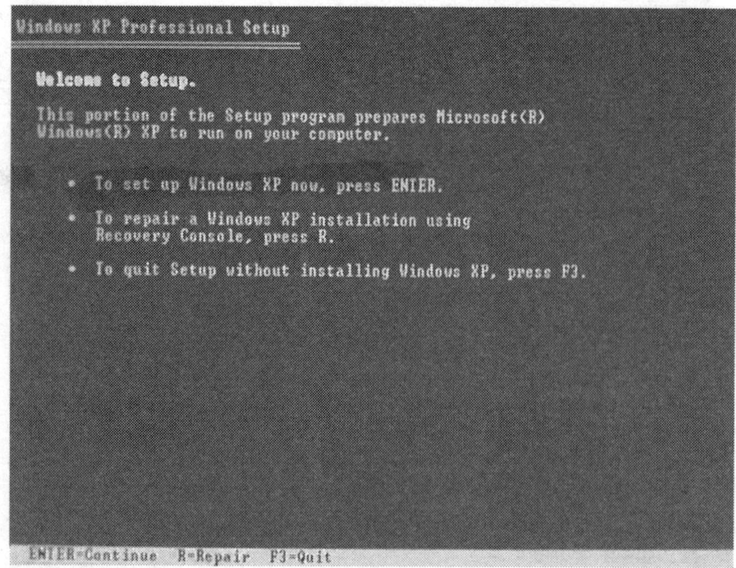

Fig.5.1 The opening screen of the Windows XP Setup program

then it is time to install Windows from scratch. The advantage of reinstallation on top of the old Windows installation is that the programs should remain usable with the new version. Clearly this will not happen if there is massive damage to the original installation, but in most cases all the programs will work fine with the refreshed version of Windows. Unfortunately, the problems with the original installation might be carried forward into the new one, and it could still be still be necessary to install Windows from scratch. A great deal of time can be saved if reinstallation on the old copy of Windows works, so it is well worth trying this method.

The process is very similar whether the operating system is installed from scratch or on top of an existing Windows installation. If Windows XP is already on the hard disc it will be detected by the Setup program, which can then reinstall Windows XP on top of the existing installation. Note that the versions of Windows XP supplied with some PCs do not have the standard installation disc. The methods described here are only applicable if you have the standard Windows XP installation disc. If your PC was not supplied with a standard installation disc it probably came complete with a recovery disc that makes it easy to return to a basic Windows installation. With a PC of this type you should consult

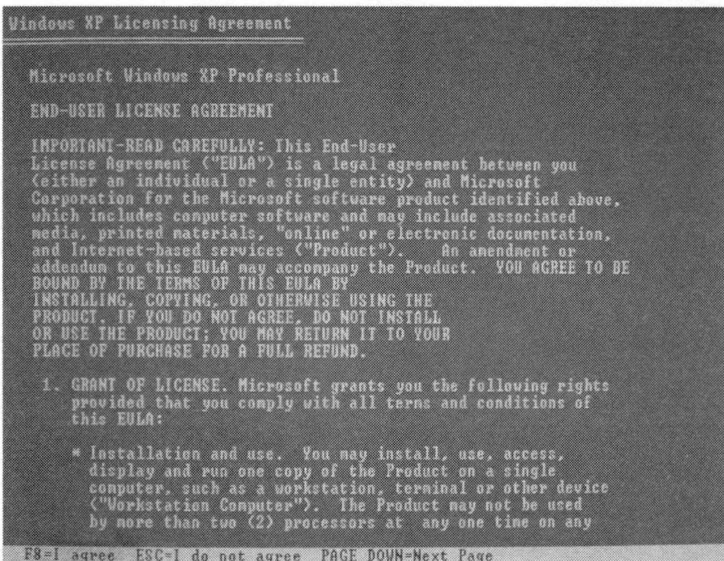

Fig.5.2 You must agree to the licensing conditions to proceed

the instruction manual, and this should give concise information about reinstalling Windows.

Booting from CD

Whether reinstalling on top of the current installation or reinstalling Windows XP from scratch, the first step is to boot from the installation CD-ROM. The BIOS must be set to boot from the CD-ROM drive before it tries to boot from the hard disc. It is unlikely that the computer will attempt to boot from the CD-ROM drive if the priorities are the other way around, and it will certainly not do so unless the CD-ROM is set as one of the boot devices. If all is well, a message will probably appear on the screen indicating that any key must be operated in order to boot from the CD-ROM drive. This message appears quite briefly, so be ready to press one of the keys. The computer will try to boot from the hard disc if you “miss the boat”. It will then be necessary to restart the computer and try again.

After various files have been loaded from the CD-ROM, things should come to a halt with the screen of Figure 5.1. The Setup program is needed to reinstall Windows XP, so press the Enter (Return) key. The

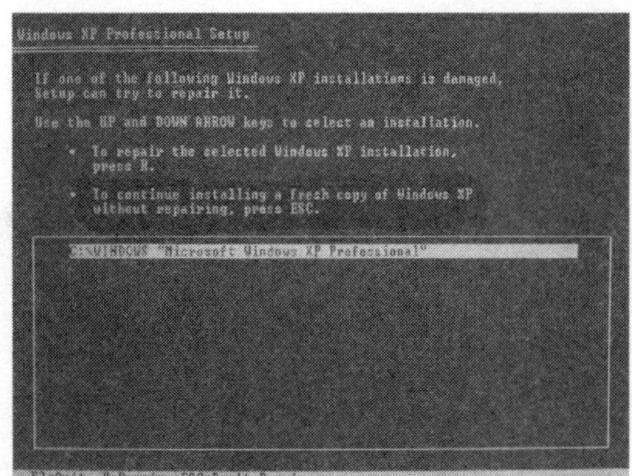

Fig.5.3 Select the correct installation

Next screen (Figure 5.2) is the usual licence agreement, and the F8 key is pressed in order to agree with the licensing terms. Note that Windows XP can not be installed unless you do agree to the licensing conditions. The installations on the hard disc are listed on the next screen (Figure 5.3), and in most cases there will only be one. Where appropriate, select the installation that you wish to repair or replace.

Repair rather than replacement of the operating system will be considered first. In other words, reinstalling Windows on top of the existing installation

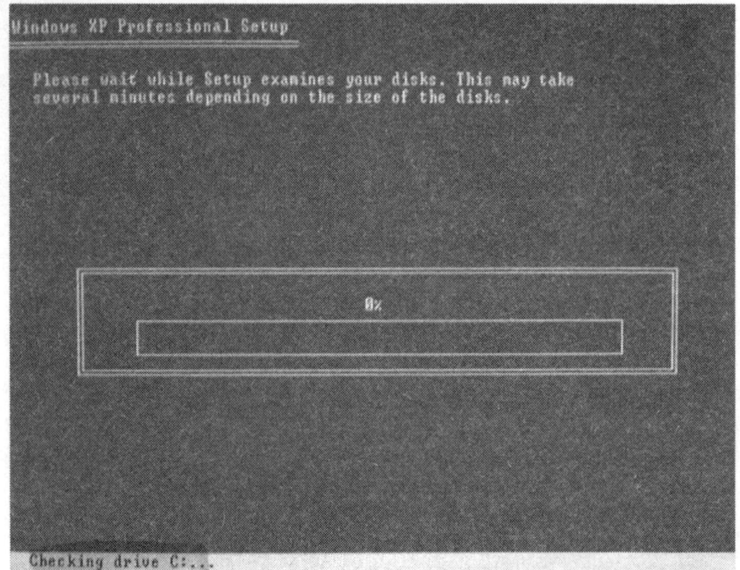

Fig.5.4 Setup will briefly examine the disc drives

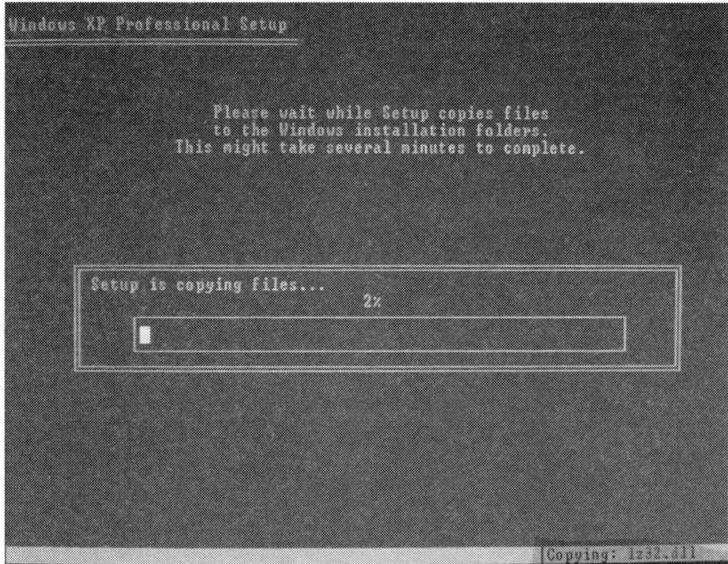

Fig.5.5 It will take some time for the files to be copied to the hard disc

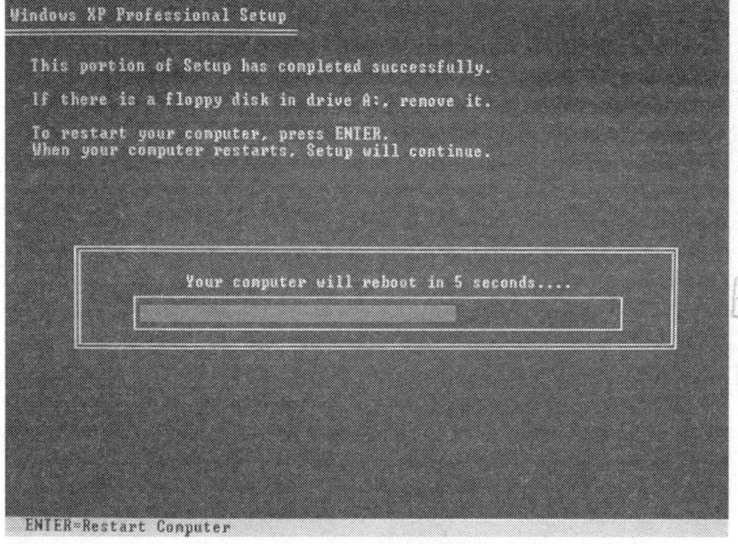

Fig.5.6 The computer will automatically reboot after 5 seconds

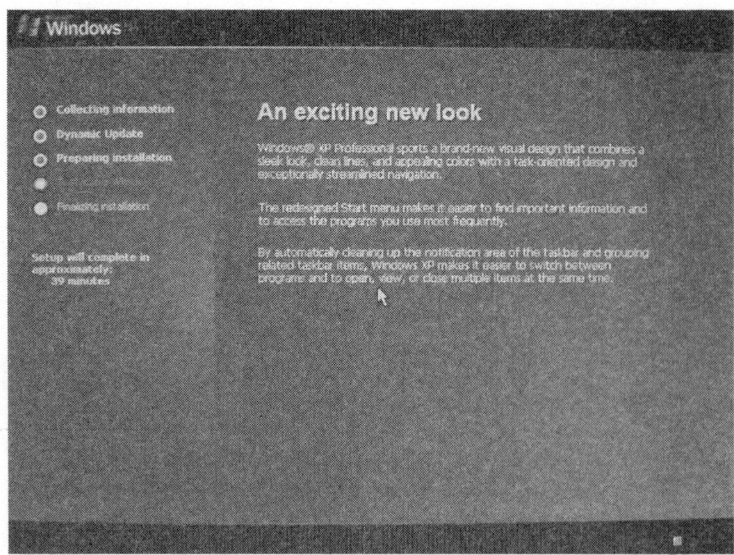

Fig.5.7 Setup indicates which stage of the process it is on, and gives an estimate of the time left until completion

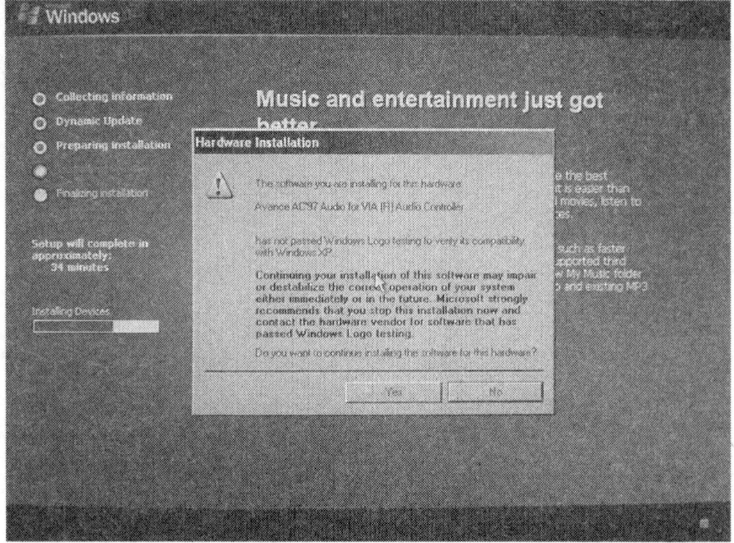

Fig.5.8 A warning message appears if a non-approved driver is found

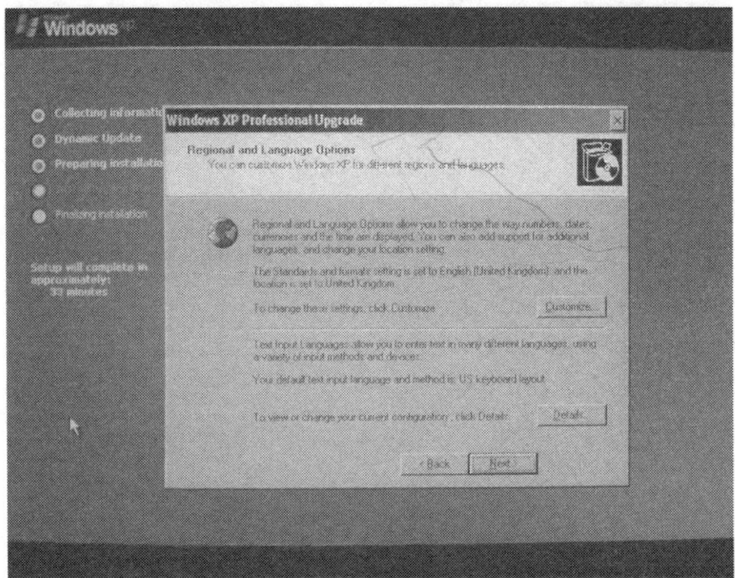

Fig.5.9 This window enables the language settings to be altered

rather than starting afresh. Press the R key to indicate that the selected installation must be repaired. The Setup program then examines the discs (Figure 5.4), and this process is usually quite brief. Next the Setup program copies files from the CD-ROM to the installation folders on the hard disc drive. This will take a few minutes, and the usual bargraph display shows how far the copying has progressed (Figure 5.5). Once the copying has finished it is time for the computer to reboot for the first time. You can press the Return key to start the reboot (Figure 5.6), but after 5 seconds it will automatically reboot anyway. Make sure that there is no floppy disc in drive A:, as this would prevent the PC from rebooting properly. Also, when the message appears on the screen, do not press a key to cause the system to boot from the CD-ROM drive. At this stage it must boot from the hard disc drive.

A screen like the one in Figure 5.7 will appear once the reboot has completed, and this keeps you informed about the progress of the reinstallation. A warning message like the one in Figure 5.8 might appear during the reinstallation. This points out that one of the device drivers in use on the computer is not one that has officially passed the Windows XP compatibility test. This does not necessarily mean that it is the cause of the problems with Windows XP, but it is obviously a possibility that

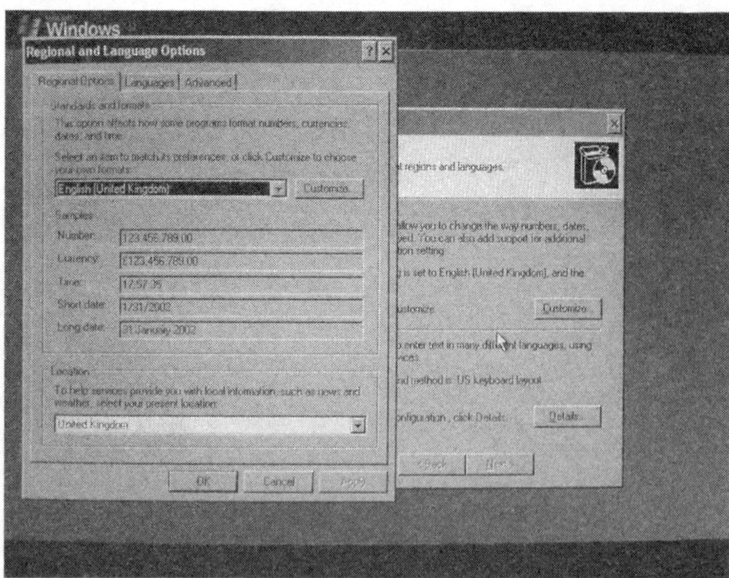

Fig.5.10 These settings determine such things as how large numbers and the time will be displayed

has to be given serious consideration. In this case the audio driver in question had been in use for some weeks without any problems arising, so it was unlikely to cause any problems. If you operate the No button so that the driver is not loaded, the corresponding piece of hardware will be rendered inoperative until a suitable driver has been installed.

Language settings

Eventually a screen like the one in Figure 5.9 will appear. This permits the language settings to be customised, and it is advisable to operate the Customise button and check that the settings are suitable. This brings up an initial window like the one on Figure 5.10, but further windows and menus can be brought up by operating the Customise buttons and the tabs. Figures 5.11 and 5.12 show a couple of examples. Look through the various windows and menus, changing any settings that are incorrect. Mistakes here will not have dire consequences, but there could be a problem such as the keyboard producing some incorrect characters. It should be possible to correct any mistake of this type once Windows XP has been installed.

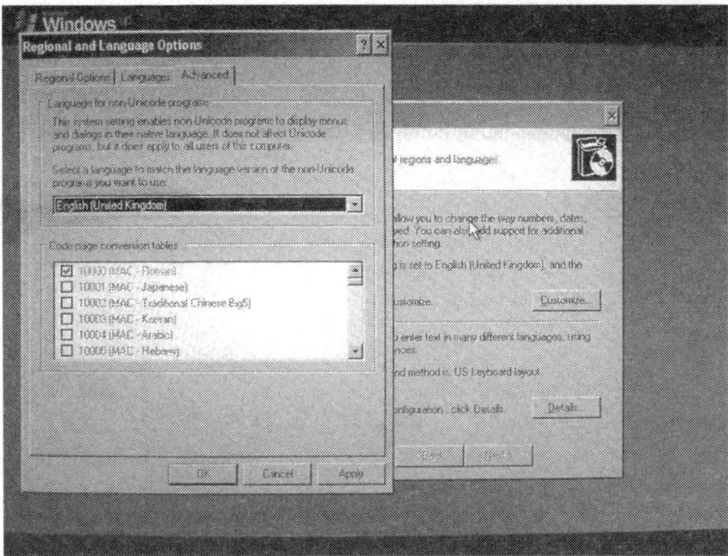

Fig.5.11 Various Regional and Language settings are available

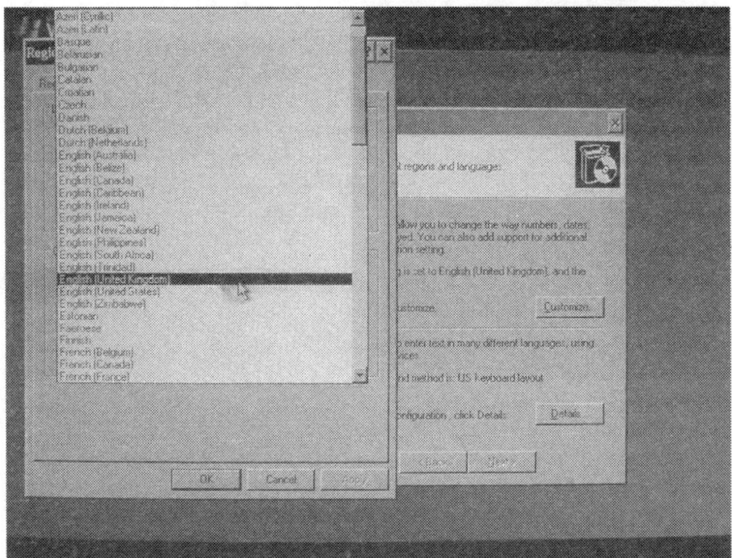

Fig.5.12 Setting the correct region

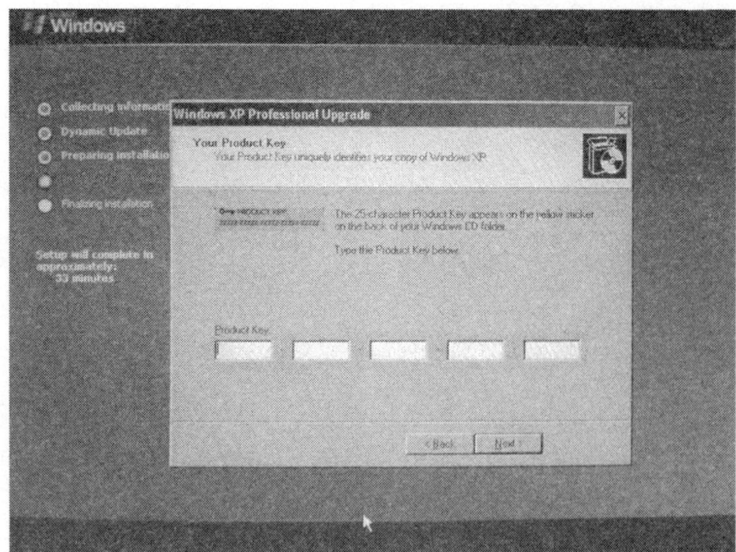

Fig.5.13 The product key is still needed when reinstalling Windows XP

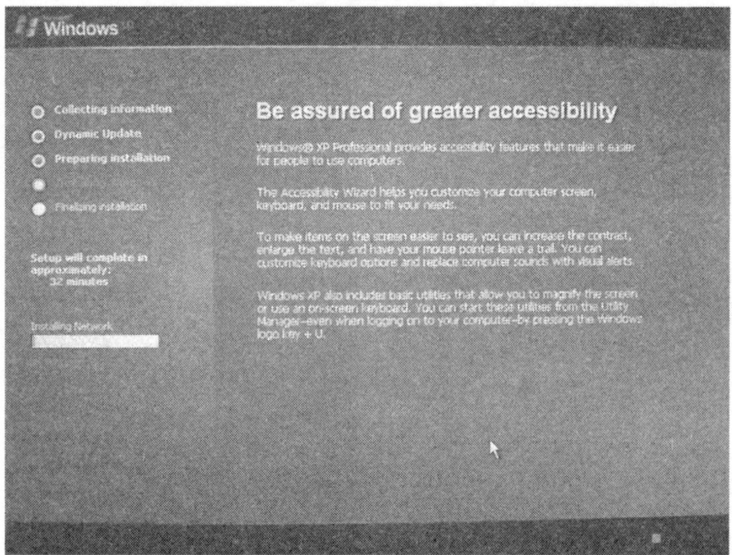

Fig.5.14 The reinstallation process resumes

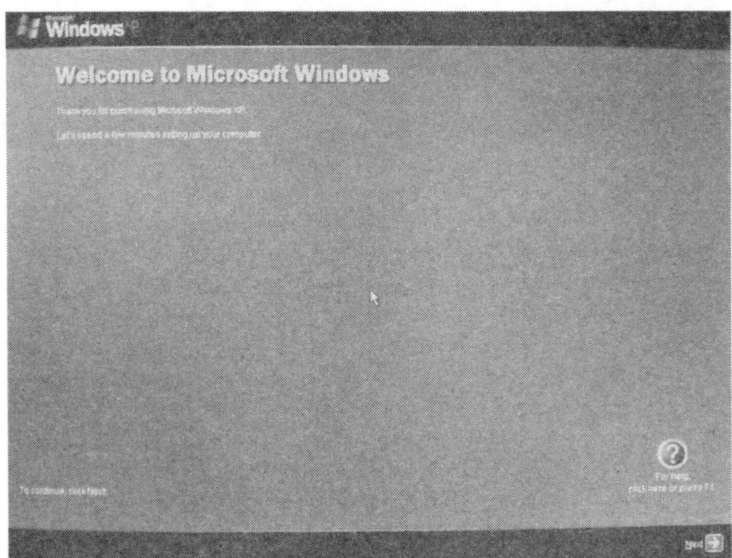

Fig.5.15 With reinstallation complete, the Welcome screen is displayed

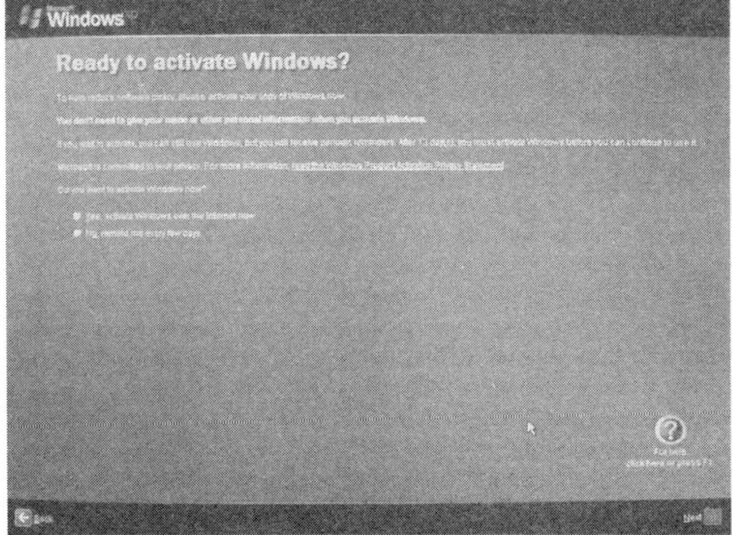

Fig.5.16 It is not essential to activate Windows XP at this stage

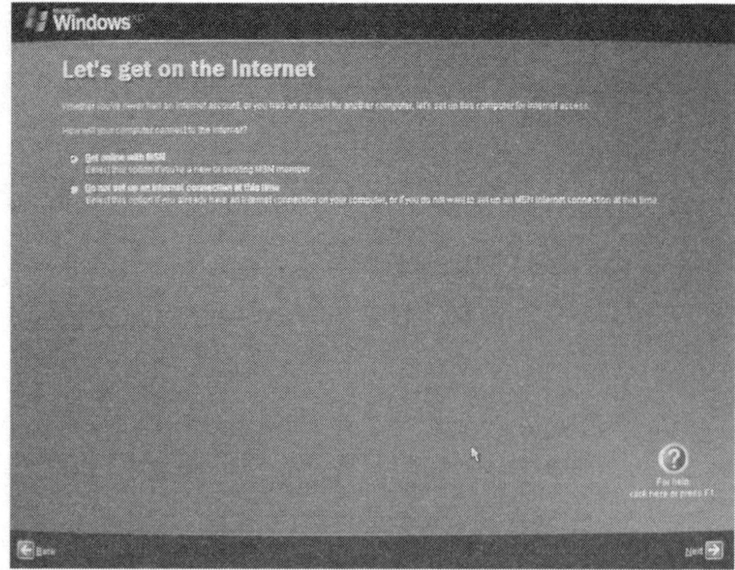

Fig.5.17 You are given the opportunity to get online with MSN

Even though Windows is being installed over an existing installation, it is still necessary to enter the product key when the screen of Figure 5.13 appears. The Windows XP installation disc is supplied in a cardboard folder rather than the usual jewel case. The 25-digit product key is on the rear of this folder. Keep the folder safe because it is not possible to reinstall Windows XP without it. With the correct product key typed into the textboxes, operating the Next button will produce a screen like the one in Figure 5.14, and the installation process will continue. The computer may then reboot, and the Welcome screen of Figure 5.15 will appear.

Operate the Next button to move on to the screen of Figure 5.16. Using the two radio buttons you can opt to activate the new Windows XP installation or leave this until later. It is probably best to defer the activation process until the PC is fully operational again. Activating Windows via the telephone method is a bit awkward, so in due course it is best to opt for the web option if you have an Internet connection. At the next screen (Figure 5.17) you can sign on to MSN or continue with reinstallation. It will be assumed here that the second option is taken. The Windows reinstallation is then finished, and the screen of Figure 5.18 will appear to confirm that the process has been completed.

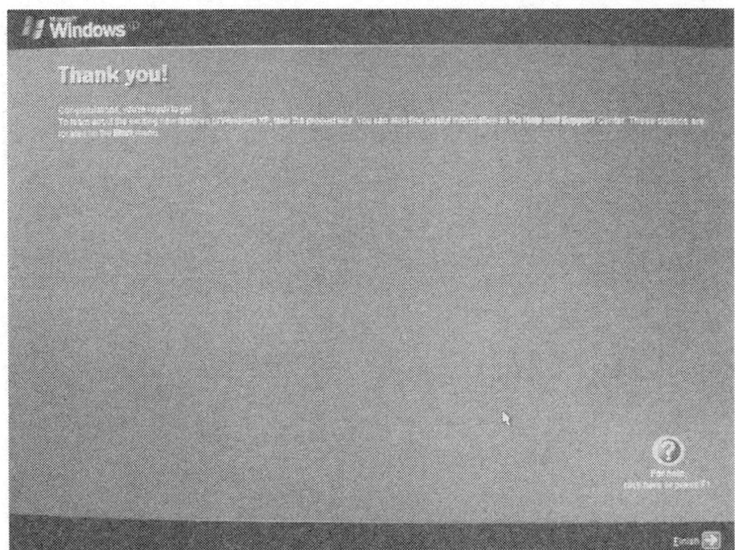

Fig.5.18 This screen confirms that reinstallation is complete

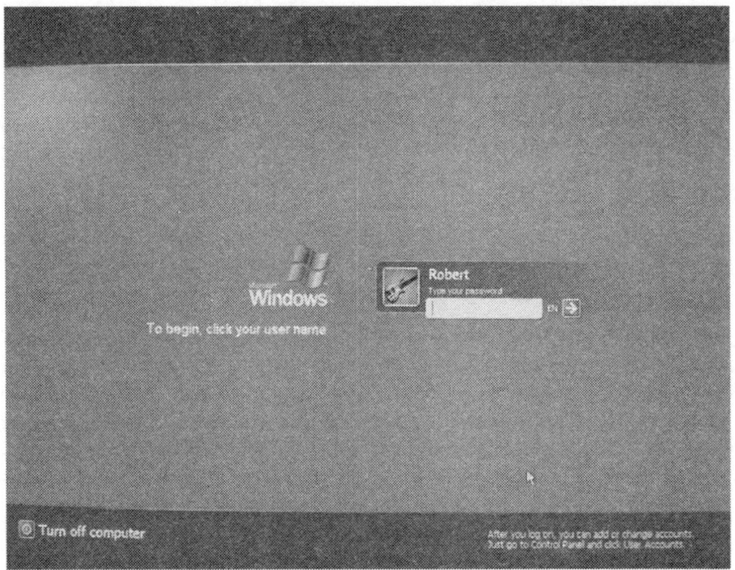

Fig.5.19 The next screen is the usual login type

Fig.5.20 The Windows desktop should look the same as it did before

To try out the new installation, operate the Finish button. The computer should then boot into the usual login screen (Figure 5.19). Login using your normal password (where appropriate), and the computer should go into the Windows XP desktop (Figure 5.20). After reinstalling Windows 9x it is necessary to adjust some of the settings in order to provide normal operation. In particular, the reinstalled version of Windows uses very basic video settings, which have to be adjusted to your normal settings. As can be seen from Figure 5.20, Windows XP uses the previous video settings, and the new installation should be usable without any adjustments.

The applications programs should remain installed and fully usable. Of course, any programs that were damaged by the virus might be unusable, and will not have been fixed by reinstalling Windows. It is then a matter of uninstalling and reinstalling any programs that are damaged. It is possible that the uninstall routines will have problems fully uninstalling damaged setups. Simply reinstalling programs over the remnants of the original will usually be possible, or you can manually delete any remaining files and folders. If there are any major problems with reinstallation, as a last resort a program can be installed to a different folder.

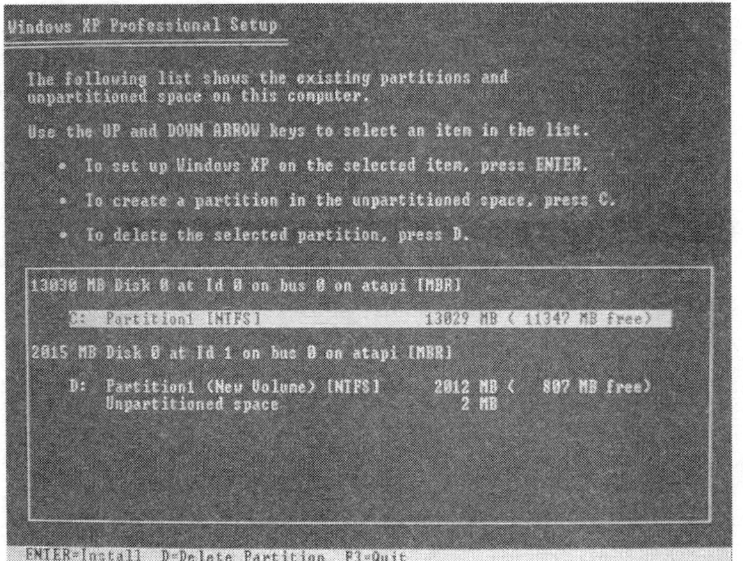

Fig.5.21 Three options are available from this screen

From scratch

The initial stages of installation are much the same if it is necessary to install Windows XP from scratch. As before, the computer is booted from the installation CD-ROM and it is only at the screen of Figure 5.3 that things change. It is a fresh installation that is required and not a repair, so the Escape key is pressed. This moves things on to the screen of Figure 5.21 where there are three options. Two of these permit the disc partitioning to be changed, and you will presumably wish to retain the existing set-up.

On the face of it, the best course of action is to make sure that the correct partition for the installation is selected in the lower part of the screen and then press the Return key. However, this will produce the warning screen of Figure 5.22. Although you are not trying to install two operating systems on one partition, the existing Windows XP installation (if still to some extent intact) might give problems with the new one. After all, the idea is to completely do away with the old installation and start afresh with a new one. Therefore, the D key is pressed so that the partition used for windows XP is deleted. This will delete everything in the partition, and a warning message to this effect appears when the D

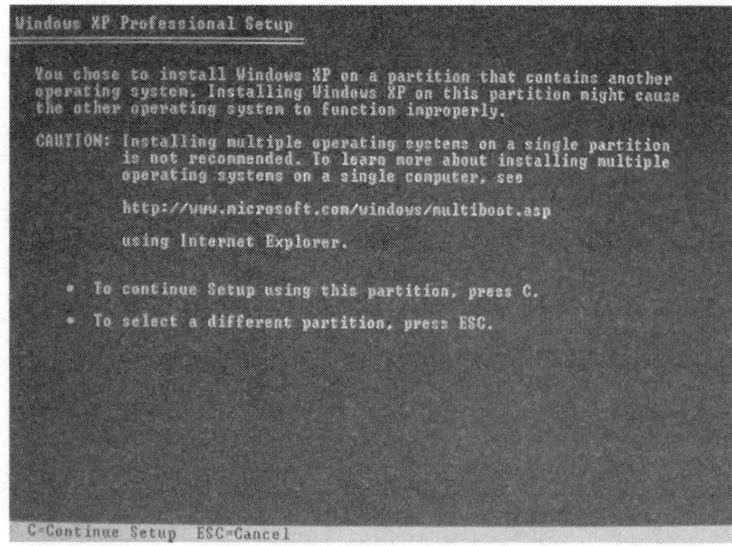

Fig.5.22 Remove the old Windows XP installation before proceeding

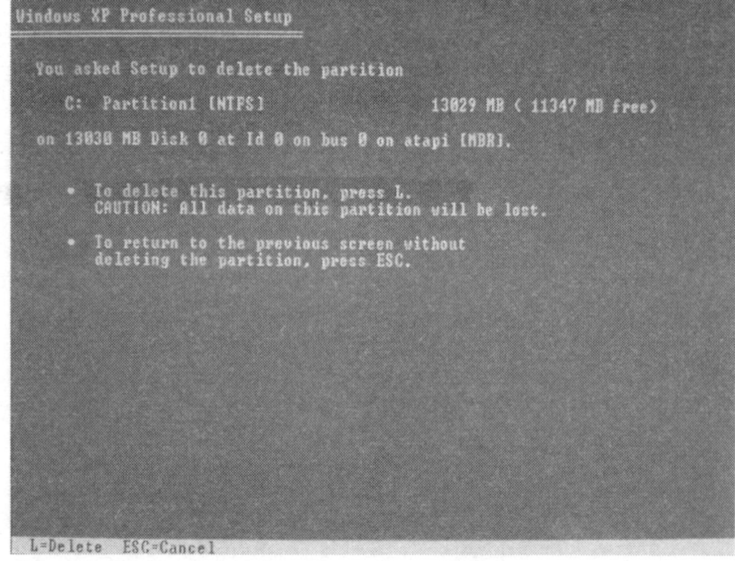

Fig.5.23 All data in the deleted partition will be lost

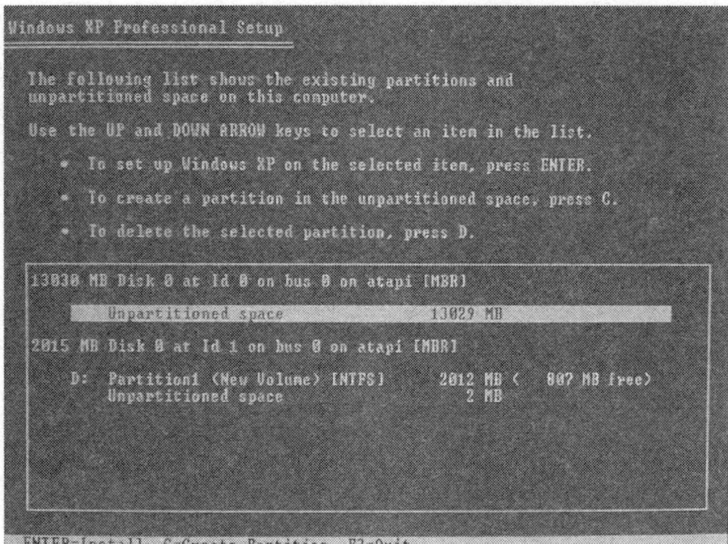

Fig.5.24 Disc C: now has unpartitioned space available

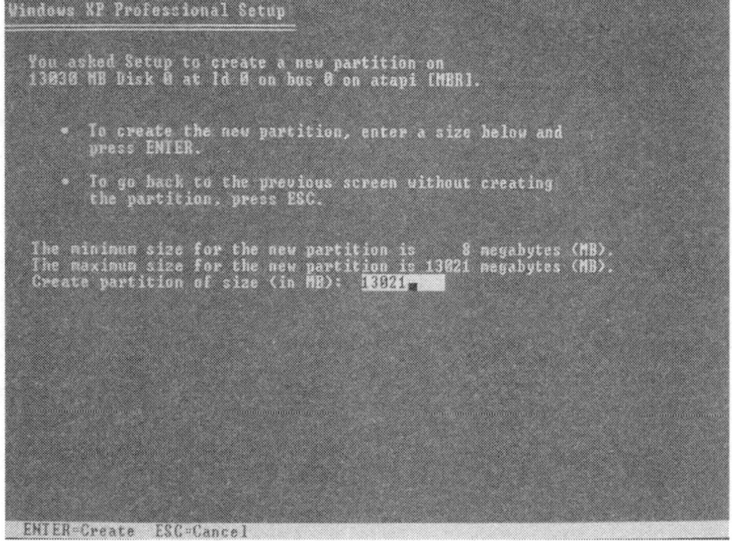

Fig.5.25 The partition will normally be set at the maximum size

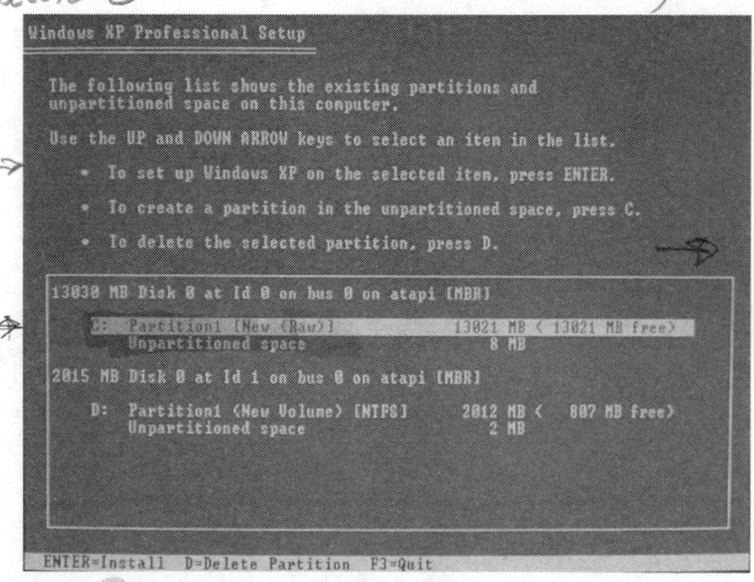

Fig.5.26 Drive C: now has an empty partition

key is operated (Figure 5.23). Assuming that you have previously rescued any important data on the partition, press the L key to go ahead and delete the partition.

The previous screen then returns, but this time it indicates that disc C: has unpartitioned space (Figure 5.24). The next step is to create a partition for the new Windows XP installation, and to format that space. With the unpartitioned space selected in the lower section of the screen, operate the C key to create the partition. The next screen (Figure 5.25) enables the partition to be set at the required size. Presumably you will simply wish to reinstate the previous partition that used all the space just vacated. In that case, simply press Return to accept the default partition size. This returns things more or less to the way they were originally (Figure 5.26), but the partition is now empty. It is not even formatted, which is why it is described as "Raw" in the partition table.

Formatting

Next press the Return key to go ahead and install Windows XP on the partition. This produces the screen of Figure 5.27, where the desired file system is selected. Unless there is a good reason to use the FAT or

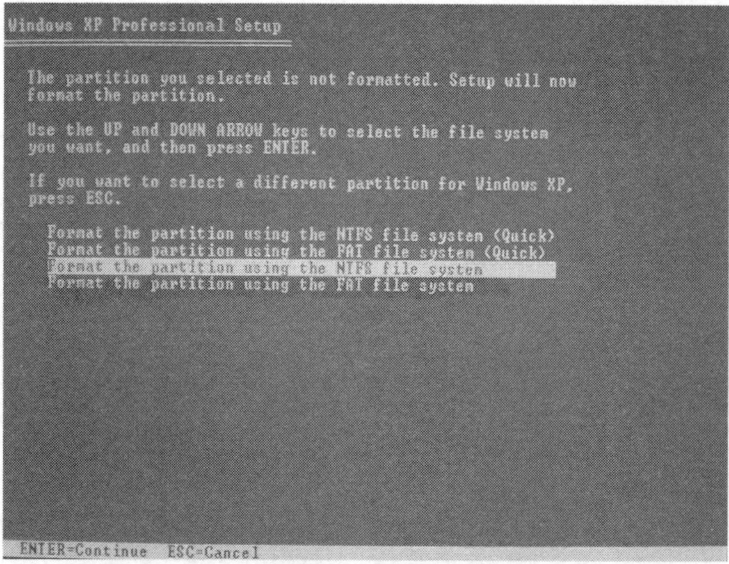

Fig.5.27 The partition is formatted using the selected file system

Fig.5.28 Formatting a large partition can take a long time

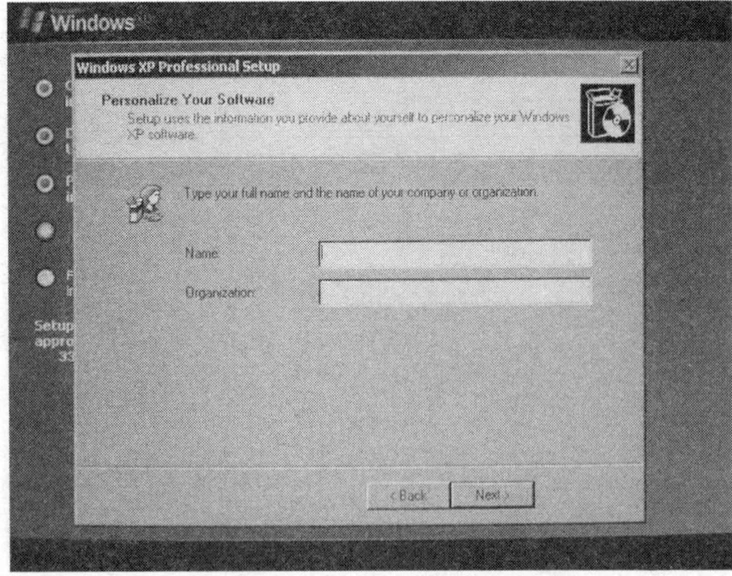

Fig.5.29 Add your name and (where appropriate) organisation in the textboxes

FAT32 file systems, such as compatibility with another file system, choose the NTFS option. This file system makes the best use of Windows XP's capabilities. Having selected the required file system, press the Return key to go ahead and format the partition. This brings up the screen of Figure 5.28, complete with the usual bargraph to show how far the formatting has progressed.

Once the partition has been formatted, the Setup program will start copying files to the hard disc, and thereafter the process is much the same as when reinstalling Windows XP on top of an existing installation. There are one or two differences though. As the original installation has been cleared from the hard disc, it is not possible for the new installation to read any information from it. You must re-enter your details when the screen of Figure 5.29 appears. The same is true of the passwords, and a new administrator password must be used when the screen of Figure 5.30 appears. Some general information has to be entered at the screens of Figure 5.31 and 5.32.

Near the end of the installation process there may be a small window that asks if Windows can automatically adjust the screen settings.

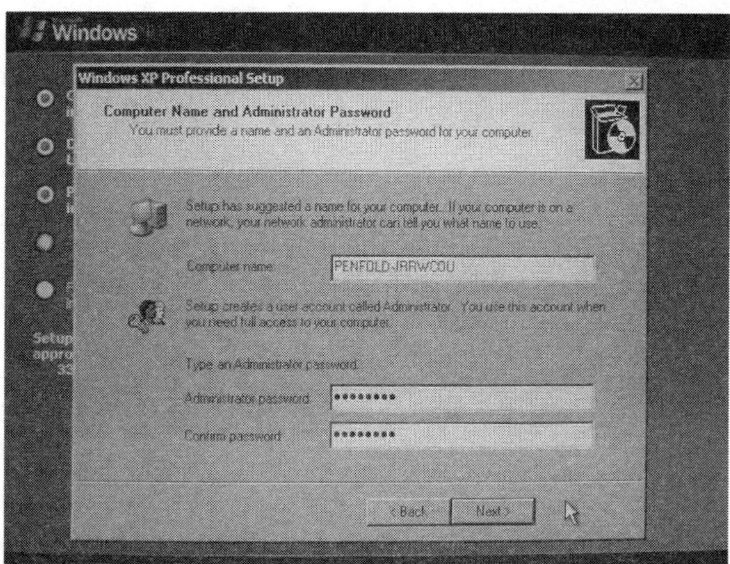

Fig.5.30 Type the administrator password into the textboxes

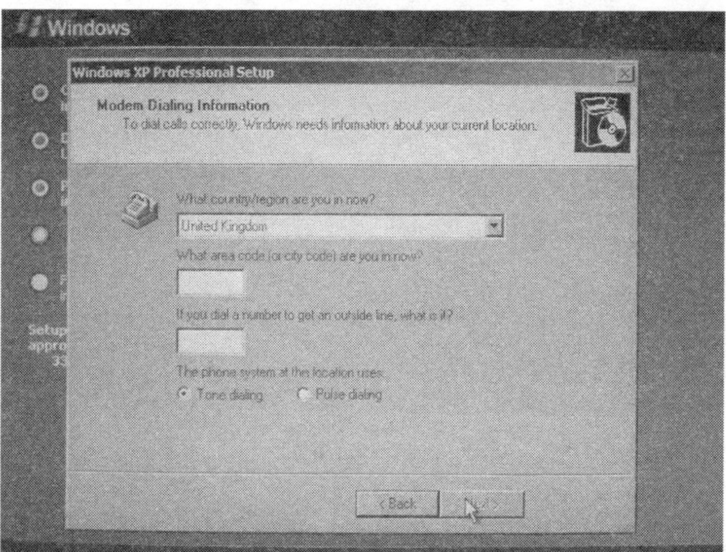

Fig.5.31 The modem dialling information is added here

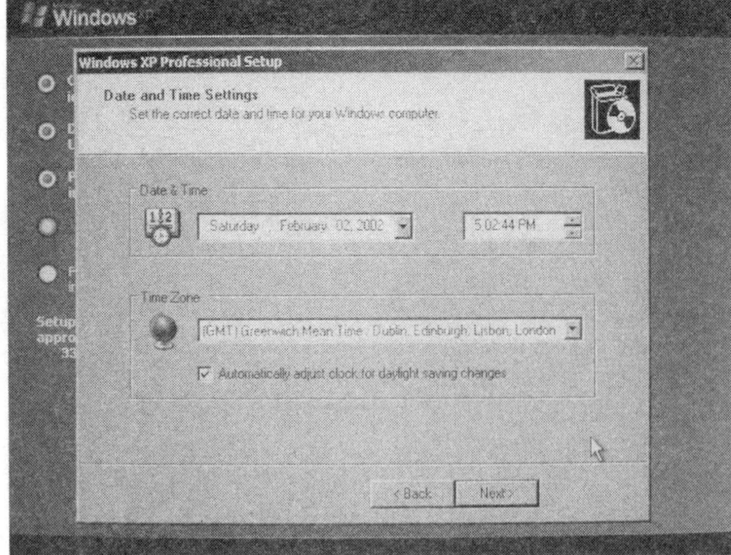

Fig.5.32 Use this window to set the time zone, etc.

Fig.5.33 Finally, you are into the newly installed Windows XP

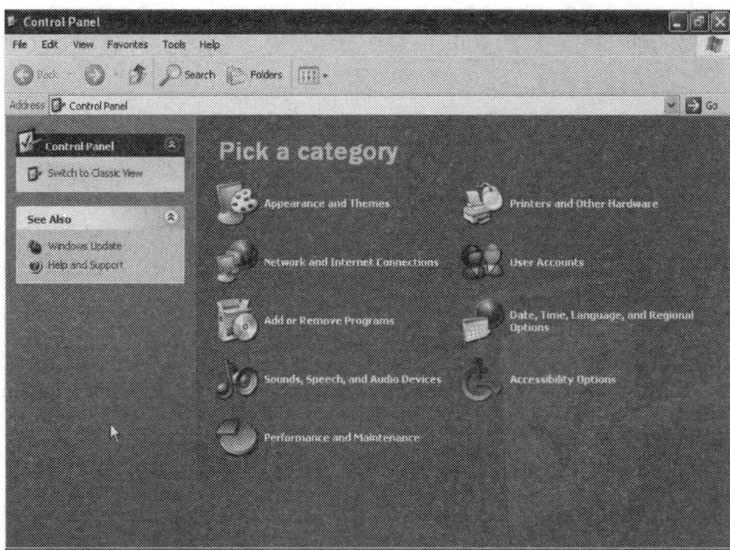

Fig.5.34 The default version of the Windows Control Panel

Normally it is best to operate the OK button if this appears. Windows will then start in something better than the basic 640 by 480 pixel resolution. It will probably opt for only 800 by 600 pixel resolution, but this is still much more usable that the basic 640 by 480 pixel mode. After negotiating the usual login screen the computer should go into Windows XP (Figure 5.33). A window asking if you wish to activate Windows XP might appear, but it is probably best to leave activation until you are sure that everything is installed and working perfectly.

Hardware drivers

At this stage you have Windows XP reinstalled, but it is likely that some items of hardware will be either partially operational, or will be simply ignored by Windows. It is possible that Windows will detect all the hardware on the motherboard and install the necessary drivers. If the motherboard hardware is more recent than the version of Windows XP that you are using, then Windows is unlikely to have the correct drivers in its standard repertoire. It is virtually certain that proper video drivers will be needed. Even if the graphics card can be set to use high resolutions and colour depths, it is almost certainly using a generic driver

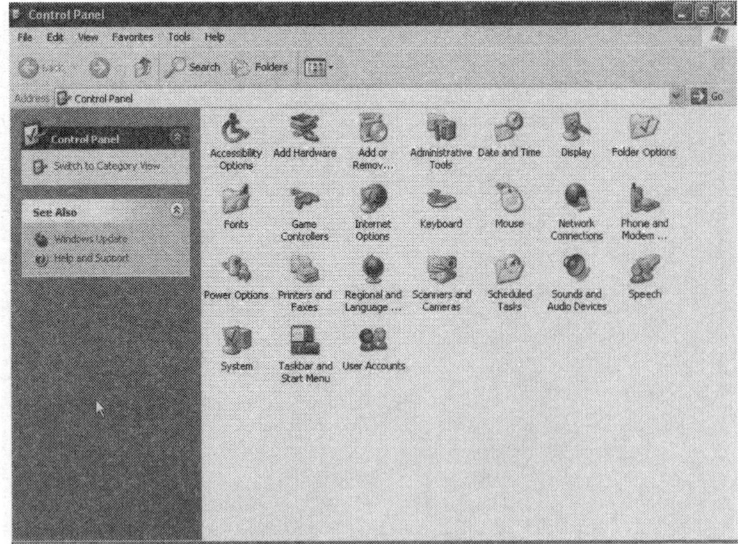

Fig.5.35 The Control Panel using the Classic View

rather than one designed specifically for the video card in use. Although high resolutions and colour depths can be used, the video system will probably be very slow in operation. There might be other items of hardware that Windows has missed completely, or has been unable to identify.

The first step is to go into Device Manager to look for any obvious problems with the hardware. First choose Control Panel from the Start menu, which will produce a window like the one in Figure 5.34. It is advisable to left-click on the Switch to Classic View link, which will change the window to the familiar Control Panel layout of Figure 5.35. This provides easy access to the hardware settings and other useful facilities. Launch the System Properties window by double-clicking on the System icon and then operate the Hardware tab. Left-click the Device Manager button, and a window similar to the one in Figure 5.36 will appear.

The important thing to look for here is the yellow exclamation marks that indicate problems with the hardware. In this case the hardware appears to be trouble-free apart from the integrated audio system and the video card. It is worthwhile double-clicking some of the other entries to check that the hardware has been identified correctly. Internal modems can sometimes be troublesome, although the modem has been correctly identified and installed in this case.

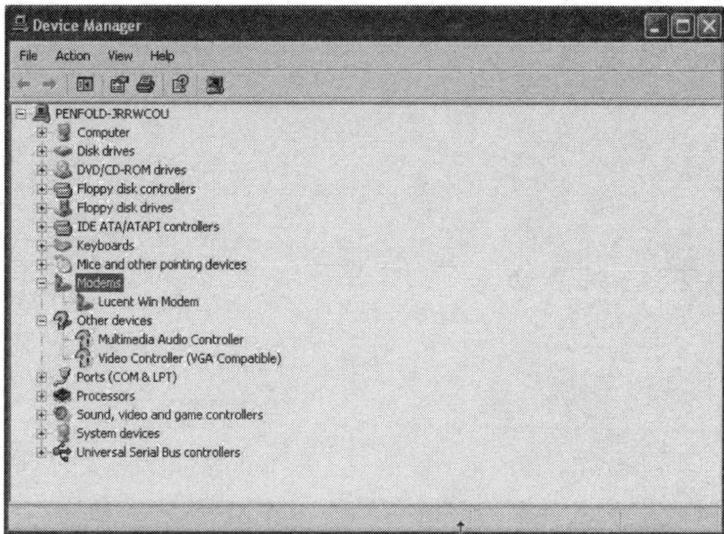

Fig.5.36 Check Device Manager for hardware problems

If there are any problems with the main hardware on the motherboard, it is advisable to install the drivers for this hardware first. The main hardware means things like the IDE controllers and the PCI slots, and not integrated hardware such as audio systems and network adapters. Where appropriate, your PC should have been supplied with a CD-ROM containing the device drivers for the hardware on the motherboard. Next the video drivers should be installed, and then the device drivers for other hardware such as audio systems and modems.

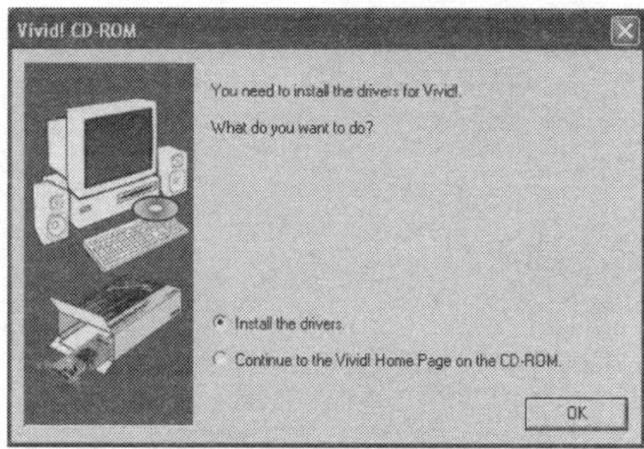

Fig.5.37 The initial screen of the installation program

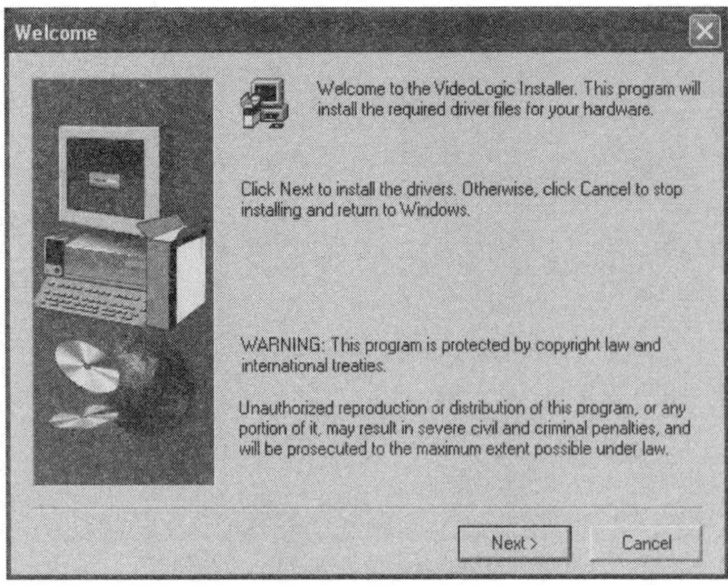

Fig.5.38 The Welcome window includes the usual copyright notice

Driver installation

Windows has built-in facilities for adding device drivers, but few manufacturers seem to make use of these. Most hardware has its own installation program. This copies the device drivers onto the hard disc, and then the computer is restarted. The device drivers are installed automatically during the boot process. The instruction manuals for the hardware should give concise information about installing the device

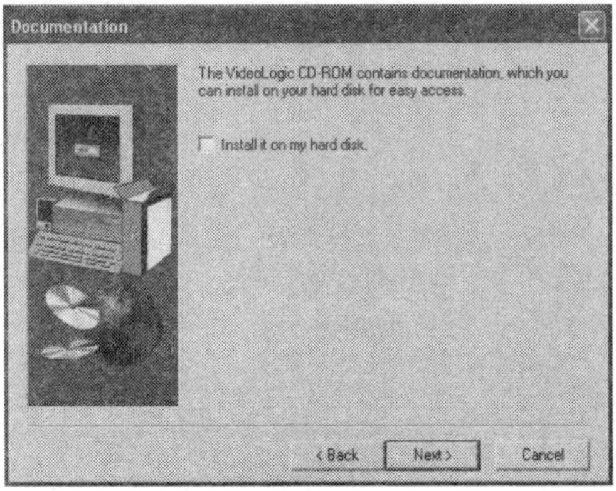

Fig.5.39 It is advisable to load the manual

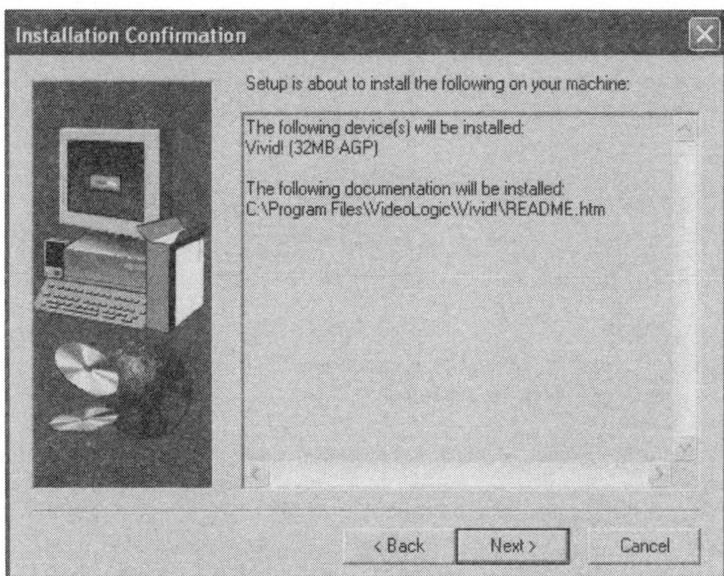

Fig.5.40 This window gives you an opportunity to review the options that have been selected

drivers, and the installation instructions should be followed "to the letter". Note that the installation process is not always the same for each version of Windows, so make sure that you follow the right instructions and use the Windows XP device drivers. Windows XP will almost certainly spot the error and display a warning message if you try to install inappropriate device drivers.

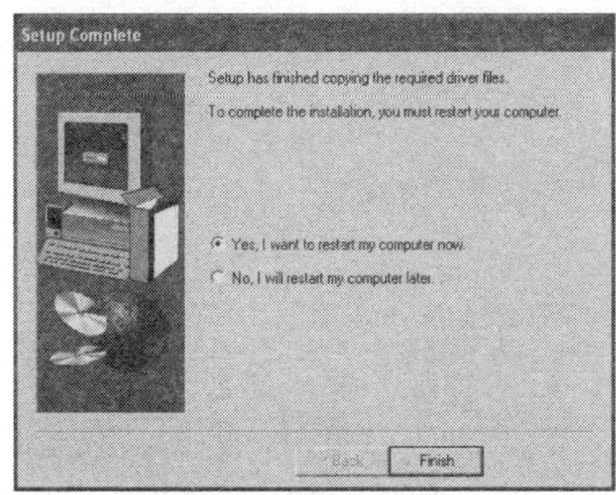

Fig.5.41 Restart the computer to complete the installation

In this example there is no need to install any additional drivers fo the motherboard's system hardware, so the first task is to install the proper video drivers. The installation CD-ROM will usually auto-run, as in this case, and Figure 5.37 shows the initial window. This provides two options, and in this case is clearly the default "Install the drivers" option that is required. The next window (Figure 5.38) has the usual copyright notice, and operating the Next button moves things on to the licence agreement. Left-clicking the Yes brings up a further window (Figure 5.39), and this one gives the option of loading the on-disc instruction manual onto the hard disc. Since the manual is unlikely to require much disc space it is a good idea to install the documentation onto the hard disc when this option is available.

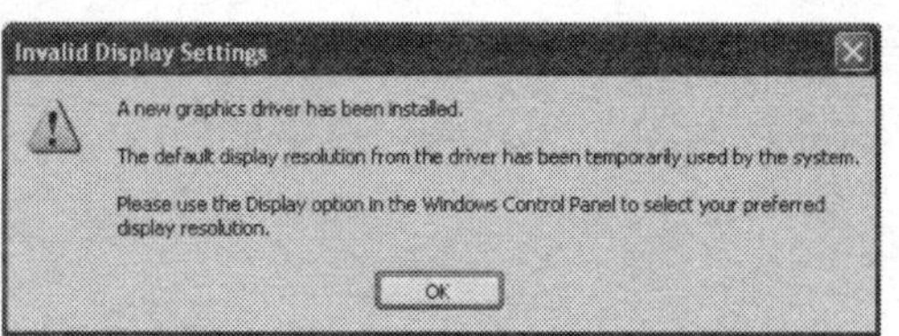

Fig.5.42 Windows will probably detect the newly installed video card

The next window (Figure 5.40) simply shows the options that have been selected, and assuming everything is in order it is just a matter of left-clicking the Next button to start installation. Once the files have been copied to the hard disc, the window of Figure 5.41 appears. It is definitely advisable to restart the computer immediately rather than waiting until later. This finalises the installation of the drivers and gives you an opportunity to check that they are functioning correctly. Installing several sets of device drivers and then restarting the computer might seem to be a more efficient way of doing things, because the computer only has to be restarted once. In practice it is not a good idea and is simply inviting problems.

Video settings

Windows will almost certainly detect that a new video card has been installed, and it will then produce the message window of Figure 5.42 when the reboot has been completed. Operate the OK button and then adjust the video settings using the Display Properties Window (Figure 5.43), which will be launched automatically. If the newly installed video card is not detected by Windows, the display settings window must be run manually. Launch the Control Panel, double-click the Display icon, and then operate the Settings tab in the window that appears.

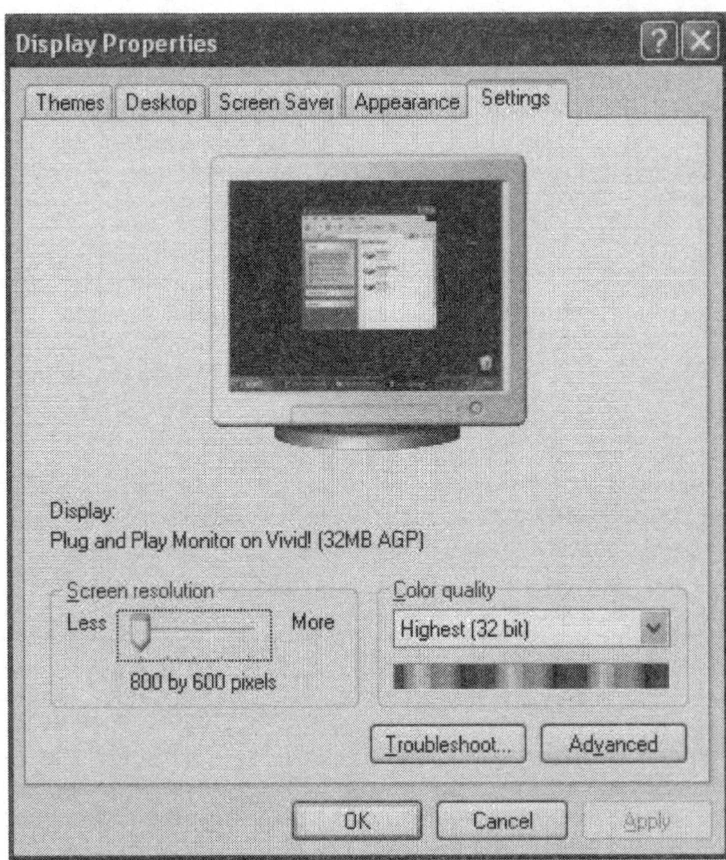

Fig.5.43 Set the required screen resolution and colour depth

Having set the required screen resolution and colour depth, operate the Apply button. It is likely that Windows is overestimating the abilities of the monitor if the screen goes blank or produces an unstable image. The screen should return to normal in a few seconds though. One way of tackling the problem is to operate the Troubleshoot button, which launches the Video Display Troubleshooter (Figure 5.44). By going through the questions and suggested cures it is likely that the problem would soon be solved. However, the most likely cause of the problem is

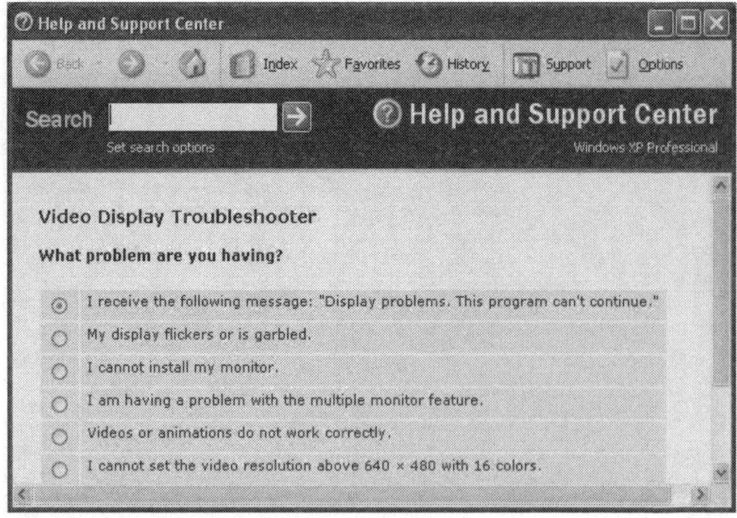

Fig.5.44 The Video Display Troubleshooter

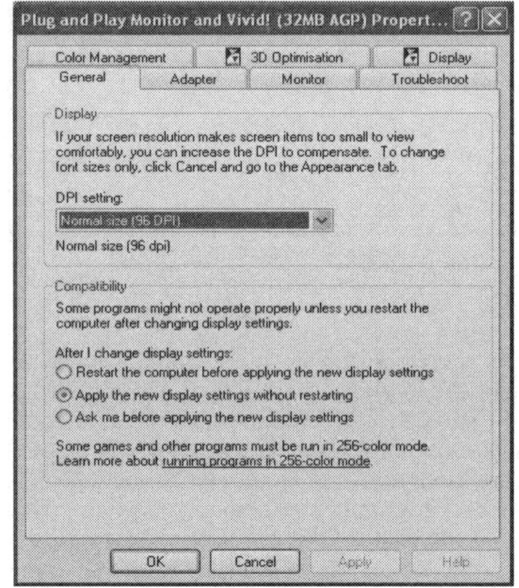

Fig.5.45 The Advanced Settings window

Windows setting a scan rate that is too high for the monitor, and this is easily corrected.

First set the required screen resolution again, and then left-click the Advanced button to bring up a window like the one in Figure 5.45. Next, operate the Monitor tab to switch the window to one like Figure 5.46. Activate the Screen refresh rate menu, and choose a lower rate than the one currently in use. In

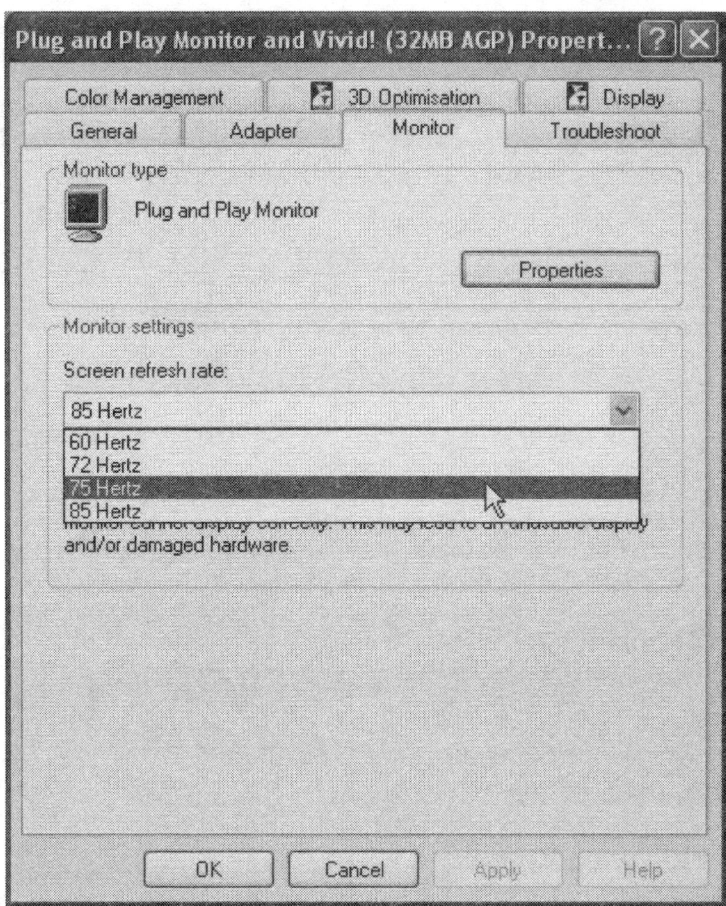

Fig.5.46 A lower scan rate should cure the problem

this example the rate was reduced from 85 hertz to 75 hertz. Left-click the Apply button and observe the screen. With luck, this time a small window like the one shown in Figure 5.47 will be visible on the screen. If so, operate the Yes button to keep the new scan rate. If not, wait for a proper display to return and then repeat this process using an even lower scan rate. Note that the maximum scan rate for a monitor generally reduces as the screen resolution is increased. Consequently, the higher

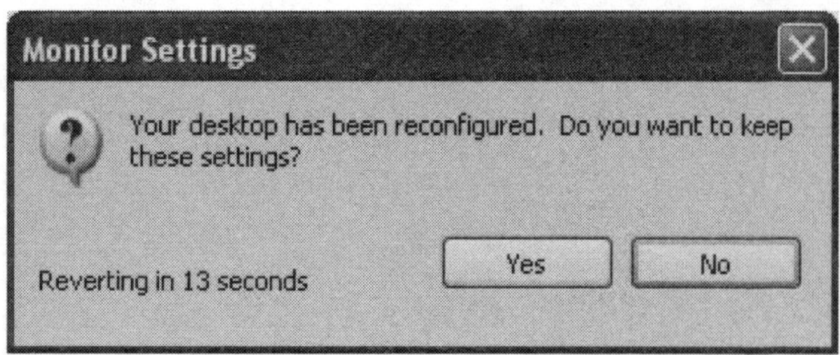

Fig.5.47 The settings return to normal unless the Yes button is operated

the screen resolution used, the lower the scan rate that will have to be set.

Obviously the installation of the video card will vary slightly from one card to another, but most cards are installed using the general method outlined here. With the video card installed and set up correctly, any further drivers that are needed can be installed. In this example it was only necessary to install the device drivers for the audio system. Device

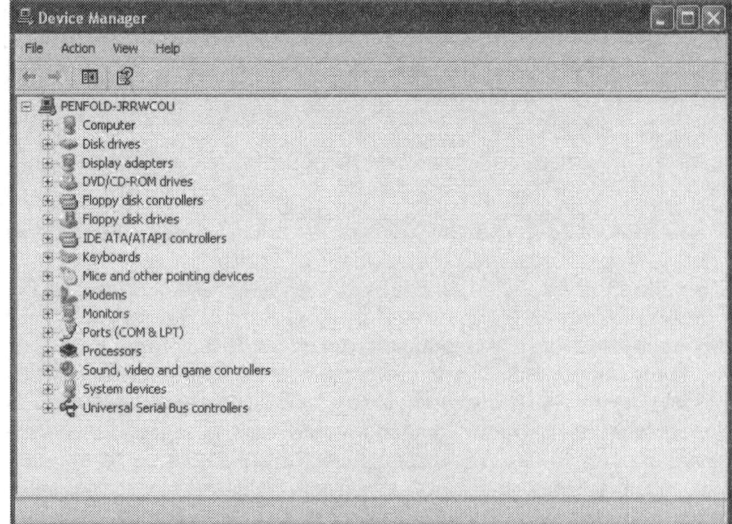

Fig.5.48 The problems with the hardware have been cleared

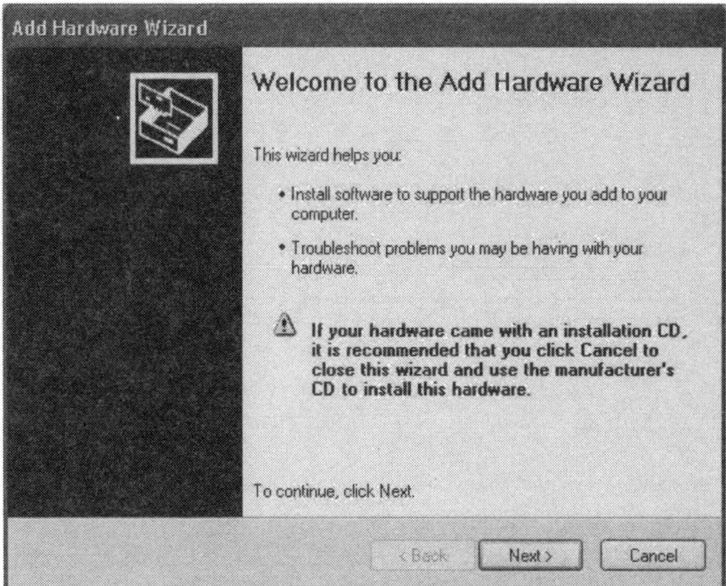

Fig.5.49 The Add Hardware Wizard

Manager then showed no problems with any of the hardware (Figure 5.48), indicating that the hardware was all installed successfully. With the hardware installed properly, it is then a matter of installing all the applications software, undertaking any customisation of the software, and then reinstating your data files. The PC is then ready for use again.

Correct channels

The installation CD-ROMs supplied with most hardware includes a Setup program. However, in some cases the disc contains device drivers but it does not include a program to install the drivers. If the instruction manual gives installation instructions, then follow them. With some low-cost hardware you are simply left to your own devices. One way of tackling the installation of hardware of this type is to launch the Add Hardware Wizard. Go to the Control Panel, double-click the System icon, and then operate the Hardware tab in the System Properties window. In the upper section of this window there is an Add Hardware Wizard button, and operating this launches the wizard (Figure 5.49).

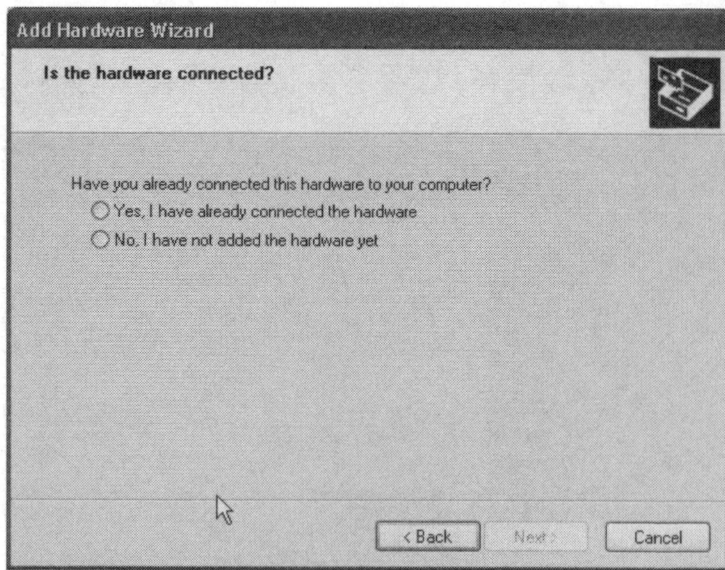

Fig.5.50 The first check looks for the hardware

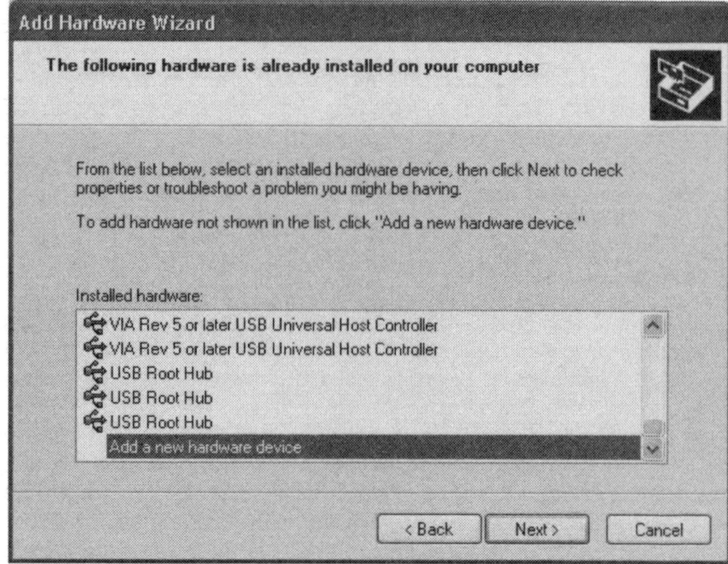

Fig.5.51 Select Add new hardware device

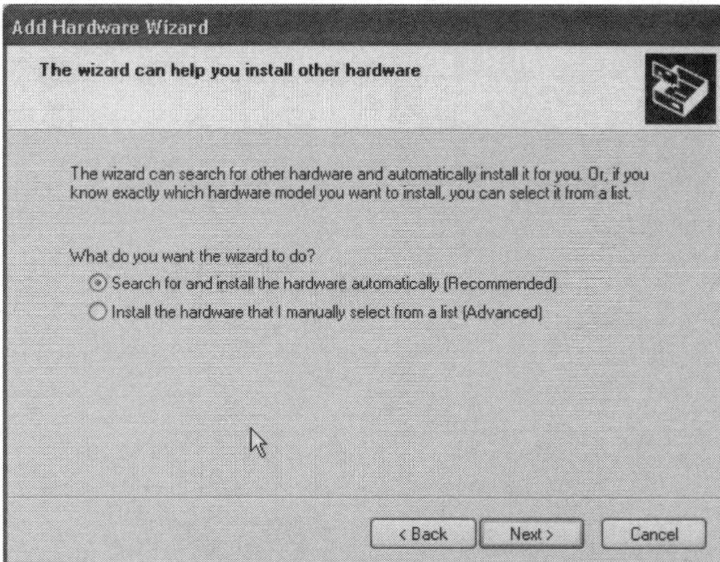

Fig.5.52 Manual installation is probably the best option here

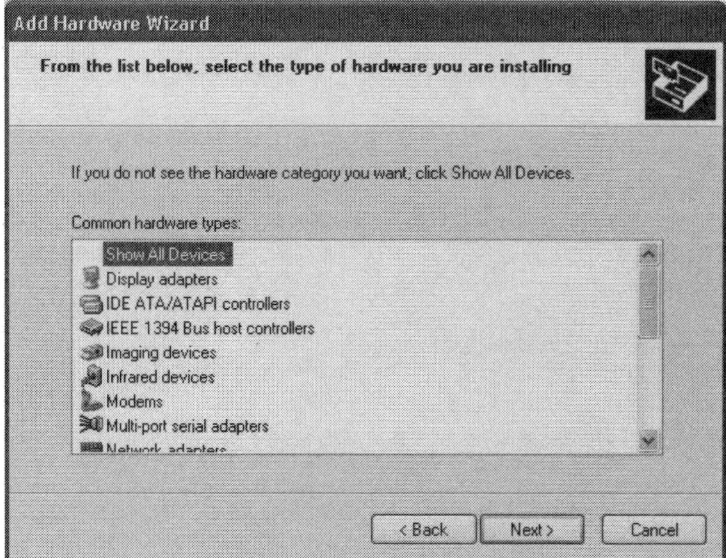

Fig.5.53 Select the correct category for the new hardware

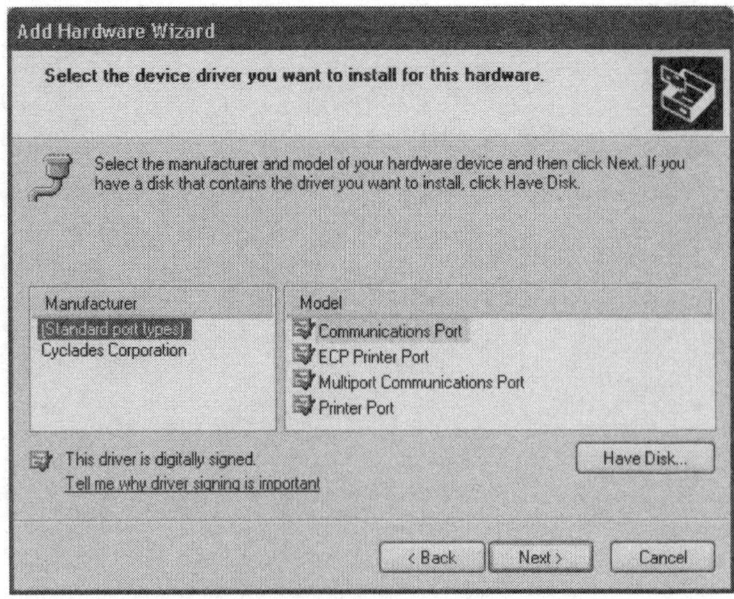

Fig.5.54 It is normally the Have Disk option that is needed here

Heed the warning notice about using the manufacturer's installation program wherever possible. Check the installation CD-ROM to ensure that it does not contain an Install or Setup program. If you are sure that it does not, operate the Next button to move the wizard on to the next stage (Figure 5.50). The Add Hardware Wizard uses the normal technique of suggestions and questions to (hopefully) find the right answers. The first screen simply determines whether the hardware is already connected to the PC. Unless

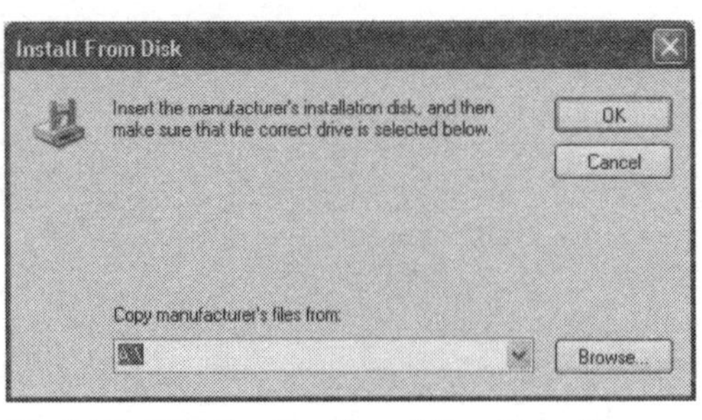

Fig.5.55 Give the location of the driver files

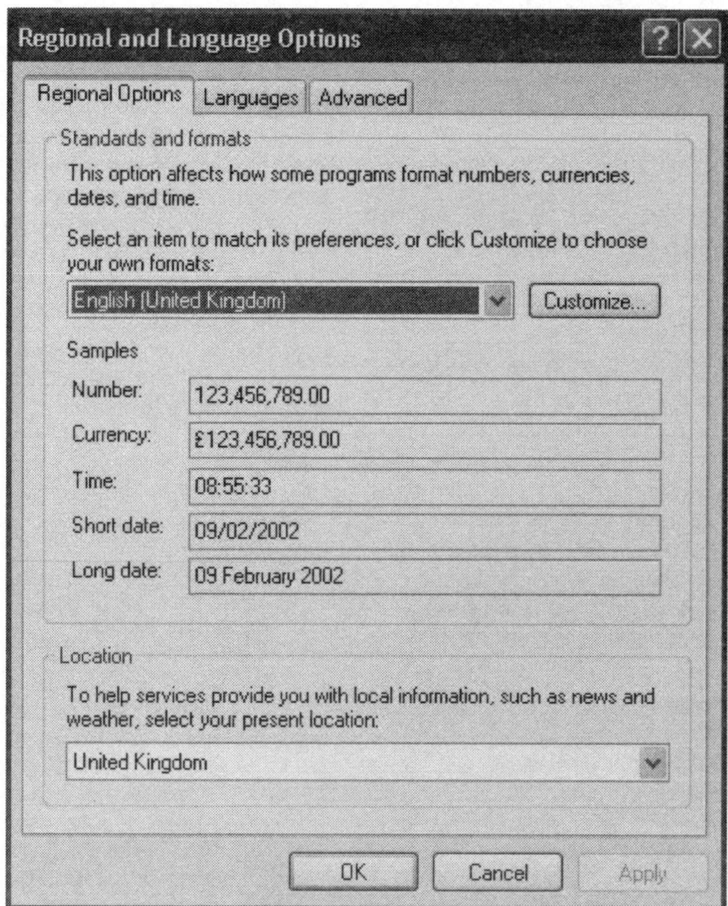

Fig.5.56 Check the the Regional and Language settings are correct

the manufacturer specifically advises otherwise, the hardware must be physically installed before the device drivers are loaded.

Assuming that the hardware is already connected, the next window provides a list of the detected hardware. Obviously the entry for the hardware should be selected if it is found in the list. If it has not been detected and listed by Windows, select the Add a new device option (Figure 5.51). The next window (Figure 5.52) gives the option of installing the device manually or having Windows try to detect it. There is no harm in trying the detection method, but it is likely Windows is incapable of detecting the hardware if it has not done so already. Taking the manual route produces a window like the one of Figure 5.53). This gives a list of hardware types, and you must select the correct category for the device you are trying to install.

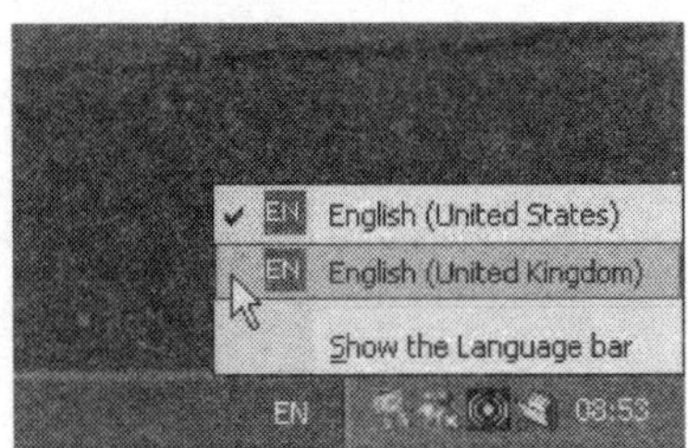

Fig.5.57 Choose the correct language version

Moving on to the next window (Figure 5.54) gives a list of manufacturers in the left-hand section, and devices for the selected manufacturer in the right-hand section. Obviously you should select the appropriate entry for your device if it is listed, but this is unlikely. It is normally necessary to operate the Have Disk button, which brings up a window like the one of Figure 5.55. Either type the path to the disc and folder containing the device drivers, or use the Browse option to locate the drivers. Having pointed Windows to the drivers, the installation process then follows along normal lines.

Language problems

Back in the days of MS-DOS it was often quite tricky to persuade the operating system that you were using a keyboard having the English version of the English layout, rather than one having the US English characters and layout. The differences are quite minor, but they result in the double quotes and @ symbol being transposed. Also, the pound sign (£) tends to disappear or be replaced with the hash (#) symbol. Some of the little used symbols also disappear or become assigned to the wrong keys.

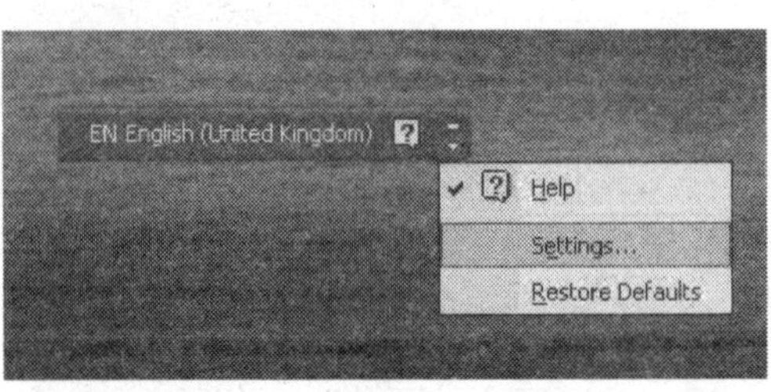

Fig.5.58 Choose the Settings option from the popup menu

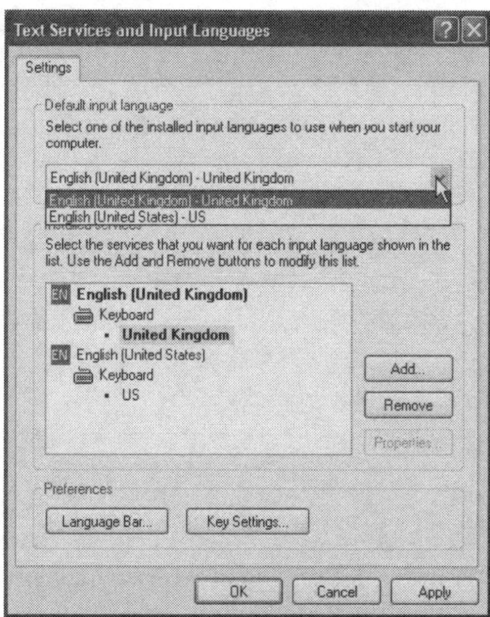

Fig.5.59 Set the correct default language

Windows XP can suffer from a similar problem after it has been reinstalled from scratch. The obvious first step is to go to the Control Panel and double-click the keyboard icon. This is the first thing to try if the keyboard is not working at all, but with a language problem it is unlikely to be of any help. It is better to start by going to the Control Panel and double-clicking the Regional and Language icon. This produces a properties window like the one in Figure 5.56, which is essentially the same as the one that appears during the installation process. Check the various sections to make sure that the correct language is set.

If everything is correct, look at the bottom right-hand corner of the Windows desktop. Here there will be a button that indicates the language in use. This will usually be marked EN for English, but more than one version of the language will probably be available. Left-click the button to produce a small popup menu (Figure 5.57), and then select the English (United Kingdom) option. The keyboard should then function properly, producing the pound sign, etc. However, the wrong version of English will be set as the default.

To correct this, activate the menu again and select the Show the language bar option. This removes the button and produces a small floating bar instead (Figure 5.58). Operate the tiny button in the bottom right-hand corner of the bar and select Settings from the popup menu. This launches the Text Services and Input Languages window (Figure 5.59). Use the pop-down menu near the top of the window to select the correct default

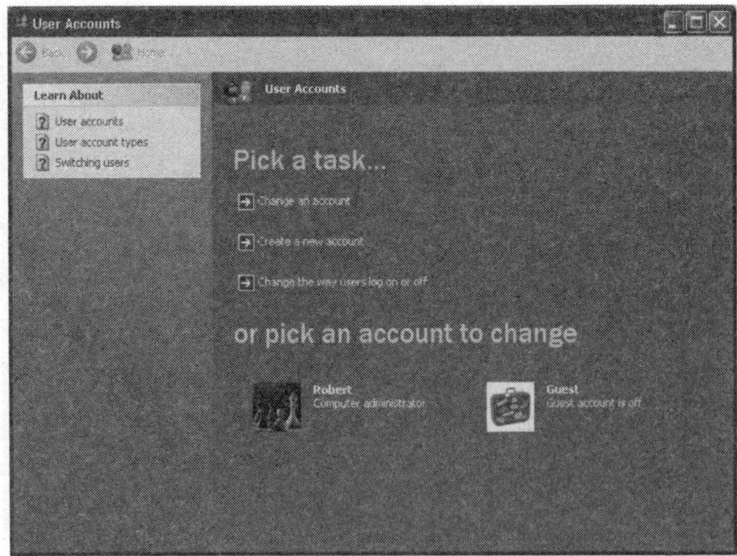

Fig.5.60 The initial version of the User Accounts window

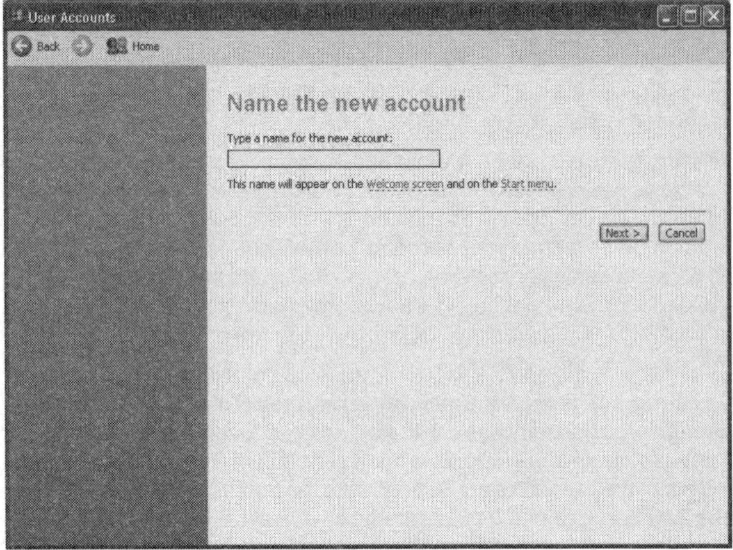

Fig.5.61 Type a name for the account into the textbox

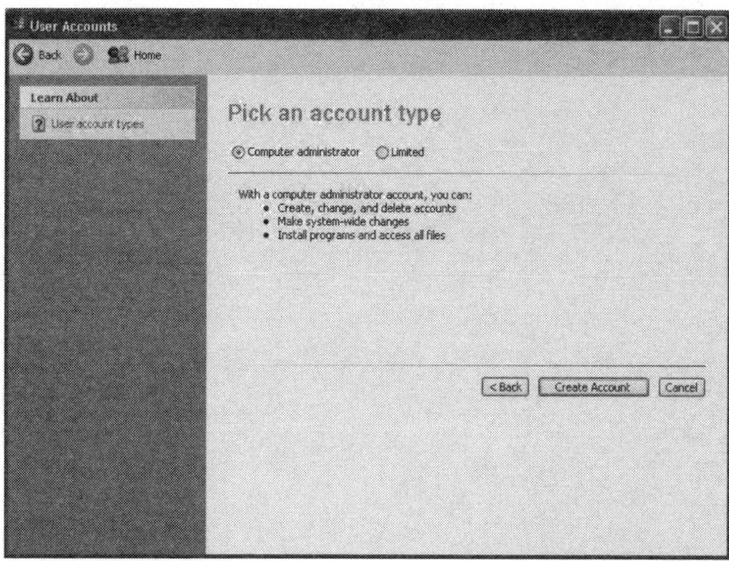

Fig.5.62 Use this window to select the most suitable type of account

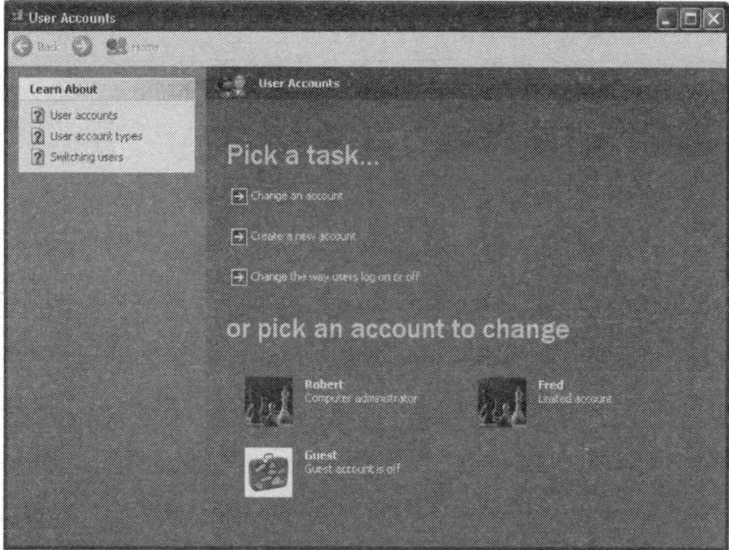

Fig.5.63 An icon has been added for the newly created account

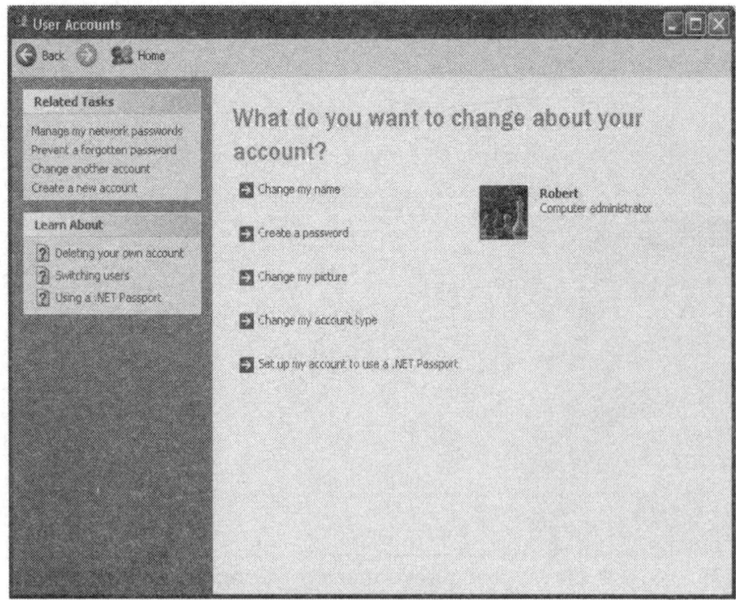

Fig.5.64 Operate the Create password link

language. Next operate the Apply and OK buttons, and then restart the computer to check that the default has switched to the right language.

User accounts

At least two user accounts would have been produced automatically if the original Windows XP installation was an upgrade from Windows 9x. The Administrator account and one for the name used during the upgrade process. Both accounts are assigned the same password. Some computer retailers supply their PCs completely set up and ready for use, sometimes complete with one or more user accounts installed. Only an Administrator account is produced when Windows XP is installed from scratch. Any other accounts you require have to be set up manually.

The Administrator account is usually reserved for making changes to the system or troubleshooting, since it gives full control over the system. As a minimum, you should install one additional account for normal use. The first step in adding a new account is to go to the Control Panel and double-click the User Accounts icon. This launches a window like

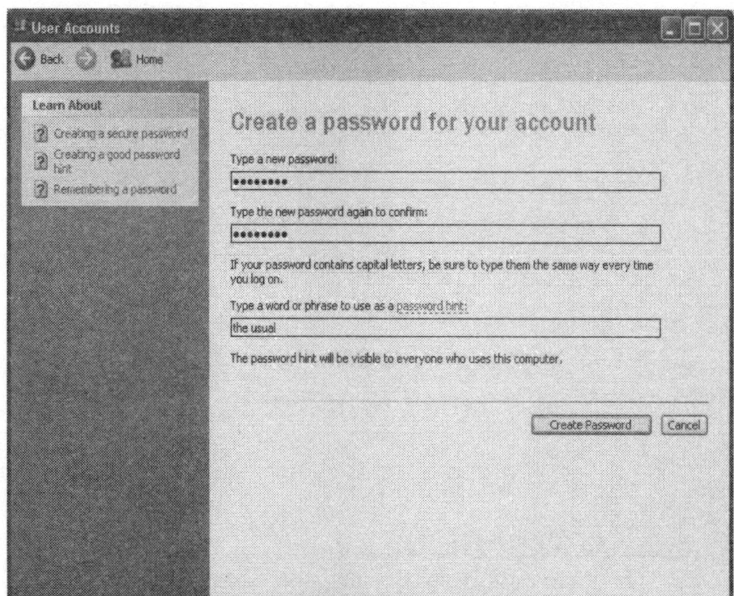

Fig.5.65 Type the password into the top two textboxes

the one in Figure 5.60. Left-click the link for Create a new account, which switches the window to the one shown in Figure 5.61. Type a name for the account into the textbox and then operate the Next button.

The type of account is selected at the next window (Figure 5.62). An administrator account provides freedom to make changes to the system, but these abilities are not needed for day to day use of the computer. A limited account is generally considered to be the better choice for normal use, since the restrictions reduce the risk of the system being accidentally damaged. Note that you might not be able to install programs when using a limited account. Also, some programs produced prior to Windows 2000 and XP might not be usable with a limited account. Consequently, there is no alternative to an administrator account if maximum flexibility is required.

Having selected the type of account using the radio buttons, operate the Create Account button. The original User Accounts window then returns, but it should now contain the newly created account (Figure 5.63). There are other facilities in the User Accounts window that enable the login and logoff settings to be altered. By default, the Welcome

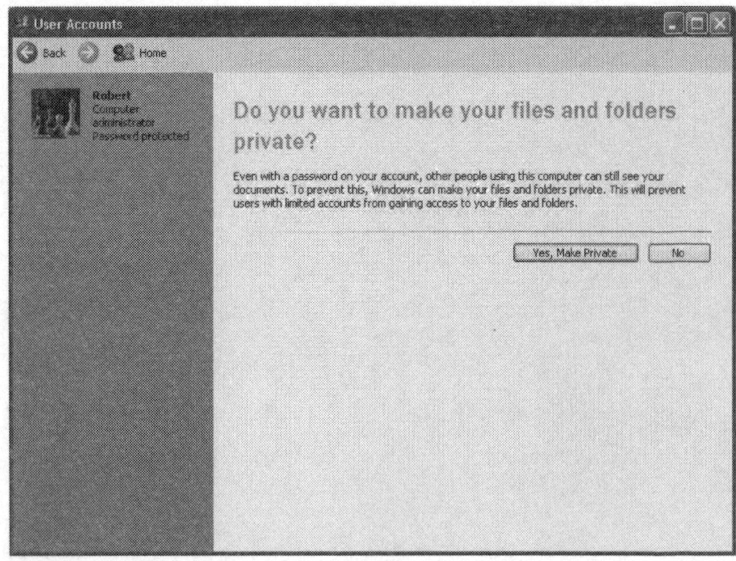

Fig.5.66 If desired, your files and folders can be kept private

screen is shown at startup, and you simply have to left-click the entry for the new account in order to use it. Note that the new account will start with a largely blank desktop. Each account has its own desktop and other settings, so each account can be customised with the best settings for its particular user.

Accounts are not password protected by default. To add a password, go to the User Accounts window and left-click the entry for the account that you wish to password protect. This switches the window to look like Figure 5.64, and here the Create password link is activated. At the next window (Figure 5.65) the password is typed into the top two textboxes, and a hint is entered into the other textbox. The hint is something that will jog your memory if you should happen to forget the password. Next operate the Create Password button, which moves things on to the window of Figure 5.66. This window explains that password protection does not prevent other users from reading your files. Operate the Yes Make Private button if you would like to prevent other users from accessing your files. This completes the process, and the password will be needed the next time you login to that account.

Points to remember

PCs that are supplied with Windows XP preinstalled are not necessarily supplied with a normal Windows installation disc. Windows then has to be installed in accordance with the computer manufacturer's instructions. The exact method of reinstallation varies somewhat from one manufacturer to another.

Installing Windows XP on top of an existing version might cure problems with the operating system, but it is not guaranteed to do so.

Installing Windows XP "from scratch", with all the previous files removed from the hard disc should effect a cure to any Windows problems. If it does not, the computer probably has a hardware fault.

When reinstalling Windows XP from scratch it is not necessary to reformat the hard disc prior to reinstallation. The appropriate disc partition can be deleted and then added again during installation. This clears away any trace of the original Installation, but all data will also be removed from the partition.

Make sure that any important data is reliably backed up prior to installing Windows XP from scratch. Data should not be lost when reinstalling Windows XP on top of the existing version, but it is a good idea to backup any important data in case there are problems.

The process is largely automatic with either type of reinstallation. The user provides some basic information and then the Setup program installs the Windows files and sets up the essential hardware.

Once Windows XP has been reinstalled, some further work is required to get all the hardware properly installed, the screen resolution and colour depth set correctly, etc. Some hardware has its own installation routines and does not go through the normal Windows routes. In fact, most hardware is now installed in this way. Always install hardware in accordance with the manufacturer's instructions.

Install the device drivers for system hardware on the motherboard first, followed by the video drivers, and then any other drivers that are needed. Do not install applications software until all the hardware is installed and working properly.

The Text Services and Input Languages window can be used to correct things if the computer defaults to using the US English keyboard layout.

Any user accounts and passwords are lost when Windows XP is installed from scratch. These can be rebuilt by going to the User Accounts window, which is accessed via the Control Panel.

6

Reinstalling ME

MS/DOS boot

The method used to reinstall Windows ME and its predecessors is rather different to the one used for Windows XP. It is perhaps rather more crude, with no option of booting from the installation CD-ROM. Instead it is necessary to boot from a floppy disc that contains the MS/DOS operating system, or the Windows version of it. I would not recommend trying to reinstall Windows by booting into Windows. With Windows seriously damaged this will probably not be an option anyway. If you can boot into Windows but only in Safe Mode there will be no CD-ROM support, so it will not be possible to install Windows from the installation CD-ROM.

Where the PC can be booted into a largely working version of Windows, an installation started from within Windows will simply place the new version on top of the old one. Unfortunately, it will not necessarily repair any problems in the existing Windows set-up. Unless you have definitely decided that it is time to "sweep away the cobwebs" and start from scratch, I would certainly recommend trying to fix Windows by reinstalling it on top of the broken version. If this fails to cure the problem it is time to install Windows from scratch.

Either way, I would suggest booting from a Windows Startup disc in drive A: and selecting CD-ROM support when the menu appears. The difference between the two installation methods is that when installing Windows "from scratch" it is necessary to wipe the hard disc clean first. When installing Windows over the existing version all the existing files on the hard disc are left in place. Simply run the Windows Setup program once the computer has booted into MS/DOS.

The basic installation process is much the same for Windows 95, 98, and ME. Although the description provided here is for an installation of Windows ME, the basic procedure is therefore much the same for Windows 95 and 98 (first or second edition). Also, the process is much the same whether the operating system is installed from scratch or on top of an existing Windows installation. If Windows is already on the hard disc it will be detected by the Setup program, which will then reinstall it on top of the existing Windows installation, by default. Any Windows applications programs on the disc should remain properly installed with the new Windows installation. Any data and configuration files should also be left unchanged.

It is because Windows finds any existing installation and merges the new version into it that an installation "from scratch" is sometimes needed. Completely wiping is the easiest way to ensure that there is no information left on the disc to lead the new installation astray. However, it also means that any data on the disc will be lost unless it is properly backed up. You can try a middle course with the Windows directory structure being deleted, but everything else being left on the disc. With luck this will result in Windows being reinstalled successfully, and any problems in the old installation will not resurface.

In practice there is no absolute guarantee of success though. Also, bear in mind that any Windows applications on the hard disc will not be properly installed in the new version of Windows. They will not have the appropriate entries in the new Windows registry files, and are unlikely to run properly. All the applications will therefore have to be reinstalled on top of the existing software. An advantage of this method is that any data files and templates should be left intact, but note that configuration files for the applications programs will probably be overwritten when the programs are reinstalled.

Things can be taken a stage further, with the data files and any other important files being copied to a new folder. Everything else on the disc is then deleted and Windows is installed "from scratch". Where there is no other means of backing up important files, this method has the advantage that the files should still be intact once Windows has been reinstalled, and there are no system files, etc., left on the disc that could have a detrimental effect on the new Windows installation. Backing up important files to another disc is still preferable, because the backup copies on the main disc will be lost if there is a disc fault or a major problem during the Windows reinstallation.

If you decide to delete certain directories rather than simply wiping the disc clean, it is best to do most of the deleting in Windows using Windows Explorer. Using Windows Explorer it is possible to "zap" complete directory structures almost instantly. Deleting large numbers of files and directories in MS/DOS tends to be a very long, slow, and drawn out process. Obviously you must be sure that the infection has been completely removed if you intend to leave any files on the hard disc.

The reinstallation process described here provides a true installation "from scratch", with the hard disc being wiped clean. However, the initial part of the process is easily modified to accommodate one of the alternative methods outlined previously. The main installation then proceeds in more or less the same fashion.

Booting up

The first task is to boot the computer from a Windows Startup disc. If you do not have a Startup disc, one can be made by selecting Settings from the Start menu, then Control Panel and Add/Remove Programs. Left-click on the Startup Disk tab, operate the Create Disk button, and then follow the onscreen prompts. It will be necessary to make the disc on another computer if your PC can not even boot into Windows in Safe Mode.

With the Startup disc in drive A, restart the computer and with luck it will boot using the Startup disc. The BIOS settings are unsuitable if the computer ignores this disc and tries to boot from the hard disc instead. In this event you must go into the BIOS and choose a boot-up option that has A: as the initial boot disc and drive C: as the second boot disc. Any subsequent boot options are irrelevant, because the PC will boot before it gets to them.

Once the PC starts to boot-up using the Startup disc you will be presented with a menu offering three or four choices. Select the one that boots the computer using CD-ROM support. This is important, because you can not run the Setup program on the Windows CD-ROM without the CD-ROM support. The CD-ROM support works with the vast majority of CD-ROM drives, including virtually all types that use an IDE interface. However, it does not work with all drives. If it does not work with the CD-ROM drive of your computer you must make your own boot disc with CD-ROM drivers. To make a boot disc first boot the PC in MS/DOS mode. To do this you must operate function key F8 as the system starts to boot into Windows, and then select the appropriate option from the menu that appears. Once the computer has booted into MS/DOS put a blank disc in drive A: and issue this command:

format A: /s

This will format the disc and add the system files needed to make it bootable. In Windows ME there is no option to boot in MS/DOS mode, but the computer can be booted using a Startup disc, and then this command can be used:

format B: /s

In the unlikely event that your PC has a drive B:, this will format the disc in drive B: and place the system files onto it. If there is no drive B:, the operating system will use drive A: as both drive A: and drive B:, and you will have to do some disc swapping when indicated by the onscreen instructions. The CD-ROM and mouse drivers should then be installed onto the floppy disc. The PC should have been supplied with this driver software, together with instructions for using the installation programs. Once this has been done the PC should be rebooted, and it should then be possible to access the CD-ROM drive.

As explained previously, it is necessary to wipe everything from the hard disc if Windows and the applications programs are to be installed from scratch. The easiest way of achieving this is to reformat the hard disc. It will presumably be drive C: that will take the new installation, so this command would be used to format this disc:

format C:

It does not seem to be necessary to have the system files placed on the disc, and they are presumably added by the Windows Setup program during the installation process. The "/s" switch is therefore unnecessary, although adding it will not do any harm. Before formatting the disc the program will warn that all data on the disc will be lost. Only proceed if you are completely sure that all important data has been backed up properly.

Windows Setup

Once the mouse and CD-ROM drive have been installed it should be possible to run the Setup program on the Windows 95/98/ME installation disc. If the PC was booted using a Startup disc, this command is all that is needed:

setup

If the PC was booted using another boot-up disc the CD-ROM's drive letter must be specified in the command. For example, if the CD-ROM is drive D:, this command would be used:

D:\setup

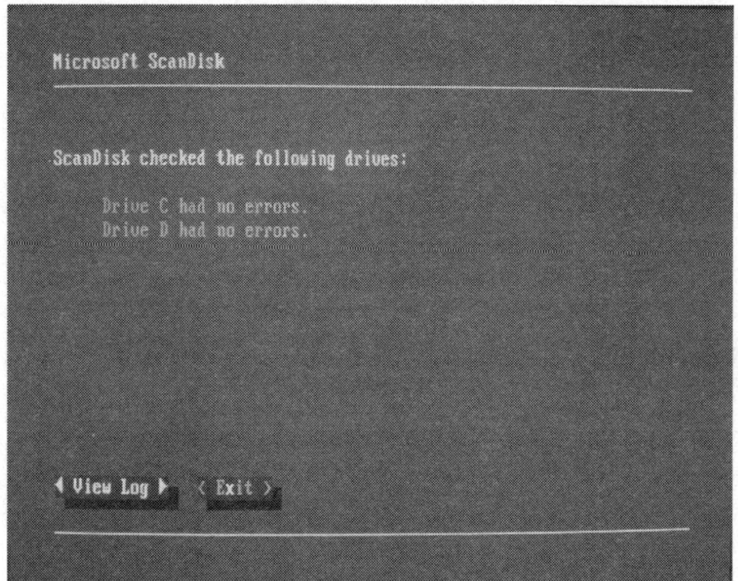

Fig.6.1 The MS/DOS version of Scandisk is run automatically as the initial stage of the Setup routine

After a welcome message on the screen the Scandisk utility will be run, and it will check for errors on the hard disc drives and any logical drives. Assuming all is well a screen like Figure 6.1 will appear. Press the "x" key to exit Scandisk and (if necessary) operate the Enter key to remove the onscreen message and go into the first screen of the Windows Setup program (Figure 6.2). It is then a matter of following the on-screen prompts to complete the Windows installation, providing the information that is requested, as described in the next section.

Note that you can install the upgrade version of Windows 95, 98 or ME onto a "clean" hard disc, and that it is not essential to load your old version of Windows first so that you have something to upgrade. However, during the installation process you will probably be asked to prove that you have a qualifying upgrade product by putting the Setup disc into the floppy drive or CD-ROM drive, as appropriate. Do not throw away or recycle your old Windows discs, as this could leave you unable to reinstall the Windows upgrade.

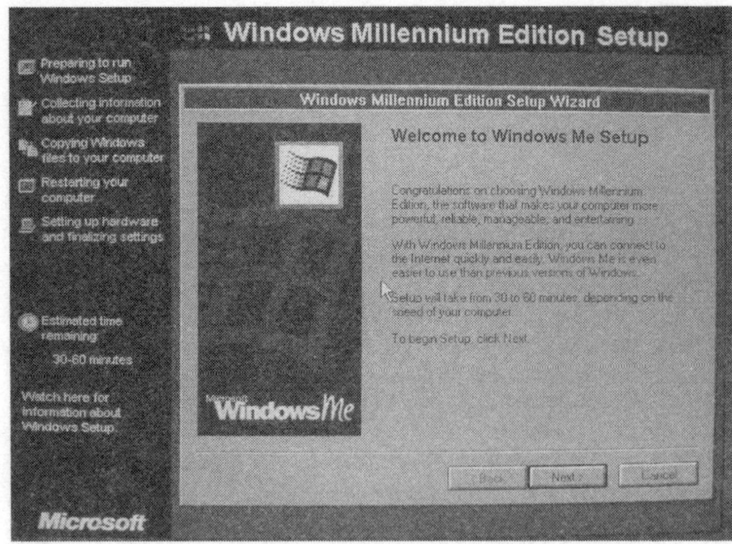

Fig.6.2 The Welcome screen of the Windows Setup program

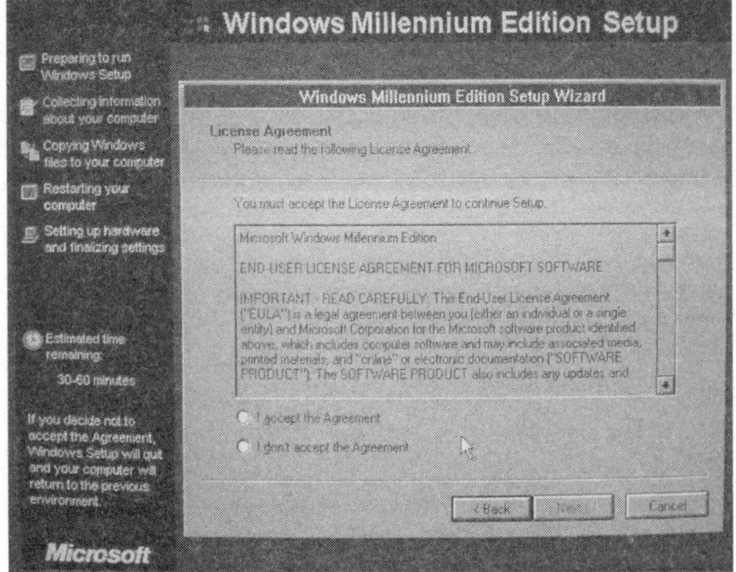

Fig.6.3 You must agree to the conditions in order to proceed

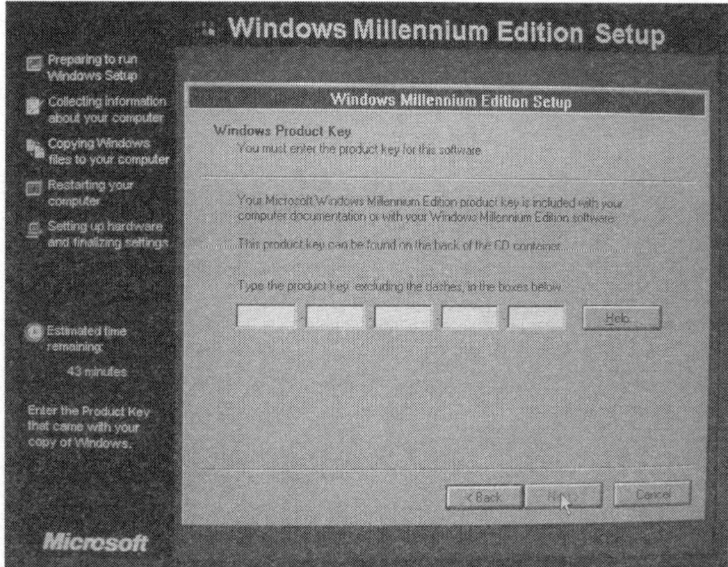

Fig.6.4 With an installation "from scratch" the product key is required

Installation

First you have to agree to the licensing conditions (Figure 6.3), and it is not possible to install Windows unless you do. At the next screen the Windows Product Key has to be entered (Figure 6.4). This code number will be found on the Windows certificate of authenticity and (or) on the back of the CD's jewel case. Next you are asked to select the directory into which Windows will be installed (Figure 6.5), but unless there is good reason to do otherwise, simply accept the default (C:\Windows). After some checking of the hard disc you are offered several installation options (Figure 6.6), but for most users the default option of a Typical installation will suffice.

Remember that you can add and delete Windows components once the operating system is installed, so you are not tied to the typical installation forever. The Custom option enables the user to select precisely the required components, but this can be time consuming and you need to know what you are doing. The Compact option is useful if hard disc space is limited, but with a new PC the hard disc will presumably be large enough to make this option superfluous. The

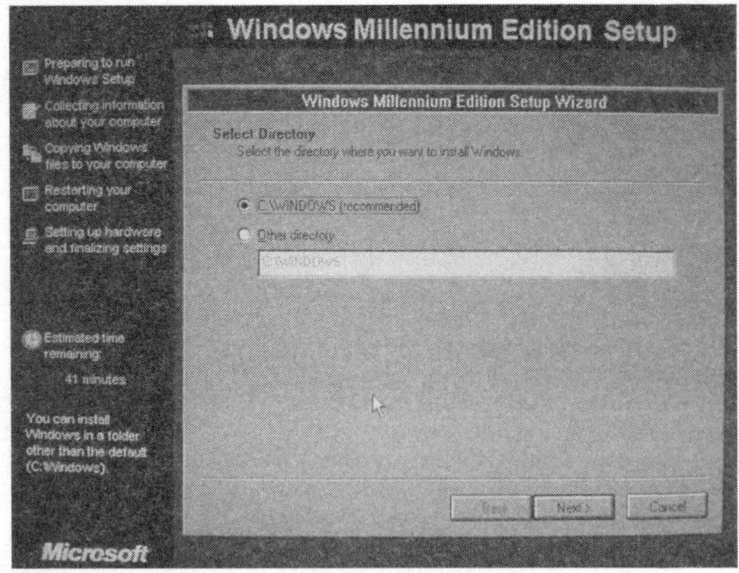

Fig.6.5 It is normally best to install Windows in the default folder

Portable option is optimised for portable PCs, and is the obvious choice if you are installing the system on a computer of this type.

At the next screen you type your name and company name into the dialogue boxes (Figure 6.7). If an individual owns the PC the box for the company name can be left blank. The purpose of the next screen (Figure 6.8) is to give you a chance to check the information entered so far, and to provide an opportunity to change your mind before moving on to the actual installation process. Operating the Next button may bring up a network identification screen (Figure 6.9). Where appropriate, make sure that this contains the correct information. In most cases the PC will not be used on a network, and the default settings can be used.

Next the appropriate country has to be selected from a list (Figure 6.10), and then the required time zone is selected (Figure 6.11). This screen also provides the option of automatically implementing daylight saving changes. The next screen (Figure 6.12) enables a Windows Startup disc to be produced. If you already have one of these you may prefer to skip this section by operating the Cancel button and then the OK button. Unfortunately, floppy discs are not the most reliable of storage mediums.

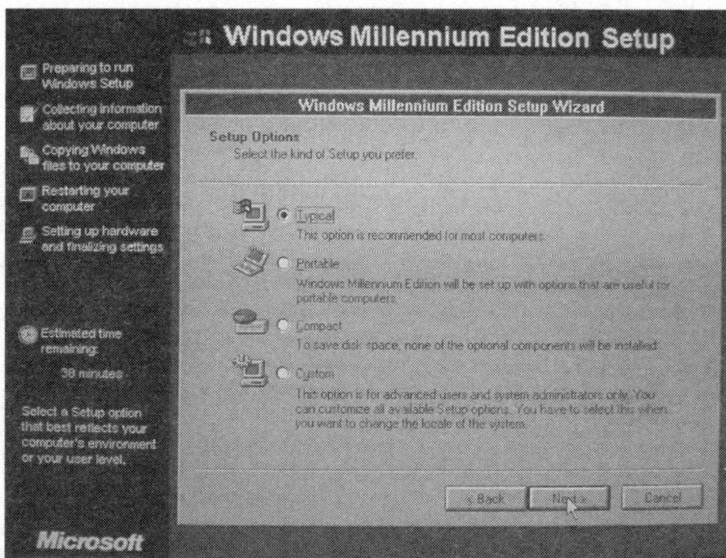

Fig.6.6 Four types of installation are available

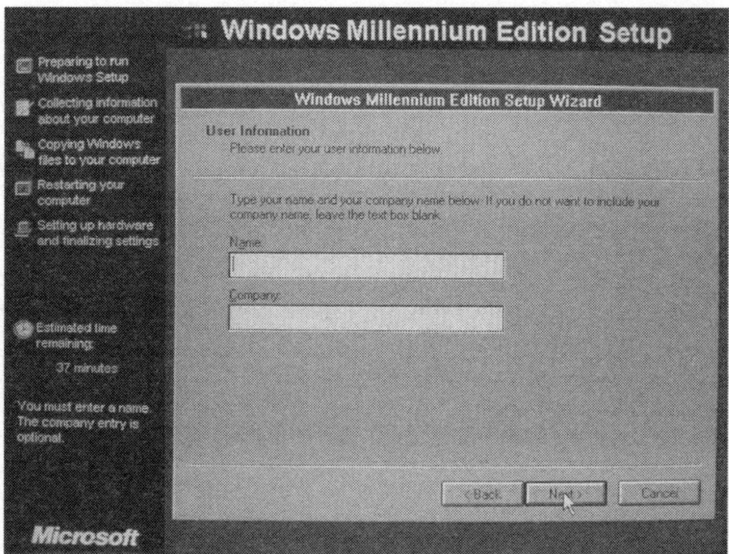

Fig.6.7 You must enter your name, but the company name is optional

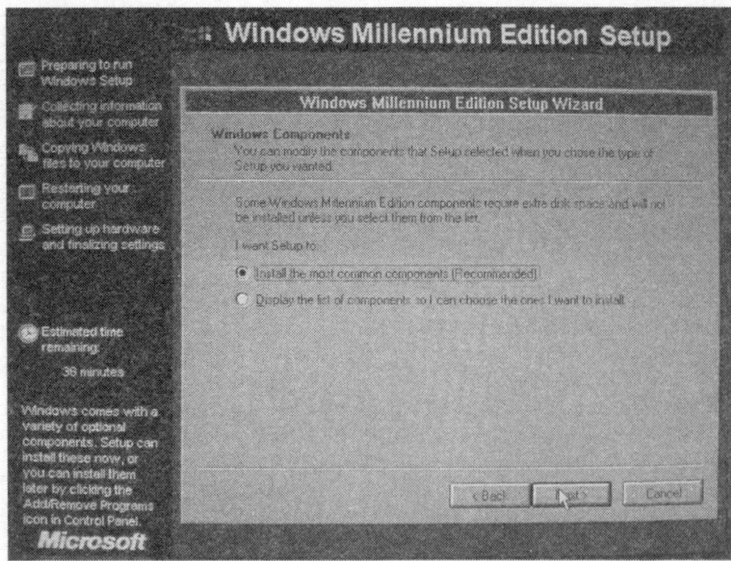

Fig.6.8 The "most common" components are normally sufficient

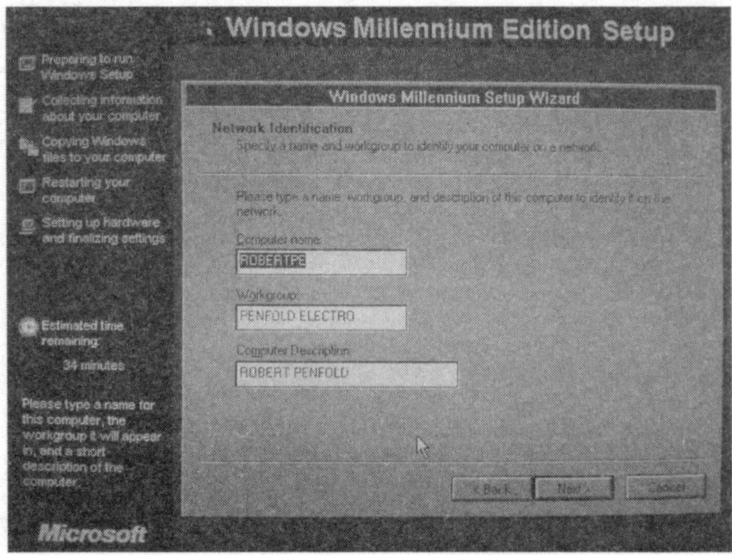

Fig.6.9 The network selection screen is not relevant to most users

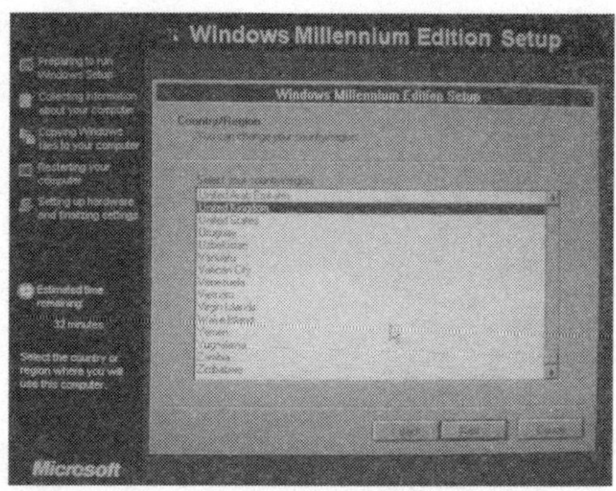

Fig.6.10 The country selection screen

If you only have one Startup disc already, I would suggest that you go ahead and make another one so that you have a standby copy.

If you are using an upgrade version of Windows there will be an additional section in the setting up procedure where you have to prove that you have a qualifying product to upgrade from. The screen of Figure 6.13 will appear, so that you can point the Setup program towards the disc that contains the earlier version of Windows. To do this you will have to remove the upgrade disc from the CD-ROM drive and replace it with the disc for the previous version of

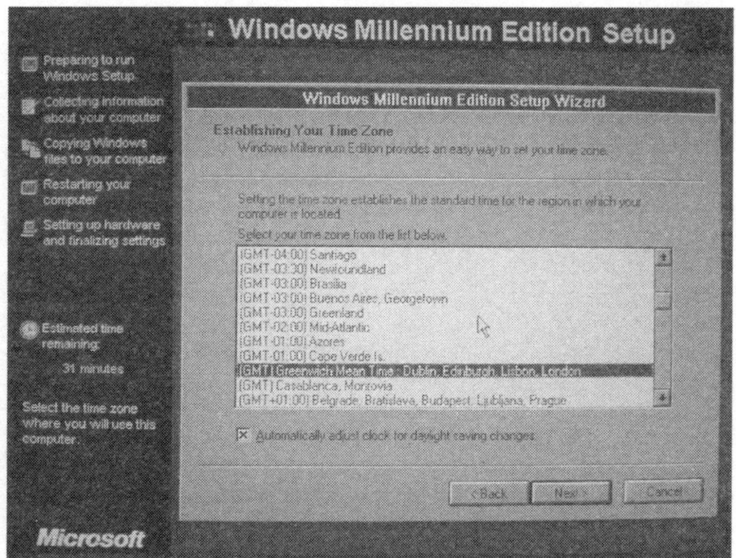

Fig.6.11 This screen is used to select the correct time zone

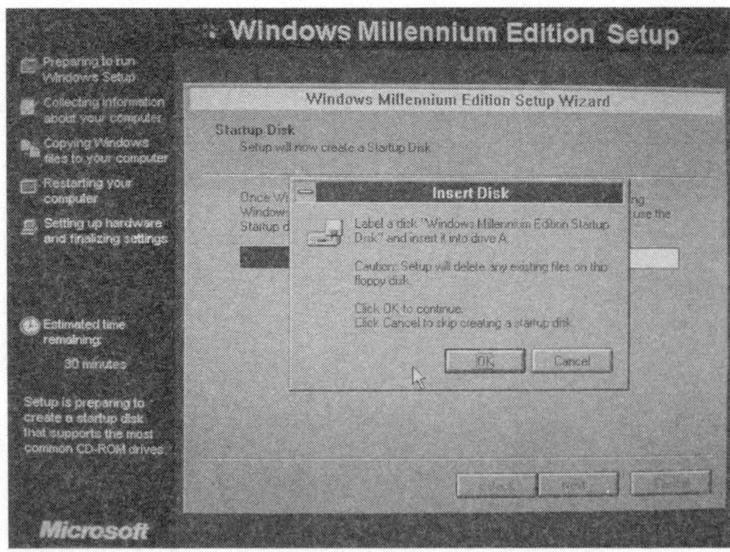

Fig.6.12 There is the option of making a Windows Startup disc

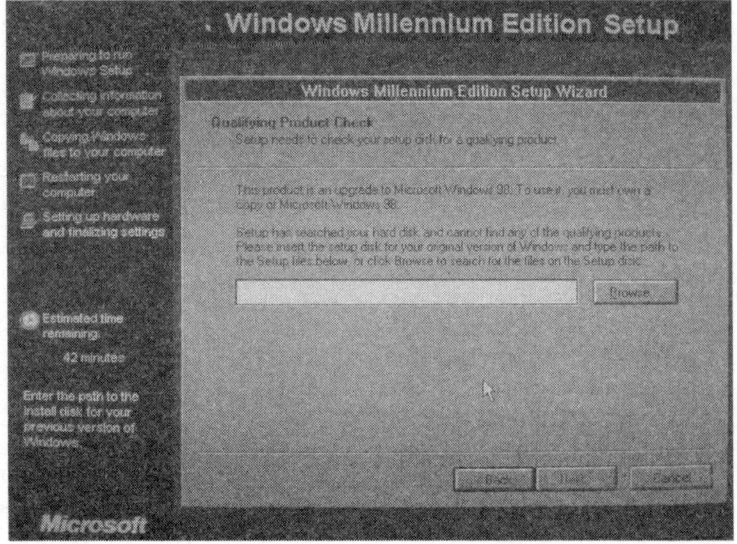

Fig.6.13 An upgrade product requires evidence of a previous version

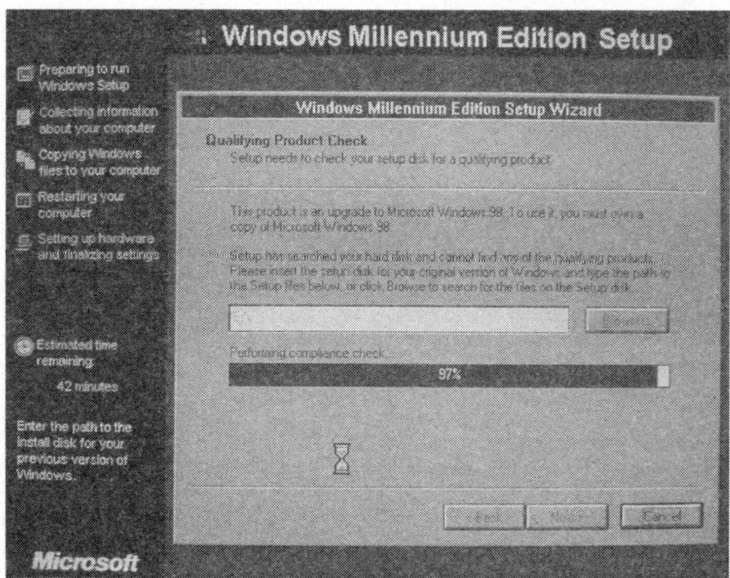

Fig.6.14 The bar shows how the (often slow) check is progressing

Windows. Then either type the path to the CD-ROM drive in the text box (e.g. E:\) or operate the Browse button and point to the appropriate drive in standard Windows fashion. Note that this stage will be passed over if you are reinstalling an upgrade version on top of an existing Windows installation.

Windows will find the existing installation and will deduce from this that you are a bona fide user.

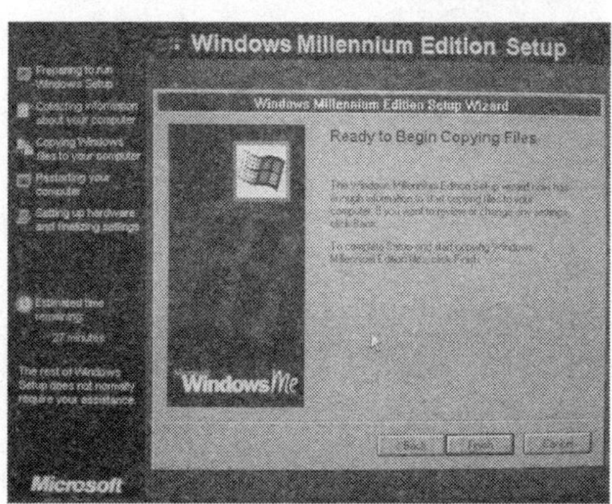

Fig.6.15 The main installation screen

Having completed all this you will have finally progressed to the main installation screen (Figure 6.15), and from thereon installation is largely automatic. A screen showing how the

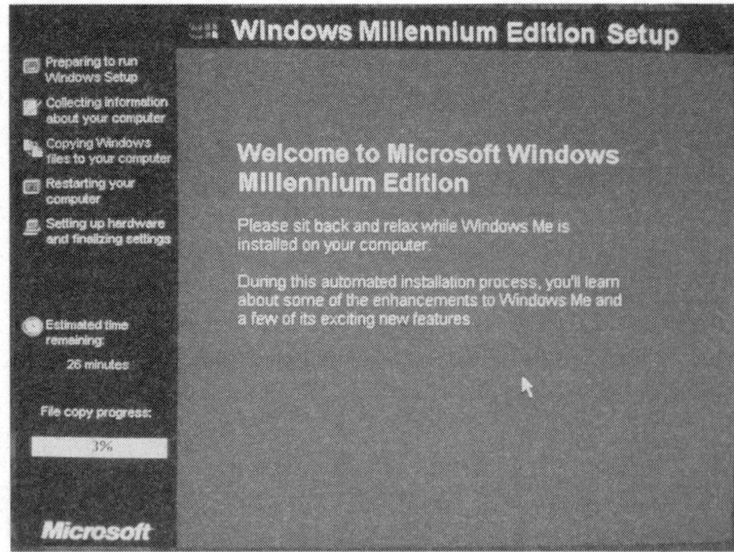

Fig.6.16 Eventually the installation begins

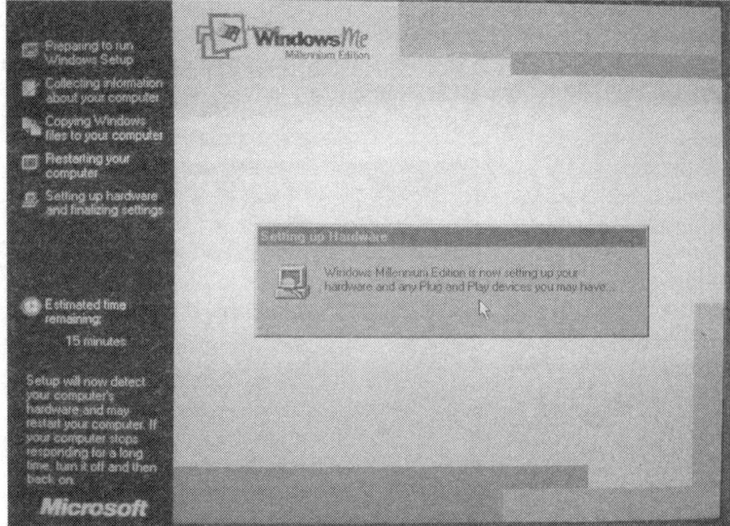

Fig.6.17 The Setup program keeps you informed of what it is doing

installation is progressing will appear (Figure 6.16). The computer will reboot itself two or three times during the installation process, so if you opted to produce a Windows Startup disc during the initial set-up procedure remember to remove this from the floppy drive. Otherwise the computer might reboot from the floppy rather than the hard disc, which would interfere with the installation process. In the later stages of the installation there will further screens telling you what the computer is doing, and giving an indication of how far things have progressed (Figure 6.17). No input is required from the user during all this, so you can let the computer get on with the installation. The one exception is that near the end of the installation process you will be asked to supply a user name and password (Figure 6.18). Simply leave the password text box blank if you do not require password protection. Eventually you should end up with a basic Windows installation, and the familiar initial screen (Figure 6.19).

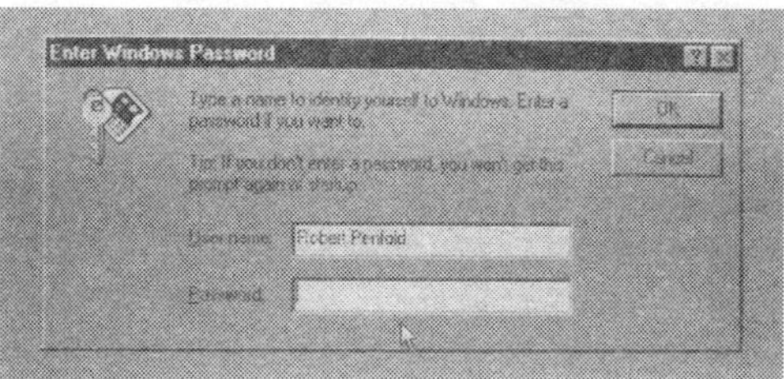

Fig.6.18 The password is optional

Sometimes the Windows Setup program comes to a halt. Either the computer shows no signs of any disc activity for some time, or there may be repeated disc activity with the installation failing to make any progress. The usual cure is to switch off the computer, wait a few seconds, and then switch on again. The Setup program will usually detect that there was a problem, and will avoid making the same mistake again. If the computer is switched on and off on several occasions, but

Fig.6.19 With installation complete, the familiar Windows screen appears

the installation still fails to complete, it will be necessary to reboot using the Startup disc, wipe the hard disc clean, and try again. If Windows repeatedly refuses to install it is likely that the PC has a hardware fault.

Hardware drivers

There will probably still be a certain amount of work to be done in order to get all the hardware fully installed, the required screen resolution set, and so on. Windows 95/98/ME might have built-in support for all the hardware in your PC such as the sound and video cards, but this is unlikely. In order to get everything installed correctly you will probably require the installation discs provided with the various items of hardware used in the PC. These discs may be required during the installation of Windows 95/98/ME, or they may have to be used after the basic installation has been completed. The instruction manuals provided with the hardware should explain the options available and provide precise installation instructions.

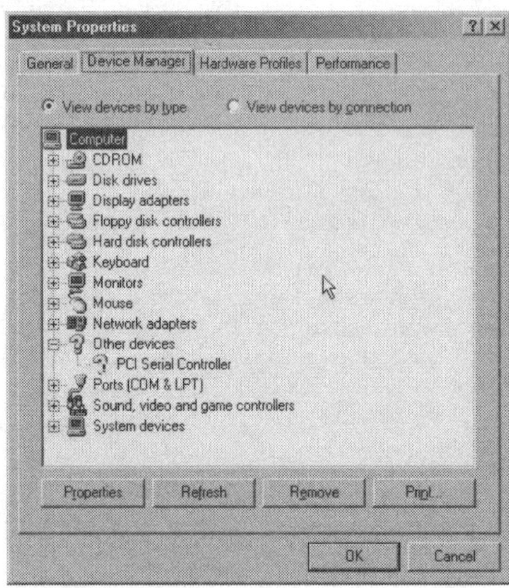

Fig.6.20 Use Device Manager to check for hardware problems

These days even the motherboards seem to come complete with driver software for things such as special chipset features and the hard disc interface. It is once again a matter of reading the instruction manual to determine which drivers have to be installed, and how to go about it. Get all the hardware properly installed before you install the applications software. It is best to start with the drivers for hardware on the motherboard. Next the video drivers are installed and then any additional drivers for a soundcard, ports, or whatever.

Once everything is supposedly installed correctly it is a good idea to go into the Control Panel program and double-click the System icon. Then select the Device Manager tab to bring up a window of the type shown in Figure 6.20. Look down the various entries to check for any problems. These are indicated by yellow exclamation marks, or possibly by yellow question marks. Certain items of hardware will not be picked up properly by Windows, and some types of modem fall into this category. The question mark in Figure 6.20 is caused by a Windows modem that the system is unable to sort out on its own. A Windows modem uses relatively simple hardware plus software in the computer to provide the encoding and decoding. Unlike a conventional modem, a Windows modem does not interface to the computer via a true serial port. It is interfaced via a sort of pseudo serial port, and it is this factor that makes it difficult to correctly identify the hardware.

If a problem is indicated, or an item of hardware is missing from the list, it will be necessary to load the drivers for the hardware concerned in order to get things working properly. This would be a good time to search the relevant web sites for updated driver software for the hardware in your PC. You may well find some newer and better drivers for the hardware in your PC. The hardware can be integrated into Windows using the Add New Hardware facility in the Control Panel. However, many items of PC hardware do not take the standard Windows route and have special installation programs instead. Read the installation manuals carefully and use the exact methods described therein.

Awkward hardware

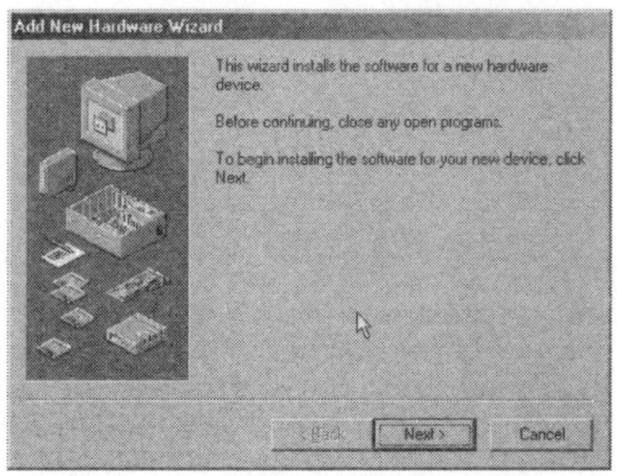

Fig.6.21 The initial Add New Hardware screen

Any awkward hardware will have to be added via the Add New Hardware facility without utilizing the Windows hardware detection facility. First Windows tries to detect Plug and Play devices, and then it can try to find non-Plug and Play

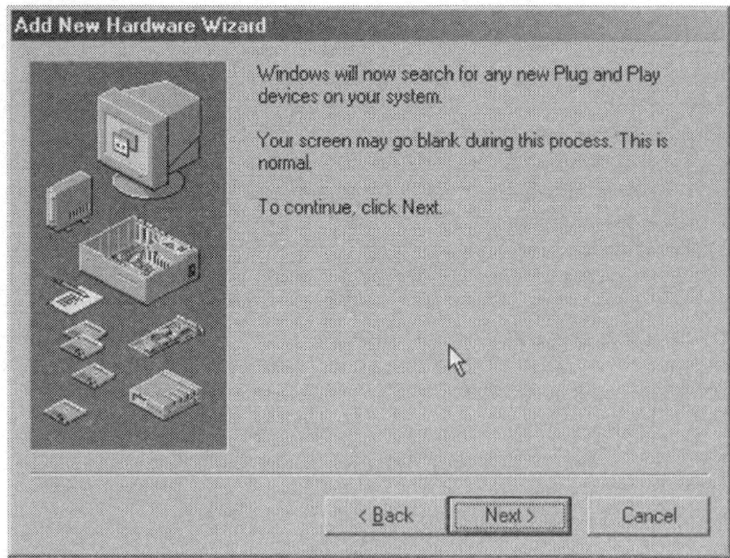

Fig.6.22 A search for Plug and Play devices is made first

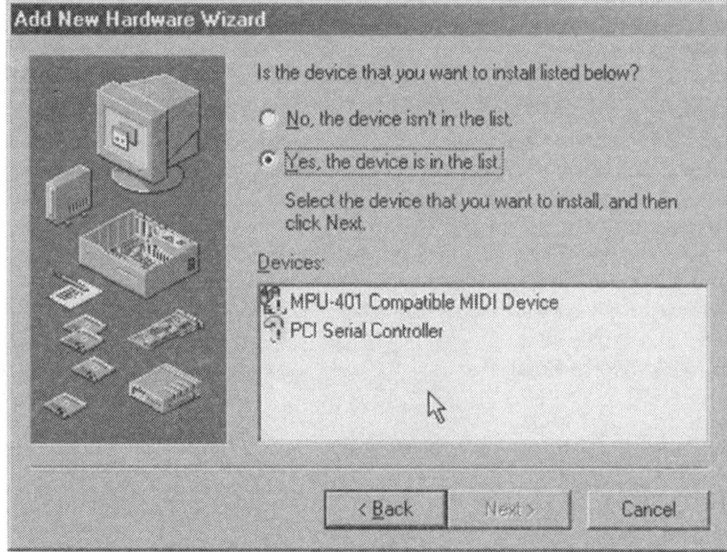

Fig.6.23 Any Plug and Play devices that are found are listed

hardware. Failing that, the new hardware has to be installed manually using the drivers disc or discs provided with the item of hardware. The process is slightly different depending on the version of Windows you are using, but the basic process is the same with all three versions. Here we will consider the Windows ME version.

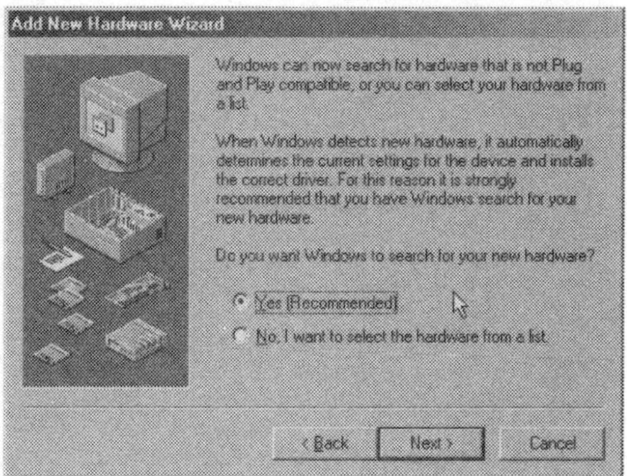

Fig.6.24 A search can be made for more Plug and Play devices

The opening screen of Figure 6.21 appears when the Add New Hardware program is run. Heed the warning and close any programs that are running before proceeding further. To continue left-click on the Next button, which will bring up a screen like the one in Figure 6.22. This informs you that the program will look for Plug and Play devices connected to the system, and not to panic if the screen goes blank for a time. Press the Next button to proceed with the search. Eventually you will get a screen something like the one in Figure 6.23, complete with a list of any Plug and Play devices that have been found. If the device you wish to install is in the list, leave the Yes radio button checked, left-click on the device you wish to install, and then operate the Next button to proceed with the installation.

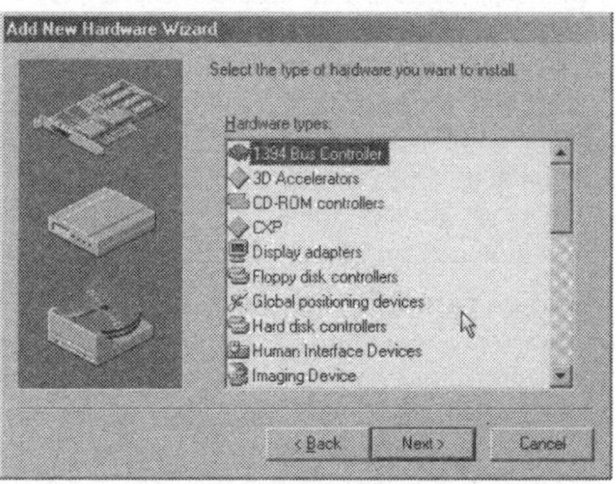

Fig.6.25 This screen enables the type of device to be selected manually

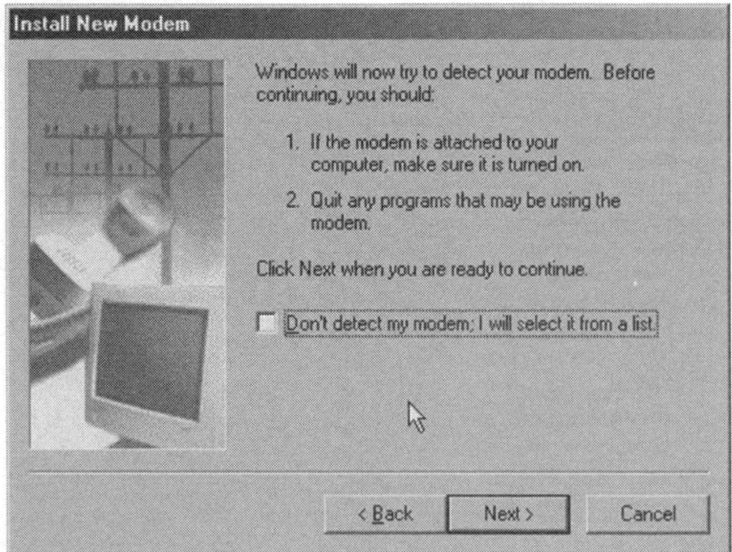

Fig.6.26 Even at this stage, automatic detection is still possible

Any non-Plug and Play devices will not be in the list, and it is then a matter of checking the No radio button and operating the Next button. This brings up the window of Figure 6.24, which provides the option of having the program search for the hardware you wish to install. There is no harm in letting the program search for the hardware, although this can be quite time consuming. It is likely that a standard item of hardware such as an additional serial or parallel port will be detected, but it is by no means certain that anything exotic will be located.

If you decide not to opt for automatic detection, check the No radio button and operate the Next button. This produces the window of Figure 6.25 where you can select the appropriate category for the hardware you are installing. A wide variety of devices are covered, with more available under the "Other" category. In this example the modem category was selected, and operating the Next button moved things on to the window of Figure 6.26. Here you are once again offered the option of automatic detection, but this does not work properly with most "soft" modems, so the No button was checked and the Next button was operated.

If you opt for manual selection you will eventually be shown a window containing a list of devices, as in Figure 6.27. The right device might

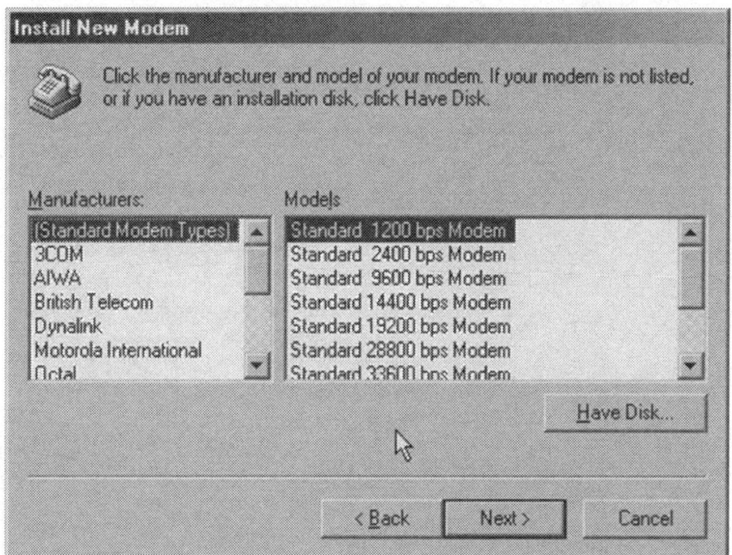

Fig.6.27 The Have Disk option is used if you have a drivers disc

appear in the list, but with recent hardware or generic devices you will probably be out of luck. It is then a matter of selecting the Have Disk option, which brings up a file browser so that you can direct the program to the correct disc drive, and where appropriate, the correct folder of the disc in that drive. With the drivers installed the computer will probably have to be rebooted before the hardware will operate properly.

Screen settings

Once the video card has been installed properly the required screen parameters can be set. To alter the screen resolution and colour depth, go to the Windows Control Panel and double-click on the Display icon. Then left-click on the Settings tab to bring up a screen of the type shown in Figure 6.28. It is then just a matter of using the onscreen controls to set the required screen resolution and colour depth. To use the new settings left-click the Apply button. It may be necessary to let the computer reboot in order to use the new settings, but in most cases they can be applied without doing this. Instead Windows will apply the new settings for a few seconds so that you can see that all is well. Simply left-click on the Yes button to start using the new screen settings.

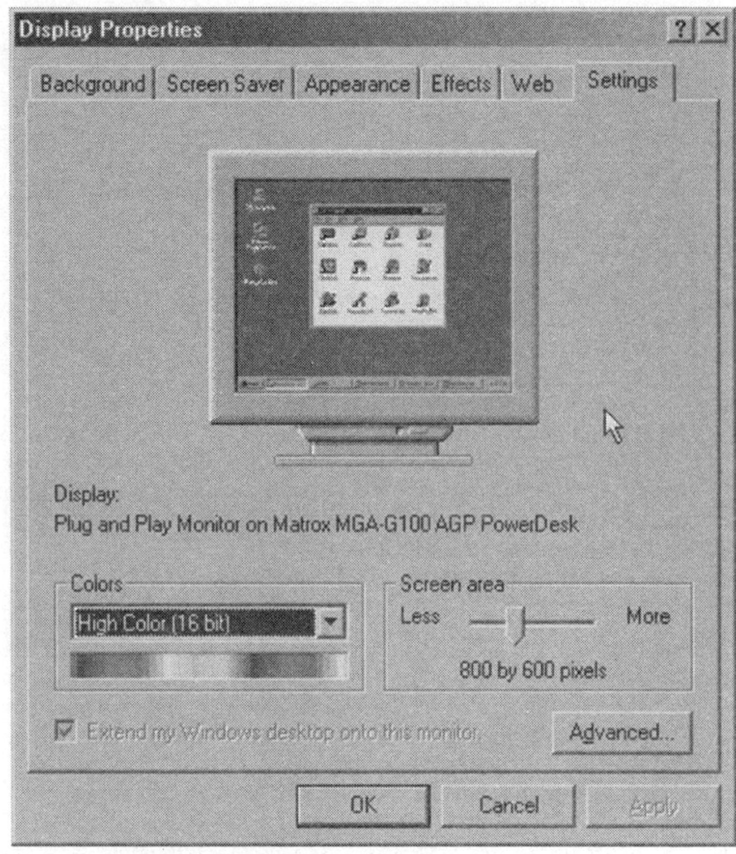

Fig.6.28 The Display Properties screen is used to set screen resolution, colour depth, etc.

If there is a problem with the picture stability do nothing, and things should return to the original settings after a few seconds. This should not really happen if the monitor is installed correctly, because Windows will not try to use scan rates that are beyond the capabilities of the installed monitor. If a problem of this type should occur, check that the monitor is installed properly. In the Display window of Control Panel select Settings, Advanced, and then Monitor. This will bring up a screen like Figure 6.29, which shows the type of monitor that is installed.

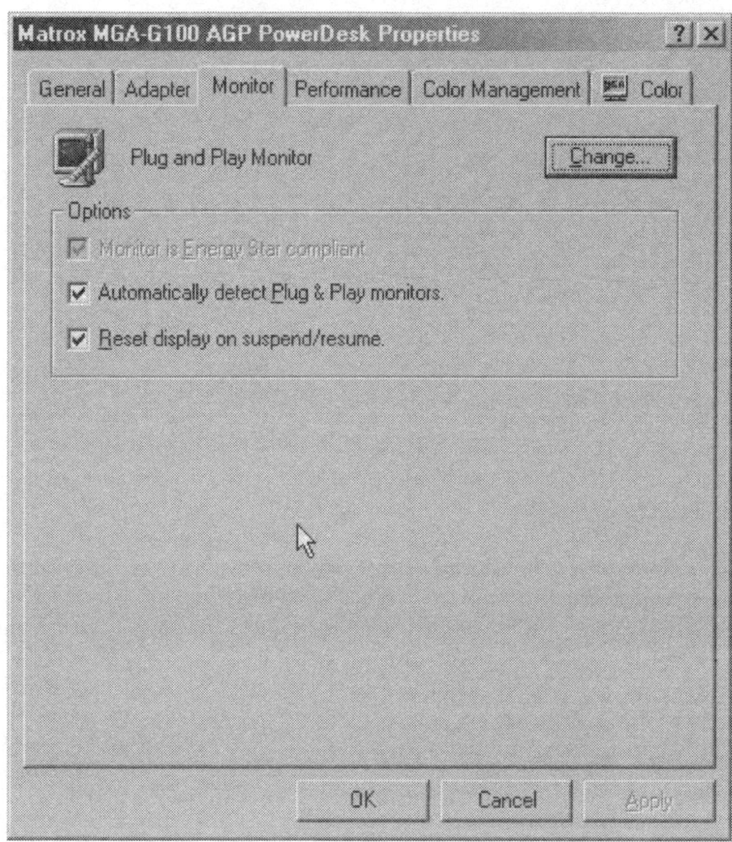

Fig.6.29 If there is screen instability, check that the right monitor is installed

If the installed monitor is not the correct one, or is just one of the generic monitor types, left-click the Change button and select the correct one. If the picture is stable with the new settings but the size and position are completely wrong, there is probably no problem. It should be possible to position and size the picture correctly using the monitor's controls. Many graphics cards are supplied with utility software that helps to get the best possible display from the system, and it is worth trying any software of this type to see if it gives better results.

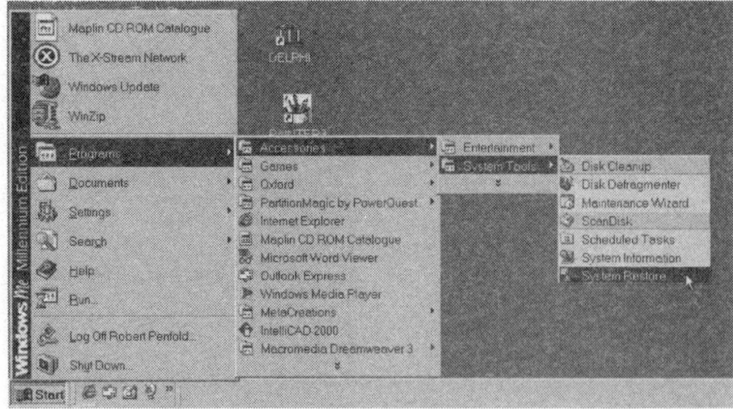

Fig.6.30 The System Restore program is deep in the menu structure

Disc-free ME

It has been assumed in this chapter that you have a Windows installation CD-ROM. Some computers are supplied with Windows ME pre-installed, and they do not come complete with a Windows installation CD-ROM. Instead, the hard disc has two partitions with drive C: acting as the main disc and a much smaller drive D: containing the Windows files. There is usually a CD-ROM that can be used to recover the situation in the event of a hard disc failure, but this is not an ordinary Windows installation disc. With a computer of this type it is necessary to resort to the instruction manual for details of reinstalling Windows.

Manufacturers are able to customise the installation software to suit their PCs and any software bundled with them. Consequently there are differences in the installation procedures, but there should be a quick and easy way of getting back to a basic Windows installation. In fact some manufacturers provide a quick means of getting back to the factory settings. in other words, the computer will have Windows installed and set up correctly for the hardware installed at the factory. Of course, if you have changed the hardware configuration of the PC, it will be necessary to install the drivers for the new items of hardware.

System Restore

The System Restore facility of Windows XP was described in the previous chapter. This effectively winds the operating system back to the system

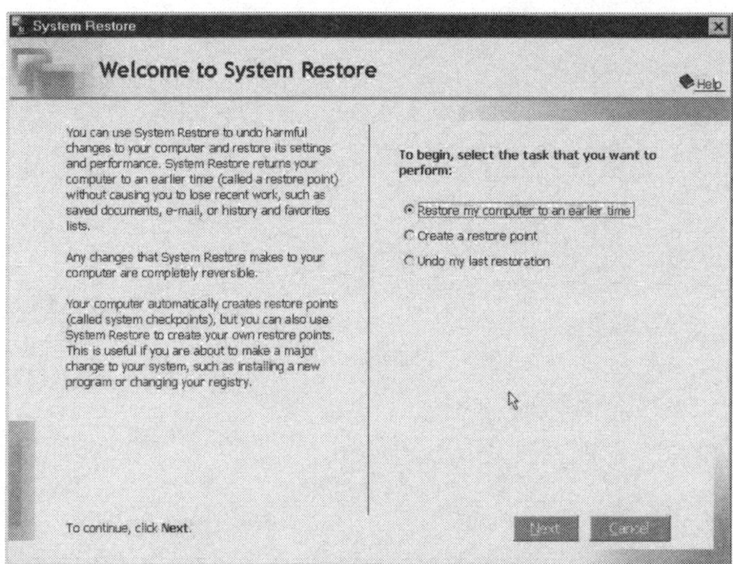

Fig.6.31 The welcome screen of the System Restore program

settings of an earlier date where the PC functioned properly. Hopefully, this leaves the data and configuration files intact and the PC working much as it did before. Any programs installed after the restoration point have to be reinstalled, and any changes made to the system have to be reinstated. As pointed out previously, a system that has been badly damaged by a virus can not always be fixed using this method, but there is no harm in trying. Obviously the virus must be completely removed from the system first.

For users of Windows 95 and 98 there is, unfortunately, no System Restore facility available. Windows ME has a facility that is essentially the same as the Windows XP equivalent, with a few differences in points of detail. The System Restore program is buried deep in the menu structure (Figure 6.30), but it can be started by going to the Start menu and then selecting Programs, Accessories, System Tools, and System Restore. Like the Windows XP version, the program is controlled via a Wizard, so when it is run you get the screen of Figure 6.31 and not a conventional Windows style interface. The radio buttons give three options, which are to go back to a restoration point, create a new one, or undo the last restoration. When the program is run for the first time there is no restoration to undo, so this option will not be present.

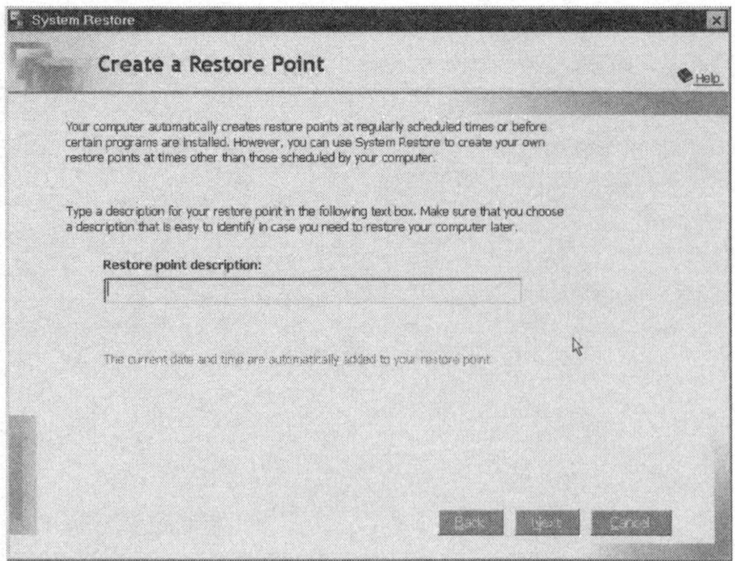

Fig.6.32 The system creates restore points, but you can add your own

As pointed out previously the system will automatically create restoration points from time to time, but you will probably wish to create your own before doing anything that will make large changes to the system. Start by selecting the "Create a restore point" option and then operate the Next button. The next screen (Figure 6.32) asks the user to provide a name for the restore point, and it is helpful if the name is something that will be meaningful. There is no need to bother about including a date, as the program automatically records the date and time for you. There will be a delay of at least several seconds when the Next button is pressed, and then a screen like the one shown in Figure 6.33 will appear. This gives you a chance to check that everything is correct before the restoration point is created. If everything is all right, operate the OK button to create the restoration point and terminate the program.

To go back to a restoration point, run the program as before, and select the Return my computer to an earlier time option. Operate the Next button, and after a short delay a screen like the one of Figure 6.34 will appear. If there are a number of restore points available you can use the arrow heads in the calendar to find the one you require. The dates on the calendar in larger text are the ones that have restore points. Left-clicking on one of these will show the available points in the screen area

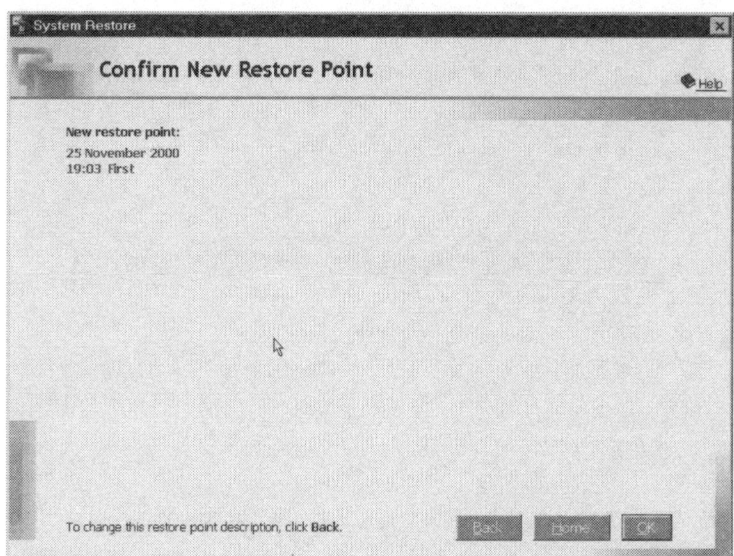

Fig.6.33 This screen gives you a chance to check your selections

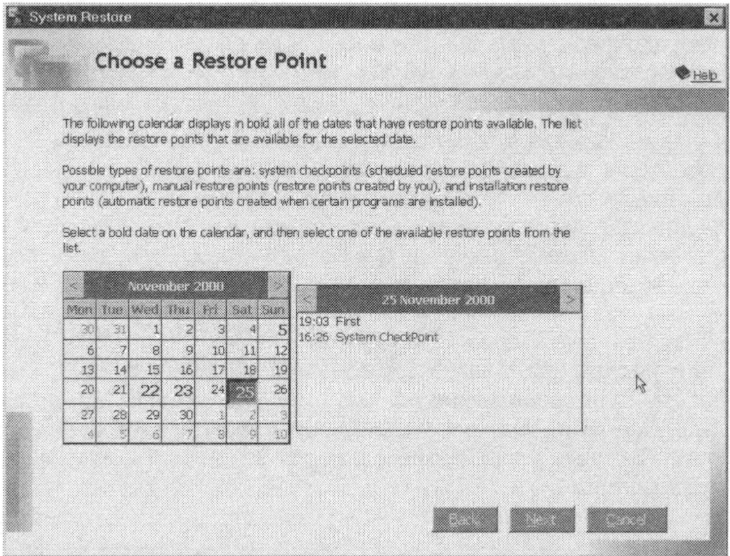

Fig.6.34 Choosing a restore point

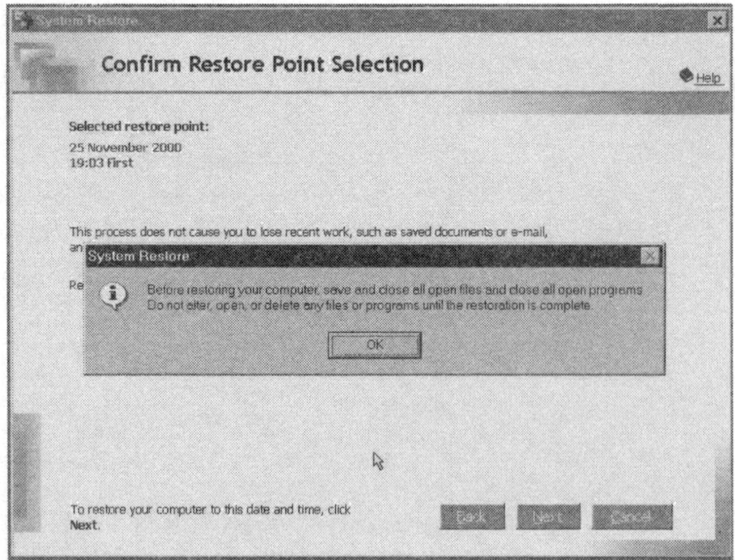

Fig.6.35 A warning message gives you a chance to change your mind

just to the right of the calendar. Left-click on the required restoration point and then operate the Next button. This brings up a screen and warning message, like Figure 6.35. Left-click the OK button to remove the warning message, and close any programs that are running.

If you are satisfied that the correct restore point has been selected, operate the Next button and the program will begin the restoration process. A screen showing how things are progressing will appear (Figure 6.36). Heed the warning on this screen, and do not do anything that will alter, open or delete any files while the program is running. Just sit back and do not touch the computer until the program has finished its task. Once the restoration has been completed the computer will reboot, and a message will appear on the screen (Figure 6.37). This confirms the point to which the computer has been returned, and indicates the options if the PC fails to operate properly using this restoration point. Left-click the OK button to finish the boot process, and the computer should then have shifted back in time to the appropriate restoration point.

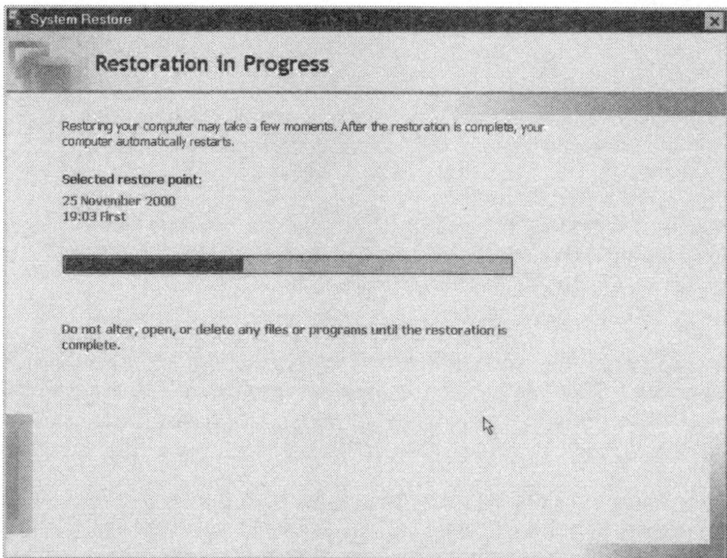

Fig.6.36 You can see how the restoration process is proceeding

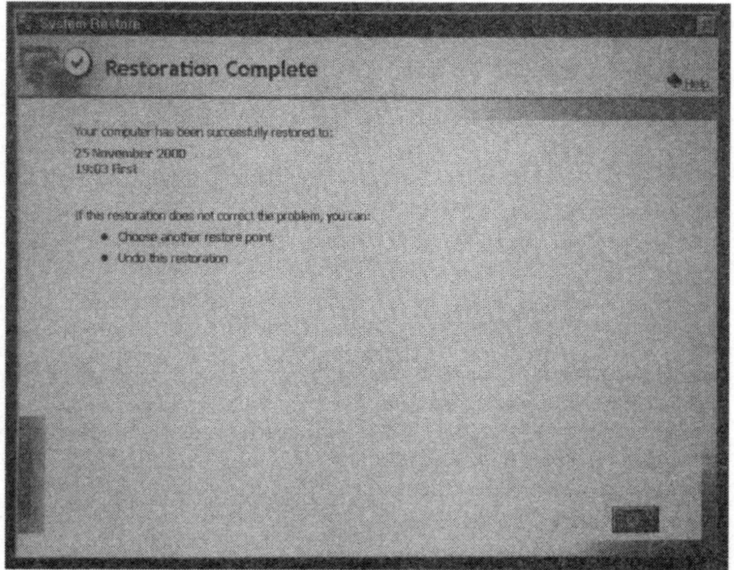

Fig.6.37 This message appears after the computer has rebooted

Points to remember

Installing Windows on top of an existing version might cure problems with the operating system, but it is not guaranteed to do so.

Installing Windows "from scratch", with all the previous files removed from the hard disc should effect a cure to any Windows problems. If it does not, the computer probably has a hardware fault.

You can erase the existing Windows folder structure and then reinstall Windows. This will usually remove any problems with the original installation, but all the applications software will still have to be reinstalled.

Everything but data files can be erased from the hard disc prior to reinstalling Windows. Unless you are very unlucky, this will give a fully working Windows installation and your data files will remain intact. This method is worth trying if you have no way of backing up the data files.

Whether reinstalling Windows over an existing installation or "from scratch" it is advisable to boot from a Windows Startup disc, opting for CD-ROM support.

The basic installation process is largely automatic. The user provides some basic information and then the Setup program installs the Windows files and sets up the essential hardware. Some further installation is then required to get all the hardware properly installed, the screen resolution and colour depth set correctly, etc.

Not all hardware can be installed with the aid of the automatic detection facilities. Manual installation of hardware drivers is not difficult, but where appropriate, make sure that items of hardware are supplied complete with a disc or discs containing the driver software. Some hardware has its own installation routines and does not go through the normal Windows routes. Always install hardware in accordance with the manufacturer's instructions.

PCs that are supplied with Windows ME preinstalled are not necessarily supplied with a normal Windows installation disc. Windows then has to be installed in accordance with the computer manufacturer's instructions. The exact method of reinstallation varies somewhat from one manufacturer to another.

Windows ME has the System Restore facility, but it is not a feature of Windows 98 or 95.

7

Email and encryption

Spam

Some say that the term "spam" is a contraction of "spurious advertising material", but the more generally accepted explanation is that it is derived from a Monty Python sketch. If you have an Email address then it is odds on that you receive at least a small amount of spam. It is quite likely that you receive large amounts of it every day. In fact spam now accounts for more than half the Emails sent, and spam is still on the increase. This has sparked very real fears that the Email system or even the Internet as a whole could eventually be brought to a virtual standstill by the sheer volume of junk Emails.

It would perhaps be a good idea to define exactly what is meant by spam, since this term does not really cover every type of advert sent via Email. Some people do interpret it this way, but this is a mistake. If you deal with companies via Email, advertising Emails they send you will probably not count as spam. It is likely you will have agreed to accept Email promotional material from these companies, and it is therefore perfectly acceptable for them to send you this type of material via an Email. On the day I am writing this piece the EU law has changed and it is now illegal to send spam from within EU countries unless the recipient has given consent. Unless you are dealing with companies outside the EU it is therefore an offence for them to send you spam unless you have specifically opted to receive it. It is no longer acceptable for an EU based company to send spam because you have not opt out of receiving spam from them.

Most of the spam received by a typical Email account is the real thing, and it is unsolicited material from companies the account holder has never dealt with. The larger Email account providers such as Hotmail and Yahoo! have systems that try to block the more obvious batches of spam. In the past it was common for spammers to send their material to a range of Email addresses, trying every possible address in that range. Of course, most of the names did not match up with an account at Hotmail, Yahoo!, or whatever provider was under attack. Some would match an actual account though, and the cheapness of mass Emailing is such that the small percentage of successes made the enterprise worthwhile. These days the Email companies have systems that soon block this sort of thing and block further Emails from that source.

Other methods are used in an attempt to filter junk Emails. If an address is used to send Emails it is likely that it will soon be put on a blacklist and blocked. This makes life difficult for the spammers, but it does not halt their activities. Spam is often sent via a hijacked system. Before too long the owner of the system will notice the attack and take counter measures, or the hijacked address will be blocked by the Email companies. The spammer then moves on to another system, and so it goes on.

A variation on the hijacked system is to use a spoof Email program together with either a genuine or fictitious "from" address on the junk Emails. The idea is for the program generating the spoof Emails to make it appear as though they are coming from another source. Usually the Email addresses used as the source are not genuine, but occasionally the address used is real. This is probably by accident rather than design, but it is unfortunate for the owner of the Email address. They often get large numbers of complaints about spam that they have not actually sent. Apparently some users have abandoned Email addresses due to this problem. The advantage of this system for the spammers is that it is very easy to switch from one dummy source address to another, making it more difficult for automatic filtering to deal with the junk Emails produced.

Another technique used for filtering spam is to look for a particular set of words in the title of Emails. Junk Emails tend to promote a relatively limited range of products, such as get rich quick schemes, devices or drugs to make bits of your body get bigger, pornographic web sites, and medicines without a prescription. The same words therefore tend to turn up in the title fields of the junk Emails, and the filtering systems search for them. The spammers answer to this is to deliberately misspell words or use extra spaces so that "sex" could appear as "s e x" for example. Another ploy is to use odd terminology. This might get the spam through automatic filtering systems, but it does at least make the junk Emails easier for recipients to spot.

Spam senders are aware that most people will scan the contents of their Inbox in an attempt to identify the junk Emails so that they can be deleted without ever opening them. Many spammers now try to make it more difficult to spot junk Emails from their titles by using something totally misleading. Here are a few typical examples:

Re Reservation #12398965

Re your recent order

Re I have still not had a reply

Re Your In Box has reached its size limit

Re Here is the information you requested

Re Returned mail – user unknown

Of course, in most cases you do not have to look too hard to see that the Email is of the junk variety. It is quite likely you will not have made a reservation, placed an order, and so on. Also, the "from" address will probably not be that of a company you deal with. However, this type of spam is more difficult to spot and probably a significant proportion of the recipients open them. In order to make these junk Emails look more authentic, some spammers use false "from" addresses that look very similar to the Email address of a large and well know company. In some cases the actual address of the company is used.

Getting addresses

As already pointed out, most Email account suppliers have largely blocked the system of sending Emails to a large number of addresses in the hope that some of them actually exist. Therefore, spammers need large numbers of valid Email addresses in order to make their systems work. Sophisticated techniques are used to trawl the Internet for Email addresses that appear on web pages, so having your Email address on a web page more or less guarantees that you will receive plenty of spam. Usenet newsgroup postings are another source.

If you deal with respectable companies they will have agreed to respect your privacy and not pass on your Email address to other companies. Some, provided you agree, will pass your Email address to other companies that are offering goods or services that are likely to be of interest to you. Letting them do this is a bit dubious, because it is possible that the companies they sell your address to will in turn pass it on to others. In theory this should not happen, but in practice you can find your Email address being passed along a chain of companies.

Giving your Email address to a company that is not well known to you is definitely not a good idea. Most companies will not pass your Email address on to others, but some will certainly do so. Some freebies on the Internet are probably put there specifically to gather Email addresses for spamming purposes. The way to "have your cake and eat it" is to have a main Email address that is used as your main address plus a second account that is used only for free offers and the like.

If you should find the second Email address is getting bombarded with spam it will not really matter, since it is not used for normal personal business contacts. Periodically clearing the accumulated Emails should not take long. It is easy to set up free Email accounts with the main providers, so if one dummy account becomes unusable you can always close it and open another one. You can give a company your proper Email address should you decide that they are trustworthy.

Blocking

As explained previously, many Email account providers use a certain amount of built-in blocking in an attempt to reduce the amount of spam reaching their client's Inboxes. Checking the title field or other parts of an Email for certain words or phrases is known as content blocking or content filtering. It is not very effective in practice. As already pointed out, many spammers use deliberate misspellings to circumvent this type of filtering. The other problem is that taking this type of filtering to the point where it is effective at filtering spam is likely to result in many legitimate Emails being blocked as well.

The main weapon against spam at present is address blocking, where the Email companies have lists of addresses that are used as the sources for junk Emails. Any Email traffic from these addresses is blocked. This method can block many Emails, but it will never be totally effective because those compiling the lists of banned addresses are inevitably one step behind those sending out the spam. An address must be used to send out at least one batch of spam before it can be detected and added to the blacklist. The spammer can then switch to a new address. Some spam is blocked and the blacklists make life difficult for those sending junk Emails, but this method can never block all spam.

Some Email companies provide their clients with customisable blocking facilities. This type of thing is likely to have limited effectiveness against spam in general, but it can be totally effective in combating the same old junk mails turning up in your Inbox time and time again. The obvious form of filtering to use with persistent junk mail is to simply filter its source address. As pointed out previously, spam often originates from dummy addresses that are changed frequently, so blocking an address might not block further occurrences of the same Email. This system can be very effective in cases where a company keeps sending you details of their latest special offers (or whatever) despite your repeated requests for them to desist. They will presumably send the Emails from their legitimate address, and blocking this address will therefore stop the junk Emails from finding their way into your Inbox.

Some Email companies permit a degree of content filtering. This is again something that can be useful for combating persistent spam, particularly if it has the same or largely the same wording. For example, a while ago I had problems with a company selling off the shelf university degrees that seemed to Email me at least twice per day and three times per day at weekends. The title field of the email always contained the word "diploma", so I was able to halt the flow of Emails from this source by setting up the Email system to filter any Email with this word in the title. Obviously some persistent spam will not be this obliging, but it is a useful system in those cases where it can be applied with at least partial success.

Setting up

The spam and general facilities on offer vary from one Email system to another. With the popular Yahoo! Email service the Mail Options link takes you to a page where various facilities can be accessed (Figure 7.1). The Spam Protection link is the obvious starting point, and this takes you to the page shown in Figure 7.2. Yahoo! has a facility that it calls Spam Guard, and its basic function is to look for what are likely to be junk Emails. Any that the system finds are placed in the Bulk folder. They will be deleted after 30 days unless you move them or delete them first. The first page enables the Spam Guard function to be switched on or off.

The checkboxes near the bottom of the page provide a couple of options. One of these automatically adds the sender's Email address to your blocked list when you mark an Email as spam. As pointed out previously, spammers tend to change the sender's address quite often, so using this facility might just produce a large but ineffective list of blocked addresses. Using it will not do any harm though. The second option automatically moves a message to your Inbox if you mark it as not being spam. This saves you the bother of having to move it manually, so it is probably as well to tick this checkbox.

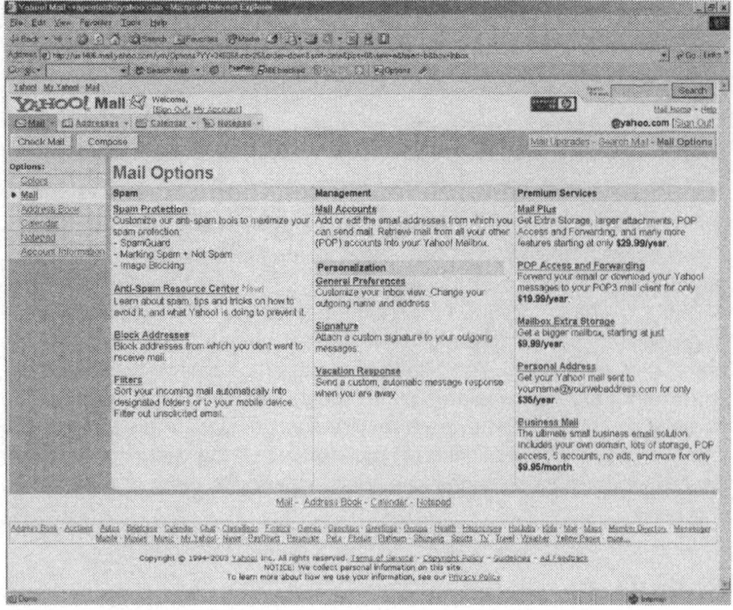

Fig.7.1 The Mail Options page is effectively a large menu

The radio buttons at the bottom of the page provide the option of displaying graphics in bulk Emails or suppressing them. The graphics content is not necessarily in the Email itself, but instead the Email carries the address of a web page that contains the image files. When you open the Email, the web page is opened and the graphics content is displayed within the Email. This assumes that your Email client is one that can handle HTML, as most can these days. With a text-only service the Emails will not appear on the page, and the web address for the page that contains them will be displayed instead.

Obviously the Yahoo! Email service can handle HTML and graphics, and normally any graphics will be displayed when you open an Email. Although this might not seem to be of any importance, it can potentially alert the sender to the fact that you have opened the Email, and that your Email address is an active one. This is likely to result in an increase in the amount of spam directed to your Email address. It is therefore advisable to switch off the display of any graphic content. Note that this

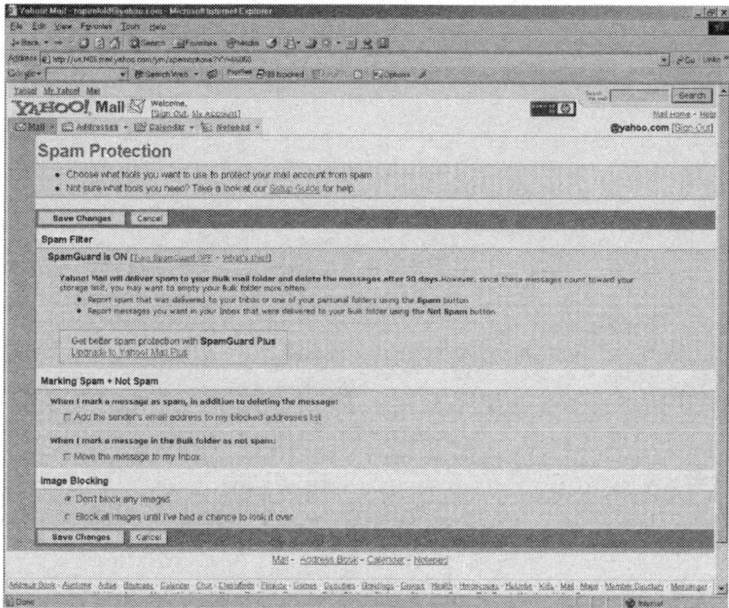

Fig.7.2 The Spam Protection page of Yahoo!

option only affects mail in the Bulk folder and that Emails in any other folders will still have the graphics displayed in the normal way.

In use the Spam Guard feature will not be perfect. A certain number of junk Emails will probably find their way to the Inbox, and it is then just a matter of ticking the checkbox for that piece of mail and operating the Spam button near the top of the window. Alternatively, if you have opened the Email, simply operate the Spam button near the top of the page. Either way the Email will be sent to the Bulk folder.

The opposite problem is likely to occur, with Emails you wish to receive being consigned to the Bulk folder. This is likely to happen with any Emails that are sent out as part of a mass mailing. For instance, I get financial news reports sent to me by Email, and details of all the latest special offers from several companies that sell computer bits and pieces. These Emails are also sent to thousands of other subscribers, but it is impossible for a filtering system to distinguish between legitimate bulk mailings and those from spammers.

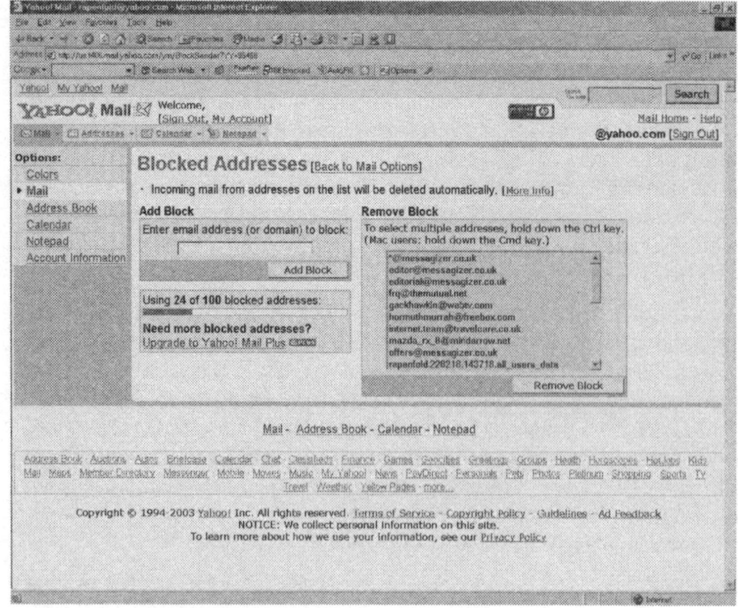

Fig.7.3 The Block Addresses page. The blocked addresses are listed on the right

Fine tuning

The way around the problem is to go into an Email that has been sent to the Bulk folder by mistake, and then operate the Not Spam button near the top of the window. Any further Emails from the same source should then be directed to the Inbox. It might take a week or so to get everything working correctly, but thereafter you should find that the bulk Emails that you wish to receive are directed to the Inbox.

It is still necessary to check through the contents of the Bulk folder from time to time just in case something has been sent there by mistake. Where large amounts of junk mail are sent to this folder it might be necessary to check through it occasionally and then delete all the unwanted Emails. They will be deleted after 30 days anyway, but you could find that this is long enough for a considerable number of Emails to build up. This could result in a large percentage of your available storage space being taken up by the Bulk folder. In an extreme case it could result in the available space being used up.

An address can be added to the blocked list by going to the Mail Options page and left-clicking the Block Addresses link. This produces a page like the one shown in Figure 7.3. In order to block an address it is just a matter of typing it into the textbox and operating the Add Block button. The address will then be added to the list of blocked addresses in the right-hand section of the window. With a long address it is easier to cut and paste it into the textbox, which should also guarantee that errors are avoided. In order to remove an address from the blocked list, first select it using the normal left-clicking method and then operate the Remove Block button.

What actually happens to blocked Emails? It depends on the Email company you are using, but most operate in the same way as the Yahoo! system. Blocked Emails are not bounced back to the sender, and are actually accepted by the system. The system checks each Email to see if it needs to be blocked for some reason, and if it does, then it is deleted. Some systems place blocked Emails in the Trash folder, but it is more normal these days for block Emails to be deleted. Consequently, there is usually no way of retrieving a blocked Email so you have to be careful not to accidentally block anything important.

The Yahoo! blocking system, in common with most others, does require a complete Email address. Suppose that you are receiving nuisance Emails from a company, and that the domain name is common to all the Emails but the name ahead of the domain is different for each one. For example, these Email addresses all have the same domain name but are (supposedly) from a different person or department within the company:

fred@wxyz.co.uk

judy@wxyz.co.uk

customersupport@wxyz.co.uk

despatch@wxyz.co.uk

It is not possible to block these Emails using the full address, because it changes slightly each time a new Email is sent to you. However, if any Emails from an address ending wxyz.co.uk are blocked, then all the offending Emails will be filtered. Due care needs to be taken with this system, because it is easy to block rather more than you intended. I was once asked to assist someone who having problems with a substantial number of missing Emails. A little investigation showed that she had blocked all addresses ending "hotmail.com", not realising that Hotmail provides Email services to millions of people. This method of

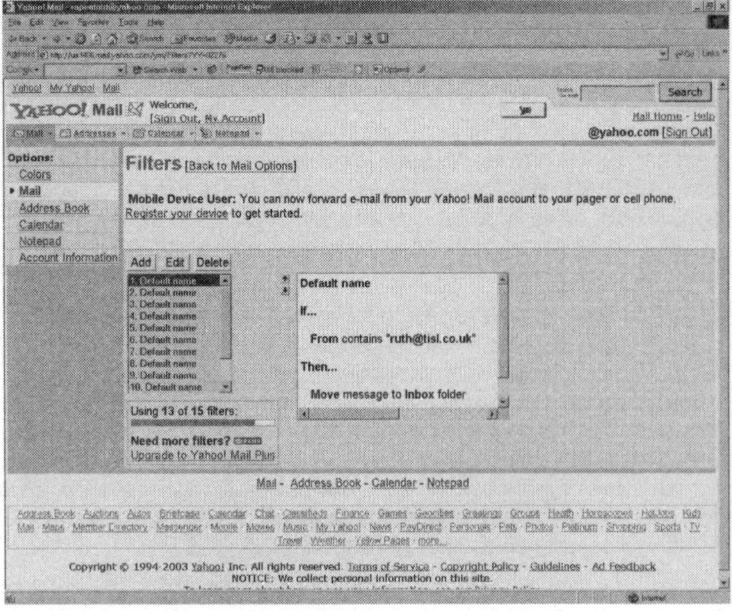

Fig.7.4 The first page shows the filters already in use

blocking is really only of use with companies that have their own domain name.

Filtering

The Filter link on the Mail Options page gives access to a blocking style facility, but strictly speaking it does not actually block anything. What it actually does is to permit Emails to be scanned, and those that meet certain criteria are redirected to another folder. This enables, for example, Emails that are erroneously being sent to the Bulk folder to be redirected to the Inbox. It can provide a pseudo blocking action by redirecting Emails to the Trash folder where they will in due course be automatically deleted.

The first page in the filter section (Figure 7.4) shows the filters that are already in use, and it enables them to be edited or deleted. Operating the Add button switches to the page of Figure 7.5 where the settings for a new filter can be selected. The system can be set to look for a certain

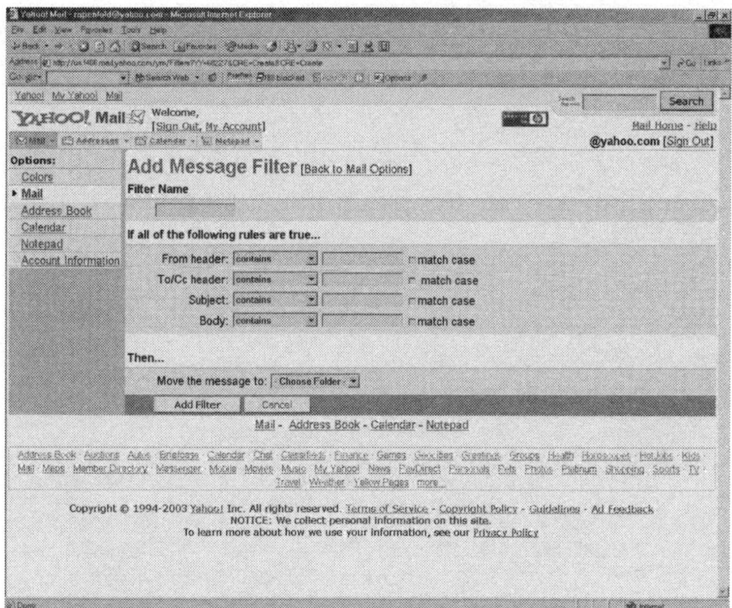

Fig.7.5 This page is used to create new filters

Email address, but it is also possible to have it search for a string of characters in other parts of each Email. In other words, it can provide content filtering if required.

Earlier I mentioned a problem with junk Emails trying to sell me "off the shelf" diplomas, and content filtering is good at dealing with this type of thing. The word "diploma" always appeared in either the subject or body fields of the Email, and usually in both. Therefore, these Emails could effectively be filtered by using the word "diploma" in both of these fields in the filter. Trash is selected from the Move message to menu, so that the offending Emails are redirected to the Trash folder and, in due course, automatically deleted. The filter can be given a name in the textbox near the top of the window. This makes it easier to find the filter if you need to edit or erase it at a later date. Finally, operate the Add Filter button and the newly created filter will be added to the list of filters (Figure 7.6).

Of course, this type of filtering will not always be effective. As pointed out previously, some spammers now try to hide keywords from this type

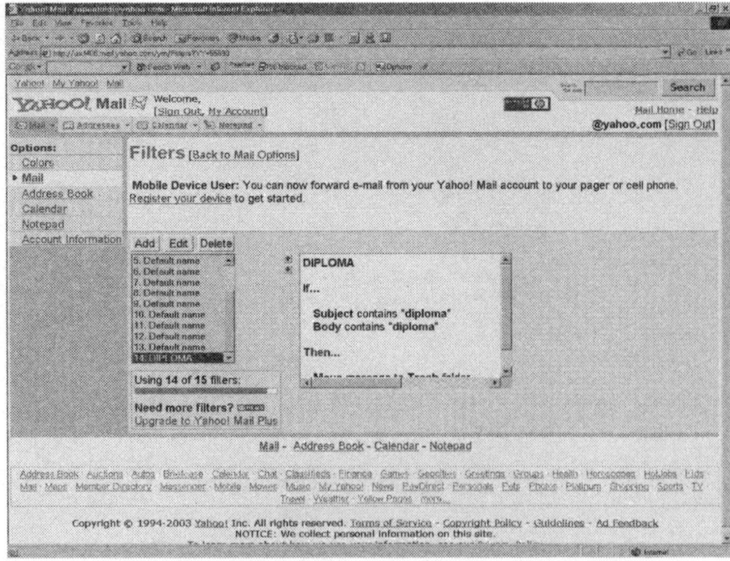

Fig.7.6 The newly created filter has been added successfully

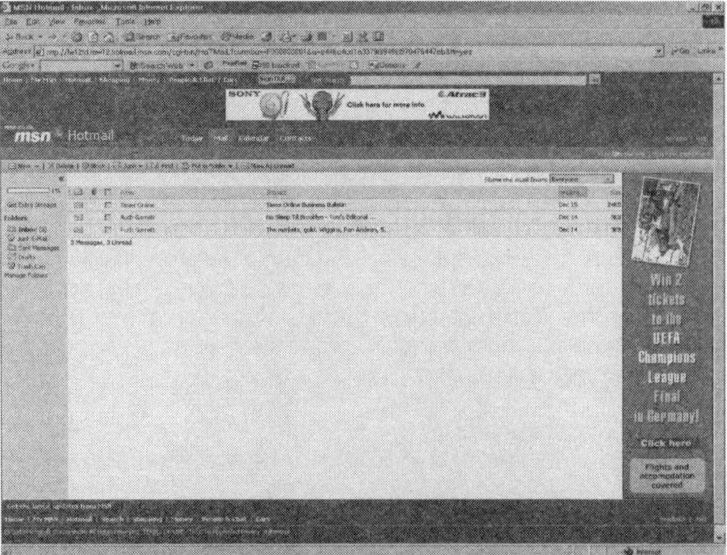

Fig.7.7 The Hotmail system includes a Block button in the Inbox

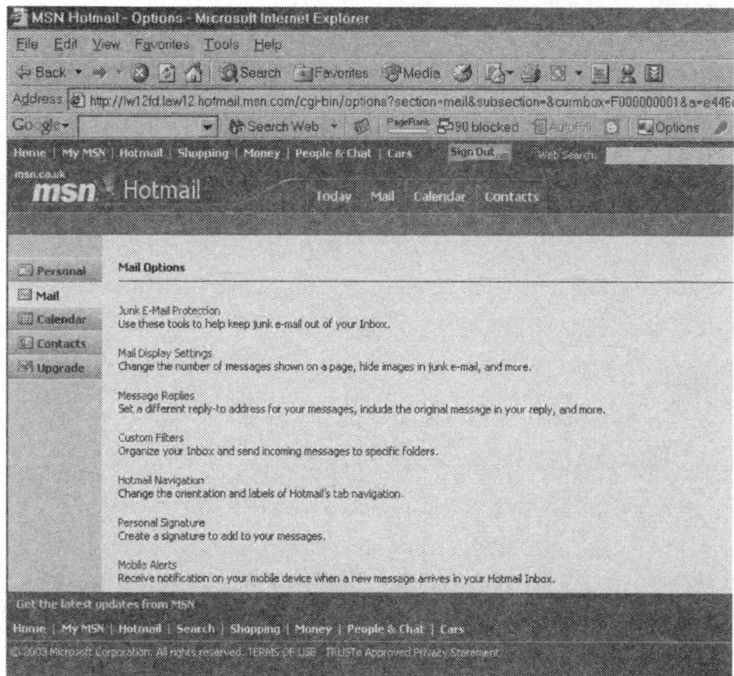

Fig.7.8 More features can be accessed via the Options link

of filtering by using deliberate misspellings and similar tricks. In this example the filtering would not detect the word “diploma if it was disguised, as in these examples:

dipl4oma6

dipploma

d-i-p-l-o-m-a

d I p l o m a

It is not really practical to add filters for all the possible variations. Nevertheless, this type of filtering can still be useful in combating a significant proportion of junk Emails.

The exact facilities on offer with obviously vary somewhat from one Email service to another, as will the way in which those facilities are accessed. With the popular Hotmail service it is easy to block further Emails from an address. There is a Block button in the toolbar of the Inbox (Figure

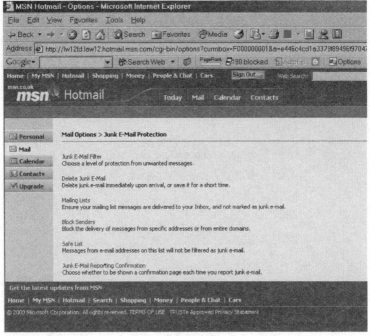

Fig.7.9 Selecting the Junk Email Protection link produces this page

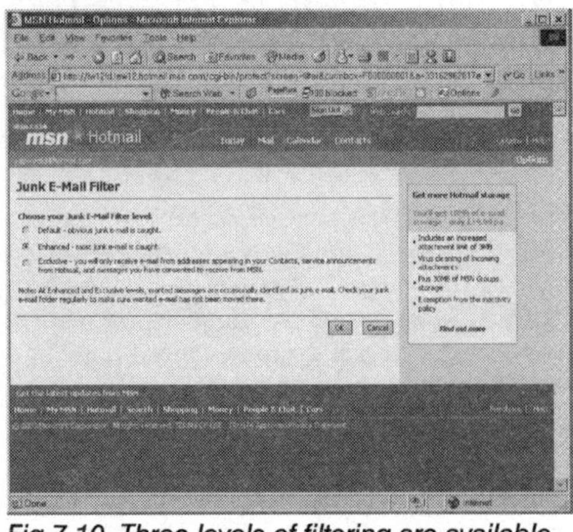

Fig.7.10 Three levels of filtering are available

7.7). Simply tick the checkbox of the offending Email and then operate the Block button. The relevant address will then be added to the list of blocked addresses.

More facilities can be accessed by activating the Options link, which produces a list of additional features (Figure 7.8). In the current context

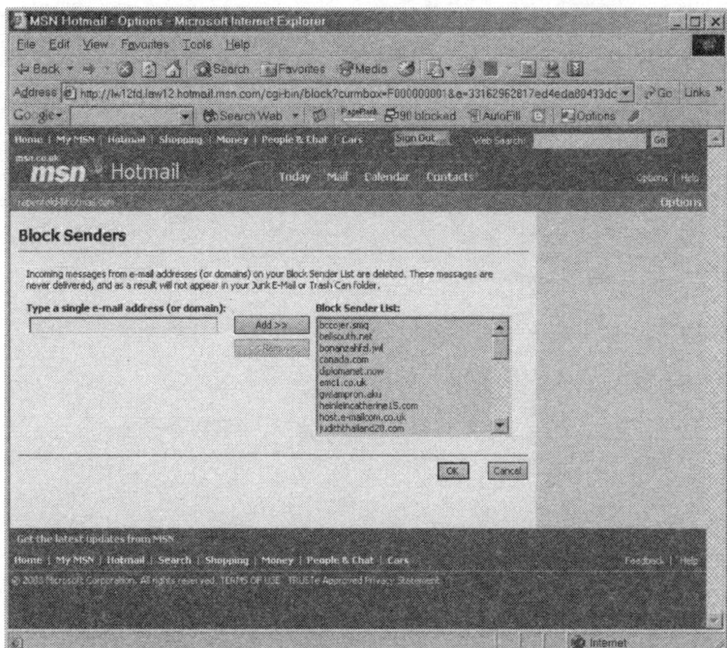

Fig.7.11 Addresses can be added to the list of blocked addresses using this page

it is the Junk Email Protection link that is of interest, and this produces the page of Figure 7.9. The options on offer include a Junk Email Filter page where three degrees of protection are available (Figure 7.10). Another option enables addresses to be added to those that will be blocked (Figure 7.11). It is also possible to have Junk Emails deleted immediately rather than being deposited in the Junk folder.

The Excite mail order service includes a Block button as part of the Inbox (Figure 7.12), and it also has a Report as Spam button. A reporting feature of this type is quite common, and the idea is to show the programmers at the Email company the types of junk Email that are getting through the built-in filters. This should enable them to improve their systems and defeat a greater percentage of the junk Emails.

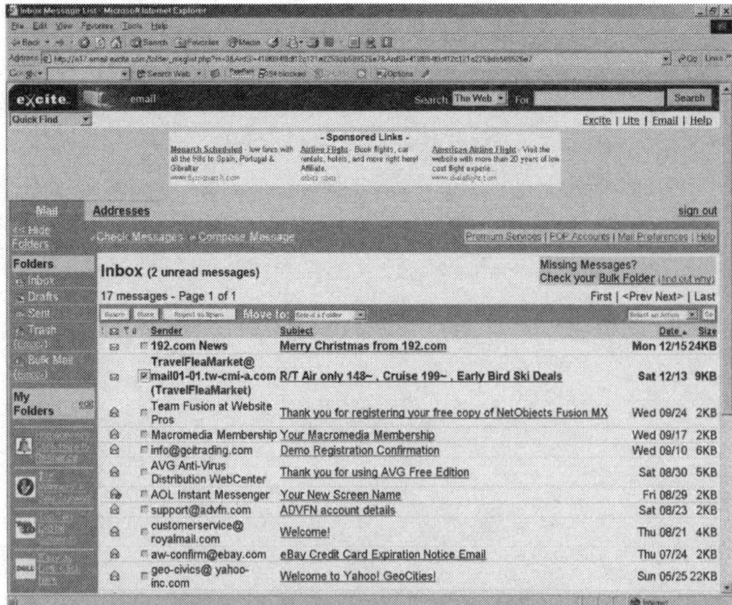

Fig.7.12 The facilities at Excite include a Report as Spam button

Filter programs

There are several good Email programs available that can add filtering facilities not provided by your Email service, but note that these programs are not usable with all Email systems. Few seem to work with Yahoo! for example, and some do not with Hotmail either. MailWasher Pro is an example of an add-on filter program, and this one does work with Hotmail. As far as I can ascertain, it is not usable with the Email service offered by Yahoo!

Once MailWasher Pro is installed and run, the opening screen of Figure 7.13 is obtained. In order to set up a filter the Spam Tools button is operated, and this produces a window like the one shown in Figure 7.14. Here the My Filters button is pressed, and the window then changes to look like Figure 7.15. There is a couple of default filters listed here, and the Add button is operated in order to define your own filter.

This launches a new window (Figure 7.16), and the rules for the added filter are defined in the lower section of the window. There is provision

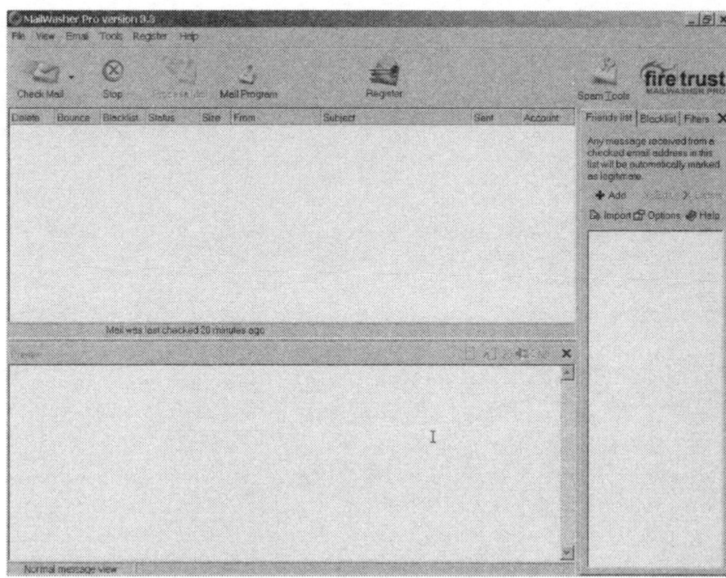

Fig.7.13 The opening screen of MailWasher Pro

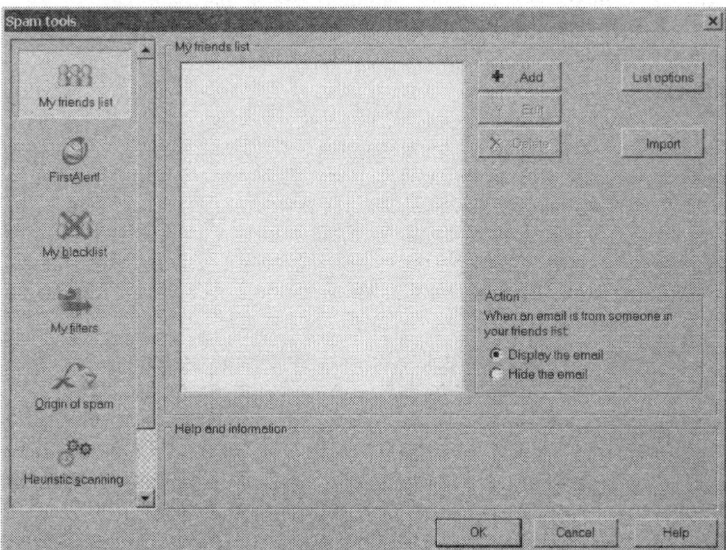

Fig.7.14 The first step in producing a new filter

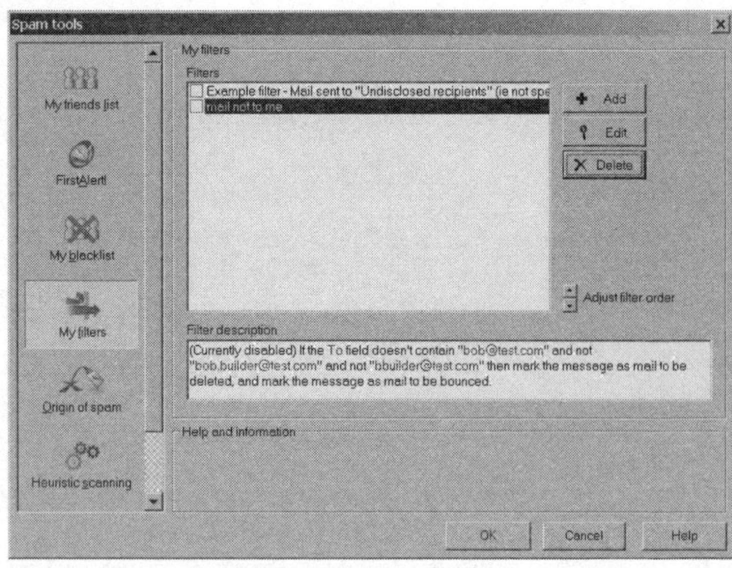

Fig.7.15 Operate the Add button to start defining a new filter

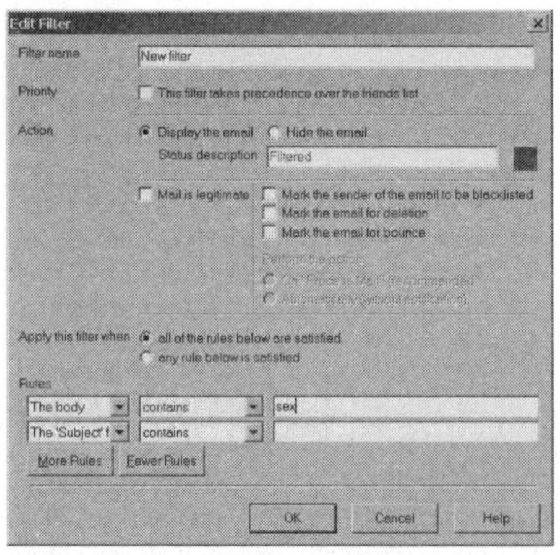

Fig.7.16 The rules for the filter are defined in the lower part of the window

for two rules by default, but the buttons permit the number of rules to be increased or reduced. The rules operate in a similar way to the Yahoo! filtering, and it is basically just a matter of giving the program a text string to search for and telling it which field or fields to search. The radio buttons give the options of the filter being activated if any one rule is met, or only if all of the conditions are

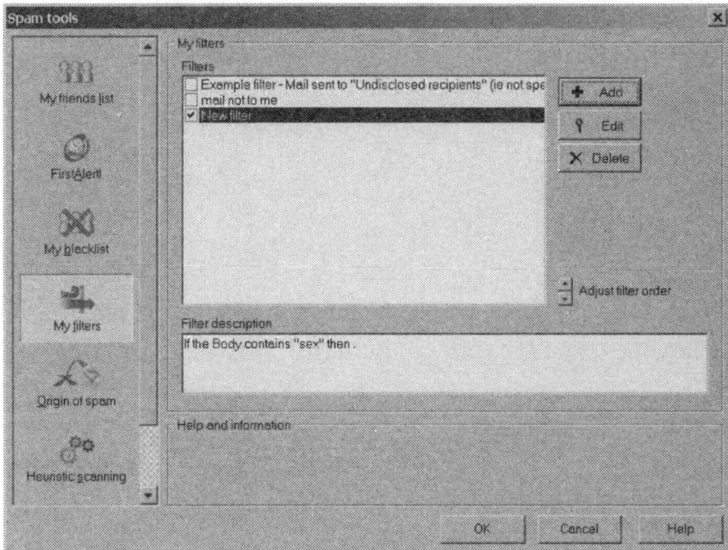

Fig.7.17 The new filter has been added to the list

satisfied. The upper section of the window gives various choices about the way in which a filtered Email is treated.

The OK button is operated when the rules and other options have been set up correctly, and the new filter should then be added to the list (Figure 7.17). In this example the filter is set up to look for the word "sex" in the body field of the Email. I then sent two Emails to myself, with one having the word "testing" as the body text and the other one having the word "sex". As can be seen from Figure 7.18, the program has correctly filtered the second Email containing the offending word.

Heuristic scanning

Some Email filter programs, including MailWasher can provide heuristic scanning, and this technique is also available in some antivirus programs. It is a technique of looking for files that have the characteristics of viruses, or Emails that look like they are probably spam. The advantage of the heuristic approach is that it does not leave you one step behind the virus writers and the spammers.

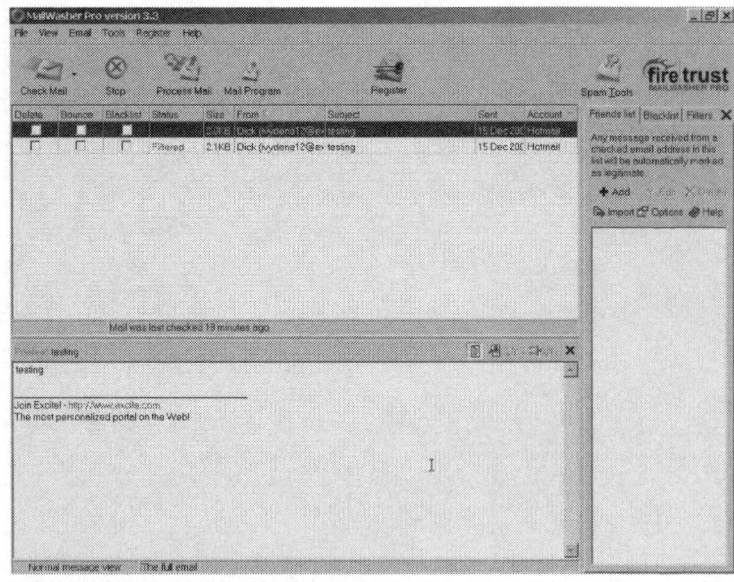

Fig.7.18 The filtering has redirected the "sex" Email

Most viruses are actually just minor variations on those already in existence, but a normal matching process will not detect them. The new viruses are similar to existing ones, but are sufficiently different to prevent a match from being obtained. A heuristic approach is more likely to find these variations since it is looking for certain tell-tale pieces of code rather than a perfect match overall. Potentially, the heuristic approach can find new viruses that are not yet in its virus database, giving better protection. It will not find genuinely new viruses, but it will detect most of the recycled ones. The situation is similar with junk Emails, where many of them are just minor variations on previous

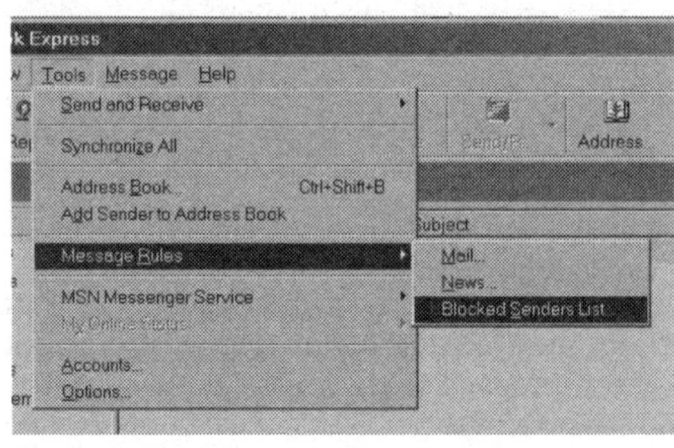

Fig.7.19 The Message Rules submenu

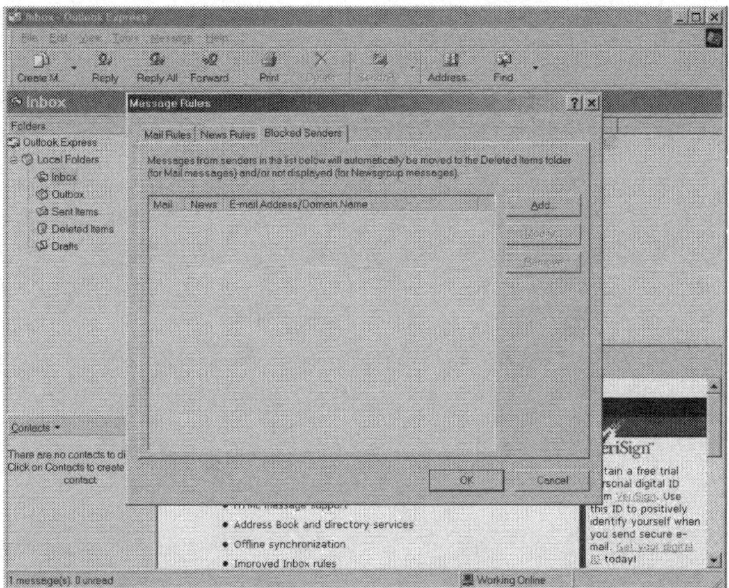

Fig.7.20 Operate the Add button to add a new new address to the list of blocked addresses

versions in an attempt to "fool" content filtering. Again, a heuristic approach can pick up this type of thing.

Inevitably there is a drawback to this approach, and it is simply that there is a greater chance of an innocent file or Email being picked up by a system of this type. If applied too strongly to Emails you could find that many legitimate Emails are being automatically deleted or dumped into the Trash folder. MailWasher has Careful and Strong heuristic settings, and it is probably best to opt for the more cautious Careful setting.

Outlook Express

Users of Outlook Express have only very limited filtering facilities built into the program. However, it is possible to block addresses. Select Message Rules from the Tools menu, followed by Blocked Senders List from the submenu that appears (Figure 7.19). A new window then appears (Figure 7.20) and the Add button is operated. A third window

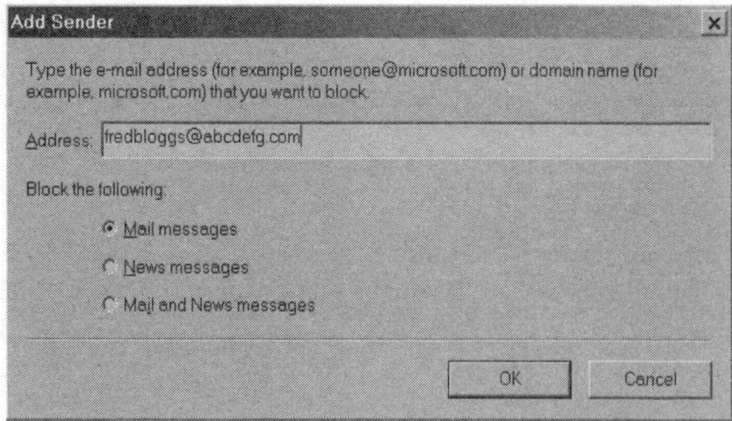

Fig.7.21 The address to be blocked is entered in the textbox

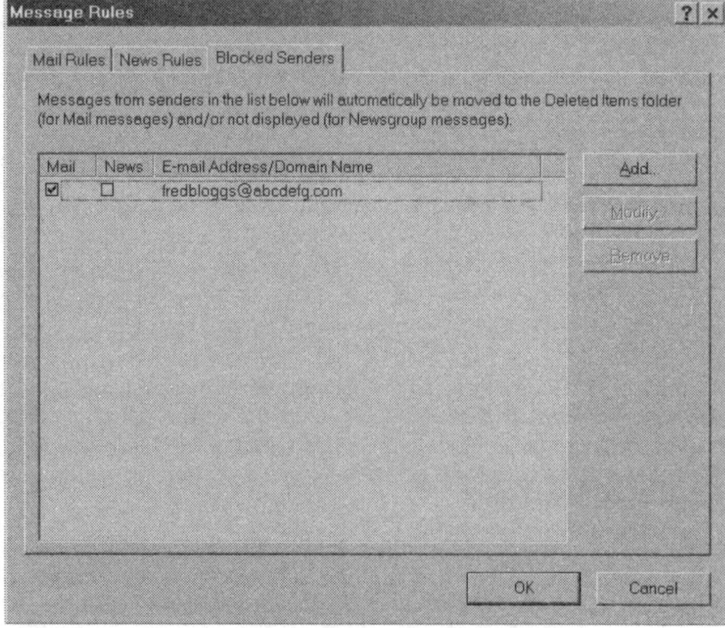

Fig.7.22 The address has been added to the list

then appears (Figure 7.21), and the address you wish to block is entered into the textbox. The radio buttons enable new message, mail messages, or both of these to be blocked. Operate the OK button to close the window, and the newly blocked address should appear in the list displayed in the Message Rules window (Figure 7.22).

Unsubscribe

Sometimes junk Emails have a link that you can click in order to unsubscribe from the service. It should be possible to unsubscribe to a service in cases where you have genuinely subscribed to something in the first place. It can sometimes happen that when you join some form of online club or service that you subscribe to something without realising it. Few of us take the bother to read the "fine print" when joining this type of thing. There is no risk in unsubscribing to a service that you have actually joined in the first place.

In general though, it is advisable not to activate one of these links. Many of them will not unsubscribe you from anything if you do active the link. Just the opposite in fact, and by operating the link you will probably just be indicating to the spammer that he or she has found an active Email account. That account is then likely to be targeted with large amounts of spam. It is very tempting to activate these links, but it is nearly always a mistake to do so.

For the same reason it is important not to respond to spam. By doing so you are making it clear to the spammers that they have found an active account. Worse than that, you are making it clear that they have found an account that is owned by someone that is susceptible to spam. To put it bluntly, you are letting them know that they have found a mug. This more or less guarantees that you will receive ever increasing amounts of spam.

It is as well to bear in mind that the companies promoted by junk Emails are usually something less than respectable. Some are legitimate businesses of sorts, but many of the offers are bogus and you are unlikely to receive the goods if you should try buying something in response to a junk Email. Giving credit card details or other financial information to one of these companies is just plain daft.

Encryption

Many people are unhappy about sending personal or any form of sensitive information via Emails because this method of communication

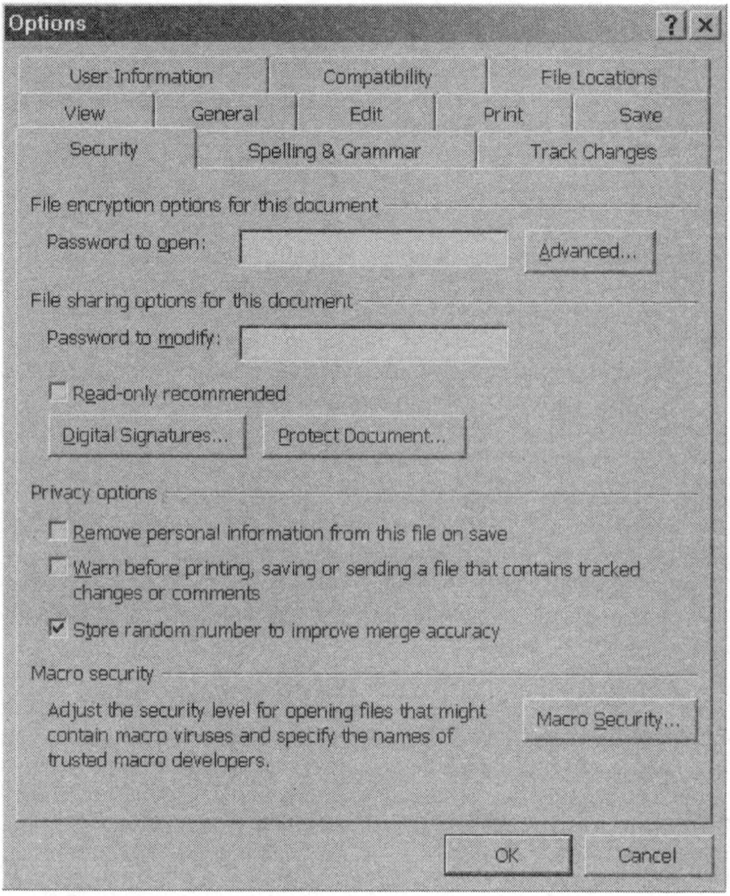

Fig.7.23 The Security section of Word's Options window

is something less than totally secure. There is a way around this problem in the form of encryption. The subject of secure web sites has been covered previously, and the same technology can be used to scramble an Email before it is sent. In order to descramble the Email its recipient must have the same program that was used to encrypt it, together with the correct password.

Most programs of this type are not only suitable for sending Emails, and can also be used to encrypt any form of data file. You can, for example,

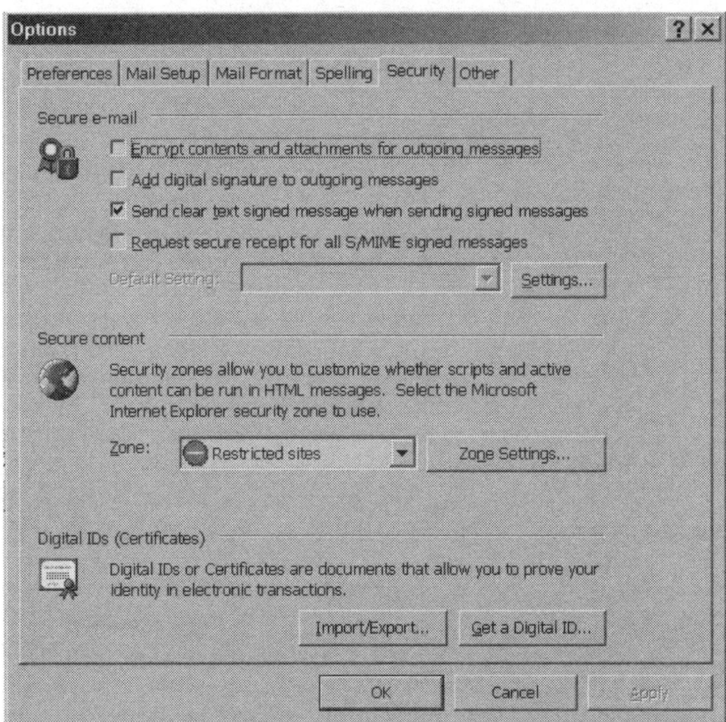

Fig.7.24 The Security section of Options window in Outlook Express

encrypt word processor files so that anyone gaining access to your PC will not be able to read them. In fact this is doing things the hard way, because many word processors now have some form of built-in encryption facility. With Microsoft Word for instance, documents can be password protected. This operates at two levels, and at the highest level it is not possible to open a document without giving the correct password first. At a lower level of security it is possible for anyone to open the document and look at its contents, but only authorised users can make any changes to it.

Before using any form of password protection for data it is important to realise that modern encryption techniques are extremely powerful. Should you manage to forget the password it is unlikely that you will ever see your data in readable form again. Writing down passwords is not normally considered to be a good practice, but the reduction in security it provides is probably better than finding yourself locked out of you own documents. Those with poor memories would be well advised to write down the password and hide it away in the bottom of a drawer where no one can find it easily. Many passwords are case sensitive, so it is as well to work on the assumption that they are all case sensitive. That way you should never be caught out by using any letters of the wrong case.

In order to password protect a Word document the document must first be opened. Then select Options from the Tools menu and operate the Security tab on the new window that appears (Figure 7.23). Type the password into the appropriate textbox for the level of security you require, and then operate the OK button. You will have to enter the password into a small pop-up window in order to go back to the document. It will also be necessary to enter the password into a small popup window each time you try to open the file or alter it, depending on the level of security selected.

There are alternatives to using special encryption programs when sending information via Emails. Many data compression programs can provide password protection, so it is possible to use one of these to compress and encrypt a file which can then be sent as an Email attachment. Unfortunately, the free versions of these programs often lack the ability to password protect files, so it might be necessary to buy the full version in order to use this facility.

Users of Outlook and Outlook Express have a built-in encryption facility, but it is of no real use to most users. In order to encrypt a file select Options from the Tools menu and then operate the Security tab in the new window that appears (Figure 7.24). Tick the top checkbox in order to use encryption on your Emails and any attachments. Unfortunately, this method is only usable if you purchase a digital certificate from a company such as VeriSign. The cost is not that great, but probably few private users are prepared to go to the trouble and expense of obtaining one and keeping it up to date.

XP encryption

As explained previously, there are programs that can encrypt files on the hard disc of your computer so that they can not be read by others. Windows XP has a form of built-in encryption facility, but it does not operate in quite the same way as most encryption programs. Although encrypted, the files are still perfectly readable and can be used in the normal way from within Windows XP. This does not necessarily mean that they are accessible to anyone that gets hold of your PC, because Windows itself can be password protected. Also, if hackers should gain access to the computer over the Internet, they will not be able to read the encrypted files. Similarly, if someone should copy any protected files to a floppy disc or CD-ROM, the copied files will not be readable on another PC.

In order to protect a file or folder it is first located using Windows Explorer and its entry is then right-clicked. This brings up a small menu where the Properties option is selected. The file's property window will look something like Figure 7.25, and the Advanced button near the bottom of the screen is operated. The new window of Figure 7.26 will then appear, and the bottom checkbox

Fig.7.25 The file's properties window

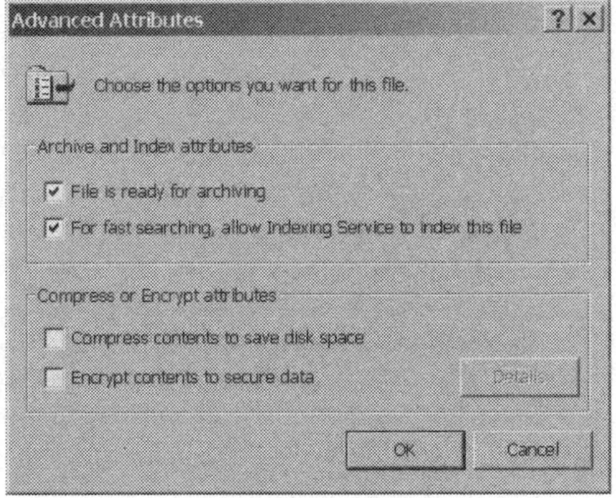

Fig.7.26 The Advanced settings

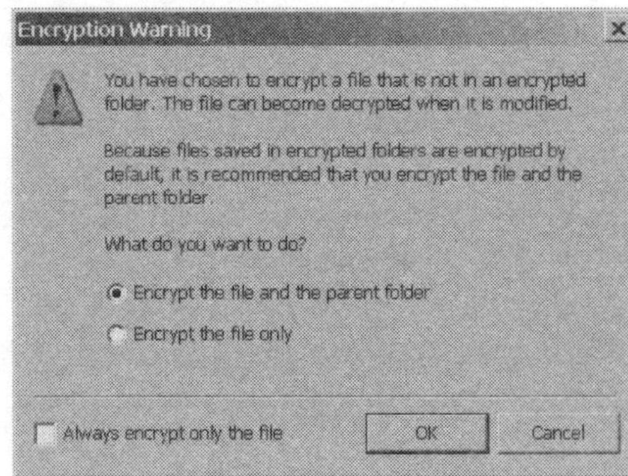

Fig.7.27 Accept the suggested setting

(Encrypt data to secure contents) is ticked. Operating the OK button will produce a warning message (Figure 7.27) if a file rather than a folder is being encrypted, and it is advisable to accept the default and let Windows encrypt the parent folder.

Encrypted files and folders are shown in Internet Explorer in the normal way, but the name of the file is in green text to indicate that encryption has been used. The encryption is to a large extent transparent to the user. Double-clicking on the Jpg image file used in this example resulted in it being displayed in the usual way

Fig.7.28 The file can be opened and displayed in the normal way despite being encrypted

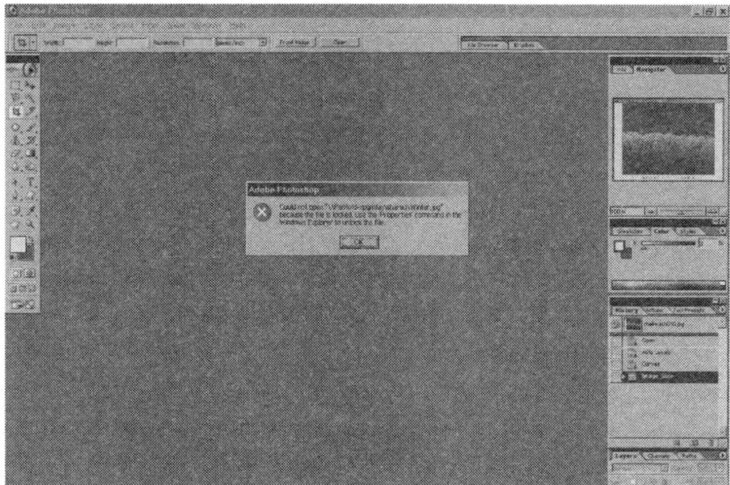

Fig.7.29 The file can not be opened over a network or if it is copied to disc and transferred to another PC

(Figure 7.28) with no password being required. Remember that Windows itself must be password protected if you need the files to be inaccessible to anyone gaining access to the computer.

Figure 7.29 shows the result of trying to open the encrypted image file using another PC with the file accessed over a network. The file is encrypted and Photoshop has therefore been unable to open the file. It has therefore produced an error message to this effect. Hackers accessing the computer via the Internet would have the same problem. Even if someone was to steal the PC they would not be able to put the hard disc in another computer and read the encrypted files. Provided Windows itself was password protected they would not be able to boot the PC into Windows and access them either.

An advantage of this built-in encryption is that it is very easy to use. Everything is protected by the Windows password, so there is only one password to remember. Having entered Windows there is no need to use a password when saving or loading encrypted files. They are accessed in exactly the same way as non-encrypted files. In order to remove the encryption it is merely necessary to go back to the properties window again, operate the Advanced button, and then remove the tick from the encryption checkbox.

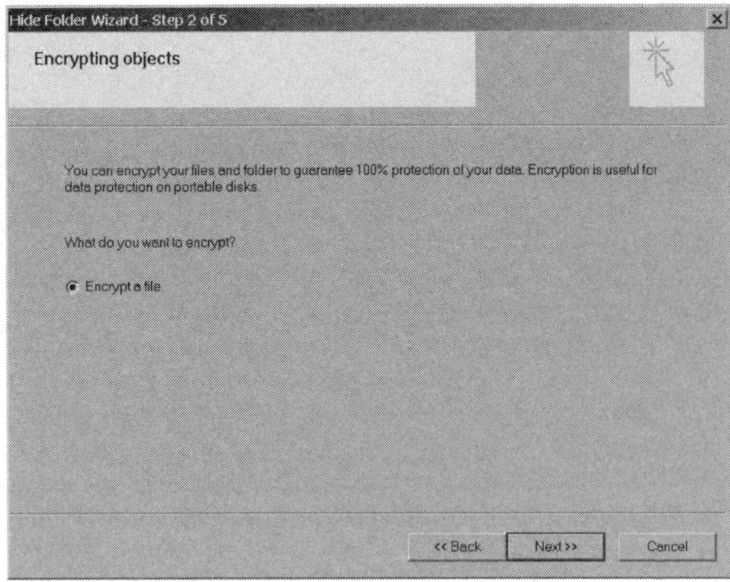

Fig.7.30 The opening window of the Encryption Wizard

Stealth

Some programs offer a facility to hide folders or files as an alternative to encryption. The hidden files do not show up in Internet Explorer or in the file browsers of applications programs. If prying eyes do not know that the files exist they can not view or alter them. Hide File 3.0 is a program that offers both file encryption and hiding facilities. Using the encryption is very straightforward and an encryption wizard can be selected from the Encryption menu.

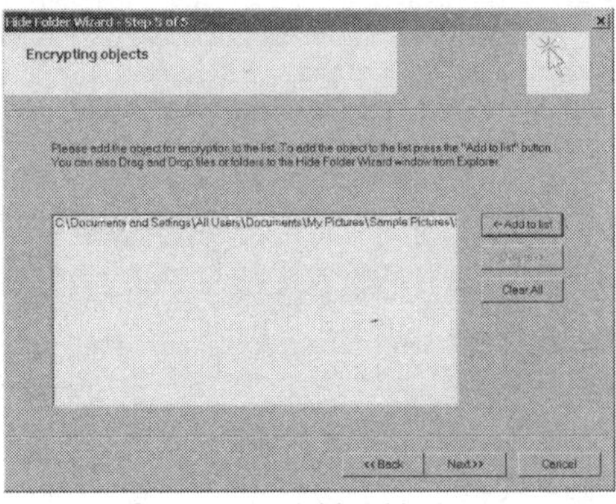

Fig.7.31 Operate the Add to List button

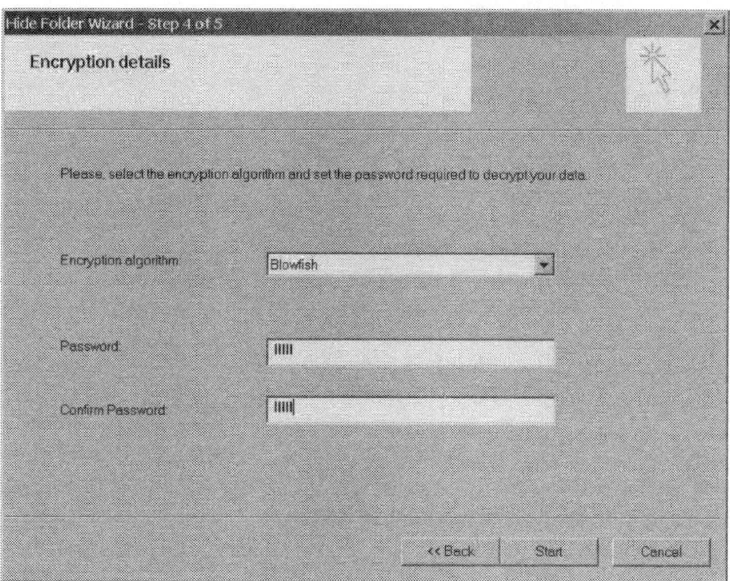

Fig.7.32 Select the required type of encryption

The first window (Figure 7.30) has only one option (to encrypt a file), and it is really just an introduction to the wizard. At the next window (Figure 7.31) you operate the Add to List button, which launches the usual Windows file browser. This is used to add the required file or files.

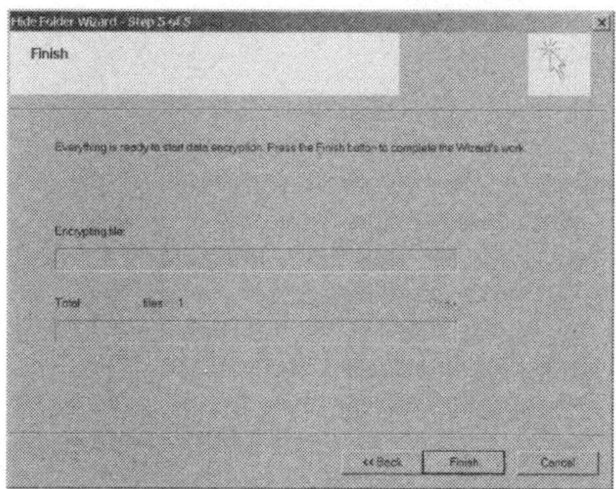

Fig.7.33 You have a chance to change your mind

Next the required type of encryption is selected (Figure 7.32), and it is advisable to simply accept the default type unless there is a good reason to do otherwise. The password is also entered at this stage, and to avoid mistakes it has to be typed

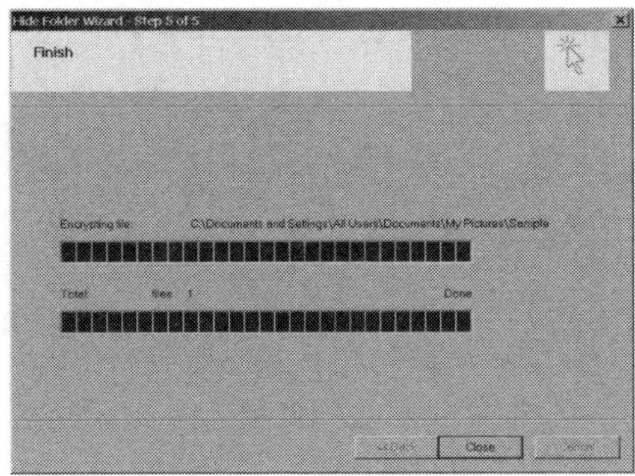

Fig.7.34 *The file has been encrypted*

correctly into both textboxes in order to proceed to the next stage. Bear in mind that there is little chance of decrypting a file if you should manage to lose the password. The window of Figure 7.33 gives you a chance to change your mind before going ahead with the encryption process, and operating the Finish button completes the process (Figure 7.34). The encrypted file is then added to the list in the main program window (Figure 7.35).

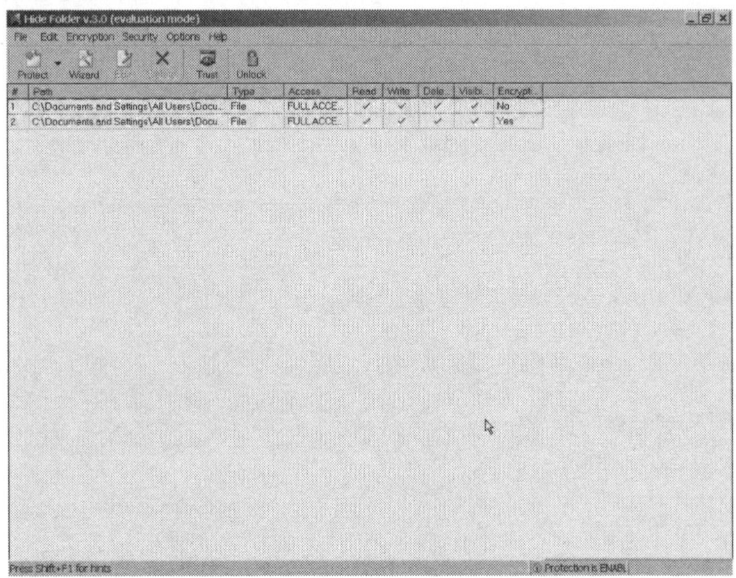

Fig.7.35 *The encrypted file has been added to the list in the main program window*

In order to decrypt a file it is just a matter of left-clicking its entry in the list, selecting Decrypt from the pop-up menu, and then adding the correct password into the window that appears (Figure 7.36). Operate the OK button and the file will be decrypted. The file's entry in the list will then change to show that it is no longer encrypted.

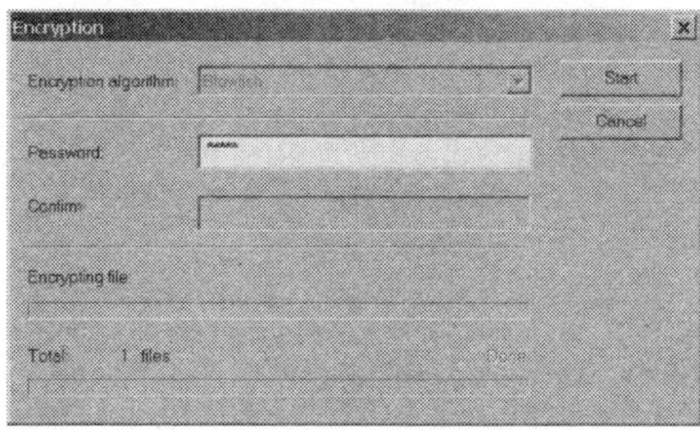

Fig.7.36 The file can not be decrypted without the correct password

To hide a file the Wizard button is operated and the top radio button is selected when the wizard appears (Figure 7.37). At the next window (Figure7.38) you select the type of object to be hidden, which can be a file, folder, disc, or a

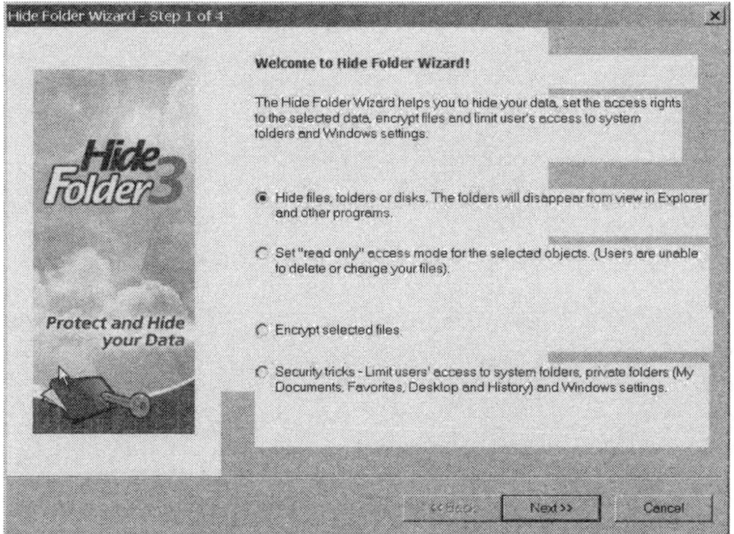

Fig.7.37 The first window of the wizard gives four options

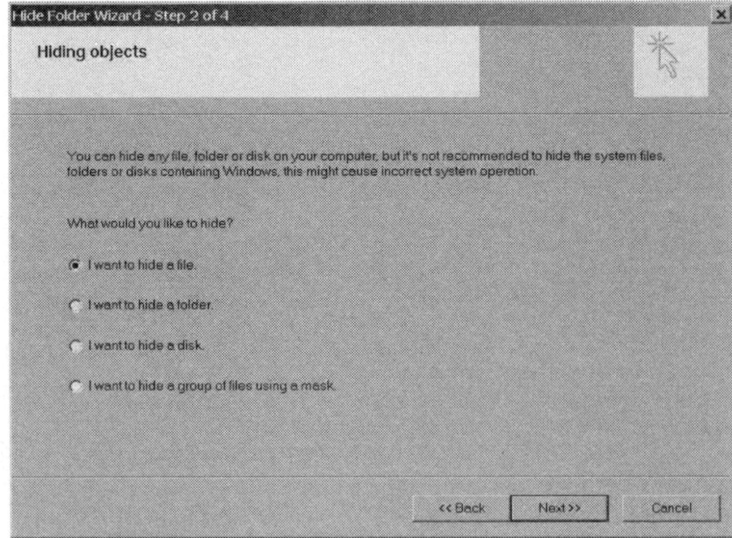

Fig.7.38 Select the type of object to be hidden

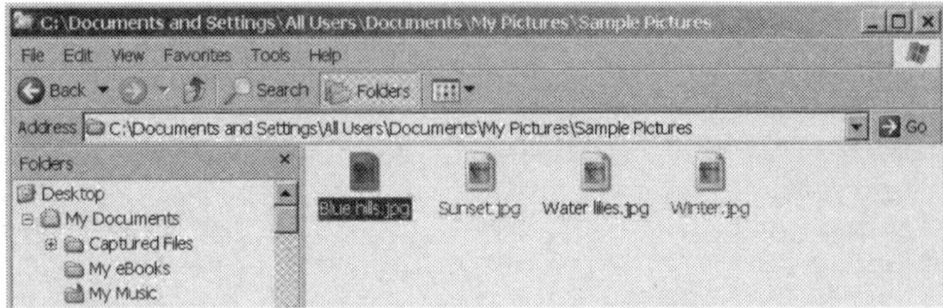

Fig.7.39 The "before" view shows all four image files

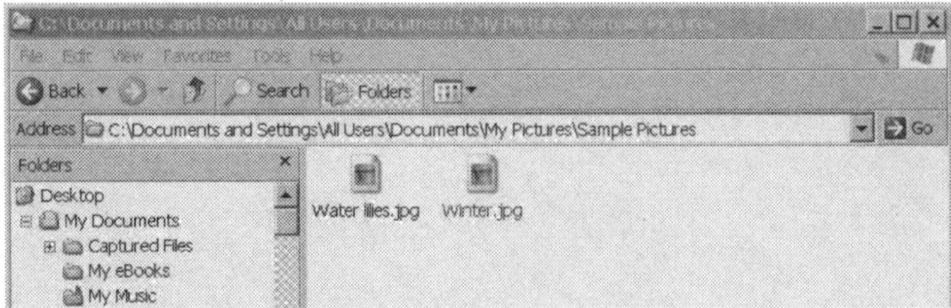

Fig.7.40 Two files have been successfully hidden, but they are still in the folder and intact

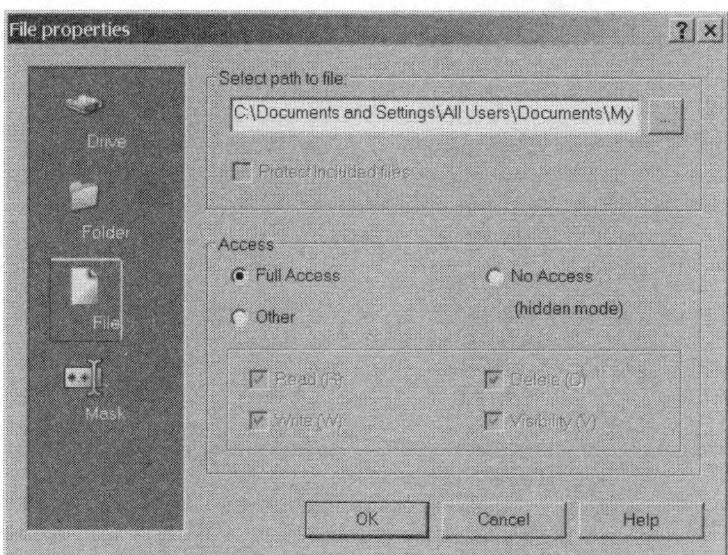

Fig.7.41 Operate the Full Access radio button to reveal the file

group of files. For this example the file option was selected, and two files in a folder were selected and hidden.

Figures 7.39 and 7.40 show "before" and "after" versions the folder when viewed using Windows Explorer, and the two hidden files have disappeared from view in Figure 7.40. They are still present on the disc and have not been erased. In order to make a file visible again it is just a matter of going into Hide File 3.0, right-clicking the file's entry in the file list, and selecting Properties from the pop-up menu. This produces the window of Figure 7.41 where the Full Access radio button is selected. Operate the OK button to exit the window and the file will then become visible again.

Points to remember

Most Email services have built-in facilities that help to block much of the spam directed at your Email address. One system they use is to have a blacklist of addresses that are known to be used for sending spam. Another is to block Emails that contain certain words and phrases.

There are programs available that can be used to reduce problems with spam. These enable you to block mail from specific addresses and (or) mail that contains certain words. These facilities are built into some Email services.

Heuristic scanning filters Emails that have various characteristics associated with spam. It can work quite well if used in moderation but can filter too many legitimate Emails when used strongly.

Clicking on the unsubscribe links in spam is not a good idea. In many cases the links are "blind" and clicking on them has no effect at all. In other cases you are simply alerting the spammers to the fact that they have found an active Email account.

Do not reply to spam. The chances of getting ripped off in some way are quite high and some junk Emails are completely fraudulent. Replying to spam simply encourages the spammers to continue in their activities. If there were no replies to spam there would be no more spam.

The Email system is not totally secure, but it is possible to encrypt the contents and (or) attachments using an encryption program. The recipient usually requires the same program in order to decrypt the files. Most of these programs can be used to encrypt files on a hard disc. Windows XP Professional has a built-in facility of this type, and password protection is also available in many file compression programs.

Many word processors have a built-in password protection facility. This can be used to prevent others from altering your documents, and can also be used to prevent others from viewing them. Ideal if you wish to keep a personal diary on a PC that will be used by others, for example.

8

Pop-ups, Filtering, Auctions

Pop-ups

I suppose that pop-ups do not rate highly as a security risk, but they certainly rate at or near the top in the annoyance league. They were originally associated with pornographic sites and other web sites at the less than respectable end of the market. Some sites were deliberately misleading and lured users via search engines using popular search terms. On arriving at a site of this type users found nothing of interest, but would find that numerous pop-up advertisements appeared. The owners of the web sites were paid a small amount for each pop-up that their site produced.

Apparently it was possible to generate quite large sums of money in this way, but those paying for the pop-up advertisements gradually realised that they were not really getting anything for their money. Most people simply closed all the pop-ups without paying any real attention to what they were advertising. Having been tricked into going to the advertised web site it was unlikely that anyone would consider doing business with it. To a large extent the mass of pop-up advertisements were counterproductive for the advertisers.

This type of trickery has not totally disappeared from the Internet, but it is nothing like as prevalent as it used to be. This is not to say that pop-ups are now something of a rarity. If you surf the Internet for a few minutes you will almost certainly encounter several pop-up advertisements. Pop-ups have moved upmarket, and they are now to be found on many of the more respectable sites on the Internet. The usual banner advertisements tended to pass unnoticed by most users, rendering them largely ineffective. Flashing lettering and moving graphics

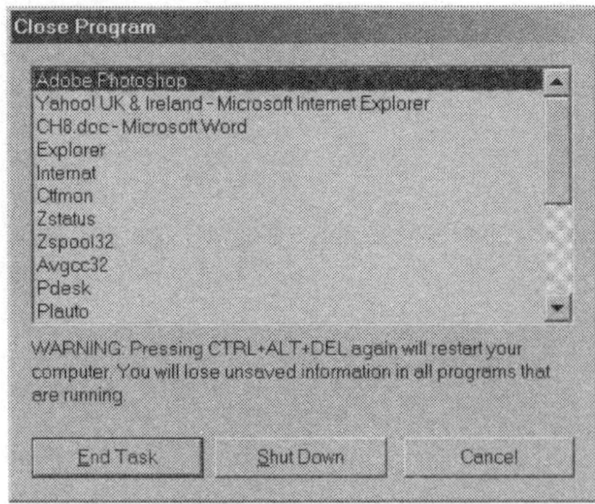

Fig.8.1 The Close Programs window

gave these advertisements a new lease of life, but they were still not effective enough for many advertisers. Hence the move to pop-up advertisements that the user can not overlook.

Most of the pop-up advertisements are now for respectable products and services such as Internet auction sites, mobile phones, credit cards, and other financial services. Some advertise the types of products and services associated with junk Emails, and should be ignored. There are still plenty of pop-up advertisements for pornographic sites, which is the type of thing you do not need flashing up on the screen when surfing the Internet with your children or the vicar's wife!

Some sites seem to take pop-ups to excess, with a new one appearing on entering the site, switching to a new page, and on leaving the site. No matter how innocuous the advertisements, a constant barrage of them makes these sites virtually unusable. Matters are not helped by the fact that small pop-ups now seem to be out of fashion, and most now seem to be in the form of full web pages.

Closing

Most pop-ups appear in a standard browser window or one that lacks the menus and toolbars. Provided the usual cross in the top right-hand corner of the window is present there should be no difficulty in closing a pop-up. Unfortunately, some pop-ups lack this small close button, or any other button to close the window. It should still be possible to get rid of the window without taking drastic measures such as rebooting the computer.

The first thing to try is to left-click somewhere on the window to make it the current one, and then operate the Control and W keys simultaneously. This will usually do the trick, but there are other things you can try. The

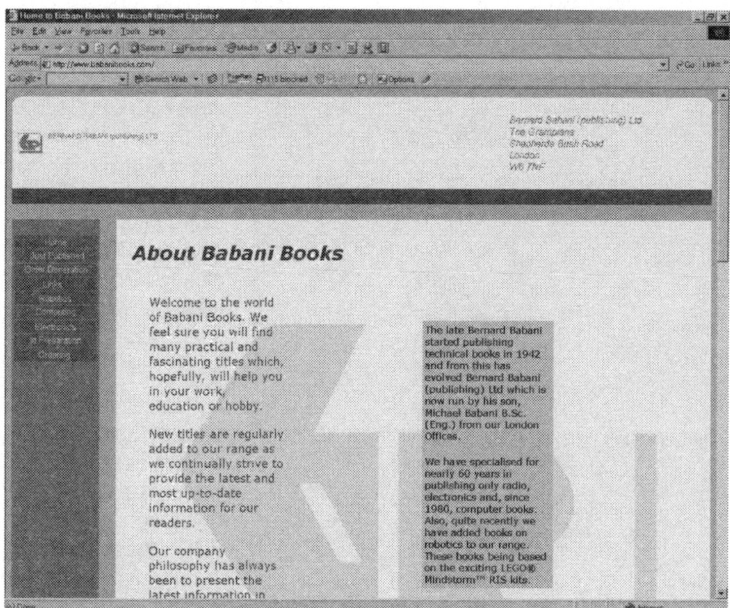

Fig.8.2 The Google toolbar includes a pop-up blocker

window should have an entry on the taskbar at the bottom of the Windows desktop. Right-click on its entry and choose the Close option if there is one.

Another method is to operate the Control, Alt, and Delete keys simultaneously. This will bring up a window like the one in Figure 8.1. It lists all the programs that are running on the computer, including any background tasks. Find the entry for the offending window, left-click its entry to select it, and then operate the End Task button. After a few seconds a new window will probably pop-up, asking for confirmation that you wish to close the program. Operate the Yes button and the unwanted window should finally close.

Pop-up blockers

There are programs that will block pop-up advertisements, but some of these are more successful than others. Unfortunately, some of these programs seem to let most of the pop-ups through while blocking a proportion of your normal Internet activity. Two main approaches are

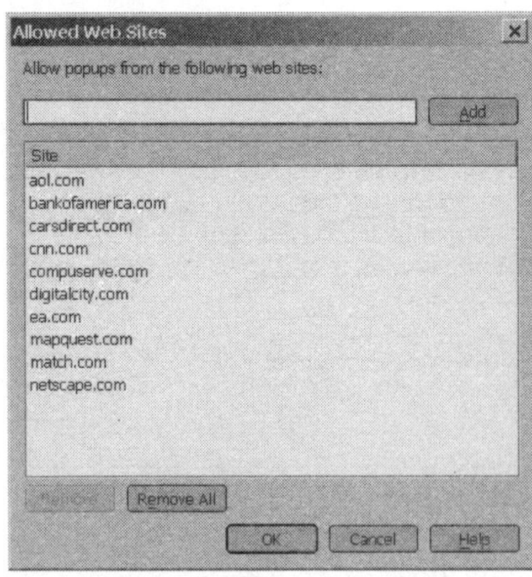

Fig.8.3 Managing pop-ups with Netscape

used by these programs, and one is to block the JavaScript code that is normally responsible for generating the pop-ups. The other approach is to block access to a list of known advertising sites. A mixture of the two methods is often utilised.

One of the best pop-up blockers I have encountered is the one that comes as part of the toolbar that is available from the popular Google search engine (www.google.co.uk). It is a reasonably small download and it has the advantage of being completely free, so there is not a lot to lose by trying it. Once installed, the toolbar appears below the other toolbars in Internet Explorer (Figure 8.2). Like any normal toolbar in Internet Explorer, it is easily switched off. Just select Toolbars from the View menu followed by Google from the submenu. Do the same again in order to reinstate the toolbar.

There is no need to switch off the entire toolbar in order to permit pop-ups. They can be toggled on and off simply by operating the pop-up button in the toolbar. There might seem to be no point in allowing pop-ups, but they are sometimes used to perform useful functions, so you might actually need them from time to time. On the other hand, I have been using the Google toolbar for several months and have not yet found it necessary to enable pop-ups.

New browser

Pop-up blockers are probably the best choice for most users, but there are alternatives. One of the more drastic of these is to switch to a new browser. Internet Explorer does not have the ability to enable or disable pop-ups, but this feature is available from some browsers. One of these is Opera, which is available in free and normal commercial versions. Unfortunately, the free version has built-in banner advertising so you have to trade banners for pop-ups if you use the free version.

The later versions of Netscape Navigator have built-in pop-up suppression, but the Pop-up Manager enables pop-ups to be enabled for a list of addresses. If you find that a facility you require is being blocked by the pop-up suppression it should therefore be possible to correct the matter. To launch the Pop-up manager select Popup Manager from the Tools menu and then select Manage Popups from the submenu. The Popup Manager (Figure 8.3) is very easy to use. To add a new address just type it into the textbox near the top of the window and then operate the Add button. In order to remove addresses from the list it is just a matter of selecting them using the normal Windows methods and then operating the Remove button. The list can be cleared by operating the Remove All button. Another way of adding addresses to the list is to go to the relevant page and then select Popup Manager from the Tools menu, followed by Allow Popups From This Site in the submenu (Figure 8.4).

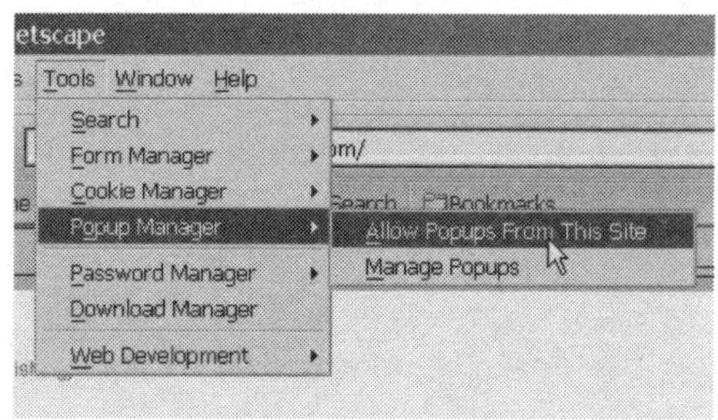

Fig.8.4 A simple way of allowing pop-ups

Another way of preventing most pop-ups is to disable JavaScript. As pointed out previously, most of them are produced using small pieces of JavaScript code, so they will only appear if your browser has JavaScript enabled. To switch off JavaScript in Internet Explorer 6 start by selecting Options from the Tools menu. This launches the Options window where the Security tab should be operated. This gives a window like the one shown in Figure 8.5. Next left-click the Custom Level button to bring up the Security Settings dialogue box (Figure 8.6). Finally, scroll down to the Scripting section, find the Active Scripting section, and set it to Disable. The problem with switching off scripting is that it will disable most “clever” facilities and not just pop-ups. Scripting can be switched back on again by selecting the enable option. There is also a Prompt option. With this selected you will be asked whether or not you wish to run each JavaScript program.

Things can be taken a step further and you can try to eliminate banner advertisements as well. Whether it is worth the effort is another matter, because banner advertisements do not really have the same nuisance value as the pop-up variety. Banners are usually in the form of an image file, and some users object to them on the grounds that the image files increase the loading times for web pages. This is probably not that important to broadband users, but it can significantly slow things down when using an ordinary 56k Internet connection.

The "sledgehammer to crack a nut" method of removing banners is to disable all graphic content on web pages. Of course, this means that no images will be displayed, and that a lot of normal page content will disappear together with the banner advertisements. However, with a slow Internet connection this method should speed things up quite noticeably. To switch off graphics in Internet Explorer 6 select Options from the Tools menu and then operate the Advanced tab of the Internet Options window. Scroll down to the Multimedia section and remove the tick from the Show Pictures checkbox (Figure 8.7).

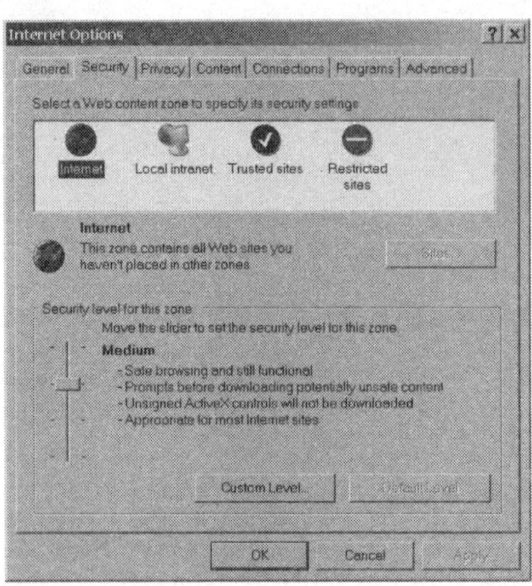

Fig.8.5 The Internet Options window

The more sophisticated method is to use a banner blocking program such as AdDelete or WebWasher. These try to distinguish between banner advertisements and other graphic content so that web pages are displayed normally apart from the missing banners. It is doubtful if programs such as this can ever get it right 100 percent of the time, but they are probably a better option than simply suppressing all graphic content on web pages.

Adult filtering

I do not know whether it is true, but the general consensus of opinion seems to be that most of the money to fund the Internet in its early days was provided by companies dealing in pornography. While the Internet is certainly less pornography oriented than it used to be, it is still easier to find smut on the Internet than it is to avoid it. For many Internet users it is something they would rather avoid, and for those with surfing children it is clearly a major concern.

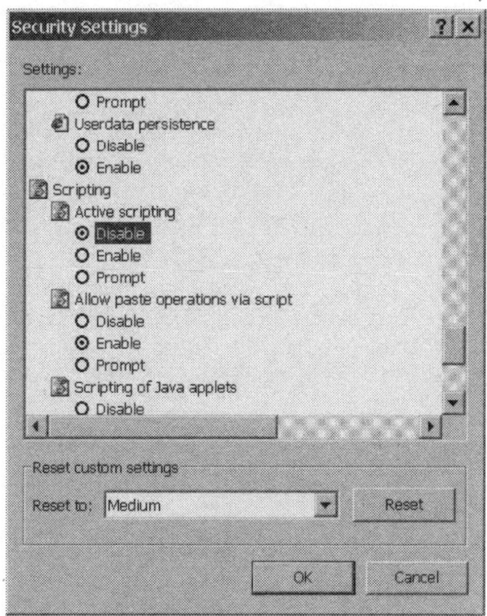

Fig.8.6 Active scripting can be disabled

When using search engines it is very easy to produce some surprising results, and even quite innocent search strings can sometimes produce matches with sites that have a strong sexual content. When searching for web sites supporting the Flash MX graphics program I was not surprised that some

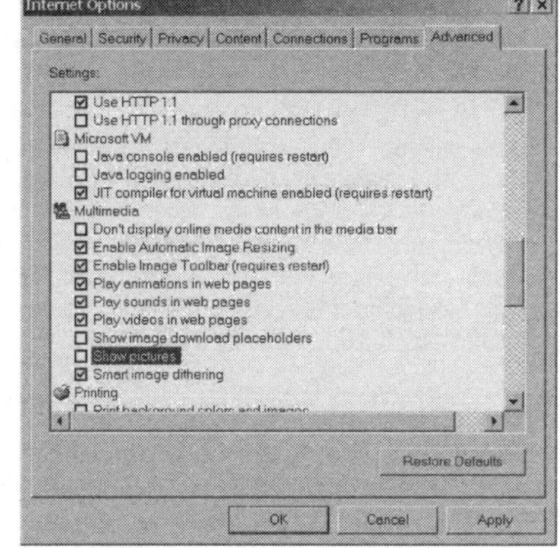

Fig.8.7 All pictures can be filtered

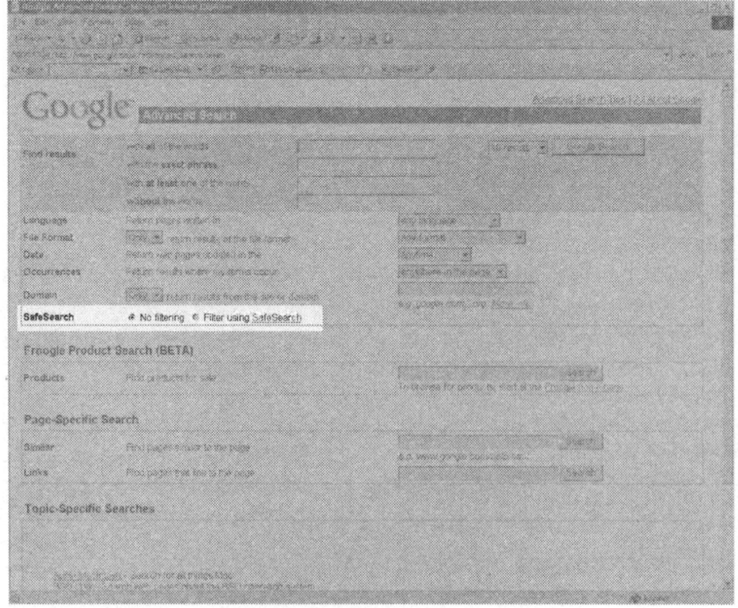

Fig.8.8 Google's advanced facilities include adult filtering

of the matches were for sites having photographs of streakers in action. It was more surprising when a search for information on a graphics tablet called a Pen Partner produced a number of matches for pages giving details of a sex aid!

This can all be a rather unfortunate if you are helping children to search the Web, and search for cheesecake recipes provides matches with some hardcore pornography sites. However, it is a problem that is easily avoided, since some search engines have a facility that tries to filter out matches with pages that have a strong sexual content. In the case of Google's Advanced Search page there are two radio buttons that permit the SafeSearch adult filtering system to be turned on and off (Figure 8.8).

If you look for similar facilities on other search engines you might find them, but adult filtering is by no means as common as it used to be. You may have to do some delving in order to unearth any filtering options that are available. A feature of this type is available from the Lycos engine if you go to the advanced search page (Figure 8.9). If an advanced

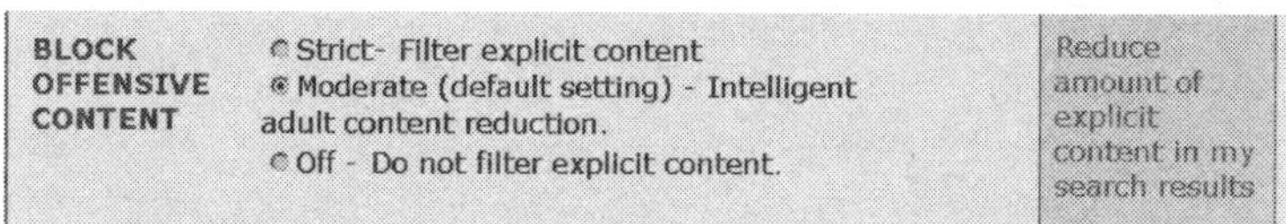

Fig.8.9 The Lycos search engine also includes adult filtering

search facility is available, it is probably the best place to look. Where appropriate, only use a search engine that does have these facilities.

It is only fair to point out that no adult filtering system can be guaranteed to be 100 percent effective, but a system of this type should filter the vast majority of potentially embarrassing search results. There is also a slight risk that this type of filtering will remove useful links. These systems operate by looking for "naughty" words in the scanned pages, and in some cases a page will be filtered if it contains a word that in turn contains a "naughty" word, even if the whole word is totally inoffensive. Some words can be "naughty" or inoffensive depending on the context. With a search for Mary Poppins you might find pages containing the name Dick Van Dyke were filtered out! However, the number of suitable matches removed by adult filtering is usually very small.

Content filtering

There are browsers specifically designed for children. These attempt to avoid inappropriate content using filtering systems that are similar to the ones used to filter junk Emails. Note though, that these browsers do not normally cover Email and chat systems, and that these have to be dealt with separately. Many add-on filter programs do now attempt to deal with Email and chat systems, albeit with some restrictions. Note that users having AOL as their Internet service provider (ISP) can utilise the filtering facilities built into their browser and system. For others it is necessary to use a special browser that has these facilities built-in, or to use an add-on filtering program.

One type of filtering relies on a list of addresses for sites that have inappropriate content. Access to all the sites on this blacklist is blocked. This is essentially the same as the blacklist method of filtering spam from your Inbox, and it has the same shortcoming. It is probably not practical for the blacklist to include all sites that have adult content, or to keep it fully up-to-date. The other main method is a form of content filtering where pages that contain certain words are blocked. Content

Fig.8.10 As one would expect, the KIWE browser for children has a simple and straightforward user interface

filtering can even be applied to images. If a page contains an image that is predominantly flesh coloured it can be blocked.

Many of the browsers for children are very safe, but rather restrictive. Figure 8.10 shows the KIWE browser in operation. Users can browse the Internet after a fashion by using the links in the main window, which in turn lead to further links for museum sites, computing sites, and so on. All these sites have been checked and will not contain any unsuitable content. New sites can be added to the Web menu, but this facility is password protected so that only the parents can add sites.

This type of browser makes surfing the Internet about as safe as it can be, but only by imposing major restrictions. Software of this type uses what is sometimes called the “whitelist” approach, where it is only a list of acceptable sites that can be accessed rather than having a blacklist of sites that are blocked. Safety should be guaranteed using this method, but many acceptable and useful sites can not be accessed unless they are added to the list by the parents. Browsers of this type are fine for younger children, but are unlikely to fulfil the needs of older children.

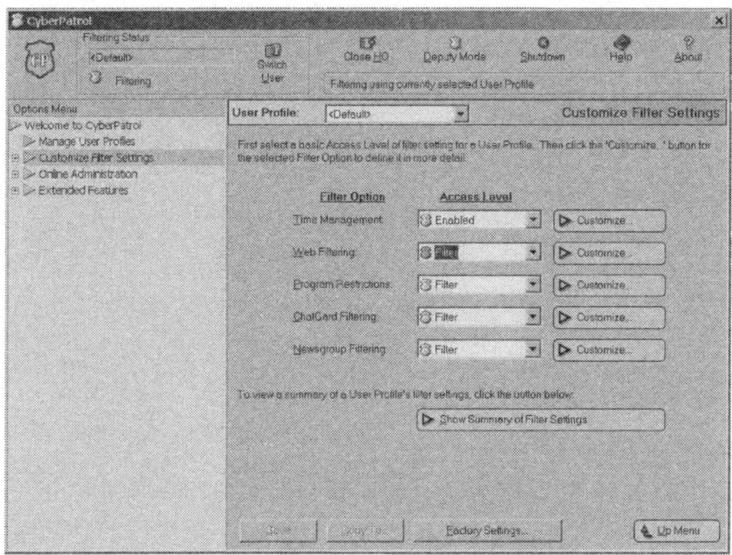

Fig.8.11 CyberPatrol offers filtering and many other facilities

Figure 8.11 shows CyberPatrol in operation, and this is a popular choice. It has a wide range of facilities and can be set up to suit most requirements. Web, chat, and newsgroup filtering are included, and it can also restrict access to programs installed on the PC. It can be set up to operate with several users, giving each one different degrees of filtering. Figure 8.12 shows the result of trying to access a porn site using Internet Explorer, and CyberPatrol has correctly identified the risk and blocked access.

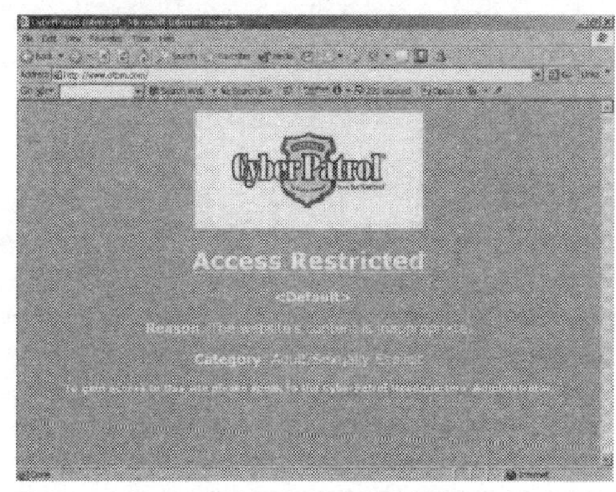

Fig.8.12 An adult web site has been successfully blocked

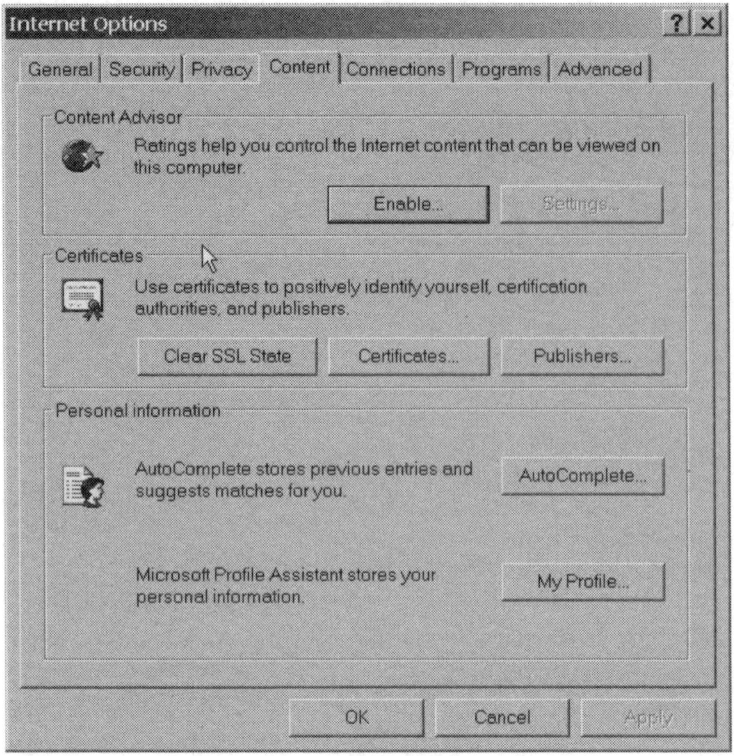

Fig.8.13 The Content section of the Internet Options window

Content Advisor

Recent versions of Internet Explorer have a form of built-in content filtering in the form of the Content Advisor facility. This is switched off by default but it is easily activated and the settings can then be customised. To switch on the Content Advisor facility, launch Internet Explorer and then choose Internet Options from the Tools menu. Operate the Content tab when the Internet Options window appears, and it should then look like Figure 8.13. Operate the Enable button in the top section of the window, and where appropriate supply your supervisor password.

A new window (Figure 8.14) will then open, and this has four types of content listed in the upper section. Below this there is a slider control that governs the degree of filtering. Select each type of filtering in turn

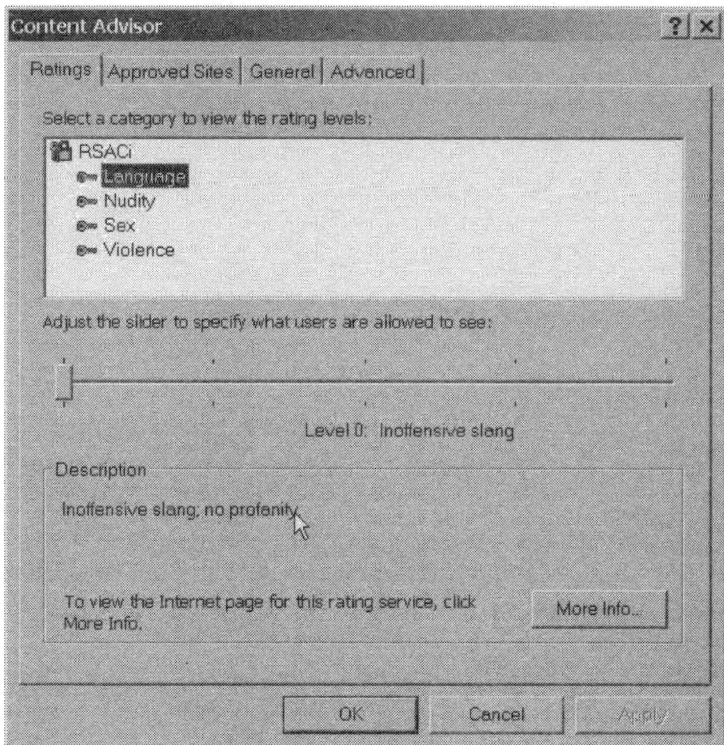

Fig.8.14 Four types of filtering are available

and adjust the slider control for the required degree of filtering. The lower section of the window indicates the type of content that will be filtered at a given setting of the slider control for the selected type of content. Obviously this can only give a rough guide, but it should make it easier to find suitable settings. If necessary, some "fine tuning" can be applied later.

Note that if Windows is not normally used with a password, one will have to be supplied when you operate the OK button to exit the Content Advisor window. This password will be needed in order to make any changes to the settings or to disable the filtering. The filtering can be disabled by going back to the Content section of the Internet Options window and operating the Disable button. Operate the Settings button to return to the Content Advisor window and make changes.

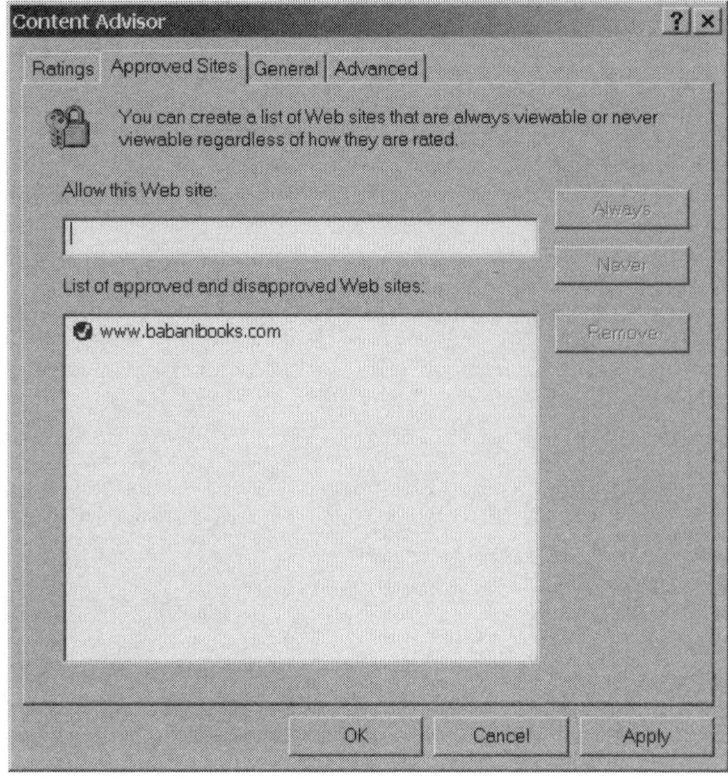

Fig.8.15 Web addresses can be blocked or always allowed

It is possible to approve or block sites using Content Advisor. Operating the Approved Sites tab switches the window to look like Figure 8.15. New addresses are typed into the textbox and then the Always or Never button is pressed depending on whether you wish to block the site or ensure that it can always be accessed. The new address will then be added to the list, complete with a marker to indicate whether it has been blocked or enabled.

Logging

An alternative approach to filtering or restricting access is to have a program that keeps a log of the web sites that have been visited. The list of sites can soon grow quite large, so some of these programs automatically flag sites that look as though they probably contain inappropriate content. Clearly this method does not stop children visiting any sites, and the idea is to enable parents to see what their children are up to when they are online. The subject can be discussed with them if there is evidence of them visiting dubious sites. Programs of this type also make it easy to check whether the amount of time being spent online is getting excessive.

There is a wide and ever growing range of software designed to keep children safe online, but surveys generally show that only a few percent of parents actually have a program of this general type. This might seem surprising given the modest cost and widespread availability of these programs, but it probably reflects the limitations of the current technology. Some programs are very effective but restrictive, while others are less restrictive but not guaranteed to block all sites that have dubious content. There also tend to be disagreements over what constitutes inappropriate web content. The programmers' ideas on the subject are unlikely to match those of everyone that buys their software.

Probably many parents simply feel that educating their children to avoid dubious web sites is a better way than trying to screen them from what is out there on the Internet. It would certainly be naïve to expect software alone to handle the problem, but a mixture of software filtering and education might provide the best answer. It is certainly necessary to educate young Internet users of the dangers if they start using chat rooms, bulletin boards, newsgroups, or anything of this nature. The potential problems have been highlighted by some recent cases. These are some important dos and don'ts.

Never give out any information that could be used to identify you. Using your real name or a thinly disguised version of it should always be avoided. A screen name such as "djames" is fine if you are called Fred Bloggs, but not if your name is David James. Do not give out any personal information such as telephone numbers, full addresses or even postcodes, school attended, or anything that could aid identification. When joining something like a bulletin board service that includes a user profile it is important to ensure that no information of this type is included in the profile. Sensible adults keep to these rules themselves as well as educating the children to do so.

Children should be taught to end contact and report the matter to their parents if someone starts probing for personal information or behaving in an inappropriate fashion. Swapping pictures is something that should only be done with parental consent, and is probably best avoided altogether. Obviously children should not arrange meetings over the Internet without parental consent, and parents should attend any meetings that are arranged. Again, it is probably something that is best avoided altogether.

Auction problems

Most of the dotcom companies failed to live up to early expectations, but some of the Internet auction sites have been very successful. Ebay in particular, has been a huge global success. It was inevitable that auction sites would attract those who cheat slightly and those who are out and out fraudsters. Recently the most contentious issue in the world of Internet auctioning is the practice of what is termed shill bidding. This is where the seller either places bids on their own items or gets a friend or relative to do it for them. Obviously a seller can not openly bid on their own items, but they can open a dummy account and use that for shill bidding. The Internet auction companies have a ban on shill bidding, but this has not stopped its widespread use.

There are actually two different versions of shill bidding. One method is for the seller to bid on the item with a view to raising its price, but (hopefully) stopping short of actually buying it and having to pay the auction company commission on the sale. This is similar to an illegal system that has been used from time to time in conventional auctions. A variation on this scheme of things is for the seller to place a fairly high bid on the item. With luck someone is then keen enough to outbid them. If not, after the auction has closed they contact the highest legitimate bidder and say that the winning bidder has withdrawn from the deal, dropped dead, or whatever. The losing bidder is offered the item at the maximum price they bid.

When used skilfully it is difficult to spot the first type of shill bidding, and even harder to prove that any wrongdoing has taken place. Some auction sites now have software routines that look for likely shill bidding so that further investigations can take place, but most bidding of this type probably slips through the net. The second type of shill bidding is easier to spot. It pays to be suspicious if you lose an auction and are then offered the item by the seller.

The feedback system used by most auction sites is very helpful when trying to spot attempted fraud and bending of the rules. Sellers and buyers are encouraged to leave feedback for each other once a deal has been completed. The feedback is good, bad, or indifferent depending on how well or otherwise the deal went for each party. It is made freely available to all users of the auction site. To say the least, it looks very suspicious should you find that the original buyer of an item that has been offered to you has previously bought a number of items from that seller.

It would obviously be advantageous for shill bidders to know the value of the highest bid near the end of the auction. They could then bid just below that amount, pushing the winning bidder close to the maximum amount they have bid. However, the amounts are hidden until the auction is over. The current price of each item is displayed, but there is no way of knowing whether the current high bid represents the maximum that has been bid, or just a fraction of that amount.

Some shill bidders try to find the amount of the maximum bid by using a dummy account to place a very high bid. This becomes the winning bid at an amount just above the amount bid by the previous high bidder. It effectively reveals the value of the highest genuine bid which can then be calculated quite easily. Next the fraudulent winning bid is withdrawn and another account is used to place a bid that is just too low to win the auction. This forces the winning bid as high as possible. The auction companies have made this type of thing more difficult by tightening the rules governing bid withdrawals, but it is as well to be on the lookout for this type of thing.

Fraud

Internet auction sites are sometimes the targets of straightforward fraudsters. Goods are advertised, money is sent off to the seller, and the seller promptly disappears. Fraud is not usually a problem with inexpensive items because the amounts gained from the fraud are out of proportion to the risks involved. The situation is different when the amounts involved get into the hundreds or even thousands of pounds. Much greater care then has to be taken, should you decide that it is worth taking the risk at all.

Once again, feedback is important when trying to avoid fraudulent sellers. Do they actually have any feedback? A seller should really gain some feedback buying and selling a few cheaper items before moving on to more expensive items. A recent fraud involved items such as expensive digital cameras worth a few thousand pounds being sold for about a third or a quarter of that price in a so-called fixed price auction. In other words, the items were offered at a certain price on a first come – first served basis. On the face of it, the goods were on offer at prices that were too good to be true. Of course, they were too good to be true and the buyers never received any goods.

There are often clues to the fact that not all is well with these fraudulent auctions. As already pointed out, the fact that the goods were on sale at such low prices was a good indicator of likely fraud. Why would someone sell something for a thousand pounds when there is a ready market for it at three or four times that price? In all probability they would not do so. Many of the fraudulent sellers are based overseas, which, even in this day and age, makes it much more difficult for the authorities to apprehend and prosecute them.

Often the fraudulent sellers have what at first appears to be impeccable feedback. In some cases they have stolen someone else's auction identity and their feedback, giving them a plausibility that they do not deserve. In most cases though, the feedback was genuine, but did not stand up to close scrutiny. For example, the seller could have feedback from hundreds of satisfied people, but when you delve more deeply it turns out that they have been buying lots of cheap items such as low value stamps and bulbs to plant in the garden. It requires some time and money to get the feedback, but presumably the rewards from the frauds are sufficient to make it worthwhile.

A seller being defrauded is more of a rarity, because they can make sure that they have the money before they hand over any goods. When selling anything expensive it is as well to make sure that the cheque has been honoured before sending off the goods. I do not always bother if the buyer has good feedback, but as explained previously, you need to examine the feedback to ensure that it is as good as it first appears to be.

Although auctions attract a certain number of fraudsters, it is only fair to point out that the vast majority of users are legal, decent, and honest folk. Online auction sites would not be doing such good business if this was not the case. Having used Internet auction sites extensively for a few years I have not yet had problems with any fraudulent deals. I did encounter one rather inept example of shill bidding which went badly wrong for the seller, so there was no harm done. You do need to proceed carefully, as you do when buying any second-hand goods. The auction sites contain masses of information about buying and selling in safety, and prospective users should certainly read this information. Like many aspects of Internet security it is a matter of proceeding cautiously and using some common sense.

Points to remember

There are a number of ways in which pop-up advertisements can be combated. A good pop-up blocker should suppress all or most pop-up advertisements while letting you use the Internet normally in other respects.

Some Internet search engines have built-in filtering that prevents matches being obtained with pages that have pornographic or other inappropriate content. No filter of this type can be guaranteed to be 100 percent effective, but most seem to work quite well.

There are browser programs specifically for children that use the so-called "whitelist" method of filtering. In other words, the only sites that can be accessed are those on a list of sites that have been checked for inappropriate content and found to be all right. This gives close to complete protection, but is restrictive in that many good sites are not on the list and are therefore inaccessible.

Most browsers that have content filtering work on the blacklist principle, as do most add-on filter programs. The list contains sites that are known to be unsuitable and are therefore blocked. Most of these programs also filter sites that contain unsuitable words, and some even try to identify images that are possibly pornographic in content. These methods are less restrictive than the "whitelist" variety, but can never be totally effective.

Content filtering can not provide a complete solution to keeping children safe online. It is important to tell them about the potential dangers, especially if they use chat rooms, bulletin boards, IRC, or anything of this type.

Make sure that children never provide real names online or other information that is likely to be useful to an Internet predator such as a telephone number, address, or even a postcode. Encourage them to report anything suspicious such as someone probing them for this type of information or behaving in any sort of inappropriate manner.

Most Internet auctions are free from fraud or any form or wrongdoing. As when buying or selling any second-hand goods though, you need to keep your wits about you and use some common sense. If a deal looks to be too good to be true, then it probably is, whether it is on offer at an online auction or elsewhere. Read and digest the safety information provided by the online auction sites.

Index